Handbook of
Team Design

Other McGraw-Hill Books of Interest

Handbook of Team Design

A Practitioner's Guide to Team Systems Development

Peter H. Jones

McGraw-Hill

New York   San Francisco   Washington, D.C.   Auckland   Bogotá
Caracas   Lisbon   London   Madrid   Mexico City   Milan
Montreal   New Delhi   San Juan   Singapore
Sydney   Tokyo   Toronto

Library of Congress Cataloging-in-Publication Data

Jones, Peter H.
    Handbook of team design : practitioner's guide / Peter H. Jones.
        p.   cm.
    Includes bibliographical references and index.
    ISBN 0-07-032880-3
    1. System design.   2. Software engineering.   3. Management
information systems.   I. Title.
QA76.9.S88J66   1997
005.1′2′0684—dc21

                                                            97-17652
                                                            CIP

McGraw-Hill

A Division of The McGraw-Hill Companies

1 2 3 4 5 6 7 8 9 0   DOC/DOC   9 0 2 1 0 9 8 7

ISBN 0-07-032880-3

The sponsoring editor for this book was John Wyzalek, the editing supervisor was Caroline R. Levine, and the production supervisor was Clare Stanley. This book was set in Century Schoolbook by Teresa F. Leaden of McGraw-Hill's Professional Book Group composition unit.

Printed and bound by R. R. Donnelley & Sons Company.

McGraw-Hill books are available at special quantity discounts to use as premiums and sales promotions, or for use in corporate training programs. For more information, please write to the Director of Special Sales, McGraw-Hill, 11 West 19th Street, New York, NY 10011. Or contact your local bookstore.

 This book is printed on recycled, acid-free paper containing a minimum of 50% recycled, de-inked fiber.

For my best friend Rosemary and my parents,
Betsy and Hayward.

Contents

Preface

Handbook of Team Design enables facilitators, project managers, and other organizers of software teams to create better group design and development processes. Systems analysts and design practitioners are also served with useful approaches and new methods to enhance their toolkits, especially for the requirements and design of software-based information and business systems. I encourage all readers to discover how the guidelines and structures are used to engage workgroups or customer teams in effectively planning and designing systems and information products.

At first glance, *Handbook of Team Design* might resemble a manual for facilitating development teams, with effective software engineering practices neatly integrated across team activities. With deeper examination, you'll notice that flexible organization of design processes lets you choose how to organize team workshops and processes for systems projects. You might also find the handbook useful as a project management guide, with its templates for building software projects and entire project life cycles. Work your way through the sections you find most applicable and consider the book a resource for planning your design efforts and team processes.

Although there are many books available covering software design and development methods, and excellent books on teamwork abound, there is a paucity of good advice integrating the two different worlds. With so many organizations acknowledging the benefits of development by team, as well as with increased use of sound project management, the effectiveness of sharing the Team Design approaches becomes clear. Consider this book a starting point for your teamwork in development, and not as "the answer" to group-oriented development needs. As with unpublished, proprietary development process and lifecycle methodologies from consulting companies, the structures in this book must be customized somewhat to your unique organization. But unlike most consulting methodologies, the rules for organizational adaptation are included.

No one book can support the design practices for all organizations. Any organization using group techniques conducts its practice in a way that fits *its* culture and *its* users. This handbook addresses the needs of facilitators, project managers, and technical leaders with a comprehensive treatment of adaptable team methods already tailored to fit the context of certain development and organizational environments.

Consider the purposes for using *Handbook of Team Design*. If you are an experienced systems developer, you may already be familiar with many of the techniques covered in the book. If you find new methods, you should have little trouble picking them up and adapting them. References are provided for all methods, if further details are required.

More importantly for the systems developer, the book offers ways of integrating analysis and design techniques into other project phases or applications. The formats integrating these methods are like crib sheets for complete usage of analysis and design methods. Details about facilitation and processes that you might not find elsewhere are also provided. Consider your primary purpose for using the handbook as improving your own ability to offer excellent service in design, team facilitation, and project management.

If you come from an administrative or managerial background, you might not have specific experience in building systems. However, as information technology commands a greater role in the work lives of everyday people, it creates the new tools, the new everyday jobs of our information-based world. Because of the demand for more information management systems throughout the worlds of business, government, and all enterprises, many of us now find ourselves in the role of developer or specifier of systems to support our work or that of others. Sometimes with very little formal training or background, we are given the task of defining a workable process for handling information requirements. *Handbook of Team Design* offers you a crash course in understanding all the structural aspects of a business process or systems project, in which you can find the roles and requirements most applicable to you.

Group facilitators will notice that most of the facilitation and workshop techniques are not described in extensive detail. A step-by-step approach to every process would have resulted in an encyclopedia, whereas balanced coverage across a comprehensive range was my goal. If you are an experienced facilitator, you will find the strength in the defined workshop structures, the detailed process life cycles, and the relationships of facilitation and development methods to the structure and to each other. Other texts are available to the new practitioner if in-depth facilitation procedures are required.

Project managers typically require an overview of entire development processes, to establish scope and to size an effort. Project managers also need a clear idea of the value of design and teamwork methods, and the expectations of difficulty or involvement to use them. *Handbook of Team Design* offers project managers this type of guidance for structuring projects, and allows them to adapt the project life cycle to fit the natural flow of the design process. Project managers will find the structured agendas for development processes, and supporting detail, useful for selecting appropriate activities when scoping and sizing. They might also find the teambuilding and facilitation approaches useful in their work with project teams.

This book integrates a number of current and traditional influences into its design approach, serving the larger purpose of a handbook that brings forth the best available methods for creative group design and problem solving. Each influence is introduced and credited where it first appears in the book. Joint application design (JAD) and participatory design are integrated throughout, and these are treated as general approaches rather than methods per se. Concepts and methods from the traditional systems analysis and design literature are assimilated, as they have much value to bring as fairly stable, somewhat standard design approaches with perhaps the broadest understanding. Contemporary business process analysis and reengineering methods are brought in mainly in the business orientation sections. Collaborative work processes and group-oriented computing and communications are discussed. Methods from business process analysis and quality management are introduced and discussed within a larger framework of group design processes.

This book is dedicated to your success within your unique situations, and not to bringing about another new or proprietary way of doing design and development. *Handbook of Team Design* offers:

- A comprehensive set of methods from which to choose, not just a step-by-step or "cookbook" approach.

- Both group workshop activities and individual analysis deliverables that support ongoing workshops and team development.

- Methods for use across four basic organizational *contexts* (business, user, systems, product), addressing a wider band of teams and applications.

- A consistent design model that fits software design, product design, and group planning and decision making. The phases of scoping, visualizing, usage, and packaging scale to workshops, team development, or individual work.

- Five formats providing complete design models and lifecycles for business process design, requirements definition, application design, planning, and decision making.

Several corporate audiences are addressed in this book: the information systems (IS) world, the software engineering community, and product development. Although there are distinctly different needs in these communities, the needs of articulating and executing effective design are fundamental in each world. Very similar techniques can be applied to the work of these general communities, as well as to other communities where creative problem solving and interactive group processes can be used.

In modern systems design, the voice of the *user* is taken seriously, and the Team Design approach provides mechanisms for drawing out user requirements in a creative yet disciplined process. In today's business environment, the voice of the *customer* is primary. The customer is tightly woven into the development process, more than possible with traditional methods. For some businesses, just this aspect of group design brings the partnership with customers that is so desired and necessary for successful design.

This book should be used as a handbook, as a set of tools and guidance from many perspectives brought together to serve the practitioner. Although not a theoretical book, *Handbook of Team Design*'s foundations are constructed from bands of contemporary research in systems analysis and design practices, human–computer interaction, organizational development, team behavior, and group process study. As these strands of related disciplines appear throughout the text, notice how your personal experience informs or argues with the notions. This is not an "exact" science, and *Team Design* is not the definitive treatment. As a handbook, use it for what you can get out of it, use what works, and share ideas with others. Make the ideas part of your practice and they will make a difference.

Peter H. Jones

Handbook of
Team Design

The Practice of Design

The Culture of System Design

Teams pervade every organization involved with designing and building software and systems. As the information industry has matured, the team model has not only become acceptable, it is ubiquitous. Talk about teams is everywhere—in management thinking, industry news, and current articles. For all the interest in teamwork, have our organizations *created* appropriate teams, or are we calling workgroups "teams" to be current? Is there anything really new in development team collaboration? Haven't we "done teams" all along? Are we building new teams to satisfy project managers, to increase productivity and control? Why are teams important in design and development?

In his book *I Sing the Body Electronic,* Fred Moody describes the culture of software developers working in the unique product development environment at Microsoft. An overabundance of highly educated, high-IQ software engineers, perhaps more of them than at any other location on earth, are engaged in the excitement, long hours, and tedium of the software craft. The anecdotes of software development teams in this successful product machine are telling. The ability to produce software code is considered to be of the highest technical value, and the ability to create the most innovative code is presented as a kind of standard of creativity. Developers are assigned to development teams, and workers feel separated into one of two categories: technical versus nontechnical (or coder versus designer/manager). This modern corporate fable makes hard points about the conduct of work in software system development today.

Even though a team model is espoused, team members work against each other. Alliances are formed among individuals against team leaders, and team leaders seem frustrated in their inability to inspire solutions or gain agreement. The central development team described in the story could be considered a model of constant organizational chaos. Team members are described as physically segregated from each other in isolated offices with closed doors, doing highly specialized jobs. In the end, a product is built and shipped, leaving the exhausted and apparently dissatisfied remnants of the development team moving on to the next project.

Is this example of an intensely driven, competitive software factory a fair depiction of a design culture? What are the values and desired behaviors in this type of environment? How can teams be organized and facilitated to promote coordination and cooperation? How does the design process differ for different organizations?

Who establishes the vision for a product, and how is it known when that vision is reached? Is a shared vision brought forward by a team of equal participants? And who represents the (eventually) satisfied customer? These are some of the questions we'll be thinking through during this exploration.

First, we must explore and uncover the development processes and group interactions of design *as an activity of organizations*. Adopting the attitude of an interested and unbiased observer (like a social scientist) is a useful approach; by simply observing the work and interactions of people engaged in design activities we can see how some collaborate and others isolate. Our work together in this book requires you to "try on" questions as an inquiry into design practice. In this chapter we inquire into the impact of culture on our ability to design in collaboration. We lead to such questions as: What is the impact of a corporate culture on the design process? How does the process of design itself construct the culture of work? How does the organizational and social culture influence design practices? Can we—or should we—design "culture-free" systems for managing information or work tasks?

The organizational environment—the context of its culture— affords some styles of team cooperation and constrains the possibility of others. Before taking any recommendations or using any design guidelines, look closely at your current culture, the workers and the management. What kinds of teams are used now, and how are they accepted? What types of design processes are used, and how well do they work for building quality systems? How informal or rigid, adopting or cautious is the organization regarding development teamwork and new design methods? First understand the mind-set of your work, and then evaluate the Team Design processes accordingly.

Design and team discipline

People working in groups design and develop all major products and systems today. Think about it—every information systems integration, software development project, or even the installation of an accounting package requires the buy-in, discussion, and decision of many organizational stakeholders. Yet, the training and background of people managing systems teams do not *typically* include understanding and leading group processes. Usually, the project team leaders and systems analysts leading the charge have backgrounds in business or computer science, with strengths in quantitative disciplines. We talk glibly of "people skills" being missing in the management of design and development, acknowledging that some qualities of communication are not available when required. Well-developed interpersonal and group communications skills are often missing from the skills mix of development teams. Are they required for effective group creative design and problem solving? As practitioners and facilitators, we must look at the impact of good and bad team communications on the design process, and must often create our own means of motivating people to work together.

Why should an organization invest in changing the structure of design processes? What are the advantages of working in teams that individuals working and sharing do not provide to the organization?

Even the Microsoft example described previously shows the extensive use of a team concept, even if a somewhat disorganized team is exemplified. Moody allows that the company's corporate culture is organized around small teams, without exception. Self-managed teams are given complete responsibility for a product and are left to work together as effectively as is practical. The teams are relatively unsupervised, and although some teams may demonstrate a complete lack of team cooperation, they usually manage to build something that succeeds in the marketplace. The documentary doesn't speak about other development teams, however, and Microsoft cannot be underestimated in this regard.

Almost any conference dealing with cutting-edge design methods will have Microsoft researchers and project members in attendance, and more than a casual discussion with most of them will demonstrate their keen grasp of issues and direction. In other words, your competition is probably improving its team and design processes, allowing for faster releases and higher quality. What is your organization going to be doing?

Almost all systems design and development and work are done by groups of people—not necessarily teams, but always groups with defined or not-so-defined roles to play. A major premise of this book holds that *teams* are significantly more productive and creative than other types of groups for work of this type. Although this may appear to be either a representation of the obvious or an untested popular expression, research on teams has shown that cooperative behavior is impressively more productive than merely having groups of people working on the same problem. Therefore, the way we define *team* is important to understanding superior group performance.

Driskell and Salas (1992) distinguish team behavior in sports and complex work by the notion of *collective behavior,* as distinct from *individual behavior.* They describe how national championship basketball teams typically demonstrate high levels of team cooperation, with all players contributing to a great extent to the overall performance. Losing clubs often have one or two talented star players who behave in a self-centered way and do not encourage the high level of cooperation found on the winning teams. Driskell and Salas propose that a *team* is present to the extent that a group's members function as an *interdependent collective.* Collective behavior, they assert, "refers to the tendency to coordinate, evaluate, and utilize task inputs from other group members in an interdependent manner in performing a group task." In other words, team players work together toward common goals and build upon contributions from all members in pursuit of a collectively held goal.

When we start to look at cultural and organizational influences on team behavior, collective interdependence is not a common result in practice. Product-producing companies and service organizations are typically structured in a top-down hierarchical fashion, and horizontal structures like teams present formidable challenges for traditional management. But the team approach has been growing in favor and is becoming, if not widespread, at least a metaphor for productive organizational behavior and a model for decentralized innovative working.

Drucker (1992) describes three kinds of teams. On small teams, such as in tennis doubles, each member adapts to the other to strengthen the overall team. On larger, coordinated teams, such as in soccer or hockey, each player has a fixed position, but the whole team moves together down the playing field. The third type of team is like a baseball team or an orchestra—all members have fixed positions in the performance.

Drucker describes how American corporations relied on the baseball-style team for product development. Each department developed an internal product that was handed off to the next team member when done. The Japanese institutionalized the soccer team model, where all disciplines worked together from the beginning. Drucker indicates that they took 15 years to learn this practice, but once it was in place, they shaved their overall development time by two-thirds. American companies have started moving in the soccer team direction, but have not caught up with the Japanese. The team model is essential for businesses, as they become information based and team members must act as responsible decision makers. According to Drucker,

> All members, in other words, have to see themselves as "executives."
> At any given time, an organization can play only one kind of game. And it can use only one kind of team for any given task. Which team to use or game to play is one of the riskiest decisions in the life of an organization. Few things are as difficult in an organization as transforming from one kind of team to another (p. 101).

Many organizations have instituted the *notion* of teamwork from the top levels of management. Expectations are filtered down through the work force for employees to work together in blissfully productive harmony. People are not often provided a strong team model to follow, and they usually don't receive training in the new mode of working together. A major constraint is that executives *promoting* teamwork usually do not change reward and incentive structures to *support* teamwork. From the highest levels down, managers compete with each other instead of forming true teams across their business functions.

North American businesses also typically reward *individual* performance, not the team. Companies generally plan, track, and reinforce the working behavior of individuals. Performance appraisals and incentives are still designed to reward superior individual results. In the current appraisal/reward model, people will tend to use the team as a vehicle to maximize their individual outcomes.

However, a positive trend is apparent, with team reward structures emerging in the compensation plans of many companies in the mid-1990s. Product-producing companies and even traditional heavy manufacturers now regularly award bonuses to successful project teams rather than to all members of an organization. The message is that success of the whole team is success for the enterprise. Full participation should be fully rewarded.

Generally, though, teamwork in current business practice is a diminished version of its possibility. In creative work, such as the design phase of product development, several factors work against effective group cooperation. One is that good designs are typically produced by *good designers,* who sometimes work alone or collaborate within small groups. (However, bringing productive and creative individuals together in a room with eight assigned team members is not by itself likely to create great works.) Second, when a team culture is not the norm in an organization, team members without training or a history of cooperative teamwork do not know how to work together. Team behavior can then result in *less* than the sum total of the individuals. Finally, even effective team behavior is often influenced by social factors, such as the need for building agreement and avoiding conflict. Social influences such as these do not support good design, and they usually prohibit finding creative solutions.

As software technologies become more powerful and afford more capability, more specialized systems are invented for all areas of business, engineering, and education. Whereas only a few years ago Joint Application Design (JAD) was considered a cutting-edge approach, insufficiencies in the products generated from inconsistent and unskilled use of JAD have led to integrating newer techniques derived from other product/system traditions. JAD is considered a highly effective structured approach for meeting user requirements and generating the initial specification of an information system. As with any organized set of practices and methods, such as development methods and programming languages, the JAD process must evolve and become more robust, better able to handle a broader range of purposes.

Team Design stakeholder groups

The term *Team Design* proposes to capture as many related methods as possible in the net of discussion and application, while still conveying the essential idea of a cooperative group intentionally working together in design and analysis. By *group,* we could refer to any variation of workgroup—it includes teams of any type, such as project members on assigned tasks with consultants and clients, and internal corporate groups representing their own business functions.

For the purpose of applying the methods in this book, assume the typical group to be a collection of individuals representing the different interests involved in the analysis, design, or development phases for a significant project. Their different interests must be balanced against the overall needs of the organization. These different groups are considered to be *stakeholders,* in reference to the stake each has in the success of the whole group effort.

In management theory, stakeholders often include the community at large, employees and their families, corporate shareholders, and customers. The organization has a responsibility to understand the agendas, needs, and expectations of all stakeholders and to provide value appropriate to each group. Within the development organization, a similar balancing of needs and value is required. In project planning, resource allocation, and requirements management, decisions are continually made that affect the stakeholder groups. Team

Design, and most approaches to JAD, provide methods of group decision making and consensus that create group acceptance of decisions impacting the welfare of stakeholders. In this way, individual team members represent the interests of others who count on their fairness and understanding of the issues. Understanding the stakeholders in the organization is a primary function of any facilitator of the group process.

Typical stakeholders might include the following roles in the organization:

- Originator or *buyer* of the system or design effort (considered the *customer*)
- Management or executives from the customers' organization
- *Users* of the design or system
- Management representatives from the user's organization(s)
- Business or systems analysts
- Software or systems technology specialists

These representatives and development professionals are the stakeholders in the process and its outcome. If they do not have a significant stake in the outcome, their involvement in dedicated group design work might be inappropriate. Members not having the team's results at stake can weaken the team overall. Although development staff are not always considered to be among the system stakeholders, the principles of team organization suggest that their having a significant stake in the results is critical to project success. Having a major stake in the work is necessary to reach real agreements and informed consensus. Every member of such a group must be willing to participate and to be accountable. The success of the effort depends upon this basic understanding among the participants. The interdependence among group members is the primary reason for calling the group a team. The *Team Design workshop* expresses the nature of this team approach: a temporary, dedicated set of members working together on a project to make decisions, design processes, and achieve creative and lasting results that all can live with.

Design and the organizational culture

Does the culture of the corporation affect the products/outcomes/artifacts designed by its system building organizations? Could it possibly *not* affect its products? Robey (1986) defines culture as "the pattern of shared assumptions that aid a group in dealing with basic problems of internal adjustment and external adaptation." Shared assumptions abound within every product or system—who the customers are, the overall market, the competitors and their products. Assumptions from the culture filter down to the very features that are selected for one system release over the features postponed and saved for the next release. For our purposes as facilitators and practitioners of the designing process, we should assume that everything is affected by the predominating group mentality of the corporate culture. For how your work is received and valued will be dependent on the shared values—conscious and unspoken—at large in the organization.

Take an example from another industry. When you look at any artifact of single-purpose design—a sports car, for example—how does its design express its corporate identity? Look at a Porsche automobile: it is not just a means of transportation; it explicitly embodies its purpose and represents its culture of design. Every aspect of its production execution informs you of its form-follows-function design and of its corporation's demand for product identity. There is no mistaking the design realization of the Porsche with any other car available. It is a clear expression of its corporate identity and values. A Porsche is a highly *intentional* design. It was not designed by accident, and the over-30-year duration of the 911 model's design is a testament to its intention and design philosophy.

If your company or your clients build tractors or systems and not sports cars, the uniqueness of those traditions and history must be taken into account. As a practitioner, be aware of the way people are accustomed to working together in the organization—their comfort level with collaboration. Take into account whether people like doing work in meetings, for example, or prefer working in solitude and then sharing their personal discoveries and products. Does your organization prefer consensus building for decisions or strong leadership from a product or project boss? Do people spend hours brainstorming or do they want the "right answer," *now*? Your own observations along these dimensions are necessary to understand the organizational environment. A thorough understanding is required if you are to create and promote an effective process for collaborative design and development.

Robey describes several action guidelines for understanding and enhancing organizational culture. Like an anthropologist, he emphasizes the importance of symbols, stories, and rites in communicating and strengthening the culture. These guidelines are significant to the practice of design, since they work at the foundation of the organization and influence the style and direction of a team. Consultants and facilitators will gain effectiveness and credibility by adopting behaviors that align with the existing culture. Robey's guidelines are adapted to assist in understanding the impact of culture on teams in the design context.

Pay attention to the softer, less tangible aspects of an organization. The deep assumptions and values that people hold might endure longer than hard changes in systems and structure. Culture offers a way to understand these intangibles (p. 453).

As a facilitator of design work leading to internal systems or marketable products, your challenge entails identifying and supporting the deep values held within a team. Conversely, in a leadership role you may be called upon to bring forth new methods and processes, which might be initially rejected by team members if their value is not related to the cultural context. If democratic self-guided teams are used instead of facilitated meetings, for example, the team might perceive a facilitator as forcing behaviors on them that don't align with their cultural comfort. Be aware of a team's sensitivity to guidance, and adjust the facilitation to allow group sharing of the role, using brief sessions or other adaptations that fit your organization's style.

Be cautious of organizational "quick fixes," proposals to overhaul the corporate culture within a given timeframe, or using the latest management theory. In a leadership role or as a practitioner you will be perceived as a champion of new technologies or practices and will likely be asked by management to spearhead the latest systems or organizational trend. Learn to distinguish the probability of acceptance of these proposals, to determine what will work in your environment. Some organizations have instituted a facilitated JAD process as part of larger efforts to overhaul development processes, and set out launching new standards, controls, and metrics. As a facilitator you might become a visible target for team members who cannot otherwise express their disenchantment, and workshops will be less productive. Adopt the principles of change management, and integrate the processes you own into the larger effort following a thoughtful, planned approach. Don't adopt all the new processes at one time, and learn to distinguish when proposals are faddish "silver bullets" that promise to easily solve deeply engrained or structural problems.

Important organizational symbols express significant meaning for individuals and teams. Your awareness of organizational symbols can greatly assist in the building of team identity and in facilitating team workshops. Using important symbols and appropriate names, acronyms, and terms will enable broader acceptance of your work and your message. Recognize that using these symbols effectively in communications and in design eases the team through its transition from organizational identity to a team identity. During this transition period, use symbols as a powerful method of facilitating the team. Have the team design its own symbol (a mandala, or coat of arms) representing its purpose and identity. This new symbol will become part of the local organization's culture and will forward team integration and acceptance.

Stories carry significant meaning within the organization. Understand how stories reveal insight about your organizational culture. Storytelling and discussing meaningful history gives team members a way of sharing their values and ideals with one another. Use your role as a design facilitator to elicit stories from people whenever consensus, decisions, or new concepts confront the team. Sharing stories before encountering conceptually or historically uncharted territory serves to remind the team of cultural heroes who trailblazed before. Senge's *Fifth Discipline Fieldbook* emphasizes the use of *dialogue* and storytelling as important rituals for fostering team communication and strengthening organizational culture. Dialogue is a form of facilitated conversation among team members that is used to share and create value.

Organizational rituals are useful for expressing and sharing cultural ideals and values. Many team activities can be integrated with ritual behaviors to push organizations into a deeper recognition of their shared values and team identity. Organizational rituals or rites typically include such functions as group meetings to recognize and reward employees, social activities, and staged departmental meetings that serve specific purposes. Teams should be encouraged to design rituals that bond members and enhance their own organizational identity. Rituals can be simple activities, such as Friday lunch meetings or telling stories before design workshops. For celebratory occasions, more momentous rituals, such as recognition ceremonies or formal parties, create a strong sense of belonging and team value. Robey points out how these rites can be changed. Consider using new rituals to increase awareness of transition periods and when starting any significant change effort.

Robey's last guideline exhorts executives to *"communicate abstract ideals through a hands-on, direct approach in their daily activities."* This suggestion just makes good sense. Anyone in a leadership role should "walk the walk" as an example for others. For example, if democratic teamwork is an abstract ideal, leaders might hold open business review meetings to share information with all interested members of an organization. Allowing all attendees to share ideas and news within a cross-hierarchy meeting shows the leadership of democratic management.

Organizational and systems design processes are extensively intertwined. Organizational processes determine the affordances and constraints available to development groups. *Affordances* are the opportunities for adaptation or growth in the environment, and *constraints* are built-in limitations. For example, if your team requests an off-site work site for private project work, your affordances and constraints will show up very quickly. You may be given the go-ahead, while compromising on location. Or the organizational rules may not allow it at all. Your ability to build an effective design team might be affected by internal organizational constraints. Consider these as basic rules of the game, and learn when to selectively break them when team breakthroughs depend on it. When given the opportunity to lead, it's easier to gain forgiveness than permission.

Other organizational processes influence design work. In his contemporary business manifesto *Liberation Management*, Tom Peters (1992) describes the organizational influences affecting modern business. The primary influence is that the value added to all products and services derives from knowledge work. Much, if not most, of this added value can be considered to be *design* work—thoughtful anticipation of new product features, creating a new twist on an existing service, listening to the customer and providing something better than was requested. Peter Drucker, whose publications in management theory and practice have driven business thinking for the latter half of the century, asserts that "every organization must devote itself to creating the new." Drucker (1992) describes the three systematic practices that management must adopt:

> The first is continuing improvement of everything the organization does, the process the Japanese call *kaizen*. The aim of kaizen is to improve a product or service so that it becomes a different product or service in two or three years' time.
>
> Second, each organization will have to learn to exploit its knowledge, that is, to develop the next generation of applications from its own successes....Finally, every organization will have to learn to innovate—and innovation can now be organized and must be organized—as a systematic process (p. 97).

Drucker points out three new functions of the organization that effectively address design issues, from both development and organizational perspectives. These functions are so critical to the future success of an enterprise that Drucker insists that only those organizations that master these functions will succeed. The Team Design approach brings a toolkit of best practices for group methods that enables the organization to adopt each of these functions. It takes a dedicated group of product champions and creative developers to improve a product or service rapidly so that it transforms itself every two to three years. A team approach using creative and precise methods of design communication is required to exploit knowledge and create the next generation of applications. Innovation as a systematic process is definitely a team-level activity. None of these functions are performed as mandates from management. The successful organization does not wait for the CEO's vision statement before acting on opportunity.

Tom Peters continues to discuss how layers of structure, particularly middle management, destroy value in the knowledge-work process. Layers of structure inhibit responsiveness and individual action by requiring numerous paths of communication and oversight. An extensive chain of management creates too many points for credit taking and second-guessing decisions. All it takes is one *no* in the chain to kill a good idea or slow down service to the true customer. This trend of reducing layers is good news for teams, as it frees them from unnecessary reporting outside of the team itself.

Notice the organizational structure in the places where your work is conducted. Whether you are an internal facilitator or a consultant, you will be compelled to adapt to an organization's structure. Organizational structure forms an inescapable set of constraints within which the team must function. A brief review of structure concepts serves to relate team and design facilitation to the basic organizational structures and styles. (See Table 1.1.)

TABLE 1.1   Organizational Structure and Team Models

Structure/ attributes	Functional	Divisional	Matrix
Characteristics and typical use of model	Each department organized around occupational skills: Finance, Marketing, Engineering.	Each department organized around product lines or missions. Used in auto and retail.	Members shared across departments. Used in large project-oriented organizations.
Management style	Traditional, chain of hierarchy.	Traditional, self-contained business.	More flexible, project authority shared.
Use of teams and team authority	Occasional, cross-functional teams. Little or no authority.	Frequent use of teams within product areas. Hierarchical reporting in division.	Frequent use of project teams. Higher level of team authority.
Facilitation approach	Conservative, focus on intergroup communication and teambuilding.	Democratic, allowing team members to contribute fully.	Creative and democratic, sharing knowledge and skills.
Facilitation techniques	JAD, neutral meeting facilitation.	Focus group, participatory design.	JAD, PD, Breakthrough Thinking.
Customer interfaces	Structured, through official channels.	Integrated into organization, available to team.	Customers might be team members.

Team-based organizational designs are becoming more common, and in the six years since Peters' prophecies in *Liberation Management,* many North American companies have performed significant business process evaluations and have at least addressed the layers of structure in their organizations. Teams have emerged as much more than a fad, or even a management trend. Project-based teams are now the mode in all types of organizations, regardless of formal structure. However, as managers in matrixed organizations have warned for years, teams are not simple, and are not a cultural fix for companies with problems. Teams have a high potential for conflict, and consume resources at a faster rate than other modes of management. For the project manager, teams present a constant challenge of coordination. For functional managers responsible for personnel, having people on teams makes them unavailable for other duties. And it is notoriously difficult to track progress or productivity within the team.

However, team organization within any one of the three basic structures is not only desirable, it is necessary. Work processes that are based on using individuals as isolated contributors to a business assembly line are outmoded, slow, and inefficient in knowledge-based production. When the quality of ideas and innovation is valued more than mere physical output, the knowledge of every team member counts. Teams (or small dedicated workgroups) are essential to this process. Of course, individuals still generate the best ideas, and organizational structure is required to control business operations. But to create value for customers and put the *right* new ideas into action—and into production in the fastest way possible—a team is required.

Scope of Team Design

Team Design encompasses a range of currently used group processes for achieving design goals. A *team,* for our purposes, is any small group (no more than 20 persons) dedicated to a project with specific goals for production of deliverables or of providing a service. So, almost any software product development department would contain one or several teams, and a system integrator might construct teams to support specific projects for a client's system installation. Teams are often cross-functional, in that members are pulled from different functional line organizations with their own, sometimes competing, agendas and goals. In project-oriented companies, teams might work as dedicated organizations within a larger department. These are typical contexts for the Team Design team.

The types of teams in development practices have been articulated by Richard Zahniser (1993), drawn from his experience and research in the CASELab research group. He identifies the dimensions of group work in software development as follows:

- *Solo.* A single person, typically working with a single computer not actively shared.
- *Dyad.* Two (or three) individuals working together, usually in a sequential fashion.
- *Small group and small group, networked.* Small groups are the traditional meeting arrangement, and organizational development teambuilding approaches apply to these groups. Networking the computers of the small group (with groupware and communications tools) enhances team coordination and collaboration.
- *Large group and large group, networked.* The large group includes one or several functional organizations, or a large development team. Networking large groups can support the sharing of information and knowledge between groups and among projects.
- *Team of teams.* A team of teams is a way of organizing multiple subteams of large groups. Greater organizational role flexibility is gained when establishing a team of teams and providing networking tools.

Other types of teams are legitimate in this perspective. A continuum of group definition spreads between the extremes of partnership and assembly. Another dimension of affinity extends between low affinity (remoteness) and high affinity (interpersonal involvement). A type of "team" can fit almost anywhere within the center of this depiction. (See Fig. 1.1.)

Although these depictions of groups may be addressed as teams from time to time, are they *truly* teams? Which of these groups reach the point of interdependency and goal alignment where they function together as a whole? Team harmony, performance, or cohesion are critical factors in successfully using Team Design—or any other group process—to accomplish challenging and complex tasks. Allen Drexler (1988), author of *The Team Performance Model* and organizational development theorist, describes this aspect of team development:

> Something magical happens when a team learns to do its job well. Members are no longer just separate individuals working on a parallel course; they begin to think, work, and act as a unit. The best teams celebrate differences, take risks together, and spend time to create the bonds that strengthen team process. They respect themselves, each other, and their leader—and they get results.

In facilitation, you will find an existing high-performance team the

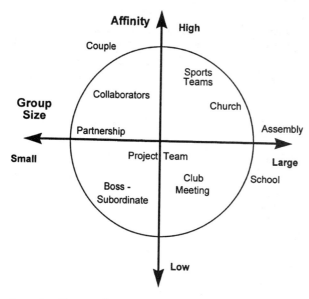

Figure 1.1 Team and organization affinities.

exceptional case. You will not always have the opportunity to work with a smooth-functioning project team, or even a formed team. Many times you may be faced with basically an ad hoc group, formed for the express purpose of meeting the development or design goals described in an agenda. Many JAD workshops, for example, are conducted with groups that are formed from representatives of several different work functions that have never worked together before. Add customers and user representatives to the mix, and the result may be an unwieldy group of well-meaning but unconnected individuals. Your participants may not expect to work together much longer than the timespan of the workshop, leading to even less team loyalty than other ad hoc teams (such as process improvement or task forces) might enjoy. These challenges are typical in design sessions, and are a significant reason for stressing the necessity for team-building activities in technical and development work.

You may have been a participant in a short-lived design workshop, or have led or participated in long-term goal-directed team activities as part of a project team. Either way, the experiences of group cohesion and effective creative problem solving are usually the rare high points in group processes. Facilitators are challenged with the daunting hurdle of bringing newly formed groups of workers, some or most of which are temporary, into a creative and productive team experience. They are faced with creating a team and quickly having the members focused on a shared perspective and producing results. With approaches like JAD, consensus is expected of the team, and with participatory design experiences, a user-centered democratic process is expected. These methods require the facilitator to help establish and maintain the team context, if it is not already present. Proceedings can easily break down in such creative group processes when members do not perceive the value in arriving at commonly shared solutions. The process of working together toward those solutions is based in the notion of teamwork, and teamwork is not a given. It must be developed by the team, usually with leadership and guidance. The Team Design approach addresses this process of working with creative groups and integrates the best practices of researchers and facilitators within a team model.

Integration of facilitated methods

Team Design incorporates structure and practices from several types of facilitated workshops and planning sessions for analysis and design, including JAD, participatory design, facilitated planning, prototyping workshops, and total quality management (TQM) processes. Some or all of these may be familiar to facilitators and business analysts; they have been used throughout many organizations with varying levels of success. Joint Application Design is the type most closely associated with the Team Design approach, which has maintained a significant following for almost 20 years since IBM first began using it. However, has JAD changed much with the times? Computer and software development technologies have changed dramatically, but JAD work in the 1990s looks a lot like JAD work in the 1980s. Perhaps it's because JAD works so well that it has not required significant evolution over the years. However, if JAD techniques work so well, why are they not universally applied in the context of system development groups? One reason may be that the style of collaborative work necessary for effective JAD-type workshops is not supported in the mainstream of everyday work at most organizations. Employees in large service corporations, such as banks and insurance companies, often are expected to work in relative isolation on specific, controllable tasks for a full working day to produce identified outputs. This approach toward worker "productivity" does not encourage collaboration, which may be seen as wasting time needed for the production upon which the job and its evaluation depend.

Due to organizational size and job specialization, we also find that customers, users, managers, and developers have widely varying perspectives on their work and their goals. Collaboration between these different groups is often difficult unless they are given business reasons or directives to work together. What are their perspectives?

- *Customers* want a system or product that supports their work needs, and their goals are "better, faster, cheaper." They expect their investments to reward their business and work processes, to provide substantial improvement over their current systems.

- *Users* have a job to do using your system. They want a system or product that makes their work lives easier, and their goals are satisfied by something that is easily learned, easily used, and saves them time and trouble.

- *Managers* want to have a reliable system implemented on time that meets the requirements, and pleases the primary customers. Of course, meeting the budget is high on the list, so productivity tools are considered essential.

- *Developers* want to build a product that demonstrates technical excellence and realizes an effective solution within the constraints of the requirements.

Collaboration among these different team members is often uneven, fraught with communication gaps. True collaboration is more often found *within* the members' groups or disciplines, since their professional colleagues understand their tasks and can contribute immediately. Collaboration as a team is more of a challenge.

According to Michael Schrage (1995), the key to collaboration is shared space:

> Shared space exists wherever there is effective collaboration. Whether we collaborate to discover something that we don't know, to create something new, or to solve a problem that confounds individual solution, shared space is invariably an indispensable tool...you find it expressed in the prototypes of nearly every significant invention of this century.

Schrage's concept of shared space involves physical, symbolic, and interpersonal sharing. Collaborative sharing of ideas, work, designs, and expressions requires an intimate concept of space, a situation where the team or collaborators are completely free to follow their best professional opinions and share and build on work with those they respect.

> Shared space literally adds a new dimension to conversation, a dimension embracing symbolic representation, manipulation, and memory. Participants must have near-equal access to the shared space—or else it isn't really shared, is it?

In fact, Schrage's thesis in *No More Teams!,* as expressed by the title, involves the notion that sharing in collaboration is what drives results, and not some possible synergistic output of an organized team structure. Through his research, Schrage describes how most teams—as well as most meetings and other organized group events—fall short of their possibilities. He finds that most breakthroughs occur through the intimacy of collaboration between two or three people, and not from the group. It requires a unique and powerful team to support collaboration as presented in Schrage's thesis. Such a team is not created in a day through a single facilitated effort, or even in a few days of team building. But a team can be nurtured in this direction, and facilitation is one of the means available in the contemporary workplace to promote the social engineering of an effective design and development team. This is the point from which Team Design starts.

Types of workshops

What *types* of workshops will Team Design support? Will a JAD approach suffice? Will this approach satisfy defined goals and requirements? Ten workshop types represent the most significant uses for workshops in product and development organizations. These 10 fulfill most of the needs across the life cycle as well, an aspect covered in Chap. 5. They are discussed as examples throughout the book, and most of them map directly to the Team Design formats in Chaps. 6 to 10. The workshops are as follows:

Project planning.   Project planning involves defining the scope, budget, and schedule for a project (a complete major task with a defined start and finish). Project planning should also cover the areas of project organization and communication, quality, human resources, and even contracting approach, but scope, budget, and schedule are essential to the basic plan. Project planning is also the process used in developing most major *proposals,* since a complete effort must be scoped and priced for comparison with other bids. Project planning requires the input of a team of people who provide the planning effort with the necessary range of technical skills and project management experience.

Strategic planning.   Strategic planning defines the long-term plans for organizations, large-scale information systems, or an enterprise's infrastructure. Strategic planning is based on shared goals, critical business decisions, and preferred direction for meeting the organization's goals. It usually defines the key activities required to meet these major long-term goals, and provides members of the organization with plans and guidance to pursue the strategy. Strategic planning requires a team of leaders and key technical members of an organization with sufficient authority, insight, and vision to set goals and define direction. A structured workshop process is often used to guide strategic planning, to generate inspired thinking through the group process, and to facilitate the achievement of consensus among conflicting approaches.

Product planning. Product planning workshops can support planning and direction for existing products and services, for generating new product concepts and idea testing, or for long-term product evolution. Product portfolio planning is also supported, as a process for designing product strategy to engineer the growth and evolution of a family of products (such as the Microsoft Windows products, which represent a complete product portfolio). Product planning requires a cross-functional team of planners, leaders, and executives to work through ideation sessions, focused discussions, and decision making. As with strategic planning, the structured workshop is extremely useful for bringing together the diverse team members required to move creatively and decisively forward.

Process analysis and redesign. Analysis and evaluation of business processes is often conducted by systems/functional analysts, but in current business thinking this area is becoming cross-functional. Process analysis and redesign refers to the substantial redesign of processes for significant business advantage. This also includes business process reengineering and its related methods. Workshops supporting this process involve in-depth knowledge and evaluation of current business practices, technical skills for focusing on key areas of analysis and design, and creative sessions for rethinking the business from new perspectives. All of the aspects of Team Design are involved in this type of workshop. Process analysis requires a varied crew of team members bringing current process knowledge, business skills, reengineering experience, analytical and creative skills, and systems thinking skills. Facilitation is recommended for these sessions at least as much as for the previous processes.

Decision support. Decision support refers to any group process where the primary objective is to reach decisions acceptable to the group of stakeholders or participants. Decision support workshops or conferences might involve a small group of executives working together to reach consensus or negotiate on projects or budgets, or a large group of line managers and project leaders attempting to hash out priorities for a limited set of corporate resources. In fact, almost any of the group processes detailed here will involve some degree of decision making and decision support. Facilitation of decision support is highly recommended, as it removes or lessens the personal biases and political influences that affect traditional decision meetings.

Process improvement.   Process improvement involves a wide range of organizational activities intended to enhance an existing business or technical process. Process improvement greatly differs from process redesign, in that it maintains the existing process in recognizable form and proposes incremental improvements instead of total overhaul. Also, this process is conducted at lower organizational levels, where reengineering efforts occur with top-level sponsorship. Process improvement workshops must often show rapid results, since process change is often based on a fairly narrow scope and human resources are not dedicated full-time (as is typical in reengineering). Process improvement teams require a mix of people from across the organization, to integrate the varying points of view of members representing different business functions. A designated team leader is typically sufficient to conduct these workshops, since facilitator bias is not as much of an issue as it is in JAD or reengineering. Facilitation is often required mainly to engage the team participants in creative thinking and design exercises.

System, user, or product requirements.   Requirements analysis and management involves numerous processes, and is a difficult area for many organizations, since project dysfunction usually starts at this point. User requirements sessions are distinguished by the emphasis on specific user needs or tasks that are (typically) redesigned using computer technology. Product requirements are usually specified by business analysts or product managers responsible for the corporation's product marketing, definition, and execution. Similar group processes are used in these two areas, although the team membership, organizations, and workshop approaches might be very different. Requirements processes focus on three key areas: (1) requirements elicitation, or gathering of valid requirements; (2) requirements definition, or identifying and specifying the requirements in language acceptable to all participants; and (3) requirements management, or reviewing requirements and negotiating any changes to agreements. All three areas can be handled effectively by facilitated workshops, as long as the user/product team participants are well-informed, representative of their organization, and authorized to become fully involved and make decisions as part of the team.

Selection of software packages.   Selection involves identifying the requirements for an off-the-shelf software package to be implemented as a business solution. This activity has become so frequent among North American organizations installing automated systems that it deserves its own workshop process designation. A complete workshop process can be organized to identify user requirements and negotiate priorities, discuss research findings on software packages, identify vendors and solicit demonstrations, evaluate packages, and make consensus decisions. A workshop process might also be used for planning the implementation of the package and new processes across the organization, providing training and support, and customizing the package to adapt to planned business processes. This approach is more typical of selection of major packages that affect the business, such as project or cost accounting, administrative functions, payroll, and financial management. A workshop process is also effective for smaller package decisions that affect a technical group. The same process can be used for a shorter period of time, perhaps without formal facilitation methods.

Make-or-buy decisions.   This class of decision making requires detailed specification and evaluation of requirements, and compares development versus purchasing business strategies. Especially for a major effort, such as a key product decision or foundation technology, the make-or-buy decision requires extensive engineering, marketing, product management, and project management expertise. Because the divergence of opinion and approach is so extreme among these functions, the facilitated workshop approach is of considerable value.

Application design or prototyping.   The application or software system design process is probably the best known class of workshop, for those following the JAD school. This broad area includes all the traditional JAD processes of requirements analysis, architecture design, external design (initial user interface, reports, and data definition) and preliminary system design (system interfaces, data storage, data conversion, and migration). Prototyping is commonly part of the application design process, as it effectively conveys the requirements and design at the user's level of understanding. This process requires involved and informed user participation, and skillful facilitation to manage the conversational balance between technical considerations and the user's needs. The format for this process in Chap. 9 specifies numerous team workshop activities.

Facilitators can organize variations and combinations of these workshops as required for different projects. For example, a project planning process held over a two-day workshop might be extended with a two-day requirements definition session. A requirements session might be expanded with vendor demonstrations, and then might break into decision making or even make-or-buy sessions. Flexibility is explicitly designed into the process to enable organizers and facilitators to build the workshop process required.

The sections that follow describe current facilitated and user-oriented design approaches that have been successfully followed over a decade or more. JAD and participatory design approaches especially provide a foundation for the Team Design workshop techniques.

Joint Application Design (JAD)

Joint Application Design is the original process of group-based design upon which many of the assumptions, techniques, and processes described here are based. The general purpose of JAD is to bring together developers and users to jointly define an application or a system. In practice, the JAD meeting is a structured workshop used in many business situations for group input and discussion, usually around requirements and decisions, and for reaching consensus or planning for organizational action. The JAD is conducted to define enough detail to move to the next stage of an effort, or as defined by the key stakeholders. This is its simple purpose—each JAD will have its own unique purpose that fits the goals and needs of the organization.

Joint Application Design has always been based on the format of a facilitated meeting. A group of *stakeholders* are authorized to make plans and decisions, guided by a *facilitator,* and supported by people in specific relevant roles. Nonmanagement facilitators, sometimes technically oriented and usually neutral to the project, guide the traditional JAD meeting. Trained and experienced facilitators are necessary to elicit productive interaction from team members. In practice, this is not always possible or practical for all organizations. Facilitators from other disciplines are brought in, nonneutral team members might be used, untrained analysts give it their best try when asked to lead a JAD, or consultants are hired to provide facilitation for critical JAD workshops. However, an uneven but dedicated attempt is usually better than no facilitation, and using a good reference and guide is better than going in cold. Therefore, one of the goals of this book is to assist both the experienced and the new facilitator in delivering results from a design workshop.

As indicated previously, JAD has been around since 1977. IBM invented and trademarked the term, and JAD has since grown into widespread application. Many offshoots of JAD are used, and consulting companies have designed and produced their own methods, such as Gary Rush's FAST, Tony Crawford's JAD, the Method (ATLIS, formerly Performance Resources, Inc.), and Odyssey (APLAN Information Services), as well as IBM's original Joint Application

Design. Some of these variations use specific software tools to capture information in a repository and generate deliverables from the session. Some recommend using standard computer-aided system engineering (CASE) tools, or even provide tools to build applications as part of the JAD. All varieties of the JAD approach claim to generate highly productive and effective sessions resulting in specific required deliverables.

JAD facilitates technical communication among all points of view among members and organizations. The facilitator becomes a translator of perspectives during the session. JAD facilitators bring together the practices of small group team building, organizational boundary crossing, coordination of purposes and goals, group decision making, creative problem solving, and guiding creative collaborative design.

The purposes of Joint Application Design include the following:

- *Streamline interactions.*   One workshop is used to handle all user/customer and stakeholder issues and discussion.

- *Identify and resolve issues.*   Issues are discussed in an open facilitated session with the user community and other stakeholders. Reactions are immediate and can be handled in the session.

- *Generate initial design or prototype.*   The session is often used to develop the first cut of a process model or system prototype, saving much time that would otherwise be used to present and modify a concept prepared in isolation.

- *Gain agreement.*   The session is used to obtain the group's consensus or, at least, inputs on business processes and system requirements

- *Produce deliverables.*   The JAD approach is often used to initiate a project or the development process and to produce initial documentation.

Joint Application Design can replace numerous meetings that might normally be scheduled to accomplish some of the same goals. However, typical meetings do not accomplish much of the communication that has to happen.

Very little discussion of JAD is found in academic or research papers on collaborative development after 1993. It is a practice that developed outside traditional academic orientations, but has been amplified by research in the areas of social computing and groupware, organizational development, and systems engineering methodology. Some might think that since JAD is considered a mature methodology, it has little research value. It might also be considered to be too bound by structured design methods that are becoming outdated as object-oriented methodologies become more widely used, or too tightly bound to information system design practices such as are used for MIS installations in large corporations. As practitioners, we must ask whether a future turning point is apparent for the acceptance of the 20-year-old JAD process. Or is it, perhaps, a chance for renewal, regenerating methods, updating its applications into new areas of creativity and problem solving? *Yes* to both is a possible answer.

Is JAD the best answer for some development groups? Joint Application Design is probably least effective when major organizational or team-building work is required of the project/stakeholder team. Merely gathering a group of loosely related systems consultants or developers with the target users does not guarantee a productive session. Trained and experienced facilitators are essential to producing worthwhile results, and a formal JAD should not be attempted if facilitation is not available. Also, if a creative process or a breakthrough product is required of the team, a JAD approach is typically too highly structured to lead to innovative new designs. Finally, although JAD is consensus oriented, it is not designed to be democratic. JAD goals and scope are typically predefined in advance of sessions, and alternative methods are not readily available to practitioners.

Participatory design (PD)

Participatory design is a discipline of design practices based on complete inclusion of the users or intended work community in the design of their tools and processes. Participatory design (PD) differs from JAD and other approaches in that the users are more than stakeholders in the design and development process—they share responsibility with the developers for the quality and performance of the delivered system. They also share much more broadly in the development process itself, by participating with developers and as designers themselves (a process sometimes referred to as *codevelopment*). PD is more a philosophy of total user involvement with the systems they will eventually use in their role as producers of value for the organization. In practice, this philosophy extends far beyond design workshops and JAD sessions—it becomes the way of doing business for all systems development.

Participatory design originated in Scandinavia in the 1980s as an outgrowth of the democratic philosophy of work fostered in northern Europe. Since PD is so strongly user-centered, it represents a major philosophical change from the consulting model of system design favored by U.S. corporations. One of the tenets of PD is that system workers should be given better tools instead of having their work mechanized. Another is that the users' perceptions about technology in their work are as significant as the technical requirements for the technology. PD is oriented toward improving social factors in the workplace, which is considered a major purpose of design in Scandinavia. As a design approach, it has been favorably received in Europe, and has been used in numerous projects reported in international journals. Participatory design has evolved over time from a worker-centered intervention to a more integrated system design approach, incorporating a wider range of team members, such as analysts, developers, and managers. Participatory design showed up later in the United States, as an outgrowth of user-centered system design practices facilitated by human factors practitioners. The North American PD approach is more focused on integrating users into the design process and less oriented toward workplace issue resolution or organizational design. PD is considered different from JAD in that it allows users to share responsibility for design with the project and development teams.

Carmel, Whitaker, and George (1993) compare JAD and PD design approaches, and discuss two broad themes they believe demonstrate PD principles. *Mutual reciprocal learning* is present in PD projects, wherein the design team and users learn from each other about system design and work practices. A mutual learning is gained, allowing both sides to understand and work with one another in ways that respect their own unique goals and circumstances. The other theme is *design by doing,* engaging users directly in low-fidelity prototyping, hands-on creative design work, and workshop participation exercises. These themes are borne out in the following examples of North American PD practices.

A good example of a PD method is PICTIVE, developed by Michael Muller of U.S. West, who has innovated and published other techniques over recent years. PICTIVE was applied in several projects during its development, and has since been used in large projects, such as a facilities allocation system. Muller (1991) describes PICTIVE (Plastic Interface for Collaborative Technology Initiatives through Video Exploration) as follows:

> The purpose of PICTIVE is to facilitate the design of systems by heterogeneous groups. In order to include the contributions of all of the participants on an equal-opportunity basis, PICTIVE uses deliberately low-tech design objects that are familiar to anyone in office environments. These include colored pens and papers, removable tape, scissors, and Post-It™ Notes or other removable labels and papers. This is an extension of the mock-up work in the UTOPIA project, but with greater attention paid to bringing the users directly into the design process in terms of the user interface and system capabilities that they will encounter in use.

Karen Holtzblatt developed the process of Contextual Design, a methodology for engaging users' participation in the design of their systems and tasks by fully involving their work experience. By interviewing users in the context of their work environment, and treating them as the experts in the work processes to be designed, a *contextual* view of the system is developed. This substantially differs from traditional requirements approaches, as it places much of the control for information collection in the hands of the users. Contextual inquiry is typically conducted as a set of processes adapted to the environment, and does not consist of specific steps. Traditional design methods, such as prototyping and diagramming, can be integrated into a contextual inquiry approach. Contextual Design has grown into a useful methodology with applications throughout the development life cycle, and has achieved fairly regular use among practitioners.

Various product companies ranging from consumer products (Thomson-RCA) to software (Microsoft) and data services (LEXIS-NEXIS) engage users in interactive methods derived from PD. Design consulting firms such as Fitch actively use PD-derived tools as a primary design approach with clients and their users.

Although some specific techniques and user interaction approaches are associated with participatory design, it has become more a way of organizing the people involved with democratic problem solving and design. It is a way of bringing together people in the "shared space" of collaboration as described by Schrage, where the *shared space* is the workshop or other environment created by the design team to support creative collaboration in the design by all participants. It is shared because all the participants have equal access, not just the professional designers. Participatory design advocates have traditionally resisted imposing the structure and strict methodology associated with JAD and other system-oriented approaches. The shared space concept is typical of PD approaches, allowing the group to create its own design processes in a shared model of design.

Team Design provides guidelines for working in this way as appropriate for the team, without requiring specific design tools or procedures. A "pure" PD approach is not accessible to all organizations. Clearly, its best practices are effective, and by involving users more fully into the design process, an organization gains the possibility of evolving in the same direction as those using full participatory approaches.

Facilitated planning and decision making

Executive and management decision-making processes have also benefited from the use of facilitated meetings. Whereas management decision processes have traditionally been fraught with conflicting agendas, biased toward special interests, and dragged out with end-less proposals and spreadsheet numbers, the emergence of facilitated conferencing has helped managers sort through especially tenacious decision problems. This parallel trend of facilitated meetings with direct participation from stakeholders has arisen throughout business to support the needs of groups making complex decisions in such areas as product research and development spending, business case selection, and process reengineering cases.

Decision process facilitators, such as Patrick Sepate of TASC, use multiple techniques for decision support conferences, sometimes several processes within one conference. Sepate has conducted decision meetings with clients ranging from the U.S. military and government to Fortune 100 companies. He relies on the Analytic Hierarchy Process (AHP) as a central tool for group decision making and uses Ventana's GroupSystems for managing distributed workshop participation across organizations and networks. Sepate's organization developed a Windows-based software tool to acquire group inputs for decision processes and help the group analyze its cases to make decisions involving hundreds of alternatives and thousands of variables. The Resource Allocation Decision Support System (RADSS) was code-veloped with Texas Instruments, and is used by TI specifically for resource planning and decision making. A generic version of the tool was developed for use by TASC to assist in other decision processes, and is used for decision conferences on complex decisions in budgeting, project portfolio management, and long-term planning and decision making.

Although techniques such as AHP and tools such as RADSS are breakthroughs for organizations with complex multivariate decision processes, many organizations merely require effective decision consulting. The facilitated processes traditionally pursued by JAD meetings have been worthwhile for many organizations seeking to improve the way they resolve differences or to arrive at an unbiased selection of alternatives. The Team Design decision support cycle described in Chap. 10 provides a framework for decision-making workshops that allow for integration of known methods and your best practices.

Development life-cycle approach

Team Design offers a design framework and should not be considered a specific methodology. There are no steps to be followed, no mandatory procedures. Instead, it integrates design methods across the development life cycle, and offers guidelines for selection of design methods. These distinct differences tailor Team Design to fit the various uncertainties and unique aspects of each development project. These differences can be summarized as follows:

- *Full development life cycle.* Team Design covers the full system development life cycle as appropriate for each design format.

- *Design cycle.* A general four-phase design cycle orients practitioners in the selection of methods and identification of appropriate design artifacts and deliverables for each phase of design.

- *Organizational contexts.* Four organizational contexts are considered within each format, allowing practitioners to orient toward an appropriate type of workshop and facilitation environment.

Chapter 3 discusses applications across the full development life cycle, presenting a life-cycle model and its associated activities. This life cycle reveals a structure supporting the entire life span of a product into distinct phases, with activities that apply uniquely to each phase. The general development life cycle applies to both products and systems, allowing the practitioner to map the organization's life cycles and its tried and true methods. For example, even though an apparently static life cycle is presented, it allows for mapping iterative, evolutionary, and rapid development approaches.

Very few methodologies can apply to all organizations, and Team Design does not attempt to do so. Instead, design methods and design *formats* are mapped to general types of organizations, to explore the differences in approach the practitioner might use when starting out with Team Design workshops. In Chap. 3, these are presented as four organizational contexts, which cover organizational environments oriented toward *business* goals, *systems* goals, *user* goals, and *product* goals. Although these might not cover each unique organization, they allow Team Design approaches to be tailored to better match the current organizational context.

2

The Joint Application Design Process

The Joint Application Design (JAD) process has a tradition of structured workshops that has been effective for its purposes, and JAD is the foundation for Team Design. This chapter discusses the fundamentals of the JAD process, and can be bypassed by those with experience and background in JAD. However, for facilitators from other backgrounds, and those with JAD experience who are interested in further learning in the basics, this section should be considered worthwhile background.

The JAD process has been discussed in various books and articles, and is typically presented from the viewpoint of management information systems (MIS) practices. The original adopters of JAD found the process useful for addressing both the organizational and technical difficulties of corporate information systems. Corporate applications, then and today, involve a cast of hundreds, with both development and user organizations as well as a multitude of business analysis, corporate policy, and staff offices involved. MIS applications are typically developed by internal (or, often, outsourced) corporate departments that serve to maintain corporate information standards, data management, and a host of other responsibilities. MIS typically supports numerous customers or users within a large organization. Where financial systems are the primary customer, the explosion of desktop and client-server technology has often seen MIS responsible for networking, databases, and desktop PC support, leading to a diffused customer focus at times. And outsourced MIS projects are often conducted in the cost-cutting 90s without true user representation or understanding of tasks. With the emergence of standardized platforms and packaged software for client-server systems, creative implementation opportunities can be missed, and analysis and design can be overlooked. JAD has emerged as a valuable approach to managing requirements and design issues in MIS projects in all industries.

According to numerous articles, somewhere between 50 to 60 percent of all systems problems stem from improper requirements definition, the area that is most directly addressed in traditional JAD. And all systems professionals have observed for themselves that problems detected and fixed early in the development life cycle (during analysis or design) are not that costly. However, problems resulting from a bad set of requirements pushed into rapid development are extremely expensive and time-consuming. And when problems arise after installation, they become so expensive and time-consuming that they result in new projects. These problem projects are typically called *maintenance*. According to a 1995 computer industry trade article, after systems move into maintenance, 82 percent of the project's effort arises from poor requirements, as opposed to only 1 percent from poor coding (Matthews, 1995).

According to the same article, JAD is being applied throughout the systems development life cycle at Provident Mutual Life Insurance, where manager Denise Silver has used the method extensively and says, "JAD is more important now more than ever." She describes its use in systems supporting business process reengineering changes, as well as in strategic planning, software package selection, and project prioritization.

As suggested by the article, JAD has currently reemerged in corporations as a facilitated method for designing and managing information systems strategy and policy. With many organizations in North America pursuing business process reengineering (BPR) to improve business performance, the familiar JAD approach has been used by managers to redesign business processes. Following the practices of consultants who have paved the way, organizations evaluating business processes for renewal or overhaul have learned to use facilitated approaches for selecting, analyzing, redesigning, and implementing business processes. Upon gaining consensus from the team on process definition, the MIS and user organizations are well positioned to use a JAD approach for designing and implementing the information systems to support the new processes.

The Prudential Insurance Company recently reported training 45 information systems (IS) professionals in JAD, with the emphasis on developing applications for new BPR processes. Large information systems organizations often start using JAD with consultant facilitators in trial projects and, after finding that stakeholders and IS professionals obtain value and produce quick results, then choose to more fully integrate JAD into the organization and development

processes. Once the decision is made to invest in JAD, entire departments are sometimes trained in facilitation and in participation. The
facilitators are typically, but not always, IS professionals. A survey of
750 facilitators performed by Denise Silver and Jane Wood of
Provident Mutual showed that 89 percent belonged to an IS organization, whereas 7 percent were allied with user organizations, and only
4 percent were independent of either.

Wood and Silver's (1989) leading book in the field, *Joint Application
Design,* describes the classic methodology used by IS professionals
over the last decade. They emphasize the importance of JAD facilitator training, and especially advocate on-the-job training. However,
when an organization has not used the process before, or uses it in
isolated cases, it is difficult for new facilitators to apprentice with
JAD leaders as described in their text. *Joint Application Design* provides an excellent treatment of the traditional structured JAD
approach in a practical handbook style.

Team Design builds on JAD, and could easily be viewed as a JAD
methodology. Team Design is intended to move the applicable parts of
JAD into environments other than IS. Team Design also brings collaborative design techniques learned from years of JAD and other
facilitation work into other areas of business, systems, and product
development. The business organizational context presented in Chap.
3 leans toward the IS organization, but traditional IS is not its main
focus. Team Design stretches the JAD approach to encompass the creative design process itself, which is inherently valuable for solving
the right problem and designing a system that fits its own future.

Types of JAD Workshops

There are several ways to classify the different approaches to JAD
workshops. JADs can vary along the dimensions of structure, purpose,
facilitation style, and group orientation, and we could easily define
other differentiators. An organization using JAD for its first experiences should have an understanding of its desired approach. There are
definite styles in delivering JADs. A company with a traditional organizational culture could hire a facilitator who uses "touchy-feely"
team-building and imagery exercises that might frustrate a structure-
oriented group. Conversely, a loosely organized software shop comfortable with daily brainstorming sessions could engage an old-school
facilitator who pushes for group results and limits freewheeling creativity. Either way, a mismatch of organizational chemistry could lead
to unsatisfactory results and disillusionment with the JAD approach.
The Team Design approach addresses this by stipulating different
methods for workshops, selected by the organization type and the ses-

sion goals. Some basics of JAD structure are helpful in understanding the flexibility of Team Design as constructed in this book.

Joint Application Design workshops fall along a continuum of structure. Structure can vary greatly depending on the goals of the session and the style of the organization.

Highly structured. The highly structured approach regards the JAD as a set of steps that must be followed to produce an outcome. Highly structured is "going by the book" or literally following a script. For a highly structured JAD, a book such as this handbook can be used as a guide for establishing agendas and exercises to accomplish analysis or design work. A highly structured approach may be resisted by software developers, since it tends to create a less open environment for technical discussion and creative engineering solutions. It may provide a comfortable approach for teams new to using JAD or for bringing a level of comfort to uninitiated user participants. Tools used in the highly structured approach include low-tech whiteboard and flip charts, overhead displays with transparencies, prepared formats for data collection and analysis, paper prototyping, and handbook materials. Computer displays are also more commonly used in the more structured JADs, typically for presentation and demonstration rather than design.

Structured. Traditional JAD is conducted as a structured workshop, and most proprietary JAD methodologies (such as FAST and the Method) fit into this category. Structure is required in setting strict agendas, providing a safe meeting environment for users, using process-oriented facilitation, and using tried and true exercises. Team Design can be approached as a structured session, but is intended to offer more flexibility to both facilitators and participants. Tools used in the structured approach typically include documentation tools used during the JAD, presentation tools, and boards and easels. Computer tools are frequently used for demonstration of prototypes.

Structured and flexible. Team Design falls into the *structured and flexible* category if considered in relation to typical JAD. An agenda and specific goals are provided, but are open to discussion and revision by the group. This approach allows a balance between the goal-oriented structured approach appreciated by managers and users and the real-time design enjoyed by developers. It provides more opportunity for a range of facilitation and design techniques to be employed. Experienced facilitators are required for this style, as opposed to the more basic structured JADs, which can be led by more novice facilitators. Various design approaches and workshop formats can be used, given the flexibility. All the tools mentioned in the previous categories are used, except that the prepared formats are replaced with in-session guided brainstorming and other methods. Computer-based prototyping is frequently used, with PCs for information gathering and decision-support tools.

Loosely structured. Loosely structured JADs are workshops held using a JAD facilitation approach but without a strict agenda or definite goals. As some organizations adopt JAD methods, meetings are frequently held with the intention of using the new method. Untrained facilitators and novice teams initiate the workshops with enthusiasm but with little guidance. The lack of structure may lead to developer or management dominance of the proceedings. Discussions often lead into extraneous detail, losing the attention and interest of user or business participants. With too loose a structure, any meeting can be termed a "JAD," giving the impression of using a new and productive technique. JAD must lead to some agreeable and defined output products, and must provide a structure for managing team communications and decisions. This is the minimum structure under which a JAD approach is effective. Any tools can be used in a loosely structured approach, and the basic JAD room and facilities may be used by a facilitator as well. What denotes the loosely structured approach is that their usage is unplanned or arbitrary, and not always toward a well-defined goal. With creative and disciplined participants, this approach may even be the best—but, then, a dream team of excellent communicators is not the common makeup of the software development world.

JAD with CASE. JADs held with CASE technologies are often proposed for rapid application development (RAD) life cycles. The benefits of this approach are in defining a technical specification with direct user or stakeholder input during a participatory analysis process. Using a PC-based CASE tool allows the development team to capture representations of data and workflow during the JAD discussions and to rapidly generate printed diagrams and reports during the workshop. A potential issue with regard to this approach is that users may not understand the implications of designs communicated using the technical analysis and design methods in a CASE tool. Developers are capable of moving ahead with design decisions at a rapid rate, and users may not be given the opportunity to intervene. As processes are defined using CASE, the resulting diagrams present the appearance of finished, detailed work products. Users—and even analysts—may perceive that the represented process is complete, and may not wish to break the process apart under further inquiry. When using CASE as an integral part of a JAD workshop, vigilant facilitation is necessary to ensure that user concerns and implications are raised and discussed at the appropriate times.

The JAD itself is structured to control conduct of the meeting and to guide the interaction of participants. A structured approach is required for consistent results within organizations, but it may take time—often more than a year of continual use—to evolve the best structure for productive JAD meetings. If an organization is highly structured in terms of management reporting, policies, procedures, culture, and communications, less structure should be used in the JAD approach. Less structure is necessary to provide a working environment where structure-oriented team members can be allowed to think and develop solutions creatively. A less structured meeting style helps these organizations to relax the cultural constraints and to generate ideas and proposals from a more creative perspective. With good facilitation and group trust, the deliverables will still be constructed, and a higher quality of product should be expected.

Where the organization's development process is less mature, or the organizational culture is more open and flexible, more structure should be brought to the JAD approach. Therefore, even if the organization is highly structured but the development process is not, a high degree of structure should be used in JAD. This description perhaps typifies most development groups. Most large U.S. corporations engender highly structured organizations, yet their development groups persist in using ad hoc and nonstandardized methods. In consulting, we usually find that an "official" development methodology has been adopted and is considered to be in effect, but allegiance to the process among development groups ranges from none to partial. JAD and Team Design are not methodological fixes, but provide the shared space wherein both structured tools and creative design approaches are integrated into system development processes.

Roles in the JAD Workshop

The JAD approach employs a set of well-defined roles as part of its structure. At the very least, a facilitator and participants are involved. Participants include system users or their representatives or *customers* as defined by the product or system. Other participants may include business or system analysts, product specialists, and project managers, but these also fit under the role of *participant* and do not have a particular technical role. Technical participants are not accorded any more position or influence than users, but they may be accorded *less* influence as a matter of philosophy. This leveling of technical authority and decision making supports the democratic principles of the JAD approach. Users and customers are considered to be primary stakeholders, and their satisfaction with the process and the results are critical.

Other roles in the JAD process include the supporting members that are crucial to the smooth operation of the workshop. These roles are typically described as follows:

Recorder/scribe. Recorders document the proceedings of the workshop, focusing on the substantive issues covered by discussion and as directed by the facilitator, such as decisions and action items. This is perhaps the most important role other than that of the facilitator, because results and issues are not documented effectively otherwise. The recorder should not be a secretary; it is not a clerical role. A good recorder must understand the business issues and the technologies involved enough to make astute translations, "shorthand" notes, and observations that add value to the entire JAD effort. Like the facilitator, the recorder should be neutral to the participant parties. Although recorders are typically selected from the ranks of the information technology (IT) organization and are not technically neutral, they can be used in workshops for projects in which they have no development stake. Some level of objectivity is useful in the recorder role, since the JAD output documentation must be seen to reflect agreements and perspectives from all participants. Issues that might seem trivial to an IT member might be perceived as critical by the user organization—these items are better captured when the recorder is neutral to the project.

CASE operator or technographer. If CASE is utilized in a JAD workshop, a trained operator documents the diagrams and data representations as analysis and design proceeds. The operator should have expertise in the tools and methodologies used in the session, and may also be a methods consultant. Being closer to the technology than the facilitator, CASE operators may be expected to be less neutral overall, and their translation of user discussion into diagrams and structure should be monitored as to interpretation. This role is not usually joined with the recorder, since they will be watching for and documenting different activities. The *technographer* is a new role identified by Schrage (1995), used in conjunction with computer-based display of participant's inputs. As participant's inputs are discussed by the facilitator in an organized session, specific contributions by the members are entered and displayed onscreen by the technographer. This role must be more neutrally oriented than that of the CASE operator, since the technographer is responsible for encouraging participation in working on and displaying design ideas during the session. It is like controlling the whiteboard—all participants should feel free to bring forth worthwhile ideas during the proceedings.

Observers. Another neutral role, the observer is used in larger JADs for passive feedback and monitoring. Observers are often required following a session as a source of insight and detached reflection. They can be consulted during the JAD as well, but typically are not unless a hot issue or a conflict resolution requires their unbiased and uninvolved perceptions.

Managers often participate on occasion as observers—which is the appropriate role for managers, especially senior leaders, of the users or analysts involved in the session. A strong facilitation style is sometimes necessary to prevent managers from interacting as full participants, in which event their recognized organizational authority might intimidate members of the team and inhibit participation.

Cofacilitator. A cofacilitator is useful in larger workshops (10 to 20 or more participants), and can provide backup and relief to the primary facilitator. Cofacilitated sessions allow for different styles of guidance and group dynamics, and allow facilitators to provide in-process feedback to each other. Cofacilitators are also used whenever the planned JAD workshop extends over a period of days or weeks. It allows other facilitators to work with the group at different times, which is useful when their unique skill sets can be infused during appropriate activities on the agenda.

Sponsor. The sponsor of the JAD is a role as well, and must be handled as such. Usually the sponsor is an executive, and may well be the boss of over half the participants in the workshop, or the ultimate customer who must be satisfied. His or her influence is important and should be framed in appropriate perspective. Some sponsors promote the cooperation of the JAD approach, and encourage the social dimension of the team to work together and make agreements. Other sponsors, typically from the systems side, are more directive, and push for a specific result or deliverable. If more than one sponsor is involved, their goals must be discussed in advance of the JAD to discern their expectations and potential conflicts.

Finally, if you are a consultant facilitator, it is important to distinguish the sponsor from *your* customer. It may be difficult to satisfy both, and asking your client which to serve first in a conflict is in your best interest.

Stakeholders. As described previously, stakeholders typically include the customers, users, and managers who expect to use the system or benefit from its value. Stakeholders can include representatives from almost any part of the organization that the eventual system will touch upon. With systems affecting communities or larger populations, stakeholders easily extend into the public arena. With any major system affecting jobs and work processes, stakeholder investigation should initially extend as wide as possible, in order to understand the possible impacts of the system before settling on the group that will represent the design work at hand.

Preparing for the Workshop

When setting up a workshop, you coordinate a number of activities and then follow up to ensure that your requirements are met. As the facilitator or planner, you are responsible for identifying all supplies, facilities, and participants. If left to others, at least one critical item will likely be unsatisfactory. Lay out your requirements clearly, and hold people to meeting them. Experience helps in preparation—discuss the workshop plan in detail with an experienced facilitator if you are new to all this.

1. Gain real support from management.   Your first action must be to gain *management buy-in,* or support to that effect. Buy-in shows up as consensus support from the managers with something at stake. Without an appropriate level of support for a participatory approach, the results of the workshop may be unused. Building real support for the project and the team approach requires a concise yet purposeful discussion of the goals and methods of the workshop for the project. Minimizing the ever-present intrusion of politics from the design process is one of the key elements behind team-based design and decision processes. Management intervention in the process or results of the JAD or Team Design project could subvert the current development effort and might extinguish enthusiasm for using team approaches in the future. In gaining buy-in, remind yourself that you are not seeking permission to perform. What you seek is active support and sponsorship for a new way of doing business, which can potentially solve deep organizational problems while building a foundation of trust and commitment within the design team.

Gaining support requires that you make the case for adopting a partnership approach to development, which managers may see as relinquishing their control. Managers may be inclined to direct the team toward a specified result or management goal. For the design team leader or facilitator, the temptation arises to accept the managers' mandates in order to move forward with their own design goals. Be cautioned that this may lead to false expectations on the part of participants and, eventually, to veering off track from the original purpose. Management issues are part of the landscape in facilitation and design work. Be prepared to work through numerous issues that might arise during your preparation and information gathering. Collect these concerns and issues and present them to your management team in a forthright manner. Ask which issues should be handled outside of the session and which might be brought forth to the team. Discussing management's specific concerns raised over the design effort with your team can often improve the candor of the team as a whole. If your team members were selected for participation in the design workshop, they are probably close enough to the action to know of the issues' existence in the first place. Your frankness in dealing with potentially political conditions will enhance your respect within the team.

Visit and interview executives and managers involved with the workshop participants and deliverables. Listen to them and understand their concerns, and be clear in describing design and team issues that may not be known to them. Once these issues are defined and discussed, they might not be perceived as a threat to management goals. If you can resolve conflicting purposes in advance, a crucial step will be made toward the long-term success of the project.

2. Define the workshop requirements. Work with the immediate team to define known requirements for the workshop (not for the project or system). What are the purposes and goals as described by the project team? What, at a minimum, must be accomplished for the session? What deliverables must arise from the JAD? Who will be the recipients of the deliverables? Who are the customers, and what do they want from the workshop? Who are the intended users, and what would they like to have?

Start off the conversation by discussing the customer-supplier perspective for the workshop and its deliverables. Ask the sponsors what they expect to get from the session, both overall and the specific deliverables. What must they be able to do with the deliverables? Who is the next customer in line from the sponsor? How do the requirements of the sponsor's organization or team members differ from those of their manager? What do they see as the service to their organization?

3. Define customer expectations for the workshop. What expectations do the information systems (IS) staff or developers have for the workshop? Even if you are from that group yourself, do you consider them customers? (You probably should—even though they may consider themselves to be the service organization to the customer/user group, there will usually be a handoff of some product to IS.) In other words, will the quality of your job in the workshop affect the quality of their work to follow? There may be other internal customers involved downstream from your process—perhaps other development staff, human factors or usability engineering, training, and documentation. Sometimes marketing and sales staff are *very* interested in your results—particularly when the workshop involves *their* (real, external) customers. Finally, business process reengineering (BPR) work is typically conducted as a team process, and team sessions are often facilitated, especially when numerous organizational stakeholders are involved and neutrality is critical. If you organize BPR workshops, *every* organization is a potential customer. The attitude of total customer service cannot easily be separated from effective workshop conduct.

Therefore, an indefinite, possibly large, number of potential customers might exist for your workshop and its deliverables. When the internal customer relationship is especially sensitive, consider constructing a simple internal contract for the workshop with both user management and development sponsors. An internal guarantee is an organizational commitment used to define a significant customer-supplier relationship. A JAD or design workshop is not like a training class or presentation—it is a service to organizations. The guarantee puts the expectations and understanding of service desired by the customer in writing. As an organizer or facilitator, it also protects your interests by defining the extent of responsibility for your service. For example, if decisions are made by the group consensus that one of the stakeholder managers does not approve, it should not reflect negatively on the *process* or the service. The contract can describe the nature of your service in a way that supports realistic expectations for the outcome and for responsibility.

4. Identify appropriate stakeholders and select participants.   Who are your major stakeholders? As discussed previously, your stakeholders include all those affected by the planned system—within the larger organization and outside it. Organizational users, customers, managers, project teams, and "functional" organizations may all be stakeholders.

Who are the end users for your particular products? Are they data entry, clerical, sales representatives, or knowledge workers? Do they represent specific professional interests, or do they belong to trade unions? Are the users likely to personally benefit from the system, or will the implementation affect people's jobs?

Who are your customers? Are they the user's management, sponsoring executives, development bosses, or all the above? In the JAD world, customers are often the *buyers,* or representatives of those paying for the implementation.

These will be the primary stakeholders. Administrative staff, developers, and staff managers are usually not stakeholders. However, the workshop team must not be too full of stakeholders to make progress, discuss critical issues, and move toward consensus. Work with management and project leaders to include all those necessary into your planning. If too many different individuals are identified, select representatives for stakeholder groups, with no more than 15 in any given workshop. Representatives are often selected from among the following categories:

- End user (representatives of actual user groups)
- Customer (buyer of service, manager of user groups)
- Sales (sales representatives with direct field contact with customers)
- Customer service (service representatives or technicians who directly assist customers and users)
- Marketing (product promotion and customer contact)
- Product management (product line managers, business area managers)
- MIS analysts or software developers (technical leads, IT project managers)
- Executives (senior managers for any of the groups)

Would you want all these parties in your JAD? At the same time? Consider some of the methods for organizing workshops to incorporate a larger scope of stakeholders, using multiple sessions, parallel workshops, or multiple phases in a series of sessions.

Restricting participation is sometimes necessary, and rationalizing participation is important. In large organizations it is too easy to expand the list to include tangential organizations, MIS staff, analysts, and others when only a core team is required to do the work. If there are more than 15 to 20 actual *stakeholders* (those who depend on the JAD's outcome for their work), consider creating parallel JAD groups instead of including them all in one meeting.

5. Conduct necessary pre-JAD activities. Allow at least a week in advance of the workshop to plan and organize, and to gather the inputs from all parties. The following activities are typically performed:

- Pre-JAD: gather information for JAD planning for a week or so.
- Conduct executive interviews and survey stakeholders.
- Gather the latest system documentation.
- Arrange for facilities, refreshments, and materials.
- Develop the JAD plan and agenda.
- Review the JAD plan with the sponsor.
- Arrange for participants.
- Train the recorder.

Use the pre-JAD period for conversations with sponsors and managers to identify and discuss their expectations. Expectations may run high when organizations first try new development or organizational development tools. As a facilitator, plan to handle issues in advance, before unrealistic goals and expectations are set through unseen and internal channels of communication.

6. Set up the meeting room and the schedule. Finally, visit the meeting area at least the day before and prepare it for the workshop. Arrange the tables into an open semicircular configuration (such as a U shape) with plenty of room for all participants to move on both sides of the tables. The semicircle enables participants to face forward and focus on the common tasks presented by the facilitator, yet still maintain effective contact with all individuals in the room. Make sure that materials and tools are available or will fit into the space provided. Set up the room and spend some time in it to determine if your arrangement will work effectively. Review the schedule and agenda, and make any adjustments as required. Draft a final agenda and ensure its delivery to all participants.

JAD Technology and Tools

When the JAD approach was first employed by IBM, personal computer technology was not yet available. Computer and software tools were not accessible as truly useful adjuncts to facilitated workshops until several technologies matured to enable PC-generated display. The JAD workshop model was not initially designed to integrate these tools into its process. In the 1980s, as computer-aided systems engineering (CASE) tools and computer projection became more readily available, different tools were brought into the JAD toolkit. Starting with simple large-screen monitors displaying text and graphics, and then with CASE tools and group communications, computer tools have grown to become extremely useful in all group design sessions. Though not in principle necessary for conducting effective JADs, the tools have become basic for the practitioner. Even the simplest toolset for conducting and documenting an effective JAD or design workshop includes hardware, software, and the availability of conferencing tools. With the introduction of any tools into group sessions, skilled (or, at least, knowledgeable) facilitators and operators are necessary. The facilitator must understand the purpose and best use of the workshop tools across the activities proposed in the agenda. The recorder (or technographer) must know the computer-based tools thoroughly, to provide competent and nonintrusive service to the team throughout the sessions.

Although a workshop may be scheduled for only a day or two, thoughtful integration of tools can provide the extra productive facility that makes a real difference for the customer. Even if only providing rapid turnaround of JAD minutes or proceedings, it might be the service-oriented timeliness that convinces a management team of the workshop's usefulness. JAD workshops are often distinguished by their use of computer tools to augment the group interaction, especially in documenting design details as they are discussed and realized by the team. In other (non-JAD) workshop approaches, a less technical orientation is preferred. Certainly, not every JAD session calls for a high-tech implementation, but even a minimal use of special tools can lessen the overall documentation burden or improve the timeliness of deliverables.

Every workshop organizer is encouraged to understand the usage and applicability of a basic set of tools. It is not necessary as a *facilitator* to personally use these tools, but as the organizer you should be aware of their effectiveness and incorporate them as necessary. When working as a consultant facilitator or analyst, these tools are essential, allowing you the flexibility to work with a wide range of clients and situations. The following JAD workshop tools are described by category, but not by specific example. Since different vendors and packages emerge on the market and disappear fairly quickly, the utility of vendor or product name references is questionable.

Software support tools

Software tools are used to support almost all aspects of the JAD group process in design workshops. Some facilitators expand the use of computer-based support to all practical areas, while others restrict their use to diagramming and documentation tasks.

Several broad types of tasks are supported by software packages, effective for all design workshops that might be conducted. The facilitator might research and select at least one appropriate tool from each category for use in all types of workshops.

1. *Documentation.* Word processing and specialized documenting tools are used for documentation in advance of, during, and following the workshop.

2. *Presentations.* Presentation packages are used to create effective presentations, print out paper handouts or packages of information for participants, and to give slide presentations during workshops.

3. *Analysis and design.* Although presentation software can be used for simple design diagrams, analysis and design is better supported by using CASE tools or specialized diagramming packages.

CASE tools automate the standards and notations for drawing data, function, and process diagrams, and adhere to standards that support readability and acceptance. Diagramming packages that support fast freehand symbols can also be used in sessions and, with documentation tools, for precise rendering of design work.

4. *Communications and group interaction.* This large category includes tools to support team member communications during the session and while working individually. Group decision support systems allow the JAD team to record and display team inputs during exercises, and facilitate the team decision process. In addition, any types of groupware, electronic mail, and Web- or Internet-based communications can become powerful process facilitation tools.

5. *Prototyping and demonstration.* Interactive prototyping is used during and between JAD sessions to design and show application screens and to mock up system ideas. Building advance prototypes helps in presenting initial system concepts and in encouraging users to think about how technology might be used to improve work processes. Prototyping software can be used to develop application screens during the JAD workshop, and to finalize the design prototype after the session.

Software package preferences are both a personal and a corporate decision, and general recommendations from any source are not productive. You should use what works for your chosen or known analysis and development methods, not because a method is currently popular. Don't fall into adopting the latest method and tool fads; be prepared instead to evaluate and select tools that support methods your customer understands. Unfortunately, software is often selected well in advance by corporate standards groups or purchasing agents who don't understand your requirements. Don't cripple your presentation by using the drawing package bundled with a word processor when you really require a CASE tool. Consider the business investment in the workshop itself—a solid week of high-priced intellectual teamwork in a JAD makes the several hundred or thousand dollars for the right tool seem insignificant. Get the best tools for the job, and don't wait until the week before the session. Ask around, evaluate, and buy what works well in advance.

Use of CASE tools

With the portability of PCs and displays, CASE tools are more easily and frequently used in JAD workshops. CASE tools are used throughout information technology organizations to capture the products of analysis in diagrams, so as to formalize the analysis in readable representations. The CASE tools automate many other functions, such as maintaining data dictionaries, holding a common database of functions and definitions for use by multiple team members, and generating specifications, reports, or code from the database of design elements.

The key benefits of CASE for JAD workshops can be listed without expanding into the technical world of CASE tools too deeply. Among the three major types of CASE tools available—*upper CASE* for analysis diagrams, *lower CASE* for code generation support, and *comprehensive integrated environments*—the upper CASE tool is most appropriate for online use in workshops. Upper CASE tools support the front-end activities of development, including function analysis, data analysis, and object modeling. These are the most popular and inexpensive tools on the market, and many are highly flexible, with numerous methodologies and notations available. For JAD work, flexibility is key, since nontechnical participants care about readability, and a flexible tool allows changing the methods to reduce visual complexity for this more general use. In JAD the most commonly used CASE analysis methods include function hierarchies, flowcharts, data-flow diagrams, and entity-relationship diagrams. Other analysis methods, such as object modeling, control flow, and state-transition diagrams, can become too technically involved to use effectively in a mixed workshop setting.

The concern for JAD facilitators is not *why* to use CASE so much as *when* to use it and *where* to use it. CASE tools are very often used after workshop sessions to integrate and document the team's analysis and design work. This offline use allows an experienced analyst to reevaluate the analyses from the sessions and to construct readable diagrams that accurately document the intentions of the design team. If problems or differences of opinion arise, they can be spotted during this analysis and discussed during later team review. There are compelling reasons to integrate CASE into the workshop, and good reasons not to. These will be discussed in the following.

The CASE operator.   First of all, using CASE requires an additional element of interaction with the group—a technical mediator for the design model. A trained CASE operator must be brought into the proceedings, with a CASE toolset and a methodology that all will understand. The operator is typically a systems analyst familiar with the tool, but not usually trained in facilitation. The CASE operator can double as a methodology expert, but the operator should not be the only member with experience in a methodology. The operator must be at the service of the team, and flexible enough to support changes in methods or representations desired by the team. Be careful of the possible domination of analysis sessions by using a CASE operator—it is too easy for them to turn the focus of sessions to the use of the tool or the correctness of the analysis methodology. One approach to moderating this influence is for the facilitator to first work through analysis discussions on a neutral area, such as an easel or whiteboard. The resulting descriptions are then captured by the CASE operator online, and displayed during breaks in the analysis sessions.

The CASE tool. The CASE acronym is confusing to some, in that it refers to both computer-aided *software engineering* and computer-aided *systems engineering*. Software engineering tools are more programming-oriented (lower CASE) coding environments, and systems engineering tools are more comprehensive, with extensive analysis and design support. Although CASE often refers to analysis and design tools, it includes a wide range of design and program support tools:

- Analysis and design support tools
- Code, pseudocode, and database design language generators
- Data dictionary/repository systems
- Reverse engineering
- Software development support, including:
  - User interface prototyping
  - Compiling, linking, and editing
  - Software documentation
  - Validation and testing support

CASE tools have generally evolved toward becoming integrated project support environments, but the large price tag accompanying these comprehensive environments has increased competition for the highly effective, limited support tools. Many of the lower-priced CASE packages provide excellent analysis and design method support, which remains their primary purpose in JAD workshops.

The CASE methodologies. CASE tools support nearly all popular analysis and design methodologies, and the better packages add new methods as they become more widely used. For JAD use, adopt a tool with a wide range of methods and flexible notation, to allow local variations of the methods your team might want to use to improve usefulness or general readability. Remember, the *customer* or reader of analysis documentation is not always just development staff—especially from JADs, a more general readership might be involved, and tailoring diagrams and documents for accessibility will be necessary.

CASE analysis and design methodologies can be typically classified into four broad categories. Examples of the currently used methodologies are listed in each category:

- *Process-oriented methods:* Yourdon-DeMarco, Gane-Sarson, SSADM, and $IDEF_0$
- *Data-oriented methods:* Information Engineering, Entity-Relationship Diagramming, Bachman, and $IDEF_{1x}$
- *Real-time methods:* Hatley-Pirbhai, Ward-Mellor, and Harel
- *Object-oriented analysis and design:* Rumbaugh—Object Modeling Technique, Booch, Fusion, and Coad-Yourdon

The case for CASE. Using CASE tools during the JAD shrinks the total time required to provide a specification or other deliverable. By developing final format diagrams in the workshop, the diagrams are both created and reviewed during the same period. At the conclusion of each workshop session, a fairly complete component of the system model can be distributed. CASE tools can assist facilitators by allowing them to focus on the group process and on working with the design discussions. With the CASE operator capturing the models as they are constructed, the *methodology management* is shared, and the participants' focus is shared as well. Finally, the CASE tool can settle differences among participants and facilitators about the use of analysis diagramming methods, style, and symbology.

The case against CASE in JAD. Using CASE in a JAD workshop focuses thinking along the lines of the tool's methodologies, which might not always be the best use of participant's time. In a technical group context, CASE diagramming methods might be well understood, but in a mixed group, the use of such tools can mystify nontechnical users and diminish their participation. In other words, it might impress the IS and the more technical members, but it could easily alienate users. Even if all participants are trained to read and understand the diagrams, their use during design sessions creates the impression that the technical outcome is the workshop goal, and this should not necessarily be the case. This possibility should always be carefully considered before agreeing to use CASE during workshops.

Using CASE tools during the workshop changes the orientation of work, from the creative discussion of possibilities to nailing down hard facts. There is a difference in the way technical tools are viewed by participants, as is well understood by PD practitioners. Participants are much less likely to question design artifacts (prototypes, diagrams, documents) that are perfected and polished, as they appear to be when using CASE. When left as drawings on newsprint or a whiteboard, the softer medium affords easy modification and better reveals any flaws in the representation. The medium, as you might say, is the message. The harder the tool, the less accessible the design elements.

Finally, using CASE tools during JAD or other sessions can give the message that the team is assembled in service of the tool, not the other way around. Design discussions become oriented around the possibilities of the CASE diagrams, and the pace of work becomes constrained by the pace of the CASE operator. Conclusions are reached not by a common understanding among team members that a topic is covered, but by completing a diagram using the tool. The CASE operator can become a strong player in the workshop instead of a neutral cofacilitator.

Summary of Facilitated Workshops

Facilitated workshops bring a high degree of discipline and cooperation to development processes, and have potential for resolving the numerous conflicts in goals that arise in development work. An analogy to engineering work may be made—engineering is the discipline of designing and producing functional products to defined specifications while managing the compromises necessary in a real-world business environment. The facilitated design workshop requires the creative principle of engineering, the focus to construct useful specifications, and is fulfilled within the context of a cross-discipline group. It requires a mix of talents to succeed, including the ability to reach consensus with others and to compromise sometimes in order to cooperate. While not a perfect process, it is, like engineering, an effective, reliable process that satisfies requirements and produces tangible value for the organization.

Why use Team Design—why not just improve the traditional JAD? Those who have worked with JAD know that it works well for certain types of problems. It's useful and proven in the areas of MIS application development, requirements discussion, and process definition. Because of its traditions, however, JAD has connotations that substantially limit it to just these traditional areas. Practitioners of JAD express difficulty in applying their workshop methods to other domains of work and problem solving, such as business process redesign and decision support. Holding a JAD creates certain expectations in organizations where it is currently used, and the current methods probably hold sway.

The broader concepts behind Team Design are more applicable for many organizations than JAD, which has a more fixed definition and assumptions from its history. If JAD has been tried before and some were threatened or disenchanted by it, Team Design provides a way to gain the benefits of facilitated design workshops with customers without having to follow the JAD approach. Finally, it is a structure that supports a variety of group processes, yet still allows JAD to fit within its context.

3

A Team Design Approach

A major reengineering of information systems is planned by a telecommunications company, and an organizational staff of dozens of project managers and systems analysts, dozens of programmers, and numerous consultants is amassed within a month to undertake the job. Can you use Team Design methods to bring coordination and collaboration into this scale of organization?

A midsized software products firm adopts a companywide strategy to instill the "voice of the customer" into all its product lines. A new system development methodology is put in place, new customer contact procedures are promoted, product groups competing for resources are asked to share information to assist the greater goal. Is this an environment where you would use Team Design?

A consulting firm team kicks off a system integration planning session for a car manufacturer. An off-the-shelf project accounting system is desired to help manage project cost visibility and resource coordination across line management groups. Business planning is in charge of the effort, and all the VPs are present. Planning is initiated: the requirements must be defined and a package selected and installed within a year. Is this the ideal situation for Team Design?

The Context for Team Design

Team Design itself is a flexible approach to participatory team sessions for planning, design, and problem solving. However, it should be adapted differently for each organization to fit their particular processes. Different types of organizations provide different social structures for performing design and system engineering, and no single method will apply generally. As Bennett and Karat (1992) describe in an IBM report: "The social context in which a design activity takes place is an important factor in the quality of the resulting design...it is particularly important to achieve a *shared understanding* of the objectives and of the emerging design." The social context is both organizational (e.g., commercial product development, government contracting, and internal information systems) and functional (e.g., composed of expertise in computer science, business, and specialized knowledge). It is also stylistic, in that some social contexts might be described as strictly structured or action-oriented and others as tolerant, fluid, or friendly. A shared understanding is a group's common mental model of how work is to be performed. It is created in the group context of Team Design, as part of the process.

A view of a full development life cycle is initially established in this chapter as a mental model for guidance through the phases of any given project. Four *philosophical* approaches are introduced so the facilitator can adopt the most compatible orientation to integrate the workshops into a given organizational culture. These perspectives are provided as guidance for your organizational effectiveness and as a starting framework for using Team Design in practice.

The Team Design approach is intended to be flexible, a framework that can evolve with your use. Starting with one of the provided formats for the first several sessions, over time you may guide your team into creatively forming their own structures and inventing new methods.

JAD, development, and organizational culture

Joint Application Design (JAD) has become the most common form of user participation in the information systems design process in the North American business culture, and it fits the prevailing notions of the role of user involvement. System users are still perceived as task specialists or operators in the traditional business culture, and they are often only grudgingly accepted into the system design process. JAD provides a means of inclusion, but also offers the systems organization a structured methodology for *managing* user inclusion. Information systems managers have found that the JAD process leads to better user *acceptance* of the systems that are produced.

Joint Application Design is traditionally applied in the early phases of a project, but has been effectively used across all phases. Participatory workshops are useful in the early stages of work, since customers can be fully involved in the planning and requirements discussions. As long as the workshop is focusing on the requirements, the *what's needed* and not the *how to,* they may feel useful and involved. When discussions turn to the technical topics typically covered in the actual design work, they may be less able to follow the session, even in a facilitated setting. Holtzblatt and Beyer (1993) describe how customers are "at a disadvantage when brought into a design meeting," and explain how the users or customers involved in a JAD are taken out of the context of their real work. Removed from this context, they are less able to represent their experience to the design team.

Internal *management information systems* (MIS) development projects are often constrained by radical deadlines or immovable dependencies. A *rapid application development* (RAD) approach is often requested or required to meet the organizational demands. When a project requires a truly rapid design and development, you may find it useful to plan a single extended JAD workshop or a back-to-back series of sessions. For a smaller RAD project, one workshop of two or three days may cover the needs for all phases of the project.

Looking at a generic system development life cycle, see how JAD can be used as a technique to accomplish group work in any of the upfront phases. This approach may work well in a corporate MIS shop where a standardized user environment and well-established tools and developers exist. But will JAD work as well in the exploration of new technologies, or in the migration to object-oriented design, or in designing a new software product?

For example, it might be useful to adopt one comprehensive workshop to cover requirements and planning for all phases of a project. TASC, a large consulting and systems integration company, uses JAD workshops with State of Ohio clients as an up-front planning process. JAD planning processes makes effective use of the full stakeholder participation that's typically available at the start of an information systems project. For statewide deployment projects of this type, it's difficult to get all the participants together on a regular basis since representatives from different counties and regions must travel and synchronize schedules. When a project is first kicked off, TASC's practice has been to conduct basic planning and development scheduling with the primary client and to use a JAD approach to present the basic plan and development issues to the entire team at a project kickoff JAD. The plans for all phases of a years-long effort are discussed in the facilitated format, and agreements are made using a moderated decision process that allows all stakeholders an equal voice in the proceedings.

After these basics, the session quickly engages specific requirements and development issues from the assembled team. Processes used in these JADs include team building, visioning, quick analysis of the current process, dataflow and process mapping of the desired work process for the new system, and envisioning the ideal system, among several others. Agendas for this type of JAD can be based on the *user* context described later in this chapter.

Complex designs often require a lengthy JAD period, with ongoing sessions lasting from two to four or more weeks. These workshops will necessarily extend from the initial planning and requirements definition through the design and early development phases. As the group becomes comfortable working cooperatively as a team, less facilitation is required. A dedicated facilitator will often let the team take over its own sessions, and in the Team Design approach, facilitation will be shared among the participants. Chapter 3 covers the basic skills and approaches necessary for facilitating Team Design workshops. By developing facilitation skills and adapting methods from the following chapters, individuals from the systems or support organizations can lead effective analysis and design sessions.

Beyond JAD in development

By stretching the original JAD concept a little, the basic participatory team session can be set up as an ongoing process cofacilitated by various members of the team. Holtzblatt and Beyer recommend that the design team establish a room dedicated to the effort. They call this the *think tank,* and explain, "if you want your team to be creative, give them a room." This technique, by which a group maintains a persistent record of its design work in one place, is referred to as a *group memory.* In the workshop, the group memory consists of the chart paper, whiteboard lists and diagrams, printouts, and other results positioned throughout the workspace. In a JAD, the group memory is eventually translated to a working document, specification, and CASE diagrams. In a participatory design or Team Design approach, the session can extend into the workspace, the group memory becoming an interactive group design.

Richard Zahniser (1993) of the CASELab project at The University of Colorado describes the use of group memory as part of their *Design by Walking Around* (DBWA) methodology (now called JMPSSTART). He defines three group success factors: *cross-functional teams* (including users and development experts), *empowerment* (the team is qualified to make immediate decisions), and *group memory.* Of group memory, Zahniser explains:

> We expand this concept by using numerous storyboards (as many as six at a time) that allows us to build multiple models of the system quickly. These feed an on-line system development notebook containing all of the design and project status information. This on-line memory is one of the keys to the remarkable success of the Digital Equipment Corporation's Alpha AXP project, which coordinated 32 teams—over 2,000 people in 10 countries—and delivered its final product on schedule (p. 115).

What we might call *continuous cooperative development* has worked especially well for fast-paced development projects where results are expected in unusually short periods. In the world of government contracting, deliverables must sometimes be built against impossible schedules due to the rules of contract money and funding-based periods of performance. At TASC, a six-person development team used a cooperative approach with the user or customer, a dedicated group memory, and a team room to develop a fully functional client-server application from an existing prototype application in one month. The initial implementation of a distributed database system for a widely spread group of archaeologists documenting native American artifacts for repatriation required a rapid development process, full client and user involvement, and rapid development tools. The delivery could not have been met without the dedicated team involvement or the dedicated team environment.

The integration of different design disciplines in team development workshops addresses a weakness of JAD, in that JAD practices evolved as a business system methodology and they have not yet grown into general-purpose design tools. However, the JAD approach has been recognized for its effectiveness in bringing together disparate stakeholders to collaborate on system design. And although JAD has grown from the foundation of information systems, the cross-functional teamwork of JAD has also been recommended as a product development process. Keil and Erran (1995) discuss this distinction, comparing the customer-facing development practices between *custom* software systems and *package* software, or commercial product development. They describe the different customer-developer links used in designing software systems in these two environments. Keil and Erran found that the facilitated team approach (JAD) was primarily used by the custom software teams and was not evident in package development. They also found that fewer direct customer links were established in the package environment. The custom developers' four most effective links were all direct customer relationships, with *facilitated teams* rated as the most effective. The next two most effective methods were *user interface prototyping* and *requirements prototyping*. The package developers not only didn't use facilitation, they didn't have many direct links to customers, with *support lines* rated as their most effective link. Keil and Erran conclude that effective techniques designed for different environments should be adopted:

> Therefore we believe that development managers would do well to consider using links that have evolved outside of their particular development environment. Specifically, we recommend that development managers in the package environment consider using various facilitated team techniques as a direct link that may be particularly useful in the development of new software products or major enhancements to existing products (p. 43).

These examples of workshop-based methods indicate the direction for development teamwork beyond the JAD state of the art. The JAD process brings a well-established foundation and precedent, but Zahniser, Holtzblatt and others have shown the efficacy of integrating innovative design methods into the facilitated workshop.

Goals of Team Design methods

Participatory workshops do not always fit the JAD mold, nor do they always require a neutral facilitator. A range of participatory practices can be described across two dimensions, as shown in Fig. 3.1. This chart shows several types of group-based participatory workshops currently in use, oriented along the extent of technology involvement and organizational involvement. The vertical axis, showing the extent of *technology* involved, refers to the technological complexity of the *outcome* and not the workshop methods. Therefore, pure facilitation, such as for decision-making or arbitration purposes, is low on the technology scale, in that its results often don't apply to technical products. Training and consulting are normally much higher with respect to technology, more in the roles of education in technologies or of advice and support, as in consulting. The design team at the top of the scale represents the focused workgroup of a software or system design team, which can be "facilitated," normally by a leader. This

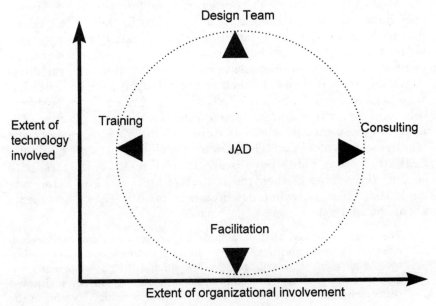

Figure 3.1 Organizational participation and technology.

team demonstrates the highest technological complexity possible in group work.

The horizontal axis shows the extent of *involvement* of the organization doing the work. Organizational involvement is quite low in training, wherein participants are actively learning but normally do not interactively influence the results and outcome of the training. Moving further to the right, facilitation is somewhat more involved with the organization using it, as it must be tailored extensively and interactively to meet organizational demands. Consulting is perhaps the highest involvement, in paying the facilitator to work with the organization in planning and implementing technological change. Consulting is the furthest along the scale of organizational involvement (or impact), as it entails making recommendations for the business or design deliverables.

Traditional Joint Application Design fits somewhere in the middle of these scales, and runs the risk of ineffectiveness whenever it veers into the other activities. Normally, the JAD facilitator isn't expected to perform training or consulting, although this may be required or requested at times. JAD teams are not always well prepared to perform the design work expected of the situation, and the facilitator is typically the first one to notice this. Also, JAD requires much more than pure facilitation. Technology-based outcomes are expected of the team, and facilitators must have the experience to recognize the development of a quality product. They must also be capable of guiding the team in the mechanics of developing the products, which is when the facilitator becomes a consultant. Likewise, the facilitator becomes an instructor when training the JAD team in the proper use of design techniques, which may also be expected.

In evaluating the roles of the facilitator, it's necessary to understand the purpose of the session and the requirements of the group. When would it be useful for a facilitator to work as a consultant or trainer? When should the facilitator step in and provide concrete advice? If a group is off track in its purpose, should a facilitator allow the group to work through its process, or is it better to risk overinvolvement and help set the design process on a more productive track?

Any facilitation requires involvement, and it's idealistic to assume that an effective facilitator can or should remain totally neutral. The myth of neutrality and objectivity in facilitation is an ideal that is untenable in practice and difficult to monitor. Twentieth-century physics has ruled out the possibility of unbiased observation in the physical universe, even in controlled experimentation. So it's unlikely that a pure unbiased neutrality is possible.

A pragmatic view holds that facilitators should use their skills and experience to the advantage of the team and its goals. An awareness of one's biases is necessary and these biases can be communicated directly with the team. With teams that are comfortable with each other and with the facilitator, the involvement or even the participation of the facilitator does not usually become a concern.

Some observers have noted that facilitator neutrality only becomes an issue in formal settings when the group is not comfortable with facilitation, or in politically charged environments where the slightest hint of favor toward a party might be construed as bias. Facilitators even worry about whether it's acceptable to offer positive feedback to team contributions, for concern of appearing to be biased! In these situations, which are not typical of design workshops, a reserved and professional style might be more appropriate.

Team Design allows the facilitator to adopt a style or level of involvement appropriate to the organizational context and to the type of design work. It provides a flexible methodology for conducting analysis and design that embraces the best of the known practices, such as JAD, and supports processes not typically considered in JAD. Further, Team Design gives organizations a framework from which to build their own custom-design practices. It's not a new system for design and development so much as a container to fit it all in. It doesn't require teams to change everything overnight, but shows them ways to start, to get moving in a productive direction, and to build and learn from the best practices of their own and other organizations.

Team Design organizational contexts

Four organizational *contexts* describe the significant variations in approach required when conducting Team Design or collaborative group work in different organizations. Context guidelines support adapting workshop models and methods for appropriate organizational backgrounds, which as defined include the business, systems, user, and product contexts. These are not all-inclusive definitions, but are constructed as descriptive categories that cover most of the organizational backgrounds expected in facilitated *development* sessions.

The *business context* is used for management information systems and business process design. It is applied when fundamental business processes are automated or redesigned. The business context is well served by the traditional JAD approach, which brings together system analysts and representatives of the user groups. It is a conservative approach, one that seeks to minimize the discord of implementing new systems impacting the business. The goals of the business approach include managing the impact of required change in the organization, improving the efficiency or flexibility of operations, and supporting more effective integration of information and individuals in the organization.

The *systems context* provides a forum for sharing design ideas and solving problems in a technological environment, where the stakeholders are those responsible for managing the technology. This is the context used for *back end* systems or large-scale software packages. However, the systems context may also serve for large systems where user involvement is universal, such as a desktop package used by everyone in an organization.

The *user context* is the primary model for Team Design. It puts users on an equal plane with the system designers. As in participatory design, responsibility is shared for the product. Roles of users and designers substantially change—in becoming partners in the project, the users agree to provide more than just information and feedback. They provide access to their work, access to their insights, and a shared commitment to the result of the system design. The goals of the user context can be considered to be the following:

- Involve the users of a planned system as much as possible in the design of their work processes and the new system.

- Produce more effective systems by fully integrating those users with task and domain knowledge into the design process.

- Enhance overall customer and user acceptance by providing continual feedback from the users to the design team, thus guiding the design to fully satisfy user requirements.

- Create productive partnerships with the customers and the user community for designing, evaluating, implementing, and using the system or product.

The *product context* incorporates aspects from all of the contexts. It supports a business-oriented model, since most products generate revenues for stakeholders. A systems approach can be taken in designing for a technical market where exacting specifications must be met. A user approach must be taken for a product to succeed in a competitive landscape. The convergence of these models supports the brute-force analysis and creativity required in product development. Goals identified for the product context include the following:

- Produce the right product for a user community by integrating users into the design process and iterating feedback into product design.

- Creatively design breakthrough products through a better team process than that possible with traditional product development processes.

- Balance the business requirements of product managers and the technical requirements of development in product design sessions.

- Create productive partnerships with customers and the user community for designing, evaluating, implementing, and using products.

The Business Context

The application of Team Design in the traditional corporate business is illustrated by an example describing an actual JAD process. A Fortune 500 corporation competing in the telecommunications and networking products market requested a JAD approach for an effort sponsored by the chief financial officer. Outside consultant facilitators for a series of JAD sessions were contracted to gather requirements among a large number of internal stakeholders and gain their agreement on priorities for a project accounting system. The customer established a very limited time period for completion of the JADs—all meetings and information would be completed within two weeks.

Each JAD or similar workshop must be evaluated in terms of the context of its customer, and in this case the customer was upper management. A top-down approach was suggested for this JAD, primarily due to its high level of organizational sponsorship. A traditional JAD workshop would have brought all the primary stakeholders together in a combined session, allowing each participant to share with the whole group and all ideas to be heard at the same time. In this business environment, a fairly large group of knowledge worker stakeholders—more than 300—would be affected by the system. The JAD approach had to account for different levels of information needs among management.

To avoid undue cross-pressure among the different levels of management, a unique approach was proposed. Each stakeholder group would have a separate JAD to discuss and agree on priorities within the more homogenous group. Therefore, separate workshops were held for a day or longer for each group. This included the business analysis group (which reported to the CFO customer), line management stakeholders, and the project management users whose work would be directly affected every day by a new system. The vice presidents of the organization were also included, but instead of conducting a JAD they were interviewed individually. The VPs responses were summarized and presented as high-level direction within each of the JADs. Rather than actually including the VPs in the JADs, this had the effect of allowing freer discussion among the groups while taking the executives' concerns into account.

The business context is used for team workshops where primary management information systems are at stake, and for business process design. The focus of this approach is on meeting business requirements, and the concerns of the users could be considered to be secondary. It is best applied when fundamental business processes are automated or redesigned, such as customer information management, asset tracking, or cost management.

Goals of the business context

The business context is well served by the traditional JAD approach based on the original IBM model, which brings together system analysts and representatives of the user groups. It is a conservative approach, one that seeks to minimize the discord of implementing new systems impacting the business. The goals of the business approach include the following:

- Manage the impact of required change in the organization.

- Improve the efficiency or flexibility of operations (sometimes cost-driven or based on growth needs).

- Support more effective integration of information and individuals in the organization.

- Incorporate the requirements of the critical stakeholders in the process.

Using a facilitated JAD session allows representatives of line organizations to voice their priorities during the planning and analysis for new processes. It also allows business leaders to stay clear of the politicking required to insert new processes into business operations.

This approach should be adopted by managers and other internal customers who call for the value of facilitated development services within traditional corporate environments, including:

- Corporate MIS managers and developers

- Business and systems analysts within corporate organizations

- Businesses teaming with other businesses that require a conservative approach to mutually beneficial or collaborative design

- Facilitators who work in these environments

- JAD facilitators who require a structured approach to design workshops

Development projects and products in the business context include the traditional information systems areas and system template pack-

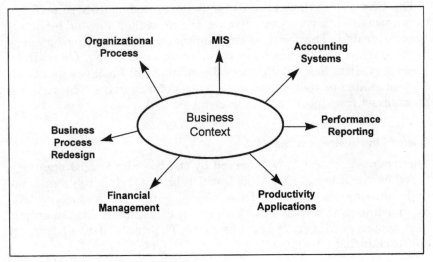

Figure 3.2   Business context applications.

ages used to automate standard business processes. Figure 3.2 shows some of the applicable domains of the business context for system development projects.

Business context deliverables

Each organizational context offers a set of preferred deliverables, often found and expected within the organizations described by the context. These deliverables are described throughout this book, are covered in more detail in the Team Design *formats,* and are only listed in this section as a reference to their applicability to the organizational context. Table 3.1 shows deliverables that should be considered for the *business context* workshop.

Organizational involvement

This context presupposes a corporate staff supporting internal information systems for the enterprise. As such, the typical customers and users for the business orientation are internal to the business. For accounting applications, customers and users are often the same, such as line managers requiring budget reports and utilization figures. For other types of applications, such as external customer databases, *customers* would include most of the upper management in customer-facing organizations and *users* might be from a completely different organization handling customer phone calls, data entry, or market research.

TABLE 3.1   Business Context Deliverables

Deliverable	Content
Workshop plan	Plan for conducting JAD or Team Design workshop Agenda, distribution, and schedules Purpose and goals Business problem statement
Business requirements	Scope of business process Process map and current process analysis Business objectives and criteria Proposed business process Proposed process diagram/map
System requirements	Scope of system Mapping of system to business process Current system architecture User/system requirements System data flow Entity-relationship model Paper prototype
Application prototype	Initial prototype for demonstration in workshop Prototype modified in the workshop
Prototype design document	Prototype design description User interface definition Database definition Program module definition
Application test plan	Test procedures mapped to requirements Usability and integration test plans
Implementation planning	Application development plan Implementation plan Release plan

Approach to facilitation.   A business-oriented approach to facilitation could be described as conservative and perhaps even cautious. If multiple stakeholders are involved, conflict is likely due to the normal conflicts in goals and incentives among corporate organizations. The facilitator must realize that participants probably view the session as an extension of their own management or staff meetings—after all, they are in attendance together and the focus is often on their business requirements.

This is not to discourage a creative approach to facilitation—the business context does not normally lead to free-for-all sessions. However, creativity exercises can and should be used to assist in getting the group to reach breakthroughs in generating ideas and working cooperatively.

Facilitators in this context should have business analysis and group leadership skills, and must be able to anticipate the group, understand the underlying business problems, and invent approaches for the group itself to solve its problems. Some of the skills required of the facilitator in this context include:

- Business systems analysis or process or industrial engineering skills, with a background in or an understanding of the organization's industry or work
- An understanding of business practices such as accounting, management processes, business metrics, and cost management
- Change management skills, with a background in social psychology, organizational behavior, team building, and negotiation

Roles of participants and leaders.   The roles of participants in the business context are typically those found in the traditional JAD. These include the sponsor, project or development manager, user representatives, and business analysts. Specialized roles include the facilitator, recorder, observers, and, sometimes, a methodologist. Technical specialists are typically brought into the sessions as needed, but can be included as full-time members depending on the inclination of the culture. User representatives should be active in or experts in the business process under design, and be supported by their management to make decisions for their organization.

Organizational dynamics.   In the business context, organizational issues often share equal significance with technical design activities. This context typically assumes an internal business unit customer, not an external client of the company. When internal customers are served, different dynamics emerge than when an external customer is driving the effort and paying for the system.

In your organization, it may be difficult to obtain additional personnel and other resources without working through channels and negotiating. Your project isn't the only one under management's purview, and your organization's processes and measurement systems may be blocks to your smooth forward movement.

Assembling a cross-functional team is not an easy task in most traditional organizations. Obtaining people with the best qualifications for the project is difficult, even with high-priority projects. Team members selected from across several organizations continue to report to managers from their home departments, and their availability may often be determined by their management. Hidden agendas and special loyalties will emerge, even in the closest teams. As a workshop organizer or facilitator, your ability to make requests of team members will be constrained by their management. Of course, the most effective and productive staff will always be busy with other duties, and your choices for a new effort may be limited. Management considerations will continually emerge, and you will find yourself with many new responsibilities. Whether you are a business analyst, facilitator, or filling another role, coordination of the design workshop requires you to function across organizational boundaries and up and down the chains of management.

In this position, pay attention to the stated and unstated objectives for the design process. In the business context, what are the critical goals? Profitability of a business unit, effectiveness of a business process, reduction of cost for internal administration? What are the desired goals—things like achieving process efficiency status by a strategic date, utilization of personnel on administrative functions, accessibility of MIS data?

The business context is among the most common orientations faced by consulting facilitators, and is probably the closest to the traditional JAD environment. If you are currently facilitating in this context, notice what lessons can be gained from the other contexts as you read through and evaluate them. The traditional business orientation probably has the most to gain from using the *techniques* of the other contexts.

The Systems Context

Development projects and workshops are frequently driven by the needs of those in the *systems community,* such as MIS managers, software product developers, and system project managers. Not all systems or product design and development work calls for significant business involvement, or even user representation. Consider the cases of design in technical infrastructure (such as networking), or the selection of database technology or development environments. In this context, technological information and technical decisions are required for projects to move forward. User requirements, if involved, will remain important, but overall less emphasis on user involvement will be found in a Team Design workshop using the systems context.

A large accounting firm moves to overhaul the complete corporate infrastructure, and one of the significant projects is the selection and implementation of desktop computing and electronic communications (such as e-mail). This might be a familiar example, since most practitioner readers have probably already survived at least one such major system conversion in their recent work lives. Although numerous *user requirements* are involved with such an undertaking, for the most part they are gathered through surveys or through a designated technical representative. The scope of the system is technical, from the design of a large-scale infrastructure to the evaluation of vendor solutions and implementation proposals.

The traditional JAD approach might not be the best approach in this case, but modifications could apply. The systems context maintains common aspects from JAD, such as organized group problem solving and decision making, group participation methods, and neutral facilitation. In fact, a Team Design approach to this systems problem might look a lot like a JAD on the surface.

Goals of the systems context

The philosophy of the systems context is to provide a forum for sharing design ideas and solving problems in a technological environment, where the stakeholders are those responsible for managing the technology. It doesn't so much exclude users as it recognizes that their participation is not critical for the context. Often this is the case for *back end* systems such as networks, database or communications servers, or large-scale software packages that manage largely invisible processes. However, the systems context may also serve the practitioner for large-scale systems where user involvement is universal, such as a scheduling system or a desktop package used equally by all members of an organization. User input and requirements are solicited, but specific end users would not be included in design and development workshops planned under this context.

The goals of the systems context include the following:

- Solve a basically technical system problem or construct a systems design, where direct user involvement is not required.
- Involve technical staff to their maximum effectiveness by applying group participation methods in a workshop setting.
- Produce a thorough system design and its documentation in a short period of time.

The systems context supports technical development projects for infrastructure and enterprisewide installations, such as networking and systems integration. It also supports installation of commercial software for office automation and standard desktop packages. Figure 3.3 shows some of the applications associated with the systems context.

Systems context deliverables

Systems context deliverables are similar to those identified for the business context, except that they support systems integration, infrastructure, and package installation instead of IS applications develop-

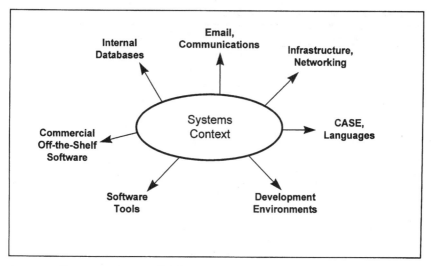

Figure 3.3 Systems context applications.

ment. Table 3.2 identifies the deliverables considered appropriate for the *systems context* workshop.

Organizational involvement

The systems context assumes a development orientation, and is much more technical in approach than the other contexts. The typical customers for this approach are internal, as in the business context, but represent the information systems organizations, not the business areas. Customers for the systems context include development organizations and their management, who are responsible for implementation of the workshop's solution.

Users for this context might include various representatives across the organization, since almost anyone could be considered a user of basic system or structural implementations. However, direct user representation can be unwieldy and unreliable in this context, depending on the system. For infrastructure, database, and server systems, users might be technical support from the major business applications, or technical user support for desktop and user applications. These representatives should always be included in systems context design sessions.

Approach to facilitation. Facilitation is often overlooked in the systems context approach, at least in traditional organizations. Systems managers and analysts bring a strong technical competence to their work, often leading to a self-reliant viewpoint. With a roomful of self-

TABLE 3.2 Systems Context Deliverables

Deliverable	Content
Workshop plan	Workshop or session plan Agenda, distribution, and schedules Purpose, goals, and problem statement
System project plan	Project definition Project scope Schedule and assumptions Costs and resources Work plan
Business requirements statement (if applicable)	Scope of business process Process map and current process analysis Proposed business process Proposed process diagram/map
System requirements	Scope of system Mapping of system to business process Current system architecture User/system requirements System data flow Entity-relationship model Initial prototype or pilot system installation
System prototypes	User interface prototype Architecture prototype Design prototype
System design model	Prototype design description User interface definition Database definition Program module definition
System test plan	Test procedures mapped to requirements Usability and integration test plans
Implementation planning	Development plan Implementation plan Release plan

reliant, analytical engineers and technicians, an outside facilitator cannot expect an invitation to assist in design sessions. An approach to facilitation in this context holds that it's a shared responsibility, wherein different team members can lead sessions where their expertise is of value, similarly to consulting. Therefore, truly neutral facilitation might not be a primary consideration, but the chances of engaging an external facilitator in the systems context are very slim. From the viewpoint of technical competence, having a facilitator lead a team in technical design decision making is tantamount to incompetence, to admitting it can't be done without help. If you're in this environment, be especially sensitive to the self-reliance and pride in workmanship brought to the session. As a technical leader, use the strengths of the team members to propel the session forward. Be willing to move quickly, and go slow on pushing group sensitivity exercises that might actually impede the team's interest or willingness to deal with team issues.

Roles of participants and leaders.   The roles of participants in the systems context are different than those found in the usual JAD. Participants in this context are more technical, and would include the project and development managers, lead architects or engineers, and development and technical specialists. Roles such as the sponsor, user representatives, and business analysts are not typical for this type of workshop, since it's dealing with fairly technical issues. Specialized roles such as the facilitator, recorder, observers, and others will not usually be used, although facilitation is often performed and shared among the team members. The project and development managers will more often perform in the facilitation or session leader role in this context than in the others, as the entire team is usually oriented toward solving a common problem without the organizational diversity and goal conflicts seen in more cross-functional team workshops.

The User Context

The user context is the basic model for Team Design. In the user context we integrate learning from user-oriented JAD with participatory design approaches. *Participatory design* (PD), although used in Europe for over a decade, has only more recently been used in North America. Although still unknown in most corporations, PD principles are easily understood and are well regarded by those organizations using them. A user context can be established without adopting a participatory design approach, but it is recommended as the model from which to work, in the way that JAD is a model for the business context.

The user context puts users on an equal plane with the system designers. As in participatory design, responsibility for the product is shared, and this is made clear from the outset. The roles of users and designers substantially change—in becoming partners in the project, the users agree to provide more than just information and feedback. They provide access to their work, access to their insights, and a shared commitment to the result of the system design. System designers bring the design process and design expertise to the project. Bjerknes (1993) describes the process as a mutual educational experience:

> The users must learn about technology from the system experts in order to understand what computer technology can do for them, and the system

experts have to learn about the application domain from the users in order to build a flexible and efficient system that fits the user's needs (p. 39).

The user context is the opposite end of the spectrum from the type of session described under the systems context. Bellcore's PICTIVE process, developed by Muller (1991), has been used with NYNEX projects where nontechnical users require a simple product interface. PICTIVE involves very simple activities presented to a group of users for building and iterating design mock-ups. Users are engaged in nontechnical design activities that fully incorporate their thinking and afford opportunities for simple creative design. However, in this context technologies that aren't directly relevant to the users' perspective (such as CASE or interactive prototyping in the session) are not used.

Goals of the user context

The user context hinges on a basic premise of human factors engineering: Design should be concerned with the role of the users of technology, and design for human use should ensure that the users' systems and environments are developed to support usability, comfort, and safety. By observing and listening to the users, we can integrate their requirements into system designs and specifications. Users typically understand the true demands of their tasks better than management and systems analysts. We can always design better systems by creating a partnership with the user to ensure that a system's design is effective for the task and that it is highly usable or even rewarding to use. By bringing the user and customer closer to the source of the product, this approach inspires a high degree of organizational involvement, and it makes business sense.

The goals of the user context can be considered to be the following:

- Involve the users of a planned system in the design of their work processes and new system as much as possible.

- Produce more effective systems by fully integrating those users with task and domain knowledge into the design process.

- Enhance overall customer and user acceptance by providing continual feedback from users to the design team, thus guiding the design to fully satisfy user requirements.

- Create productive partnerships with customers and the user community for designing, evaluating, implementing, and using the system or product.

The user context may not be an immediate fit in many organizations. To MIS departments, it may represent a shifting of power outside of their domain, and to developers, it may be a threat to their control of the process. In this context the philosophy of shared responsibility and democratic process are basic assumptions. Steven Miller (1993) points out that PD embraces two principles which apply here: (1) users and customers are intelligent and creative, and will contribute productively if given the opportunity to bring their insights and expertise forward and given responsibility for the results of their decisions, and (2) good ideas will rise up from the bottom as well as down from the top—perhaps even more so. In other words, "customers know what works, what doesn't work, and how to improve things."

A user context project is planned and managed differently to some extent. Power and decision making are likely to be shared. Workshops may include more user stakeholders and may have several sponsors, depending on the scope of impact on user groups. Schedules must allow for user review and feedback time, and perhaps allow for the cross-education required between the customer/user groups and the designer/developer groups. Functional requirements may be refocused as *user requirements,* task and work process definition may be conducted along with system analysis (as it should be), and a strong emphasis is placed on acceptance and usability testing.

The user context is found within a wide range of projects and organizations, and should be considered for any systems development of production systems used by large numbers of operators. The user context applies to most information system projects where the business processes are managed by the users, and to large-scale customer service and business operations oriented systems. Figure 3.4 shows a range of applications associated with the user context.

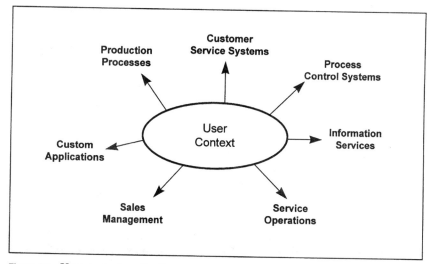

Figure 3.4 User context applications.

TABLE 3.3   User Context Deliverables

Deliverable	Content
Workshop plan	Plan for conducting Team Design workshop Agenda, advance documentation, and schedules Purpose, goals, and problem statement
Business requirements statement	Scope of business or work process Process map and current process analysis Proposed business/work process Process scenarios Proposed process diagram/map
User requirements	Scope of system Mapping of system to business/work process Current system architecture User requirements System data flow Entity-relationship model Paper prototype
User task definition	User task scenarios (business process–task relationships) Task workflow analysis User task analysis or task observations Videotape or interview protocols
Application prototype	Simulation of user interface prototype Design prototype
Acceptance criteria	Customer acceptance criteria User acceptance criteria Acceptance test scenarios
Acceptance test plan	Test procedures mapped to requirements Acceptance and usability test plans

User context deliverables

User context deliverables differ from those identified for the other contexts, and there is more flexibility for adding or removing items from the list in this context. Table 3.3 identifies the deliverables considered appropriate for the *user context* workshop.

Organizational involvement

As hinted by the name, the user context is the most involving of users of all the Team Design approaches. Derived somewhat from the original JAD approach, the user context is designed to infuse direct user participation with every element of the analysis and design process. Key users are involved early in the process and become an integral part of the team for the duration of the project. This approach is especially useful in projects where the user organization will be responsible for the maintenance and support of the application. If users are involved in the key decisions during development and implementation, they will have the intimate knowledge of the system required to manage its life cycle long after installation.

In the user context, the terms *user* and *customer* are often referenced interchangeably. This is not problematic, but it is somewhat imprecise. If an organization relies on the development group for delivery of a system, and they sponsor or fund the development effort, they are of course the "customer." Members of the organization might be users of the system when it is deployed, but this does not necessarily make the users, or even their representatives, customers. Users become customers when they are the organization that development answers to, when they become responsible for development meeting the schedule and delivery of the system.

The user context, like JAD, is more oriented toward internal information systems (IS) than product development. Product development follows the product context, in which the users are typically paying customers, and major customers are organizations representing hundreds or thousands of users. The user context supports the corporate IS model, where users represent a business process that serves the corporation. Their full involvement is critical in the design and acceptance of any system they will use in fulfillment of the business process. Using a systems context approach to develop specialized business systems for a user group can lead to unacceptable or, at best, difficult applications. The users must be fully involved in the user interface and workflow decisions made by a cross-functional development team. The user organizational context is designed for such systems where usability and user acceptance is critical to business operations, as well as where workflow inefficiency could impede the business process.

Approach to facilitation. Facilitators in the user context take a very different approach than in the business or systems contexts. The facilitator works closely with customer and user representatives during the planning period to understand the key requirements and acceptance criteria and uncover issues that will affect system deployment.

During the workshop, the facilitator encourages collaboration with the users as much as is practical. The line between collaboration and distraction can be difficult to manage—collaboration requires a willingness to share the group's space for discussion and design, and technologists and facilitators often have a strong need to maintain evident forward progress. A tolerance for ambiguous processes is necessary, as it's not always clear to nonusers when a topic is pertinent or critical to discovering design attributes of the work process. Although technologists quickly lose patience when it appears that a workshop has lost its apparent focus, users should be given a fairly broad rein to discuss issues and possibilities. It is as important to allow the user representatives the opportunity to fully belong to the design team as it is to solicit their input.

Roles of participants and leaders.   We have concentrated on the role of facilitator, which is a crucial role in the user context, in most of this discussion. The makeup of the user context team might be similar to that of the business context, on the surface. Analysts, a recorder, development leaders, the project manager, observers, and other stakeholders will be members of the team. However, the users have the most significant role in participation, as customers as well as users.

As participants, users should be willing to learn as much as practical about the business requirements and the business need for any new system project in which they will participate. They must be able to speak for the larger group, and possibly make commitments (for design or implementation) on behalf of their organization. They must be willing to participate fully in all design workshops to which they are invited. The key term is *willing*—there is not always a role for user participation in every discussion, but there may always be user impacts that should be cleared and discussed openly with involved user stakeholders.

Team leaders must be able to support the design workshops with an open mind toward including the user community, and should be discouraged (by the facilitator if necessary) from using their authority to push along the proceedings in their chosen direction. Project leaders and development managers will typically engage opportunities to make closure or to wrap up points to facilitate their forward direction consistent with their goal-oriented timeline. In a team-oriented design session, project goals aren't the only goals supported by the workshop structure. As a facilitator, be aware of the various goals and the problems to be solved by the different stakeholders. Sometimes a problem with availability of resources or organizational policy might require solution before the system design team can move forward. These are the types of issues which can be effectively handled by team leaders, and freeing up the group from organizational distractions and side issues should be a primary task of those in management or leadership roles. However, not all the team's issues will be handled in the sessions, and many issues may not be appropriate for the workshop environment.

Dynamics of the user context

The user context should be employed whenever the users of a system will be the major stakeholders for a planned system or process. Therefore, use it for any overhaul of an existing user-oriented function (such as customer service or order management). Use it for any facilitated process where any nonmanagement organizations have much at stake (such as the quality or existence of their jobs!), and where potential conflict might arise from differences in interests.

The user context is useful for any major organizational change where systems and processes are redesigned, and the users' jobs or work processes will be affected. To use the business context approach when major changes are planned to workers' jobs invites organizational conflict and the loss of productivity of dissatisfied users. Giving the user organization the responsibility to redesign its work processes using information technology supports the corporation in working as a whole, and prevents fragmenting the business in turf battles and disagreements over process. The user context, guided with experienced facilitation, allows the business process owners and the user organizations to work together in designing a system that meets business and user needs. It supports the user organization in ownership of its part of the business process, affording buy-in of the larger plan that includes the system.

The user context demands a fully involved team composed of decision makers from the various groups represented or, at least, influential stakeholders (some might refer to them as *empowered,* but as this term is frequently misused it won't be cited). If only *representative* users are involved, their decision-making power will not stand against the business process owners or development politics. The users on the design team must also be qualified to some extent to understand the impact of technology decisions and must, at least, be willing to ask the right questions when information systems technologists start "herding" toward a consensus for design or implementation. Tradeoffs between systems and users are always made in development projects, and the resolution is often determined by cost. These factors and negotiations are fair game in the user context; therefore, experienced facilitators are highly recommended for this approach.

It cannot be stressed too much that when the user context is called for, another approach will not substitute. Using a business or systems context for a new system when the users have their work lives at stake risks creating rifts between organizations that can shake every level of the enterprise. When work processes are being automated, it is tempting to leave out the very people whose work will be automated. However, no other organization in the business is as qualified to understand the scope of the work and the best approaches for redesign and, possibly, full automation than the user groups themselves.

The Product Context

How does the product context differ from the others? Consider a product to be any system, service, or software package developed for use by external customers that is packaged and sold as relatively the same product for all users. It must be a hot item its first time out in public, or soon after its release. You might know a few representative customers for the product, but as a designer, facilitator, or developer it's likely you'll never work directly with a product's market—whereas with the business, system, or user contexts, teams typically work directly with the customer and user representatives. In the product world, you might work with sales representatives. Being so far removed from the source of your product's success makes this context more difficult than the others.

The product context combines elements from the other three approaches and is also the most unique of the contexts. Most practitioners cannot easily pick up this book and immediately apply the information on the product context in their work. Methodological evolution has been documented by books and journals in areas corresponding to the business, systems, and user worlds; the product development world is always changing, is highly competitive, and doesn't follow published standards. More than the others, the product context requires adaptation to the organization's culture, development methods, and unpublished techniques of working together. Also, any organization developing software, hardware, or integrated products will use a unique, and probably proprietary, methodology. The product context doesn't scrap existing methods—it shows a framework for understanding a broader, user-centered view of product development.

Developing products with a team approach requires a willingness to be creative and audacious. The best product ideas and designs don't originate from logical reasoning, but from a synthesis of good existing ideas and taking advantage of group creativity. Breakthrough products are not the by-product of reasoning, but of flashes of insight and ingenious twists on the familiar. Most successful products are the outcome of collaborative work, in which an idea becomes a shared resource, added to and reshaped until it becomes a working model. The working model is tested and beaten on until it becomes something more solid. A software package, automobile, or motion picture is designed by a team of people, all of whom play some role in its production. The finished product reflects the coordination of many small decisions and changes, and is never attributable to just one person.

Goals of the product context

The product context incorporates all of the contexts in some ways. It supports a business-oriented model—most products are designed to generate revenues for the stakeholders, so some of the business reasoning of the business context is necessary. A systems approach can be taken in evaluating and designing for a technical market, where exacting specifications must be attained in the design. A user-oriented approach must be taken for a product to succeed in a competitive landscape. The convergence of these models supports the brute-force analysis and creativity required in product development.

The goals of the product context include the following:

- Produce the right product for a user community by integrating users into the design process and iterating feedback into product design.

- Creatively design breakthrough products better through a team process than is possible with traditional product development processes.

- Balance the business requirements of product managers and the technical requirements of development in product design sessions.

- Create productive partnerships with customers and the user community for designing, evaluating, implementing, and using products.

The product context is found in many development environments where commercial software products and package software are produced. Information services that provide data to the public require an understanding of the product context. Most Web-based systems developed as revenue-based business services are product contexts. Custom software development projects that produce software for resale apply to the product context. Figure 3.5 shows a range of product areas for this context.

Product context deliverables

Table 3.4 identifies the deliverables considered appropriate for the *product context* workshop.

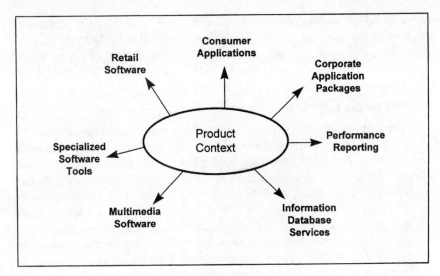

Figure 3.5 Product context applications.

TABLE 3.4 **Product Context Deliverables**

Deliverable	Content
Workshop plan	Plan for conducting Team Design workshop Agenda, distribution, and schedules Purpose, goals, and problem statement
Product vision	Scope of product and business goals Product vision statement Business requirements for product
Product requirements	Product scope or definition Mapping of product definition to business requirements Current product architecture User requirements Initial product prototype
User process definition	User's business process–task relationships User task or workflow analysis Work context analysis, videotape, or interview protocols
Product prototype	User interface prototype Product design prototype
Product acceptance testing	Market acceptance criteria User acceptability criteria Usability test plan

Organizational involvement

Customer and user involvement in the product context is as essential as in the user context, although the distinctions of *customer* and *user* are different. In the product approach, customers are typically *end users* as well, since they actually purchase and use a product or its associated service.

Since a huge range of potential customers from any market might use the product, a definition of the expected users should be constructed. Marketing research might supply some of the initial customer definition for a potential product, based on sales and competitive analysis information. This should be considered only a starting point. The product team will learn much more about the intended user by establishing relationships with people with a need for the product envisioned. By visiting user sites and meeting with potential customers and users, the team will obtain a first-hand look at the tasks and work currently done that the product might address. One hour with real users communicates more clearly than weeks of marketing research. When developing a product to help law firms sift through mountains of testimony for a large case, visiting law firms and talking with attorneys, paralegals, and legal assistants will help define the task and the need. Continuing to work with customers over the design cycle should be a regular practice.

For a new product, you will require some test bed to test the concept. Work with your most trusted current customers to select a small set of users that reflects the characteristics and interests expected for the new product. Arrange focus groups or interviews early in the process to engage their interest in the product. As the product concept becomes more focused and deeper customer interest is found, consider requesting time with these key users to engage them in design sessions with the product team. Having at least one or two actual product users available to the team at critical times can make a significant difference in design effectiveness.

Approach to facilitation. In the product context, the facilitator might work in multiple roles. Product development teams often are cross-functional, comprised of members from various disciplines reporting to different organizations and having their own goals within the product goal itself.

Dedicated facilitators are not typically utilized in today's product development environments, since product companies often build products following a sequential development model that doesn't ever bring developers and customers together in the same environment. Requirements, design documents, and communications are frequently passed between the organizations in the product development world. Sales representatives gather customer interests and needs and pass them along to marketing, which then evaluates the trends and gathers sets of requested features and identifies potentially larger needs in the market. They present a summarized notion of product features to product managers, who explore the feasibility of producing a new system or service to meet the identified need. When critical mass is achieved, the product concept might be approved, and product management brings a product team together. It's no wonder facilitators are not used, since this process might take weeks or months before a team is established. By then, a facilitated approach might be perceived as an unnecessary contrivance that could slow down the pace of meeting product goals.

However, the traditional process is slow and unwieldy. The product development process spans several functional organizations in most companies, and communication issues abound. The traditional process generates inconsistent results, depending on factors such as the level of management commitment, the quality of project leadership and programming or design talent, and schedule. Many companies have invested heavily in proprietary product development methodologies, or have spent years growing their own processes as a guide for organizations and teams. A large consulting market exists in product development due to an important and time-critical need to improve the processes. Facilitators are used more than ever in product consulting, both in creative designing and in defining and managing the development process itself. Consider the necessity for both—if a breakthrough product concept emerges from a Team Design workshop process, what are its chances for timely production if the development processes are weighed down by bureaucratic or inefficient organizational gyrations?

Roles of participants and leaders. The development team participants in the product context include many of the same roles as in the user context. The product context team includes the recorder, analysts, development leaders, project manager, and observers. In this context, sales and marketing representatives will probably be full members of the design team, with significant input to the design. Customers are included in this context to represent the potential users, and are given roles in design participation.

User participants in the product context will be in a unique situation to influence the design of a custom or commercial package. Their participation might be considered as that of potential users, or as actual user representatives. Depending on the product, they might be knowledgeable in the specific domain of the application (such as accountants, if designing a small business management package), or they might be average users, with no special skills, if designing a consumer package that must be usable on the first try. Participants for a product context will probably not be full-time team members, but will be included on the team during requirements definition, visualizing sessions, scenario definition, and prototype evaluations.

There is a high probability of conflict among team leaders in the product context, since so many perspectives are incorporated into the workshops. Project and development leads will push for scope and schedule, while marketing and sales leads will push for features and flash. Sponsors and other managers might have requirements for the product that must be met regardless of other concerns. The facilitator must be ready to address and work through the potentially conflicting agendas among product leadership.

Team Design and Life Cycles

When are the best opportunities to use Team Design? In your products or systems, what are the milestones or major meetings when the project team actually works together to sort out issues and solve problems? If your teams don't currently work together well, what can you offer to provide the opportunity for collaboration and teamwork? The place to start is by understanding the system or product life cycles in force.

The *product life cycle* is the idea of structuring the entire life span of the product into distinct phases with defined work activities allocated uniquely to each phase. Like the life phases of a living thing, a product can be born and grow through childhood into adolescence, maturity, and seniority, eventually die, and possibly even be recycled. Product or system life cycles can be defined from cradle to grave, as in today's military and major infrastructure systems, or can just be applied to the development, sales, or maintenance phases. For Team Design purposes, a development life cycle is described, since this is the prevailing structure for analysis and design work.

Product or system development life cycles are models used to plan and manage the activities required to produce automobiles, consumer electronics, software, or information systems. Many corporations invest in proprietary life-cycle models to enhance competitiveness, others adopt a standard generic model to use as a guide. The life cycle presented here describes a simplified generic system development model applicable to most types of design and implementation projects. It's provided as a guideline for understanding how Team Design fits across the activities of any given life cycle. The standardized phases can be used for invention, development, or problem solving. They include the following:

- Planning
- Requirements definition
- Solution design
- Implementation
- Distribution

Participatory workshops naturally fit within several phases of a standard development life cycle. Joint Application Design is often conducted as part of the requirements definition and into the early design phases of development. The JAD facilitation model is sometimes adopted for strategic planning or project management planning. Some proponents of JAD use it for the production of the prototype and all the design documentation. However, JAD is rarely used in the implementation phase, while the program code is being produced.

General system development life cycle

A generalized *system development life cycle* (SDLC) is described in Table 3.5 as a reference model for Team Design. The organizational contexts describe sets of deliverables applicable to projects found in their worlds, and these deliverables fit into the general SDLC defined. The workshop formats for business process, requirements, and application design assume the use of life-cycle models for performing design and development work, and these life cycles also fit into this general scheme.

However, the life-cycle model in Table 3.5 also covers any development process in which a product or plan is established by a team, requirements are defined, and a solution is designed to meet the requirements. Implementation, evaluation, and distribution processes are also accommodated in this model. Almost any plan or project could adapt this general life-cycle model for use as a checklist or guide for product and process development activities.

The table is read sequentially, but, in practice, the tasks would not necessarily be conducted in sequence. Parallel tasks and iteration are common among most specialized life-cycle processes, and these would be variations of the general model. To read the table, note that major phases of the life cycle are listed under the *phase* column. *Major activities* are the general activities performed by technical teams in each phase, and are at a typical level for project management tracking. The *description* column identifies the tasks and steps performed to accomplish the activities. Tasks in italics are supported by *facilitated* Team Design processes to involve cross-functional participation.

TABLE 3.5 General System Development Life-Cycle Model

Phase	Major activity	Description
Project planning	Planning for project and phases	
Requirements definition	User or system requirements analysis	*Define scope of requirements analysis.*
		Identify scope and elicit initial requirements.
		Describe current process.
		Identify users and user tasks.
		Identify current process or system problems.
	Requirements definition	*Define user, system, and product requirements.*
		Iteratively review requirements.
	Alternatives assessment	*Evaluate buy or build options.*
		Define alternative solutions.
		Determine buy-or-build strategy, and/or evaluate and select alternative solutions.
		Analyze selected alternative(s).
	Prototype development	*Cooperatively design concept prototype.*
	Requirements specification	*Draft initial specification. Team development of document.*
	Requirements review	*Review plans and specifications.*
		Revise plans and specifications.
Deliverables of phase		Requirements specification
		Application prototype

TABLE 3.5 General System Development Life-Cycle Model (Continued)

Phase	Major activity	Description
Solution design	Solution definition	*Iteratively revise prototype.*
	Architecture design	*Develop system architecture model.*
	Prototype revision	*Cooperatively review and revise prototype model.*
	Solution design	Produce design documents.
	Evaluation planning	Develop plans for test and evaluation.
	Design review	*Review design. Team revision of design document.*
Implementation	Development environment selection	Identify and select tools for development.
	System or product implementation	*Develop system or component products.*
	System or product evaluation	Test and evaluate system/product.
	Implementation review	*Report and review results.*
Distribution	System evaluation and distribution planning	Perform system-level tests, user evaluation, and final planning for distribution.
	System installation or product delivery	Install, test, and monitor system. Package and distribute product.
	Management change	Initiate support and change control programs.

Typical required *deliverables* are identified at the conclusion of each phase.

Although the life cycle is general, it is not comprehensive. Many activities that are not identified would be used in any specialized life cycle. This model incorporates the major activities that most product development life cycles have been found to use. Therefore, it is useful as a guideline or checklist for product development planning, project planning, and process management.

Using other development methodologies

As this is not a text on development methodologies, the range of applicable life cycles will not be discussed in detail. It would not be practical, since our points can be covered by a general-purpose model, and specialized books can more effectively cover life cycles. The general life cycle in Table 3.5 can be used as a model to apply to other specific life cycles which you might use in your organization's practice. However, if you are interested in pursuing development methodologies and the use of specific life cycles in depth, consult the following references:

- *All life cycles.* Yourdon (1993).
- *Traditional or waterfall life cycle.* Boehm (1981).
- *Incremental or phased life cycle.* Boehm (1981).
- *Spiral, iterative, or evolutionary life cycle.* Boehm (1981).
- *Rapid application development life cycle.* Arthur (1992).
- *Object-oriented development life cycles.* Coad and Yourdon (1991) and Jacobson et al. (1992).
- *Usability engineering life cycles.* Nielsen (1993).

Matrix of life-cycle activities and roles. Across the time span of any development life cycle used in a real project, some team members play an active role throughout and some team members come and go. The roles and activities that interact with our general model of development include almost every role in the team. The matrix in Table 3.6 shows the relationships among project life-cycle activities, team processes, and roles. Assume in this matrix that a facilitator (as well as facilitation support) might be used with any of the processes.

Targeting Workshop Deliverables

What deliverables are expected for each phase, and how does Team Design contribute to the development of these deliverables? For any

TABLE 3.6 Matrix of Life-Cycle Activities and Roles

Phase and activities	Team processes	Roles required
	Project planning	

Plan for project and each phase
Define project scope and roles
Select project life cycle
	Team planning and discussion of:
	  Project life cycle and schedule
	  Project timelines and milestones
	  Cost and complexity factors
	  Risk and quality analyses
		Project manager
		Lead systems analyst or architect
		Lead engineers
		System methodologist*

	Requirements definition	
User or system requirements analysis	Initial team formation and team-building processes	Project manager
Define scope of analysis Elicit initial requirements	Scoping and visioning processes Team requirements elicitation methods with customers and users	Business area analyst (IS) or product manager (product) Customer representative(s)
Describe current process	Process mapping and facilitated process redesign	Lead systems analyst or architect
Identify current process and system problems	Process and task walkthroughs	Analysts and engineers
	Construction of task scenarios	Human factors engineer User representative(s)
Alternatives assessment Evaluate buy-or-build options Define alternative solutions	Brainstorming and ideation processes Scenario design for solutions Team decision and evaluation processes for alternatives	Project manager Business area analyst (IS) or product manager (product) Customer representative(s)
Evaluate and select alternative solutions	Vendor and internal demonstrations and guided discussions	Lead systems analyst or architect
Analyze selected alternative(s)	User interface prototyping for demonstration and team discussion	Analysts and engineers
Develop prototype Review plans and specifications	Facilitated team reviews	Human factors engineer or user interface designer User representative(s)*

TABLE 3.6 Matrix of Life-Cycle Activities and Roles (*Continued*)

Phase and activities	Team processes	Roles required
	Solution design	
Solution definition Architecture design	Team analysis and design processes Prototype evaluation and revision	Project manager* Business area analyst (IS) or lead systems analyst or architect
Prototype revision System architecture model development	User scenario walkthroughs System process design and diagramming for architecture design	Analysts and engineers Human factors engineer or user interface designer
Solution design	Team document development and revision or review	User representative(s)*
Evaluation planning Design review	Team planning and decision processes	
	Implementation	
System or product development System or component products development	Team development decision making Development review processes	Project manager* Lead systems analyst or architect
System or product evaluation	Evaluation reviews and walkthroughs	Developers and engineers Human factors engineer or user interface designer
	Distribution	
System evaluation and distribution planning	Team selection of evaluation criteria	Project manager*
	Team decision-making processes	Lead systems analyst or architect Developers and engineers

*Optional role.

project, a workshop or series of sessions will generate a set of deliverables, and each phase might serve different customers. For an overview description of the major deliverables typically generated from the session, consider the following guidelines.

Business process workshop deliverables.   For the process-oriented workshop, deliverables will support the design of new business processes, new workflow and workflow systems, communications and support systems, and applications that automate the new processes. Customers of the process workshop are typically business area managers, executives, and information systems managers who must make decisions based on the process. Also, the systems and application development teams are *downstream* customers using the process definition as required input to their analysis work. For all these customers, expect to develop the following types of deliverables:

- Baseline (current) process flow, defining current process to be revised
- Context and scope diagrams, defining the scope of the design effort
- Revised (future) process flow, defining the new business process
- Process requirements definition, defining the business and organizational requirements for the new business process
- Initial functional specification and functional design, defining the basic system function requirements for the new business process

Requirements workshop deliverables.   For the requirements-oriented workshop, deliverables support the requirements of systems, infrastructure, and applications. These are not removed from the business process deliverables; they mainly present the systems view of the same story—the need for change in the process. Customers for these deliverables might include those for the business process area, but also include marketing, sales, and external customer representatives (in product design), business and internal planning areas, and software development teams that use the functional requirements deliverables as inputs to their design and development process. For all these customers, expect to develop the following types of deliverables:

- *Customer or user requirements,* defining the functional requirements from the perspective of customers and users
- *Product requirements,* for a product effort in which the new product requirements are defined for further analysis and design
- *Function hierarchy and dataflow diagrams,* as deliverables defining the scope of the system functions and functional flow

- *Data requirements,* defining the databases, entities and relationships, and data elements required for design of the system or processes

- *User interface prototypes,* visually describing the tasks and interaction for the new product or system

Design workshop deliverables. For the design-oriented workshop, deliverables support the system, infrastructure, and applications design by detailing how the systems or products will be physically organized and constructed. Customers for these deliverables will primarily be the software and product development teams—as well as the previous customers, in a review and approval capacity. The design deliverables for these customers include:

- *A complete prototype,* providing a design model that visually describes interactions and user interface details, with some refinements from user evaluation

- *An architecture design,* providing a complete system architecture plan and design to be used as the blueprint for infrastructure and data architecture

- *A system design document,* providing detailed description of system transactions, modular program definition, use of data and algorithm definition

- *An evaluation plan,* providing test and evaluation plans for system, integration, and usability testing for the product or system

4

Facilitating Team Design Workshops

Without facilitation, a design workshop can easily become just another meeting—and an average one at that. Team Design is a facilitated approach because, simply, facilitation works better. While collaboration unfolds naturally within partnerships, it does not just evolve on its own within groups. The evidence of experience and observation reveals that groups—especially larger groups—regularly function as less than the sum of their individuals. Organizations have turned to facilitation as a method for inspiring group synergy, building teams, and managing group action toward producing deliverables.

What do we mean by *facilitation?* The root word *facilitate* literally means "to make easy," and the task of the facilitator is to create an environment where complicated work is made easier for the participants. However, facilitation has different connotations in industry and government. Facilitation in JAD workshops is identified with a neutral individual who guides a group through the workshop agenda. In traditional industrial settings, facilitation is thought of as a moderating process between potentially disagreeing parties. Other facilitators are seen as process leaders or group leaders.

For much of Team Design, as in JAD sessions, a facilitator primarily manages the group *process,* allowing the participants to attend to the *content* of their work. This can be considered the traditional model of facilitation, in which the group guide shepherds the team through the agenda but remains disinterested in the content.

A further look at facilitation shows that facilitators must pay attention to at least three threads of interaction with the participants: structure, content, and process. *Structure* can simply be seen as the workshop itself, its agenda, exercises, deliverables, and formats. Typically, what most think of as process can be reduced to structural components. Most of the material discussed in the Team Design formats produces *structure* for workshops, which can be facilitated using any style appropriate for the team. Structure provides the framework for activities, leading to deliverables. It is the *what* that the workshop is about.

From a workshop and facilitation point of view, the *content* is the *why* of the workshop. Participants are most concerned with organizing, designing, and making something of value. The requirements, design, models, and processes all deal with the content, the facts and ideas of the design effort. Usually, the facilitator doesn't contribute to this area but must attend to its progress, to the productive creation of the content.

The final thread involves process. *Process* can be thought of as the *how* of the workshop—the way in which the workshop structure unfolds, the way in which content is developed. The facilitator becomes fully present to process trends in the group, along the dimensions of affinity, emotion, agreement, cooperation, values, and even spirit. Effective process facilitation requires taking the risk of dealing with human issues in the team, which raises the possibility of irritating those who merely want to proceed with business as usual. Minor detours to handle group-process concerns are often necessary, and these excursions prevent major delays caused when unmanaged issues later blow up into conflicts.

Recent facilitation approaches, evolving from team-building (Heermann 1997) and learning organization approaches (Senge 1994), have integrated the concepts of emotion and spirit into facilitation. These approaches hold that the quality of the team's working together is as important as the quality of work produced. In fact, it is doubtful that a fragmented and conflicted group is capable of producing quality results as a team.

One key to fruitful team development is in the device of the workshop. A *workshop* is used instead of a *meeting* for quite practical reasons. As noted in Chap. 1, meetings have specific connotations within most organizational cultures. The concept of *meeting* has history working against it, as well as a stigma. People don't expect to work in meetings—they expect to *meet*. Workshops carry the notion of focused work within a structure of planned activities. The expectations participants bring to a *meeting* differ from those brought to a *workshop,* even if they can be considered the same event.

As a facilitator, you probably have some influence over the presentation of your sessions. By advertising development team sessions as workshops, you signal to the organization your intention to produce something, to share the responsibility for producing with the participants. Sometimes this is enough to result in a positive attitude and a willingness to participate. Many organizations use the JAD workshop in this way, although even JAD is also subject to "meeting aversion."

JAD facilitators understand the reluctance of participants to spend time in meetings, as well as their desire to produce. Jerry Kail, senior facilitator with LEXIS-NEXIS, describes the use of JAD in a company where nonproductive meetings have been visibly reduced by a proactive corporate culture. Since the company has a cultural injunction against nonproductive meetings, some people are reluctant to participate in JAD for the extent of time required.

"There's a core set of people that understand JAD is 'not a meeting', that it's a working session, a group of people coming together to work on something. JAD is a very public type of event, and managers and participants both want to get something out of it." Kail describes how when JAD was first used in the organization (using The Method), the rules started getting in the way, and people had the impression that they were to sit in a meeting and follow a bunch of rules for their work.

"People didn't want to follow the rules and structure. It was like, 'Oh, JAD—I'd rather eat my spinach'!" The process was changed, according to Kail, "to appeal to our internal clientele," which included business-oriented product managers and technical developers. The primary client, however, was the project manager, "the bridge between product needs and what gets built." Kail expresses that since facilitation work had been accepted and actively used, with JAD sessions held on a continual basis, that the methodology side had to be developed more.

Kail's experience is typical for business facilitators working at an internal corporate level. Facilitation has been adopted and accepted into many corporate cultures, even where a meeting mind-set is not evident. Internet and interdisciplinary discussions with facilitators reveal an evolving need and stronger emphasis on methodology among those practicing. As shown by Kail's comments, participants don't especially enjoy rule-bound highly structured workshops. A key need is for flexible structure and methodology that can adapt to the context of the organization, work processes, and participants.

Flexibility in both facilitation and meeting structure is required for successful group collaboration. Structure and methodology are discussed throughout the remainder of this book. Facilitation approaches for Team Design are the purpose of this chapter. Not all the specific skills and resources of facilitation are covered in depth here, however. Many resources are available for developing facilitation skills—literature and training in group dynamics, team building and team leadership, and group facilitation. The purpose of this chapter is to tie facilitation to the context and methodologies used in the Team Design approach to development workshops.

Being a Facilitator

Should you be a leader or an unbiased guide? Should you challenge the team or merely present topics and manage interaction? Are you expected to be an expert in a given area or totally content-neutral? Misconceptions arise because opposite poles are both encompassed in facilitation, and are even expected of the same facilitator at times. Facilitators bring a tradition of their experience into the job; they grow from different backgrounds. Facilitators in JAD, organizational development, human resources, team building, conflict management, and human relations all have something to offer when building skill in facilitation.

A review of facilitation reveals as many approaches to the practice as there are disciplines avowing the use of facilitation. Rachel Vance, a facilitator for nonprofit organizations, conducted graduate-level research into the question and found a wide range of approaches and competencies associated with facilitation. Even within the literature of one organization, the American Society for Training and Development (ASTD), at least three different models of facilitation are presented. Two of the definitions support the model of the facilitator as "one who actively controls the event and group interaction although does not control the content or the outcome" (Vance 1996). In their publication on Group Process Tools, this facilitation approach is supported by a definition with the following roles:

- Management of the decision-making process
- Responsibility for establishing a climate
- Responsibility for focusing group efforts
- Responsibility for applying a variety of techniques to encourage movement toward the goal of the meeting.

Facilitator as group nurturer. Other approaches to facilitation, especially from the human relations disciplines, promote the role of the facilitator as more of a group nurturer rather than one who drives the process forward. Another ASTD definition supports this approach, wherein the facilitator does not lead or control the environment, but empowers others to control the process. Vance describes how Heron (1989) defines the facilitator as having the role of "helping participants learn in an experiential group." Both of these approaches are more suited for sensitivity training and personal growth than for development teams. Even in corporate cultures, however, this approach is fostered on occasion, and it's important to recognize when this style of facilitation is desired by your clients.

Facilitator as process guide. Moore and Feldt (1993) define the facilitator as being closer to the Team Design practitioner. They describe the facilitator as directing and tracking the processes of the meeting, including discussions, decision making, and deliberations. The facilitator is explicitly not involved in the content of the group's work, is not a contributor to the products or of ideas used in the team's deliverables. "This person is, however, a deliberate manipulator of the process and the flow of the group's work. He or she manipulates what the group does so as to maximize full participation, to minimize individuals dominating or interrupting the group, and to optimize the group's performance and satisfaction" (Moore and Feldt 1993). This definition also serves well as a baseline for development workshops.

Facilitation in Team Design. Let's look at some of the ways facilitation is used in technical and design workshops. A more significant technical responsibility is required by JAD facilitators than in basic meeting facilitation. JAD and Team Design facilitation assume competence in both the group process skills and design methodologies. So that a project team's technical members (systems analysts, developers, and technical leads) can focus on the task at hand as full participating members, facilitators are called to lead teams in producing the actual design in working sessions. The technical facilitator must have both knowledge and experience in design methodologies, at least for developing such artifacts as diagrams, graphic representations, and group documents. Facilitators organize, plan, lead, and guide teams conducting various development projects as represented by the following Team Design formats:

- Designing and automating business processes (Chap. 7)
- Capturing and defining product and system requirements (Chap. 8)
- Designing and building information system applications (Chap. 9)
- Planning and making group decisions (Chap. 10)

Each chapter describes the use of design methods appropriate for the project as well as the facilitator's approach in leading team use of the methods. Facilitators are also guided in selecting methods appropriate to the organizational context. Finally, Chap. 5 covers general workshop methods appropriate for use in any session. Chapter 5 is the starting point for new facilitators, as it covers the basic methods used on an almost continual basis and drawn upon from memory during sessions. The Team Design *format* chapters (Chaps. 6 through 10) are then used as guides to the leading methods in each area of practice.

Uses of facilitation

Team Design endorses facilitation for guidance through group processes in the various workshops described by the formats presented in later chapters of this book. For any workshop, facilitation can be used broadly in one of two ways:

1. To create an environment in which participants are fully supported to create their own work products
2. To lead development of the work products by supporting the team in using tools and methodologies, facilitating processes to organize participant inputs, and developing models for use by the team

In the general system development life cycle presented in Chap. 3, a complete range of activities is defined across the phases of development projects. Team Design facilitation is shown to have a number of opportunities for use across this life cycle. Each phase of the general life-cycle model is discussed with its relevant use of facilitation for Team Design.

Project planning. Although project planning receives very little discussion in the life-cycle model, this is because few development activities are introduced in this phase. Project planning, involving team planning for the project and its phases, presents a major opportunity for team facilitation. Planning requires the discussion of multiple activities and their priorities, and often requires negotiation and conflict resolution. After all, when a project is first established, it might be seen as a threat to the resources available to existing projects or it might shuffle organizational priorities that have favored others. Project planning, whether for an internal or client-centered project, is an inherently political process that requires sensitivity to organizational impacts on budgets, talent, and other resources.

Facilitation introduces the notion of *neutral guidance,* and can assist in managing the planning and structuring of projects with regard to both project and organizational needs. Facilitation is particularly useful for several aspects of project planning:

- Project scoping and definition
- Project scheduling and resourcing
- Development planning
- Organizational issues resolution

Facilitated project planning creates a productive atmosphere for working through technical and organizational issues. Facilitators can assist by guiding the process through defining the scope, setting priorities, handling emerging issues, and making group decisions.

Project management consultants use facilitation for project definition, schedule development, and project kickoff, providing a combination of consulting advice and methodology. For example, TASC's planning process involves facilitating consultants and scheduling specialists. Typically, a knowledgeable facilitator guides a client group through the process of defining timelines, major milestones, and initial dependencies. The scheduling specialist either works the concepts out on a whiteboard or uses a preferred scheduling software package in real time. At the conclusion of a project planning workshop, clients will have a project definition, resource plan, and bar chart schedule for the project's lifespan, all developed with consensus agreement from the parties in the process. These facilitated deliverables provide a useful starting point for the project, as well as clear steps to take for the action to follow.

Requirements definition.   Requirements definition offers significant opportunities for facilitation, and is the phase that is most identified with facilitated processes. The typical JAD workshop focuses only on the requirements phase, after all, and JAD is a recognized alternative to requirements interviews and other analyses. Requirements definition facilitation tasks based on the generic life-cycle model are shown in Table 4.1.

Note that facilitation can be instrumental in every requirements task involving team participation. Table 4.1 not only shows facilitated activities used in each of the requirements definition tasks, but also shows how facilitated sessions can include a team approach throughout a process that is traditionally considered an individual's job. Requirements work especially lends itself to teams because of the need to completely understand both the overall scope and the details of customer, user, and product needs. No one or two people ever have a grasp of all this territory, except, perhaps, in smaller-scale specialized products. A facilitated team brings all available thinking and voices to the task, whether confident, introspective, expert, or hesitant. Including a wider variety of people in the team supports finding more innovative solutions by bringing a diversity of experience, intelligences, and opinions into the workshop. Providing facilitation ensures that these voices will be heard and their ideas will be incorporated into the resulting work.

Solution design.   Solution design activities represent the invention or adaptation of a system that meets the requirements as defined. Again, note that only team tasks are shown in solution design. This is

TABLE 4.1   Facilitated Requirements Tasks

Major activity	Description	Facilitation tools
User or system requirements analysis	Define scope of requirements analysis. Identify scope and elicit initial requirements. Describe current process.	Facilitate scoping of project requirements. Lead group requirements sessions. Lead and diagram process mapping exercises.
	Identify users and user tasks. Identify current process or system problems.	Lead and diagram user groups and tasks. Lead problem assessment.
Requirements definition	Define user or system requirements. Iteratively review requirements.	Facilitate requirements processes.
Alternatives assessment	Evaluate buy-or-build options Define alternative solutions. Determine buy-or-build strategy, and/or evaluate and select alternative solutions.	Lead brainstorming of options. Facilitate discussion. Facilitate decision making. Lead alternatives analysis.
	Analyze selected alternative(s).	Lead alternatives analysis.
Prototype development	Cooperatively design concept prototype.	Facilitate prototyping.
Requirements specification	Draft initial specification. Team development of document.	Lead group development of document.
Requirements review	Review plans and specifications	Lead team review sessions

not to minimize the high degree of individual effort that normally occurs in this phase of work; it does show opportunities for team facilitation that are normally missed. Although in practice these activities are cyclical, conducted in an iterative fashion and not in lock-step sequence, the facilitation aspects can be used as a consistent form of team integration and coordination. Also, facilitation works across the multiple processes as a type of team glue, maintaining communication and feedback throughout and between phases. At this point, however, the project manager or lead analyst might facilitate, instead of a specific neutral facilitator as in the other phases. The reasons for this shift in the solution design phase include the following:

- *Team maturity.* The project team will have grown to the point where outside or neutral facilitation is not required to elicit and manage different viewpoints.

- *Responsiveness.* The project team will be moving at an accelerated pace of work at this point, with multiple work assignments and, perhaps, multiple subteams. An outside facilitator would not be a productive fit within a team working at this level of performance. Only an *internal* facilitator, or facilitating team member, will be able to maintain the responsiveness needed for on-the-spot coordination of activities.

- *Type of work.* As the team moves into solution design, team meetings require less negotiation, discussion, and creative ideation. Processes that support facilitation are shown in Table 4.2, and most of these coordinate the efforts of individuals rather than generate new design models or other creative artifacts.

Implementation. Implementation processes are not typically viewed as suitable for team facilitation. It's as if each phase further down the project timeline allows fewer opportunities for team collaboration in development. As work packages are distributed among team leaders, subteams split off from the lead team, and developers build modules individually, team leaders might assume that team-based activities have concluded for the time being. Those processes that can be aided by facilitation are shown in Table 4.3.

TABLE 4.2   Facilitated Solution Design Tasks

Major activity	Description	Facilitation tools
Solution definition	Iteratively revise prototype.	Lead team through design processes.
Architecture design	Develop system architecture model.	Facilitate group diagramming and definition of system models.
Prototype revision	Cooperatively review and revise prototype model.	Facilitate prototyping review and changes in team sessions.
Solution design	Produce design document.	Manage group document development and reviews.
Evaluation planning	Develop plans for test and evaluation.	Facilitate discussion of evaluation approaches, planning, and criteria.
Design review	Review design and design document.	Lead group review, discussions, and decision-making process.

TABLE 4.3   Facilitated Implementation Tasks

Major activity	Description	Facilitation tools
Development environment selection	Identify and select tools for development.	Lead any major decision processes for toolset choices or investments.
System or product implementation	Develop system or component products.	Facilitate as necessary for reviews with clients, feedback sessions, and walkthroughs.
System or product evaluation	Test and evaluate system or products.	Facilitate discussion and planning for evaluation execution.
Implementation review	Report and review results.	Lead group review, discussions, and decision-making process.

To the extent that coordination and communication are significant aspects of the project management, quality management, and execution of the development effort, facilitated team sessions maintain their usefulness. In implementation work, the project manager or lead analyst might continue the facilitation role, or others in the project team might accept the role on a rotating basis to foster skills growth in this area of teamwork.

Facilitator roles

Facilitators often adopt different roles during a single workshop, and can also use a single type of role throughout an entire meeting. Part of the task of facilitation requires understanding the unique role required of you by the group and bringing the right mix of roles to the session. Roles can be active or passive, involved or neutral, or anywhere along a spectrum of group-interaction behaviors. Roles of the facilitator can include that of a guide through uncharted territory, that of a group-process coordinator who keeps the team's flow of action on track, that of a gentle moderator who nudges the process along, or that of a trusted advisor with expertise in the techniques to be used in the sessions. It is useful for facilitators to be aware of the various roles they might take on—recommending a certain facilitation approach to your client can head off any differences in expectation that might arise during the session. To those who have taken a strong role in guiding the group process when a laid-back approach was desired, or who have conducted touchy-feely group sensitivity sessions when a more technical role was expected, the need for presenting these role options will be evident.

Other facilitation roles have been described in terms of problem solving, coaching, and leading into unknown territory. These roles can be summarized as follows:

- Creating a climate to foster team success
- Fostering problem solving and breakthrough creativity, by enabling teams to open up the group's knowledge and capability
- Guiding a team in using new methodologies and design processes
- Observing, coaching, and enhancing group interaction and performance
- Assisting groups in making decisions
- Helping a group move from their current state to where they want to be

Chapter 2 discusses the facilitation aspects of Joint Application Design in particular, and presents a model of facilitation and group process involvement. That model is adapted in Fig. 4.1 as a description of roles available to the Team Design facilitator. Like the original model, the dimensions of involvement represent the two directions of group influence the facilitator can offer. The technical or JAD facilitator is typically in the center, and in the Team Design approach, the facilitator is understood to be free to select the best orientation to fit

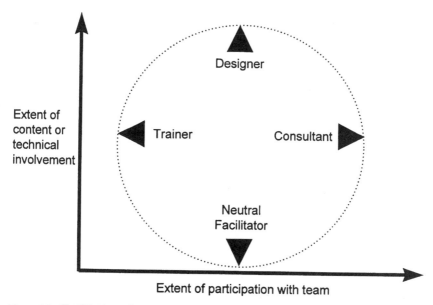

Figure 4.1 Facilitation roles.

the context and the team's abilities. It is not fair to insist that facilitation is always a neutral affair, or that it requires a specific background. Facilitation is basically a skill with many aspects, and no one facilitator will be strong in all aspects. Therefore, the diagram shows different aspects commonly associated with other professional roles that will emerge in facilitation.

Neutral facilitator. To the extent that truly neutral group guidance is required, the process-structure facilitator assumes the role of pure facilitation, with no technical or organizational influence. This is, perhaps, the traditional role expected of facilitators—it falls midway along the scale of team participation and is very low in technical involvement. Typically, *neutrality* refers to the absence of bias in conducting the session. The facilitator is expected to not have a stake in the outcome, to not have a bias toward a particular technical solution, or to care about the content developed. However, the facilitator does have a stake in the quality of the process, and must be capable of determining when team results are satisfactory. This can imply a significant role in controlling processes, regardless of content neutrality. This role, as with any other in facilitation, should be communicated with the group at the outset.

Experienced facilitators understand the difficulty in claiming neutrality. Even when sticking closely to only process concerns, facilitation involves occasional "editorial" issues. For example, when managing discussions you might handle contributions from the group by promoting input from *all* participants. While desirable in theory, this can have the unintended effect of creating a biased outcome by emphasizing the inputs of less-informed participants as much as the contributions of the group's experts. Another common process issue arises when the facilitator predominantly relies on user contributions in sessions over those of technical participants. The facilitator must, therefore, keep aware of the effect on content caused by such strong management of the process.

Trainer. The role of *trainer* is occasionally required of the facilitator. When leading group processes, a specific technique applicable to a design solution will be taught to the team. When leading discussions or conducting brainstorming, education of the team will be necessary at times to enable effective participation. Zimmerman (quoted in Vance 1996) describes the training role, as opposed to facilitation, as providing information supporting skills and knowledge by "offering understanding, initiating new skills competency, or further developing skills that participants already possess." The trainer role might usually be limited to analysis and design techniques or group processes, but could also involve domain content if appropriate. The trainer role is different from the consultant-facilitator, however, in its lesser degree of group involvement. The trainer teaches but does not recommend, and does not get involved in the solution. Trainer roles are temporary, in that design sessions that are facilitated are not training sessions. However, training is a useful role that can be applied within any of the Team Design organizational contexts as required.

Consultant. Use the *consultant* role of the facilitator with caution, but understand that it may be desired and even expected at times. Although it might appear to break the oft-spoken rule of nonbias, a consultative role can be used in many areas outside of the specific content of the workshop. The consultant role is both technically and organizationally proactive, and is one where advice and education can be provided to the team in sharing the methods, history, experience, and knowledge of competitors or other industries. A facilitator adopting the role of consultant will usually have worked closely with the project team, and might be in the position of working as a temporary member. When a facilitator has performed extensive analysis, prework, or preparation, the consulting role can be legitimately adopted within the team sessions. Sensitivity is necessary to understand when advising and informing the team is acceptable and required in a workshop. Because this role has the most influence in the organizational dimension, it can be threatening to participants if the team context is not appropriate. Be especially careful if working as a facilitator with a user community team at the behest of management, and your clients expect consulting involvement as your dominant role. The consultant role actually works best with managers and other decision makers who have some power of their own to balance the external authority designated to the facilitator.

Designer. The *designer* role is highly involved technically, and as a facilitator you might work as a codesigner of the product with the team. This role is one that is well supported by Team Design, though it is far from a traditional facilitator role. Because its organizational influence and participation is about the same as that of a neutral facilitator (in the middle range), this role does not appear to participants to be "leading the design." This is an effective and appropriate role to take on when facilitating a team of nontechnical users or a highly cross-functional team with many different disciplines. By providing techniques and design involvement, the facilitator can provide the best value of the team members' technical skills and their facilitation of group processes. However, it is a difficult balance to maintain at times, and is highly dependent on building effective relationships of trust with the team members. The designer role is best used within the user and product contexts, allowing for creative participation among all team members, including the facilitator.

Summary of roles. Regardless of the roles taken on, some basic expectations of facilitators are usually not violated. Facilitators are not technical experts, they are not business experts, and they are not organizational experts. These roles might be required on the team, but the role of *expert* is not usually offered when facilitating. Another expectation might be that facilitators do not engage as participants during a workshop. However, among experienced facilitators this is often kept open as a possibility, to briefly switch roles as a participant. This can be done to illustrate a point, to demonstrate behaviors, or to allow someone else to facilitate. Facilitators might not agree on how this is done, but many allow for the possibility.

Facilitators have a strong role in team leadership during the workshop, but only in the group process. Facilitators don't make decisions; they don't really *direct* meetings as much as organize and lead the agenda. Finally, they should not engineer specific outcomes at the request of clients. If a vice president wants a certain solution from a team, and will not accept the team's consensus offering if it differs, don't even bother with a JAD or facilitated workshop. It will only destroy morale and credibility within the organization, since participants will eventually realize that they never had a real say in the matter.

A final word on roles: Many facilitators are entertaining in their presentation style, and use humor and wit, jokes, and funny exercises. These approaches are excellent at times, and have their place within sessions. However, the *purpose* of the workshop should always be clear, and it is not to entertain the team or to keep participants amused. Keep the context of your chosen role in mind when facilitating, and use a light touch. Allow humor to play a part in facilitation; however, like other ideas and contributions from the team, it works best when arising from the team and not the facilitator.

Skills in Facilitating

A number of skills are expected of any facilitator, most of which should be present in any given facilitator. Unlike technical specialists, the facilitator must be a *generalist,* at least in the facilitator role. He or she must also bring a commitment of service to the team, a tangible and authentic guarantee of support to the group's work.

In many meetings, facilitation is only required as a communication tool, and technical work is not supported by facilitation. In Team Design, however, the facilitator is assumed to be reasonably competent in design and development processes, to be able to support the team's progress on real projects. Regardless of the type of facilitation, strong personal communication skills are required of the facilitator.

After all, what is being facilitated? Essentially, it is facilitation of *communication*.

Facilitation skills. Team Design provides a framework to support teams in their development work, and facilitation is an important part of the workshop process. However, facilitation skills are widely covered in other books (as referenced throughout this volume) which present varieties of expertise. Team Design processes require that some facilitation competency be available within your organization, or, at least, the willingness to have novices learn and undergo training to develop skills.

Facilitation skills are described differently in every approach to meetings and group work described in the literature. Some of the skill models in facilitation concentrate more on the group dynamics, human relations, or negotiation aspects of the practice. Team Design is oriented toward the very practical purpose of accomplishing system and product development, and promotes an action-oriented viewpoint.

Skills deal with both the facilitator's *actions* and the necessary internalized *qualities* of the facilitator. A skill set outlined by Zimmerman and Evans (1993) represents a view of the personal competencies of the facilitator that incorporates both areas of skill. Their framework has been expanded to identify other required skills for development workshop facilitation.

Informative skills. Informative skills involve the capability to inform, instruct, and manage group processes, including the following:

- *Establishing structure.* Defining the workshop structure and guidelines.

- *Setting direction.* Directing the group when needed, providing leadership.

- *Creating objectives.* Identifying critical issues and integrating themes.

- *Requesting and providing feedback.* Informing the group and individuals of observations and the effect of behavior.

- *Establishing and maintaining group focus.* Controlling the attention of the group to maintain a common line of reasoning.

- *Providing explanation.* Defining, advising, and informing the group to support common goals as agreed upon by the group.

Interpretative skills. Interpretative skills involve the capability to listen, understand, make interpretations of communication, and support the understanding of others, including the following:

- *Listening.* Skill in both active and reflective listening, attending to verbal and nonverbal communication, and understanding of verbal behavior patterns.

- *Flexibility.* Being able to change behavior, perspective, demeanor, and attitudes as called for during group interactions.

- *Separation of self from process.* Avoiding and releasing personal identification with group processes and interactions.

- *Openness.* Being able to accept feedback and change, and being receptive to change and new understanding of the self and one's expectations.

- *Interpretation.* Skill in understanding concepts and expressions, and making correct interpretations of behavior and notions that assist in the group process.

- *Translation.* Skill in interpreting and rewording thoughts and ideas among the group so that groupwide understanding is fostered.

Intuitive skills. Intuitive skills involve the capability to creatively adapt to and guide a group based on an immediate and deep recognition of possibilities among group members and affordances for action within the group process, including the following:

- *Creativity.* Skill in generating new ideas, images, and inventions and in working with others to promote inventive and original ideation.

- *Instinct.* Ability to act naturally on one's impulses when called for within group processes; a skill of behaving instinctually in response to new conditions.

- *Timing.* Skill in responding to and interacting with groups with respect to timing of responses, flow of group conversations, and responsiveness of feedback.

- *Empathy.* Capability to listen and respond empathically, to understand issues and communications from the perspective of the individual.

- *Synthesis of ideas.* Skill in assembling, organizing, and recombining ideas and concepts to creatively develop new and useful constructs.

- *Integration of process.* Skill in identifying and acting on group processes that fit with the purpose and goals of the workshop.

Presentation, listening, and speaking. Before the team can communicate effectively, as the facilitator you must set the example and establish the tenor of the session. You must be the first to stand up for the integrity of effective communication. That's what a meeting is all about, that's why people have made time to get together face to face. Basic presentation skills are essential to effective workshops. Skill in speaking and listening are required, and what might seem like everyday behavior is anything but common. Speaking and listening are not usually practiced with intentionality and rigor; they are taken for granted. Unless that's how you make your living, which is what you do if you're a facilitator.

Facilitation requires you to manage multiple communication channels at the same time. The practiced facilitator maintains a conference of internal and external dialogues that would confound an average human being. The typical facilitator simultaneously manages:

- The flow of the group's progress toward meeting goals
- Conversations on a one-on-one basis with each individual
- Conversations with the whole group
- Discussions and guided dialogue with the group
- Empathy with individuals and with the mood of the group
- Tracking group and individual schedules and time requirements
- Issues that arise and must be handled within the session
- Spontaneous decisions and issues within the group

Facilitation requires the ability to maintain these multiple threads while gently guiding a group through conversations, processes, and exercises that generate results. And that result in consensus agreement. And that finally satisfy the group. And that satisfy the customer.

Listening skills.   As a facilitator, you are required to maintain clear communication. Your role demands that you speak succinctly, with clarity and directness. It demands that you listen actively at all times, to check on what you've heard, to ensure that decoding of communication is effective. As a facilitator, you are never a passive listener. Both active and reflective listening are necessary for facilitation. There are several basic actions required in both ways of listening:

- *Listen to the* content *of what is said.*   Each individual may have different ways of speaking, different favorite terms and buzzwords—some of which you might not understand. It takes a focused attention, at times, to extract the content from group members. Be willing to clarify communication when it is not clear to you, even if it appears to be understood by the entire group.

- *Listen to the intent of the speech.*   What is it that the speakers want to have happen? What influence do they attempt with the group? Is the intention to move the process forward or to stop proceedings due to discomfort with direction or process?

- *Assess the speakers' nonverbal communication.*   Are they making eye contact? With you or with the group? Are facial expressions congruent with the speech? How are they sitting, are they tense or comfortable? Are they gesturing or restrained?

- *Listen to the* backchannel, *or nonspeech, communications.*   Is the speaker hemming and hawing? Stumbling over words or clearing the throat? Listen to inflections and voice pitch. What is the composite picture of the communication?

Active listening is more than a style of listening, it is almost a way of being with others. It requires a proactive attitude toward listening, where every communication is attended to and assessed for a response. Active listening, though apparently simple, provides the speakers with powerful feedback that they were heard. As other group members observe this process, a relationship of trust and respect is fostered. A basic model for active listening includes the following actions:

1. *Fully attend to the speaker.*   Listen immediately to the first words said and quickly comprehend the full statement made. Make eye contact while listening. If necessary, ask for clarification if the statement wasn't clear.

2. *Reflect and respond to the speaker's verbal content.*   Use words to the effect of "What I hear you saying is...." Respond by repeating back exactly the words you heard. If interpretation is required, say "What I take this to mean is..."

3. *Request acknowledgment or confirmation that your response was correct.*   Repeat the process if necessary.

Reflective listening is the other mode of listening, which is primarily used when participants have control over their own session and are managing group communications. Reflective listening is listening to others with empathy, with the purpose of understanding but with no requirement to respond. Reflective listening is attending without judgment, and without seeking to intervene.

In all listening behavior, the facilitator should:

- Respond to behaviors and ideas, not to the speaker personally.

- Respond in the present case, not in references to the past.

- Respond by describing, not by evaluating or making judgment.

Many times during effective workshop sessions, the facilitator may appear to be only listening, and not actively engaged in working with the process. When you facilitate your next session, notice whether this level of listening occurs with you. It is a signal that the participants are taking responsibility for producing in the session, and have created a sense of ownership. As a facilitator, the best thing to do is to appreciate the team's ability to perform in this way, and to observe for the next opportunity where your support is required to guide to the next step in the process or agenda.

Speaking skills. When *speaking* as a facilitator, always be aware of the words selected and the meaning they imply. Be aware of the correct pronunciation of words, and use words with which you are very familiar. In most facilitation, technical jargon and complicated expressions only hinder comprehension anyway, so use words that come naturally from your experience. Also practice enunciation, so that your words are heard clearly by all. Some people have accents or speech mannerisms, but these are not necessarily barriers. Using an accent to your advantage will make your presentation style enjoyable to others, if it is not overused by speaking too often during the proceedings!

Try not to rely on "filler" utterances that reveal discomfort with pauses in speech. Pauses and spaces are natural, and should be used to effect. Don't try to fill in pauses between words or phrases with *ums* and *ahs*. Most people do not hear themselves say these fillers when speaking. They are a highly unconscious means of expression, which makes it difficult to attend to them and restrict them from natural speech. Videotaping your speaking or facilitation is the most effective means of pointing out ineffective variations in speaking style. Feedback from your colleagues after internal presentations and other speeches can be of use in self-training for speech improvement.

The facilitator's most important speaking involves interacting with the group to promote discussion, to draw out and motivate others, to move the processes forward, and to promote trust. In these intentions and others, the facilitator uses questions and probing to a great extent. Questioning is a powerful facilitation tool, and can be used to draw forth participation and creative involvement. Open-ended questions that do not imply an answer are best used in facilitation, as they allow the group to respond freely. Open-ended questions are those that allow free response, such as the following:

- *Soliciting input.* "What do you think? What would you add to this? How else could this be done? What more could follow?"

- *Requesting advice.* "What do you think we might do here? What options might we consider? How has anyone else done this before? What do you think might work here?"

- *Probing others for response.* "Jeff, what do you think? Laurie, would you be willing to add to this?"

When you are asked questions as a facilitator, be cautious about responding quickly. If asked to contribute to the content, toss the question back to the group, as follows:

Participant: "What (activity, element, entity) do you think we should use in this case?"

Facilitator: "I really can't say (or "I don't know"). What does anyone else think?"

Especially if you have been carefully neutral, or if controversial areas have been discussed, some participants might want to know where you stand and put you on the hot seat. A harmless-sounding question might have the intent of drawing you into taking a side. To prevent a slip, again bounce these questions back to the participants. If asked directly, you might clarify your role by saying "Now, it doesn't really matter what I think. I'm not allowed an opinion—it's not in my job description," or something similar that diffuses the team's attention from you.

Use questions and probing often, to maintain the focus of action on the team and not on you. The goal of your speaking should always be to have the team take responsibility for its efforts and to progress on its objectives.

Facilitation Processes

Facilitation of development workshops requires the coordination of many functions at once. It calls for attention to both the here and now and to thinking ahead on several concurrent tracks. Development facilitation involves the coordination of people, information, and activities, team building and group exercises, and analysis and design work—all of which might be collectively viewed as facilitation processes.

To add to these considerations, facilitators must orient their agendas, planning, activities, and conversations toward the organizational context of the group. Facilitators do not always work in the same environment or organization as the groups they must work with. Therefore, understanding the particular microculture of the team and its parent organization(s) is necessary.

Facilitation in context

JAD workshops are discussed in previous chapters as a well-established tool for facilitating group design processes. The JAD approach to facilitation has traditionally been to use an informed guide, not a group leader, but one who controls the group processes closely. The formal JAD style of facilitation works well in many cases, but not in all. Depending on the organizational context, the facilitator's approach must be flexible enough to adapt to the organization and the specific needs of the team.

The organizational context can be used as a guideline for your style of facilitation, as well as for selecting methods and design tools. Use Team Design contexts as guidelines for understanding organizations, and not as strict categories of type. Especially for consultants starting new projects or with new clients, determining which context is most appropriate to adopt can help guide facilitation and method decisions. Each context brings its own set of assumptions that influence how team members interact, how management is involved, the pace and style of facilitation, and the deliverables produced.

The traditional JAD facilitation approach closely fits the needs and expectations of stakeholders working in the business and systems contexts. When JAD has been used effectively in the past, the basic JAD session approach will be expected in any design workshop. The JAD style of facilitation is also often acceptable in a user context, in support of more user-oriented workshops that have less influence from the IS and business departments. Since the business and systems contexts require more technical and goal-driven workshops, the fast-moving pace of the traditional JAD facilitator is more appropriate in these contexts.

The product and the user contexts both call for more of a process-oriented approach than the JAD approach, even though similar goals for accomplishment and output might be present. In these contexts, creativity and relationship building count for as much or more than technical focus. A participatory design philosophy is more congruent in these development contexts. In the user context, the user's organizational, work process, and daily task concerns are central to the design solution. In the product context, a creative user-centered design perspective can lead to more innovative consumer software products than the structured and linear JAD approach. The JAD approach assumes we have a known target as the desired completion state—the product context assumes a breakthrough target, which might contain many unknowns.

Business context.   The business context, as described in Chap. 3, supports the design of business processes and business information systems. This context assumes that business needs are central to the system, and the goals of users and other stakeholders are secondary. For example, in the design of a large-scale accounting system, the business process for accounting and its data requirements constitutes the critical function of the workshop. The traditional JAD approach is useful when facilitating the business context workshop. Typically, the business-centered workshop brings together managers, system analysts, and functional organization representatives (e.g., accounting and human resources). A business-centered group will appreciate the conservative and technical nature of the facilitation.

The business context does not reject the needs of the user community; it is basically a focus on businesswide requirements. Customer considerations might not even be involved, if there are no customer-facing processes involved in the focal business process. This context often involves numerous social, management, and process issues simultaneously, making it one of the most difficult contexts to facilitate. Involving substantial user representation in this context can mix the priorities required to establish new processes that are best planned from an enterprise level. Because of this "strictly business" approach, the facilitator must judge the appropriateness of using this context.

Managers might be tempted to impose this context to avoid the politics of user issues when significant change will impact their roles. The very reason for separating this context from the user context is to enable facilitators and organizers to distinguish when to consciously choose this approach, instead of holding JAD sessions that unwittingly exclude (or include) users based on organizational needs. The facilitator is responsible for recommending a favorable workshop approach and plan, so clearly recognizing the context for a session is necessary.

If working internally (within your own organization), a *consultant*-facilitator role can be effective in this context, since stakeholders are likely to be peers. If the workshop session includes middle management, the consultant role might even be expected, if you have the background. If the workshop supports business process redesign, however, neutrality will be of high value. Business process change affects so many organizations that a facilitator must remain uninvolved in the organizational impact that must occur. If you are not in a position to become involved with the process issues, the *designer* role is the better approach instead, bringing methodologies to the workshop and not process advice. The most typical Team Design formats using this context include Business Process Design, Planning, and Decision Making. The other formats are development-oriented and should substantially involve users and customers in the workshops.

Systems context. The systems context is primarily an *internal* workshop context, used when few organizational issues will arise. It is designed to support a focused assembly of technical stakeholders requiring a forum to share technical plans, set priorities, and make decisions to solve technological problems. Stakeholders in the systems context will be the technology managers, developers, and key functional managers. This context exists for those groups charged with infrastructure planning, installing back end database systems, or implementing large-scale software packages.

The JAD facilitation approach using Team Design methods is also fully acceptable in this context. A strong technical background will be quite useful, even if not required for facilitation. In highly technical sessions, a structured agenda and looser facilitation style will be respected by the stakeholders. If the agenda is too loose, the facilitator will appear to be unnecessary, as technologists are notoriously self-sufficient and might strain at using a facilitator in the first place. However, if the facilitation style is too structured (rigid rules, tight control over meeting processes, and inflexible style) technical stakeholders might lose patience with the process. They will normally want to move into technical discussions and solutions quickly, and a rush to accomplishment might be evident. A structured agenda with credible and current design methods will further acceptance of the workshop. In this context, team members should be encouraged to take over the meeting to lead design sessions, and the expertise in the room should be used. Facilitation is especially useful to draw out available expertise from all team members in design sessions, where nonfacilitated workshops tend to be dominated by a few members.

Both the consultant and designer roles are appropriate in the systems context, as contributions of either general technical knowledge (consultant) or methods (designer) will not normally interfere with the facilitation. Neutrality is not nearly as important in this context as in the others; since a more homogeneous group typically works together in these sessions, there are not as many organizational sides toward which a facilitator might be biased.

Finally, the systems context is found in the Application Design and Requirements Definition formats, if strong user participation is not necessary for the system. The systems context is not usually present in business process design situations. Planning and decision-making workshops are relevant when the focus is on system or architecture planning.

User context. The user context can be considered to be the core Team Design context, as most facilitated design workshops, having evolved from a JAD background, require user or customer involvement.

Whenever actual external customers are brought on site for design sessions, they will naturally be the team's focus of interest for design work. When designing information systems that substantially revise users' work processes, informed user participation is critical to both user acceptance and appropriate design. The user context assumes parity between users and system designers, and it focuses specifically on user requirements. Due to the possible conflicts between user desires and technical goals, the facilitator must adopt a highly neutral role and maintain balanced communication among the different members.

The user context can almost reverse the roles of users and designers at times. Users are asked to participate in thinking through solutions, and system designers are asked to try on the users' perspective, to understand their work processes. The customers or users are treated as partners in the project, and in return they provide access to their world. Their context of work, their environment and organization, and their ways of using information are all integrated into the solution design.

In the user context, the design team shares responsibility for the system design, as in a participatory design process. In this context, users are trained in the session to understand and even to draw out flows and object diagrams of their ideas. The facilitator might take either a neutral facilitator role or a designer approach to working with the team. The designer role is typical when the users are not technically inclined, and the facilitator can provide neutral guidance and assistance in selecting and using effective design methods. The consultant role is not used as much by the facilitator in the user context, since an advising position might be seen as offering solutions.

Participating analysts and developers can take on roles as facilitators, consultants, or coaches to assist users in articulating their concepts and requirements. If they are included in the workshop, their expertise will be expected and can add significant value. The facilitator must be vigilant to guard against undue technical influence with the user participants in this context, however. Developers often raise technical problems with ideas long before they are offered as design solutions, and this can influence and diminish creativity and enthusiasm among the user participants. It is also difficult for facilitators to challenge technical positions directly, because of the perceived expertise of these participants. The facilitator certainly can't object to the *content* of the technical objections raised, but can obliquely challenge the situation by deferring all technical issues or placing them on the parking-lot board. The facilitator issues can be prevented by working with a ground rule of withholding technical concerns from creative workshops, or by setting aside time on the agenda for that conversation.

The user context is mainly supported in Requirements Definition and Application Design formats. It is not as prevalent in Business Process Design situations. However, when new business processes have major user impacts, holding specific user context workshops for user process requirements can be key to obtaining useful real-world wisdom on the processes and to gaining user acceptance and political support. Planning and decision-making workshops are typically not user-oriented, but could benefit from the facilitator assuming this context when users are the primary participants.

Product context. In using the product context, the facilitator integrates roles and techniques from the other contexts, since it is a broadly defined context. Whereas the other three contexts have an organizational definition, the *product* approach is a hybrid, and cannot be said to have any identifiable organizational approach. As discussed in Chap. 3, product development is defined differently in each industry that considers its work to be "building products." The product context must accommodate customers and users, sometimes business processes and other times consumer needs, and still other times might be used even when the product must meet exacting engineering specifications.

Because it is a hybrid, the facilitator must take into account the unique requirements of the customers. Are they a diverse group of consumers with numerous profiles, or a distinctive niche? Do they use the product for work or entertainment? Do they depend on the product, or are there alternatives? Are the customers accessible and interested in working with you, or are they unlikely to participate in your design work?

The unique requirements of the product itself also drive the way that customers are integrated into the design process. Is the product a commodity system, or a more customized select item? Does it require a long development cycle, or is it something that must be developed and shipped within weeks or months?

The facilitator in the product context will often take on different roles as needed. The designer role is again probably the primary role, where exercises and design methods are introduced and led by a facilitator. The consultant role is of value when the product requires specific industry or niche expertise, and an informed facilitator can work closely with customers and users. The purely neutral facilitator role is not as critical in this context—the facilitation manages interactions between internal and external participants, and the internal organizational considerations are less intrusive.

The product context is found primarily in the Requirements Definition and Application Design formats, the primary formats for system design. The creativity and customer focus of this context might be productively used in any of the formats, if the facilitator considers the team to be open to creative approaches in business process design or planning.

Meeting organization and facilitation

Facilitators manage meetings and are responsible for creating the working environment that spurs team performance. Experienced facilitators make it look easy. They naturally set the tone of the session, speak only minimally to the group, and people respond and start working together as a team. Without even appearing to exercise any of the foundation facilitation skills, they generate the conditions leading to performance.

A good bit of the apparent success of facilitators early in the workshop has to do with basic meeting management. *Meeting management* involves establishing an effective structure and skillfully handling common group problems that occur in meetings. The following sections address handling problems that occur in meetings. These are common meeting problems, adapted from those listed in Doyle and Straus' (1976) well-known handbook *How to Make Meetings Work*, and are discussed here with guidelines for the facilitator.

Meeting process.   Several common issues arise around the meeting process. When conducting a workshop, *process* issues will typically arise early. The facilitator must recognize these issues and handle them immediately to maintain authority in controlling the group process. Process issues challenge the way the meeting is conducted and can lead to losing the distinction between process and content.

Participant focus.   When the team is unfocused, off track, it is obvious to all group members. Participants raise issues out of context or sequence and their direction is scattered, wandering off in different directions at the same time. Sometimes when a participant attempts to bring the group around to a specific focal point, the group argues about whether that point is the focus.

Handling the focus is done immediately, before participants have a chance to wander. Start with the agenda and ground rules. Always gain agreement on the agenda and ground rules at the very start of the session. Then enforce the group's agreement to work according to the agenda. Use their agreement on ground rules to enforce the process, and refer to any rule authorizing this facilitation role.

Always be clear about the *mission* focus. The overall mission or purpose of the team should be discussed early and agreed upon. The mission or purpose statement can then be written on a large sheet and used as the focal point for the overall process. When team members ask "What is the point?" the mission statement returns the focus to their reason for being together in the first place.

Attend to any wandering within activities and exercises. Once the agenda is followed, wandering can occur within the workshop activities. This might result from miscommunication about the activity or insufficient knowledge from group members contributing to the activity. Intervene and redirect the group. If necessary, ask "What is the current task and desired result being addressed at this moment?"

Distinction between process and content. Team members can become puzzled during any part of the workshop by losing the distinction between the process and content. This arises in the form of arguments about topics versus approach toward handling topics.

Be clear about what role you as the facilitator are to play at this point. If you are leading a team activity, be sure everyone understands how to participate. If leading an open discussion, determine whether the group is leaning more toward topical discussion or attempting to establish a better means for discussion. Ask the group, "Are we talking about *how* to discuss the topic or about *what topic* to discuss?"

To avoid this situation, prepare activities to be presented to the team. Create numbered instructions on an easel pad in advance for all to follow when conducting an exercise. When a discussion is started, start off with the ground rules for discussion, and list the discussion topic on the board or easel. Discussion processes can be facilitated by listing points and issues on the board as they are raised. Participants can observe this real-time transcript of their discussion, and are less likely to lose track.

Personal attack. Team members attacking individuals rather than their ideas is a possible group problem. This can occur when team members have significant history with each other, and is often not a conscious behavior. Therefore, confronting this behavior directly is not the best way to intervene.

This problem should be addressed up front, before it occurs, by identifying a ground rule of "No personal attacks." As the facilitator, observe for this behavior and address the emerging issue rather than the attack. Defensiveness may result if you confront the attacker directly. Instead, refocus the discussion on the ideas or position raised by the individual under attack, and hold dialogue with the group about the position or idea to clarify its intent and value.

Unclear roles and responsibilities. Sometimes the team loses track of defined role boundaries. This has the effect of undermining those accepting responsibility for roles in the workshop, and can diminish team cohesion. This shows up as the question "Who is supposed to be doing what?"

To prevent this problem in the first place, clearly establish roles up front when covering the ground rules and agenda. Roles in workshops include those specified in Chap. 2, such as facilitator, recorder, observer, and participant. Identify each role, explain why it's required for the session, and appoint or preselect members to fulfill the roles.

Consider having members rotate in and out of roles if long sessions (two or more days in sequence) are planned. When this problem arises, clarify the need for the role with the group. If the role is required by the team or to support facilitation, request that someone take on the role for the team for a specified duration.

Manipulation by team leaders. When facilitation is new to an organization, those who benefited from dominance or control in the past will sometimes continue to assert themselves on the group. Typically, this will emerge when a group leader or manager wants to push goals, outcomes, or limits on the team without considering consensus.

Prevent this problem by addressing roles and responsibilities clearly. When specifying the role of participant, clarify that all individuals have an equal voice and that no one person will guide the team during the facilitated sessions. Unless the project manager or team leader has specific project issues to handle, keep organizational and management issues out of the session. Be sure to maintain fairness as the facilitator by asking for other points of view when specific members attempt to dominate.

Hidden agendas. When issues are evident behind the scene, team members might be bringing hidden agendas to the session. This will show up when the same specific issues are continually raised by the same team member, often out of sequence with the proceedings. It may also show up as covert behaviors, such as side meetings with specific team members and withholding of information from others.

Deal with hidden agendas up front, by the ground rules—"No hidden agendas brought into the room." Of course, they will arise during sessions, and as a facilitator you must observe for the patterns of hidden agendas. When one is identified, address the issue that appears to be at stake. If it is an issue that involves the team, point it out and ask the participant to voice his or her concern. If it is a personal or politically sensitive issue, ask the participant in private, during a break, to reveal his or her concern and ask to have it resolved.

Information handling. Several common meeting situations involve the handling of content, unwieldy processes, or information overload.

Considerations for addressing these situations are discussed in the following.

Data overload. When meetings are overly aggressive in scope, or attempt to force too much information on participants, an overload situation arises. Team members might appear bored or distracted or might not participate when this occurs. This can also occur when the facilitator moves at too fast a pace.

To prevent this situation, get to know the team members in advance of the session and assess their background and ability and interest in the work you are planning. Be sure you have the right set of people in the workshop, and that they bring the knowledge and abilities required to the session. If the team members are appropriate, and planning has taken the session's pace into account, notice when the overload symptoms first start to occur. Ask for feedback from the members regarding the pace, exercises, content, or style of delivery. Use team feedback to adjust the pace or style accordingly.

Wheel spinning. This situation refers to repetition of topics and issues more than once (which is often needed just for clarification or resolution). When the team is addressing the same issues repeatedly, they may have lost focus or direction, or could be lost in the content and may not understand the topic.

Use facilitation to confront this when it occurs. Keep records of issues and decisions both on easels or boards in the front of the room and with the recorder. If an issue has been noted and deferred for later resolution, put it on an area dubbed the *parking lot* and return to it later. When the issue arises again, refer to its status as an active, deferred, or closed issue or topic.

Inappropriate content. This can be difficult for a facilitator to notice, since facilitation is fairly content-free. When more than one team member complains about the team's focus on a topic or area of discussion, it might be a signal that it's an area that doesn't apply to either the project mission or purpose of the workshop. Inappropriate content might involve side issues, topics of interest only to technical members, or similar problems.

As the facilitator, you might request consensus on topics that appear to be controversial to some. If the group maintains a mixed response, go with the topic until it can be identified and addressed for further resolution. If it is not a hot or significant issue, relegate it to the parking lot. If it is a significant issue for even some of the stakeholders, spend some time to clarify it, use dialogue to draw out its relevance to the mission or purpose, and assign a team member to investigate it further if necessary. Defer it, but do not minimize the issue;

the participants who care about the issue will remember how it was handled, affecting your performance and team cohesion.

Meeting environment. Any conditions affecting the physical environment of the meeting space must be handled by the facilitator. Several of the typical problem conditions are described in the following.

Poor meeting environment. This problem usually becomes obvious immediately. Many factors are involved in meeting comfort: noise level, lighting control, room size, seating, temperature control, and privacy. As the facilitator, it's important to specify meeting room requirements and ensure that they are met. It is difficult to change these factors after the session starts, so be sure to visit any planned location in advance of its first use. Don't let anyone manage this for you, as factors will be missed. Check the room size—is it large enough for the planned number of participants? Are you likely to have visitors, requiring extra room? Will the room be private enough, away from other activities? Will you require break-out rooms for small group work? Check whether you have variable control over lighting and temperature, to be able to accommodate the changing needs of your participants. Although some people are sensitive to lighting changes, many are sensitive to temperature. In a workshop environment, it is much safer to err on the side of cooler rather than warmer rooms—you want your participants awake, after all.

Ineffective facilities. *Facilities* include everything else in the room to support the session. Problems with tables and seating arrangements, displays and projectors, food and beverage availability, or restrooms can easily arise during long workshops. During workshops, participants might have difficulty sitting in uncomfortable chairs for more than an hour, or might be uncomfortable in seating arrangements that can't be moved.

Again, be sure to check out facilities during the advance room visit. Use a checklist of items that must be available for your workshop. Check on any electronic equipment in advance of bringing it in to the workshop. Be sure arrangements are made for lunches, snacks, and breaks as needed.

Preparation and follow-up. The facilitator is responsible for workshop planning, and usually has a role in follow-up as well. The typical workshop requires a planning-to-execution ratio of about one hour planning to four hours of workshop. Follow-up time is offered as required by the project and depends on your role in the project.

Confused objectives and expectations. This is evident when participants are not sure about the purpose and objective of the meeting. If expectations are unmet, participants might complain about agenda items or certain topics. A lack of planning and an unclear agenda is usually the cause of this situation.

Advance preparation includes proper notification of participants before the workshop. As the facilitator, develop a preliminary agenda with the purpose of the workshop and distribute it with an introductory paragraph describing the workshop approach and your role in the session. If you have the opportunity to meet with participants in advance for interviews or brief discussion, provide some explanation about the workshop process and answer any questions.

No action after workshop. Unfortunately, many workshops end with participants going back to their normal work and action items being left undone.

As the facilitator, you might not be in the best position to follow up. If you have the responsibility to do so, manage the follow-up of the workshop with assistance from the sponsor. Distribute the minutes of the workshop with an action items section assigning names and due dates. Check back with the team leader on issue and action status. Were issues resolved? Were all action items addressed as assigned? Were documents and products developed as an outcome of technical decisions?

Meeting process problems. Finally, problems arise for facilitators when handling decision and management processes within the meetings. Understanding group dynamics and team building provides an effective foundation for working with these situations as they arise.

Decision making. When win/lose approaches are taken in decision making, participants struggle to optimize their outcomes at the expense of others. Other decision-process problems include arriving at partial solutions and holding off on final decisions, compromise instead of consensus, polarization of the team, and low commitment.

The facilitator must first create a conducive environment for decision making, and team building and initiation exercises might be used early in the sessions to establish understanding among participants. In sensitive situations where this approach will not work or it has broken down, the facilitator should use decision processes that do not allow individual domination. Use of blind voting and group voting methods are useful, as is using an analytical approach that gains agreement for decisions throughout the process. Low commitment is more a cause of poor decision making than an effect, and can be addressed early on by ensuring that the right participants are in attendance and that the purpose of the workshop is clearly understood.

Unresolved power concerns. Many times teams will uncover important issues within the group process that they cannot address directly. Issues dealing with organizational structure, management, company policy, and standard procedures must often be handled outside the design workshop. When team members remain unsure of their freedom to make decisions in the workshop context, many issues will be deferred. If too many issues become tabled as such, a concern for team empowerment can interfere with team motivation and commitment.

Sometimes issues can be addressed in advance through meetings with management and the team to address the team's scope of decision making. A dialogue with one or two executives at the start of the workshop will reinforce the team's understanding of their authority. When issues arise in the workshop, do not let the team stray off the issue or avoid responsibility. Have participants suggest ways to handle the issue, or assign action items to individuals to handle or investigate issues. Even if the team doesn't have the authority to decide, recommendations that solve inherent problems should be encouraged.

Problem avoidance. When the team avoids emerging conflicts and problems, the problems can become invisible to the facilitator. This shows up as the team agreeing that the group process is satisfactory, when problems and conflict are apparent. Participants might say "Everything is fine" or "We'll address the problems later." In many organizations, the need for the group to cooperate as a team is seen as more important than challenging the problems that arise. When problems are avoided in this way, they usually return at a later time.

The facilitator will not always be aware when problems are being avoided, since discussion is limited when this occurs. Look for members changing the subject, saying an issue can be discussed later, shutting down another member's topic, or other tactics that close down conversation. When an issue has been raised and quashed more than once, it is probably an avoidance signal. Try to ascertain whether the concern is legitimate in the context of the current discussion. If its solution will bring immediate value, ask the group or individual to rephrase or reconsider the question or issue, and at least acknowledge its importance to the group.

A final word of caution on raising avoided issues: Some group concerns may deal with organizational or management problems that really do belong outside the workshop. Determine the applicability, sensitivity, and importance of any issue before raising it with the group—opening highly sensitized issues can be seen as naïve or counterproductive, especially if you are working as an outside facilitator.

Group apathy or negativity. Sometimes a team might behave in a generally negative manner or appear to suffer from a lack of challenge. If the organizations you are working with have experienced upheaval or reorganization recently, the reasons for this behavior might be obvious. These reasons are not always the case, however. The prevailing attitude of apathy and negativity is often beyond the individual facilitator. Sometimes this comes across as resignation or disempowerment, revealed by expressions such as "Who cares what we do, it won't make any difference" or "We can't do anything about it, so why try?"

These expressions and attitudes must be recognized and spoken to immediately, so the group members can be made aware of the impact of their attitude. These expressions must be questioned as soon as they appear, or the group members might transfer their attitudes onto the workshop process and the facilitator. Generally negative attitudes are often looking for a specific target, so the first responsibility is to surface the problem so the group becomes aware of the attitude. Once it is out in the open, it can be handled by the facilitator and the group—perhaps not immediately, but over time it might be resolved. Just be sure not to let your facilitation become diminished by negative attitudes.

Communication problems.   Other communication problems are common among groups in workshop situations. People become engaged in dealing with the content and fail to listen to one another. Individuals quickly start working on problem solving or generating ideas, and disregard or ignore other concerns or voices raised. Members from different professional backgrounds might have difficulty understanding what others are saying and won't ask for clarification. This can lead to making faulty assumptions and missing points of discussion.

A more subtle, embedded communication problem occurs in groups when individuals are unwilling to share or express themselves for concern of creating issues or putting others on the spot. For example, face-saving behavior among groups emerges when group members assume that the highest value in teamwork is in getting along, and that consensus requires a cheerful accommodation of group decisions. Argyris (1994) calls this set of behaviors *organizational defensive routines* that hold people to maintaining well-meaning but defeating communication behaviors.

> These consist of all the policies, practices, and actions that prevent human beings from having to experience embarrassment or threat and, at the same time, prevent them from examining the nature and causes of that embarrassment or threat (p. 81).

According to Argyris, a style of organizational communication develops that prevents organizational learning, since learning would require facing the threats and concerns that arise from revealing problems. Facilitators cannot fix this problem when it occurs in small groups—but an awareness of its prevalence can greatly assist in understanding the reluctance of people to participate fully, to communicate clearly about known problem areas, and to confront communication problems in the group setting.

Facilitation Tools

Facilitators employ specific skills, techniques, or facilitation *tools* to conduct effective workshops. Previous sections covered a minimal set of facilitation skills. However, sophisticated group management, listening, and systems thinking skills fill out the toolset for the practitioner. Some of the more advanced tools include managing conflict, gaining consensus, team building, group workshop exercises, and problem solving. A guideline approach for using these tools in Team Design workshops is offered here, at an appropriate level for practitioners. Developing these skills and using the tools requires practice and observation. Refer to some of the books listed as references for a deeper treatment of facilitation tools.

The skills and tools for dealing with difficult and unique situations require facilitators to expand their basic skills. Some skills and tools can be considered essential for working with any group, but have a wide horizon for growth and development. Other skills might be used less frequently, but apply in critical situations. The tools covered in this section include:

- Conflict resolution
- Gaining consensus
- Confrontation and intervention
- Managing group behaviors
- Problem solving

When working with groups, you will encounter unique situations that don't fit your current tools and rules. Dealing with the unexpected must become second nature. One lesson universally expressed by facilitators is that *thinking on one's feet* is a primary personal skill. Unique situations emerge with groups on a frequent basis, and facilitators must develop personal resources for managing all types of interactions. No two groups are alike, and—especially when working with other organizations or corporate cultures—sensitivity and a respect for differences must be the basic attitude of the facilitator.

Resolving conflict and gaining consensus

Conflict resolution is central to all types of group work and facilitation. In almost any group situation, conflicts will arise throughout the process in different forms. As team members wrangle with one another over control of issues and influence, conflict shows up in many minor behaviors and obvious distractions.

Conflict shows up as subtle challenges to the facilitator's authority, as when people show up late for the workshop or interrupt others in the session. Other conflicts show up as barriers to progress, such as noncooperation, unwillingness to contribute, or silence throughout a session. Some people will resist the facilitator because of a perceived loss of control, while others resist the group over control or organizational issues.

As with other workshop processes, group conflict can be divided into *process* and *content*. *Content* conflict is typical, and even productive—this is when participants argue about specific content issues and disagree on what a function should be named or what data should be described. *Process* conflict can be useful, by drawing out the various points of view participants have regarding *how* a design technique should be used, or which method will best represent an idea. But process conflict does not only arise in these benign areas dealing with methodology. It also arises in the social processes in workshops and meetings, becoming a source of disruption and shutting down communication among members.

Social conflict can arise as *blocking,* when participants take dogmatic personal positions and are unwilling to listen or accept new information. Conflict can occur when people directly *attack* the positions of others, for technical or political reasons. Conflict can lead to communication breakdown and impasse. All these types of conflict must be confronted directly by the facilitator.

Facilitators must be able to determine when conflict is healthy and when it will lead to breakdown. As conflict between two or more members arises, it should be allowed to play out to some extent, to understand the direction and intent of the issue. If arguments about process *or* content arise, use the issues to clarify things with the whole team. When it is clear that the conflict is social or personal, confrontation or intervention are appropriate.

Conflict as a process. Experienced facilitators do not avoid conflict—they learn to use it to the group's benefit. Since conflict is an expected occurrence in most groups, facilitators find ways to identify its onset and manage the group's response to the conflict. Conflict shows up as a group process, and signals that participants are confronted by issues or situations and don't have the resources to adjust.

There are several attitudes and ways of acting to consider as a facilitator. Before confronting conflict or a group issue, quickly clarify for yourself the group's mix of positions on the issues. Understand which members are taking what positions, and why. Before addressing the group directly, identify the root cause of the issue or opportunity, not just the symptoms or personalities. Mentally walk through the participants' transactions to understand where the conflict first emerged in the group.

Then be prepared to work with the group to achieve a mutually agreeable solution. Keep your perspective and neutrality, as participants will likely be taking sides and might try to pull you into one side or another. There are several approaches you might take in confrontation:

- Take ownership of the problem for the group. Identify the problem as a group problem in which all have responsibility. Ask the group for a solution to the *group's* issue. This can help when personalities are involved, by removing the personal element.

- Establish a common goal for the group, and keep them focused on it. As conflict mounts, intervene and refocus the team's attention on the purpose or mission statement. Remind them of the process they had strayed from.

- Discuss the source problem of the conflict with the team. At the end of the discussion, summarize what has been decided and who will take any next steps.

- Do not allow conflict to grow. Do not ignore team interactions that bother you. Describe your observations in nonjudgmental terms, and identify any feelings that you may be experiencing.

- If only one or two people continually disrupt the proceedings or create conflict, talk with them directly in private. Explain their behavior in observational terms, and describe the effect on the group process. Give them the option to leave if they would choose, or to continue with the agreement to work as part of the group, following the ground rules.

- If a group member approaches you with a particular issue, perhaps a private issue with another member, be agreeable to working with him or her on managing the issue. This can have an impact on total group cohesion by preventing other issues from arising.

- Ask for help in resolving the conflict only after working on the issue with the other person without any significant change. One approach is to ask the sponsor to confer with the individual directly, or a cofacilitator if you are working with one.

Conflict resolution strategy. Regardless of your facilitation approach, groups will seek to resolve the stress of conflict on their own through several behavioral strategies.

Avoidance. Members will avoid dealing with the conflict directly, and try to avoid it or deny that conflict exists. The avoidance strategy is commonly used when the conflict is between team members and their superiors. They may seek to avoid conflict to protect their standing with their bosses, and will avoid even raising conflicting opinions in discussions.

Diffusion. The diffusion strategy is used when groups try to change the subject, downplay the issue, or deny the significance of the conflict. When team members say "It's not a big deal, let's move on," or "Let's get back on the main subject," a diffusion strategy is adopted. This is also not an effective way of working through conflict, since the source of the conflict remains, at least with a part of the group.

Confrontation. A range of confrontation behaviors will be seen in groups. Confrontation can be understood as dealing with the behavior directly, and attempting a resolution of the issue causing the conflict. Figure 4.2 shows the interaction of confrontation styles, along two scales of motivation (results versus needs) and social impact (win ver-

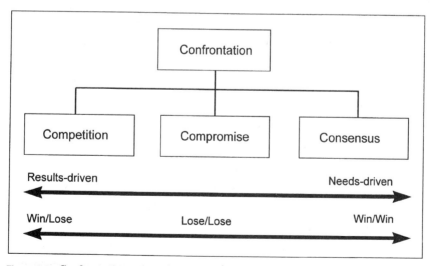

Figure 4.2 Confrontation approaches.

sus lose). The motivation scale looks at ways of achieving the goals of the group. A purely results-driven approach can damage team relationships by valuing results over team respect and cohesion. A needs-driven approach looks at both the work requirements (deliverables) and the team requirements (social goals and team cohesion) and accommodates both.

Confrontational behavior is characterized by three approaches, ranging from competition (taking sides in the conflict for a win-lose approach) to consensus (coming to agreement about the issue or the process of conflict). These are described as follows:

- *Competition.* Competition is a way of confronting others in which one attempts to win at another's expense. Competitive confrontation seeks to gain from the behavior, by having the other person lose power or control in the outcome. Competition is often very simple, as when one person fights for an issue, creating a minor source of conflict. Others might oppose the person's ideas, presenting at least one competing proposal, if not many alternatives. An attitude of competition prevails when team members use the conflict as an opportunity to make points, split into competing groups, or to win at the expense of others.

- *Compromise.* Compromise moves the group more toward agreement, and away from discord. It represents moving away from competition, but still reveals the attitude of competition, as when participants give up a position or idea to move forward with the whole team.

  In compromise, the members who gave in to the majority are rarely comfortable with the process, and might feel that their points were not fairly engaged. Because this approach is dissatisfying to most involved with the decision, it is considered a *lose-lose* approach.

- *Consensus.* Consensus is the best result the group can expect from moving through conflict, which is why it's described as a *win-win* approach. Consensus allows individuals to maintain their opinions and positions, and recognizes the group's need to identify and commit to a solution with which each member can agree.

  Consensus building is a group conflict strategy used by facilitators to prevent destructive conflict and to encourage discussion and airing of opinions and approaches. Consensus building starts at the beginning of the session, and is not an approach pulled out during periods of conflict. Therefore, when consensus solutions are reached following team conflict, the team has experience with collaborative decision making, and has the expectation that it works.

Intervention techniques. During group processes, the facilitator has the right to intervene in situations where the integrity of the group is at stake. Whenever team members act inconsistently with their stated goals or the ground rules, the facilitator must detect the situation and intervene appropriately to bring the team back on track. *Intervention* is a type of confrontation where action is taken to interrupt current group behaviors to remedy the conflict. Intervention actions range from nondirective to prescriptive, and any of them might be effective given the right circumstances. Each group and each situation must be considered new when intervening. A direct intervention that worked well with a smaller group of peer level engineers might not work with an interorganizational group of managers, or even with the same group on a different day. Knowing when and how to intervene requires learning and sensitivity on the part of the facilitator. But the basic techniques can be learned and incorporated into the facilitating toolkit.

Nondirective. Nondirective intervening is highly accepting of a person's behavior. The person is given the floor and allowed to express, perhaps within time guidelines or other guidance offered by the facilitator. This approach might be useful when customers or high status individuals originate the conflict, and a direct confrontation would cause potential harm to business relationships.

Involving. The facilitator encourages participants to become more involved in the group process. They are asked, by name, to join in on specific exercises and let go of any conflict experienced. This approach is used with individuals who become separated from the group, typically of their own choosing, and whose conflicts emerge from withheld communication or unexpressed concerns or expectations. Deliberately requiring their involvement serves to confront the conflict in a reasonable manner, while requesting their participation as a full group member.

Confronting. Direct confronting is required for situations where the conflict is obviously disruptive or shuts down communication. The facilitator stops the disruptive individual's behavior by pointing it out and addressing its effects on the team. Confronting often requires the following approach:

1. Stop the participant, and ask him or her to conclude their thought.
2. Describe the participant's behaviors that evidence conflict in objective terms.
3. Describe the effect of this behavior on the group.
4. Ask the participant to reveal the purpose of the behavior.

Ready answers are not always forthcoming, if this type of intervention is necessary in the first place. As a facilitator, you might find it necessary to ask probing questions to get to the source of the conflict. Once the source is known and exposed, others on the team can address the issue, and the problem can often be resolved. The key to effective confronting is to use the ground rules established by the team to prevent conflicts from eroding the group's communication in the first place. And be sure to rely on the explicit agreement about the ground rules to assert your authority to represent the group in confronting behaviors that impede group progress.

Prescribing. Sometimes conflicts are merely rational or technical in nature, and participants are possibly open to discussing alternatives or to listening to the facilitator. *Prescribing* is an intervention style in which the facilitator offers suggestions or solutions for the participant in conflict. A prescriptive approach might be direct, persuasive, or just suggestive. Alternatives presented to the participant should be offered sincerely for the benefit of both the participant and the team, and should not appease or justify the conflict.

Intervention requires facilitators to use their authority, and is most effective with a degree of firmness of statement and resolve to reach closure. A set of simple steps some facilitators follow for intervention follows:

1. Upon detecting behaviors inconsistent with stated agreements, ground rules and goals, stop the group conversation and ask to share your observations.

2. State the behaviors as observed in objective, nonjudgmental terms. Do not blame or attribute intention to any individual involved. Ask the individuals involved if they agree that those behaviors were demonstrated.

3. Express your interpretation of the behavior. Describe the perceived impact on the group, your inference about the values expressed, or your personal feelings arising from the behavior.

4. Ask the group members for their reaction or response. If they agree that the behavior is disruptive or incongruent, ask them to realign themselves with the ground rules or purpose of the workshop.

This intervention approach maintains objectivity and removes judgment from the social process of confronting. It allows the individuals in the group the possibility of making a choice—they are free to change their behavior or to disagree and continue.

Gaining consensus. We briefly looked at consensus when discussing how groups create win-win solutions from decision making or conflict. Consensus as a strategy enables a group to discuss all aspects of a problem, raise objections, and work toward a creative solution that satisfies each member of the team. The key point (often missed) that distinguishes *consensus* from *compromise* holds that the solution must be agreed upon unanimously, and that a lone objector is not overruled or pressured to submit to a group decision. The consensus process (over many years experience) has been shown to achieve better decisions, and people are more satisfied with consensus than with using other approaches to reach agreement. Consensus is a key strategy for facilitators, and has become the basis for reaching agreement in contemporary group decision making. Other decision/agreement approaches can generate conflict or tension within the group that undermines the ability of the group to work together effectively.

- Majority voting always cuts out the minority—a win-lose process that leaves the minority dissatisfied and sometimes unable or unwilling to buy into the decision.

- Individual decision making, often used by those in authority to settle differences, can leave members at both ends of the decision dissatisfied. After a decision has been settled by fiat, team members feel disempowered to handle issues as a group.

- Compromise encourages all members to give up something in order to make the decision. It leaves everyone dissatisfied, and as such is considered a lose-lose approach.

Consensus requires more creativity than a compromise approach, and imposes more work on the group than majority voting. Consensus asks the group to collaborate to reach a *new* solution that takes into account the needs, ideas, and objections raised by all members of the team. Where other decision-making methods dispose of new ideas or information and reject individual objections in order to move forward, the consensus approach realizes that overriding team members for the sake of quick conclusions backfires in the long run. As many workshop sessions using consensus have found, the quality of group decisions is much higher with the consensus model.

Starting sessions with consensus. In technical workshops such as are used in Team Design, participants will not always see the value in consensus. Cross-functional teams are employed to represent the business and technical functions of the organization within a single team, and members often maintain the primacy of their viewpoint.

Engineers will see consensus decision making as nonrigorous and avoiding technical issues. Business representatives view consensus as reducing their influence on product decisions. In reality, consensus is easier to reach with a homogenous group with similar goals, backgrounds, and motivations than with the multidisciplinary development team.

The key to bringing consensus into development workshops is in hooking the participants on the value of the approach, heading off the default thought processes of logical argument that dominate technical discussion. Design facilitators learn to create consensus very early in the meeting, thus encouraging a template for working through real problems later in the workshop. With new teams, the first point at which a consensus agreement is reached arises when asking for the team's buy-in on the ground rules. The following guidelines might be used to start the group started thinking from a consensus viewpoint:

1. Start off the ground rules discussion by listing a partial set of rules that most members will agree with, such as: One speaker has the floor at a time; No personal attacks (respect for ideas); Arrive and end on time; and Follow the ground rules.

2. Explain to the group the importance of ground rules, and how they support holding a smooth and productive workshop. Say how they will be enforced by the facilitator to maintain the flow and order of the group process. And describe how consensus agreement is required to make the ground rules work for them.

3. Ask the group to add any other rules to which they want to hold. Inspire some brainstorming to generate ideas for team rules. Bring up some suggestions only if the group offers none (which can easily happen in technical groups not used to a socially derived process). Suggest the addition of a rule to use true group consensus to resolve differences.

4. After five to seven ground rules have been listed, offer to close the discussion. Ask whether all are satisfied with the rules, and whether everyone can live with them. When commitment has been made, describe how they have successfully used consensus decision making, which can serve as a model for resolving issues throughout the session.

Use other opportunities early in the workshop to demonstrate the power of consensus in reaching satisfactory group decisions. Point out when consensus occurs naturally in the group process, and give the group positive encouragement for their ability to work together.

Maintaining consensus. When facilitating, stay alert for breaches of consensus. Groups can become overly comfortable with the apparent easy success of the consensus approach, and a subtle peer pressure to conform for the sake of consensus emerges. If working with a new team or an external group, this encroachment of group pressure can be difficult to detect, since very few overt statements are made to betray these dynamics. Watch for dominating team members rallying the rest of the group to reach a rapid consensus, or for a vocal majority that pushes for rapid completion of tasks. Look for the reactions of the less-involved members or anyone who remains silent. Stop the process when necessary, ask these more withdrawn team members what they think, and facilitate further discussion on any concerns raised. Often, quieter group members are holding back because they feel their opinion might not be as valid, especially with technical issues, and they don't want to slow down an otherwise productive (appearing) team. Be sure to integrate all members into the discussion to demonstrate consensus and also to maintain fairness in the group facilitation. When the group falls back into old behavior patterns, and loses some of the rigor required to maintain consensus, use guidelines to reinforce the consensus process. The following guidelines, adapted from Doyle and Straus (1976), were originally presented by Jay Hall in a 1971 article in *Psychology Today,* and they hold as well today. They are discussed here from the facilitator's perspective:

1. Minimize argumentation in the group. When participants argue for their own position, ask them to state their position clearly, and to allow others to speak. Ask the most vocal members to listen to other members of the group.

2. When the group becomes deadlocked and cannot reach an acceptable solution, ask the group members to reconsider their views of whether someone must win or lose. Remind them of the benefit of reaching a win-win solution, and ask them to find the best alternative proposal that all might agree with.

3. Remind group members not to change their minds to reach easy agreement. When the group appears to have reached a difficult solution too quickly, probe for the reasons for rapid acceptance and be sure everyone freely accepts the result.

4. Don't resort to group voting or bargaining approaches if a solution is not quickly found. Work through the dissent until common ground is reached. Take a break or resume the discussion at a later time, if necessary.

5. Allow disagreements to arise, and encourage group members to voice their differences. Differences bring new information to light that otherwise might be missed, and often lead to the better group solution.

Finally, too much of any good thing has its drawbacks. Teams can become enamored of consensus and create a working environment where disagreement is tacitly discouraged. Participants begin going along with all decisions as a habit, and the attitude of *groupthink* emerges. Groupthink starts to show up after a group has formed its identity and has established the tacit values members learn to adopt as part of the group. When members submerge their thoughts and opinions and go along with the group passively or unconsciously more than once or twice, a groupthink pattern has started to take hold.

Facilitators take different approaches to dealing with groupthink. It can be difficult to confront in some groups, especially if organizational defensive routines are also at work in the group. The simplest approach is to change the format for group discussion. Other techniques include creating a change of work mode, or "thought breaks," for the group, or using anonymous group voting and decision making. When the team realizes it's acceptable to disagree, a true consensus becomes possible again.

Problem solving

Problem solving is considered to be an important tool for process improvement and development workshops. Most treatments of facilitation in design and development workshops touch on problem solving, and numerous publications deal specifically with problem-solving methods. Rather than duplicate the discussion of tools and approaches currently available, this chapter looks at the *purpose* of problem solving and presents alternatives to the traditional approaches.

Problem solving traditionally involves a collection of analytic techniques used to identify the root causes of systemic problems and to propose best-fit solutions to the specified problem. Information is collected about a problem area, analysis is performed on the data, and alternative solutions are evaluated and selected to address the problem as defined. This problem-solving model is loosely based on the scientific method, and has grown from the rational and empirical viewpoint of investigation and analysis. Several popular approaches to problem solving are based on this rational approach, and are characterized by sequential processes (usually a five- or seven-step process) that propose a model for working through problems.

The comprehensive problem-solving approach. Many problem-solving models can be used in facilitation, and a useful approach holds that learning a comprehensive problem-solving strategy will enable the facilitator to address any emerging problem-solving situation. A comprehensive model can be pared down to fewer elements when a rapid application of tools is called for, but a more limited model might miss some of the tools and steps incorporated into a bigger framework.

Knowing the larger problem-solving model pays off when working with new teams that might use a different approach than yours. The comprehensive model allows for rapid understanding of different problem-solving methods, and supports more effective situational facilitation. When working with an external group, adapt their problem-solving model to the situation, rather than offering a known model that might be new to them. If problem-solving is required and the group does not use any particular approach, assess their need for in-depth analysis and their allowable time investment before offering a problem-solving model. Consider whether a simple problem analysis is required, or a more creative approach that might propose solutions from a different angle.

A problem-solving model. The quality management literature provides a rich source of problem-solving methodologies and tools from which to draw. Total quality management, manufacturing, and process control lend considerable depth of experience to the field of methods and tools that can be used in development and design facilitation. Selected tools discussed in Chap. 7 are drawn from this background.

A comprehensive problem-solving approach is presented here as a reference model. Adapted from a popular six-step method, this model is representative of current practice. It is not proposed as a replacement for other methods, and is meant to serve as an example of this class of problem-solving methods.

- Problem definition

   1. *Select and define the problem to be solved.* This initial step selects a specific problem from a set of potential problems, as identified by the team or as directed by management. The selected problem is clarified and defined by the team, and defined and documented as the problem to be solved.

      The problem statement should describe the current state in very specific terms and describe the desired state that the problem fails to meet. The statement should not indicate any possible causes, and should not attempt to propose a solution.

2. *Collect information related to the problem.* After defining the problem, the team collects information and facts about the problem. For simple problems, a single person might be able to collect all the data necessary. For complex problems, a small group might be required to collect information by conducting a brief investigation, using interviews or surveys, or observing a process in action.

3. *Analyze the information to assess root causes.* Analyze the data collected to determine possible sources of the problem or variation. Both qualitative and quantitative methods are recommended as analysis tools, selected as required by the type of problem. Quality management tools such as Pareto charts, check sheets, scatter plots, matrices and other diagrams are generally useful for analyzing problem data. Intensive analysis is not required, but analyze enough to identify the probable cause of the problem.

   Describe the results of data analysis using diagrams or summary documentation to clearly communicate the findings in a simple manner. Describe the probable cause in specific terms, and identify all corresponding behaviors and other variations discovered that cooccur with the problem.

- Solution generation

4. *Generate alternative solutions to the defined problem.* A creative process is recommended in this step, to produce as many alternative ideas as possible. Use a brainstorming method with the team to generate a large number of possible alternative solutions. As with any brainstorming, avoid any evaluation of ideas at this stage, and focus on gaining a wide variety of solution ideas.

   Refer to the Brainstorming section of Chap. 5 for possible methods.

5. *Evaluate alternatives.* Following the creative brainstorming step, alternatives are organized and evaluated. Organize the ideas into categories if different groupings are evident from the suggestions. If several groupings emerge, it might point to a multifaceted problem. It might also lead to a new solution proposal that combines elements from the different categories, especially if no single solution fits the problem well on its own.

   Define criteria for evaluating the solution so that a best-fit solution can be identified. Narrow down the set of solutions to those that meet the essential criteria. This should result in a small number of candidates, three to five at most. Evaluate these alternatives against the criteria to select the most appropriate possible solution.

6. *Select the best solution.*   The best solution to the problem is selected by the group following evaluation and discussion. A decision-making process or consensus can be used to select the solution. The best solution is not always the one with the best evaluation. The team should decide which solution is the best overall for the problem as defined.

- Process management

7. *Identify and assign actions.*   Plan actions with the team to implement the solution, or to implement test cases to evaluate the solution itself. The action planning should identify key individuals, actions required, and dates for each action. If additional resources are required outside the immediate team, specify all requirements and assign someone to investigate obtaining resources. A small project plan might be established as a proposal to management for implementing the proposed solution.

8. *Evaluate results and plan for process improvement.*   Evaluate the results of the initial implementation or the test case to determine whether the problem was solved. Identify how closely the solution met the target goals, and plan for continued improvement of the process. Collect information on the revised process and make small changes as required to continually improve the process.

These rational problem-solving approaches work well for certain classes of problems, such as those where a systematic source of variation exists in an otherwise well-functioning system. These problems are typically found in well-defined domains, such as manufacturing processes or mechanical systems. This empirical approach works well for locating the source of an engine misfire in an otherwise well-running car, or for identifying variations in product quality from a machining process.

It's in the messy, complex, highly interactive problems that the traditional approach is insufficient. These are problems such as complex integrated software systems and business processes, ones where extensive human interaction is involved. With numerous underlying and invisible processes, multiple human and system interactions, and highly conditional operational rules, these problems call for different types of tools.

The problem of problem solving.   A common facilitator perspective regards *problem solving* as the major work undertaken in facilitated workshops. The problem-solving perspective is rooted in management theory, and has a strong following in business literature, with problem analysis and decision-making methods focused around this approach. Every facilitator should certainly know a number of problem-solving methods for use when necessary—but the traditional perspective of problem solving itself does not apply universally. Don't allow problem solving to become the do-everything tool for workshops, the hammer in search of ready nails to drive.

In *Breakthrough Thinking,* Nadler and Hibino (1994) point out how the focus on the problem is unproductive, and can lead to new problems:

> If, rather than address purposes, you go about it the old-fashioned way and simply ask, What's wrong here? What's the problem? your answer is almost certain to cause more problems. It will be culturally skewed, historically biased, conceptually constrained, and ultimately limiting—precisely because it focuses on problems, not solutions (p. 82).

By focusing on the notion of a *problem,* a group identifies with the problem too closely, and limits the opportunities for accomplishment. In a typical situation, an identified problem emerges from an existing financial system that can't accommodate a new payment arrangement. Modifications to the software result in new bugs due to the interaction of multiple modifications. The modifications represent a patchwork of previously "fixed" problems, each designed by a different engineer, and integrated over a period of years. Which problem should be fixed? The current need to handle the new payment method, or the underlying structure of programs in the system? And, to what extent does this system drive or control the business process it supports? Should the business process be changed as well?

This is often the case with large, complex software systems that have drastically evolved from an original, smaller-scale purpose. The opportunity for breakthrough accomplishment in this context is slight—about the best that can be hoped for is an incremental improvement in system maintenance. A *whole* solution arises only by expanding the dimensions of problem solving to allow for new possibilities.

Some processes and systems should not be repaired indefinitely, but should be replaced with new ones. The traditional problem-solving process focuses on such a narrow band of evaluation that the possibility of replacing or overhauling the process is missed. It is a matter of using the wrong analysis tool for the job—some jobs require tools that work on a broader scale.

A focus on solutions thinking is not a radical change for design facilitators—it can be seen as an extension of current practices. Many of these practices are discussed throughout the book, as workshop activities and Team Design processes. The design-oriented formats, Business Process Design and Application Design, especially, introduce creative methods for visualizing and reframing solutions to produce more innovative results.

Creative problem solving. *Creative problem solving* is a class of methods for generating ideas, designing alternatives, and gaining insights using a nontraditional structure. The creative problem-solving tools do not fit a step-by-step approach, and don't have rigid rules of application. Their success depends somewhat more on the facilitator's skill than the traditional approach, due in some part to participant's unfamiliarity with them. Although not as goal-oriented as traditional methodologies, creative problem-solving methods can be used to find new ways of viewing, describing, and solving problems that lead to very different—and highly effective—solutions.

James Higgins (1994b), a pioneer and proponent of creative problem solving in business organizations, has compiled numerous creative methods in recent books. His experience with problem solving led him to conclude that creativity is not encouraged in problem solving, and is actually discouraged in most organizations. He suggests methods for creative problem solving that can be used by those of us in traditional organizations.

Higgins presents a problem-solving model called the Creative Problem-Solving (CPS) process that addresses weaknesses in the traditional approaches. Although similar on the surface to more structured methods, CPS allows for the use of a huge variety of methods and tools within the problem-solving model. The following stages are identified in CPS:

1. *Environmental analysis.* A continual process of searching for problems and opportunities for improvement, and analyzing situations for possible solutions.

2. *Problem recognition.* A process of evaluating information leading to the recognition of problems, or of allowing problems to emerge over time and become recognizable in a complete form.

3. *Problem identification.* Identifying the true problem to be solved, and understanding the purpose in solving the problem. Ensuring that organizational direction is pointed toward the real problem, and that problem-solving objectives are established. Defining the problem in enough detail to initiate organizational action.

4. *Making assumptions.* Surfacing and understanding the assumptions about the future as affected by the problem. Considering the environment and conditions under which the solution might take effect.

5. *Generating alternatives.* A creative process of defining known

options and creating new alternatives for solutions to the problem or opportunity.

6. *Choosing among alternatives.*   A systematic evaluation of the alternatives and a rational decision-making process to select the appropriate solution.

7. *Implementation.*   Planning, setting goals, and assigning action plans to accomplish the solution within appropriate implementation guidelines.

8. *Control.*   Evaluating the results of implementation, using feedback to identify issues and inconsistencies, and making continuous changes to effectively guide the solution.

The Creative Problem-Solving approach allows the facilitator to select from numerous methods for working with groups in developing solutions. The majority of the techniques described are creative methods for individuals and groups to generate alternatives and ideas in problem solving. Both rational and intuitive processes are discussed and recommended, and intuition is encouraged as a means of dealing with highly complex problems that can evade solution by step-by-step rational analysis.

The creative approach recognizes there is no single right way to develop effective solutions. Higgins' book offers over a hundred various techniques with the understanding that a large number of methods provides better opportunities for inventing creative solutions to complex problems. This source and similar sourcebooks can readily be adapted for use in design and development facilitation.

Facilitating solutions.   Facilitators are faced with major differences in perspective on a daily basis. Experience with group problem solving leads to very different approaches than group members will adopt without having had this breadth of experience. Facilitators must often hold great ideas and creative suggestions back because the job is primarily to assist groups in generating their own solutions. So, if anything can be brought to the group other than problem-solving techniques and workshop exercises, it is the unique and effective *perspective* toward problem solving. This perspective holds a *solution-focused* mind-set, and is not problem-focused.

Breakthrough Thinking™, an approach discussed in several chapters in this book, emphasizes this solution-focused perspective. The notion that problems are a primary fact of life is acknowledged, but the approach toward solving problems is turned upside down. The myths of problem solving are exposed, and we are asked to avoid the trap of finding excellent solutions to the wrong problem.

Breakthrough solutions, those that create opportunity and open up possibilities, are not found by analyzing data or following the steps of a process. Creative problem solvers use many tools at their disposal to reach apparently simple and straightforward solutions. Intuition, gut feeling, experience, rational thinking, and visualization are among the personal techniques good problem solvers bring to the group. Facilitators can learn to draw these techniques out in groups— even if no one person brings all these tools to the party, among the entire group a wide range of backgrounds and approaches can be pulled to develop breakthrough group solutions. A creative, expansive approach allows all group members to participate, with their own unique contributions—not just to perform part of a problem-solving task.

Instead of a defined process, the Breakthrough Thinking approach uses a series of principles, allowing for extensive personal and group flexibility:

- *Uniqueness.* Each problem faced is a unique situation. Solutions should not be "copied and pasted" from apparently similar situations.

- *Purposes.* The initial focus must be on the purpose for solving a problem. Then purposes are expanded into a range from large to small to identify the most effective direction and intention for committing energy.

- *Solution-after-next.* The conditions of the future situation should guide the solution selected to accomplish the primary purpose. By positing an ideal target state, the solution works backward to unravel a workable approach for achieving this ideal target.

- *Systems.* The target solution defines and details as many system elements and relationships as possible. The larger system context is understood, allowing for the solution of more complex problems that will occur in the future.

- *Limited information collection.* Before investing resources to gather and analyze data related to the problem, determine the purpose and usage of the information. The solution should be investigated, not the problem. Having extensive knowledge about a problem area might make you an expert, but can also preclude your finding creative alternative solutions to the problem.

- *People design.* The solution process should offer opportunities for people to participate in its solution and in the design of its implementation. People affected by any solution can be given roles in the implementation.

■ *Betterment timeline.*   When planning and designing the current solution, the necessary future changes must be considered as well. Schedule the improvement of the process into the solution to ensure its maintenance over time.

Other facilitation tools

Facilitation is like teaching or consulting in that new techniques can be picked up along the way during one's practice. Some facilitators' favorite tools are adapted from well-known group processes used in group work and other practices. Facilitation strategies are presented as a way of organizing all types of facilitation and problem-solving tools. The next area, *dialogue,* has grown into an appreciated facilitation tool since Senge's (1990, 1994) presentations in the *Fifth Discipline* books. Finally, icebreakers are used by public speakers, teachers, corporate trainers, and many others who work with groups. These and other techniques can be easily learned and adapted for use in almost any facilitated session.

Facilitation strategies.   Facilitation strategies enable the experienced facilitator to rapidly understand and adapt to any team direction or new management that comes along. *Strategies* are the general approach or orientation a facilitator brings to a problem that enables him or her to quickly determine the best set of techniques and steps to accomplish work with the team. A strategic view of group work allows you to deal with a small set of steps for any given problem or purpose, and to expand these as necessary based on your own unique toolkit. Once these strategies are understood, the essential structure of almost any facilitation technique is easily recognized.

The following strategies were presented and defined by Alan Scharf (1996), a Canadian facilitation consultant and Breakthrough Thinking practitioner. Scharf's Internet-based newsletter published the strategies for a set of basic team purposes, and he states:

> Nearly every one of the hundreds of techniques that you know and encounter is attempting to accomplish one of these purposes. Once you learn to look at them at this level of abstraction, a huge warm cloud of understanding rolls in and surrounds you. Here are the fundamental strategies for each of these purposes. They're easy to memorize. Do it.

Creativity strategy.   Used to generate alternatives.

1. Criticism is ruled out.

2. Free wheeling is welcome. The wilder the ideas, the better.

3. A quantity of ideas is wanted.

4. Combination and improvement are sought.

5. Use prompt words, analogies, and brain resting.

6. Use teams to get others involved.

Decision-making strategy. Used to select a choice from predetermined alternatives.

1. Identify, list, and group all possible alternatives.

2. Establish the weighted criteria which will affect the decision, and establish a scale of values for each.

3. Assess or measure the value of each alternative for each selection factor.

4. Use appropriate decision rules, and select the highest-scoring alternative.

Planning and design (or Breakthrough Thinking strategy). Used to determine the action or specific means for achieving a purpose.

1. Define the function of the system—what is accomplished, not how it is done. This is not the same as the system's objectives.

2. Develop many ideal alternatives for achieving the function under ideal regular conditions, where no exceptions or irregularities occur. (Use creativity strategy.)

3. Evolve one feasible, but still ideal, target solution. (Use decision-making strategy.)

4. Develop a practical solution from the ideal, accommodating exceptions, and implement it as planned.

Research or conventional problem-solving strategy. Used to discover something you don't know or to determine causes.

1. Get all the facts about the matter of interest.

2. Model and analyze these facts.

3. Determine possible conclusions. (Use creativity strategy.)

4. Come to a final conclusion. (Use decision-making strategy.)

Operating strategy. Used to supervise or operate a good system.

1. Gain familiarity with the system.

2. Obtain needed operating resources, people, machines, and instructions.

3. Obtain needed input resources (materials, etc.).

4. Apply operating resources to input resources according to system requirements. (Plan, organize, lead, motivate, and control.)

Control strategy. Used to maintain a standard of performance.

1. Develop performance measures for the function to be achieved.
2. Establish specific levels for those measures. (Measurable performance specifications, or objectives.)
3. Develop and install methods for monitoring performance.
4. Compare performance with objectives or specifications.
5. Determine causes, if necessary, and take action to reduce or eliminate variance.

Motivation strategy. Used to foster effort directed toward achievement.

1. Develop performance measures for the function to be achieved.
2. Design and install methods for teams and individuals to monitor performance with these measures.
3. Establish a system of rewards, meaningful to and understandable by the employees, based on measured performance.
4. Deliver rewards with minimum delay.
5. Avoid punishing for poor behavior.

Scharf comments on these strategies:

> Now look at the control strategy. This is the strategy used by Management by Objectives, Quality Control, and by your automobile cruise control! At this level they are all the same. In addition to this insight, you will now understand why MBO never produced the productivity improvement that was claimed. Look at your favorite problem solving technique. It almost certainly uses the research strategy. Look at this strategy again—perhaps you can see why traditional problem solving approaches aren't noted for innovation or optimization. (Scharf 1996. Reprinted with permission.)

Dialogue. *Dialogue* is a concept for organizational and team learning brought forward by Senge (1990, 1994) that has reached a wide audience of management and organizational development practitioners. Dialogue has not yet reached the average technical practitioner, where its value can provide pragmatic resolution of difficult team problems. It is an effective complement to various technical methods in the Team Design formats, and can be used in many situations to facilitate understanding or in resolving conflict.

Dialogue creates an environment for groups to share thoughts and values in a highly respectful climate. It allows individuals to deeply explore issues with the intentional listening of the entire group. Facilitated dialogue also provides a forum for the team to work out communications and unexpressed frustrations in a safe, guided process. Dialogue is like a structured story, and is treated as a facilitated process. It requires participants to suspend their assumptions during the process, to hold off thinking from their normal positions. Participants—both speakers and listeners—must also foster an attitude of respect, regarding all team members as equals or colleagues. The facilitator maintains the context of the process by watching for behaviors that divert from the dialogue process, and by maintaining the flow of the process along accepted lines. The essential steps to dialogue are as follows:

1. Dialogue assumes that a problem, concern, or situation has emerged that affects the group, or at least one person, significantly. As a facilitator, have involved participants describe any events that they recall taking place. Encourage them to be unattached to the outcome, to just describe the situation as they recall it.

2. Have the tellers state the problem in very simple terms. Start with the expression "The Problem is..." and have them finish the statement without embellishment. Have them state the problem with no solution or assessments.

3. Then, ask them to tell their story. Have them identify patterns of behavior and themes that emerge. Investigate both sides of the story, to look at the situation as if another stakeholder were telling the story.

4. Spell out the attributes of the problem through the story and the dialogue. Make a list of items, draw a picture of the situation, have other group members contribute to the details. As the facilitator, stay uninvolved but interested.

5. Investigate any relationships or systemic behavior that come forth from the discussion. Dialogue is a two-way conversation—work with the storyteller or tellers to discuss possible patterns in the case and any resolutions that occur. The problem does not have to be solved through this process. Dialogue is an ongoing communications process that starts the chain of effective discussions—it does not necessarily lead to a close.

Facilitators should encourage dialogue at different points throughout design sessions, not primarily to move the process forward, but to create an environment of listening and understanding within the group. This is especially important with new teams that have not worked together for more than a few days or weeks. When working with larger groups, consider the following variation of the dialogue process, allowing people to use dialogue in small breakout groups:

1. As the facilitator, organize topics for dialogue and list them on the board or easel. If a central issue is at stake, write it down on the board *in question form* for all to see and agree to its representation. Write the instructions on the board, and give the groups 30 to 45 minutes to complete the dialogue.

2. Break the larger group into small groups of four to six people. If there are multiple topics, assign a topic to each group, or have all the groups dialogue with a single issue. Have someone in each group take notes on the dialogue.

3. Using a pen or marker as a *talking stick,* have the first group member hold the stick and reflect on the question posed to the group. No other member can speak while the talking stick is being held.

4. This person continues by thinking further on the question, bringing up other questions that deepen the inquiry or meaning of the initial question. When done, the stick is passed to the next member, who initiates dialogue using the same process.

Each person should have five to ten minutes for their inquiry. At the conclusion of the period, have each group debrief and discuss their insights for five minutes. Then have each group share its experience and learning from the dialogue with the larger group.

Icebreakers.   When starting a new workshop session, facilitators often employ simple exercises to stimulate thinking and get people moving. Collectively called *icebreakers,* these exercises can be used whenever a transition or break in thinking is called for throughout a workshop, not just at the start of a session. The exercises are often combined with introductions in groups where people have not worked together previously. Often, they are simple intellectual puzzles (brainteasers), quick and often humorous, used to help start group conversation. Others prefer to engage people socially with icebreaker exercises.

Some facilitation experts do not use icebreakers, preferring to move through the agenda and allow the group to loosen up through working together. Other practitioners find them useful with newly formed groups, but do not use them with established groups that prefer to start right into business. Groups that are interested in improving their creativity will generally appreciate the light touch of icebreaker exercises. And, at times, the most serious groups will benefit from these exercises by breaking down their all-business attitude and allowing creative intellectual play.

Warm-ups. *Warm-ups* are simple physical exercises, often used at the very beginning of sessions to encourage people to relax and loosen up their bodies, minds, and attitudes. Warm-ups are also useful after breaks, and sometimes during sessions if members are losing attention and interest. Facilitators assist the group in loosening up by loosening up first—forget the agendas and serious business of the day, and be playful for the warm-ups. A few examples follow:

- *Standing ovation.* Start this warm-up as if it were a light calisthenic exercise. Instruct everyone in the room stand up and face the front. The instructions are spoken to the group while demonstrating: "Put your hands up over your head and stretch. Put your hands straight out in front of you. Bring your arms out wide." At the next instruction, "Now, bring your hands together like this!" make a single loud clap. "Now repeat! Faster!" The group will quickly catch on that they are all applauding, and you can say, "Thank you—I've always wanted to start off with a standing ovation!"

- *Hello.* Have everyone sit in a large circle. Explain to the group that each person is to make a unique "hello" to the group. Each member is to stand, take two steps and face the others, and say "Hello!" By using unique movements of hands and body, facial expressions, and vocal inflections, each person makes a special greeting. Start off with your hello first, then have each member repeat your greeting in the same way and add theirs at the end. By the end of the circle, the last member will repeat every other hello in the room plus their own unique greeting. A variation of this warm-up has participants say their name with an adjective instead of hello, such as "Bodacious Bob!" The name expression is accompanied by exaggerated body movements that demonstrate the adjective.

- *Number groups.* Create an open space and have participants gather in the center of the room. Tell the group that they will be expected to think quickly for this task. Instruct the group to form small groups of the same number that is called out. Call out a small number by saying "Make groups of three (or six, or eight)," and then give them three seconds to form the groups. If a person is left out, they get to call the next number. Repeat this process rapidly, up to 10 times.

Word games. Various word games are available in training books, newspapers, and exercise handbooks that can be used as quick intellectual warm-ups. These exercises can be collected over time to be used as needed for icebreakers, breaks, or when a breather is needed during a session. A simple word game example follows:

- *Alphabet Box.*   This is a good exercise to use during the December holidays. Create a viewgraph of a 5×5 matrix, with a total of 25 squares. Write all the letters of the alphabet in the squares except the letter *L*. Ask the group to decipher the message of the matrix. The correct answer is *Noel*.

Team relationship and group development.   These exercises are useful for groups as adjuncts to the team-building process or for understanding the extent and impact of relationships in groups. As many groups will start with a mix of members who have prior relationships and new members, icebreakers are a useful way to reveal the depth of connectedness and experience in the group. These are also useful in the social development of the team, to allow current team members to welcome and encourage the new members.

Scavenger Hunt.   This exercise helps team members learn about one another, and is useful in new teams where the facilitator and participants do not know each other very well. In groups of 10 to 20 people, find out about the professional or personal interests of about half the group's members in advance of the session. Look for special achievements, certifications, special hobbies, and things that are unique to an individual. For the icebreaker, tell or list the special backgrounds or professional interests, and have the group members mingle and talk with each other to discover the individuals who correspond to the special mentions. Give the group a fixed time limit (10 minutes or so) and have people share about how many they have found. Usually, one person will have identified more of the individuals than anyone else, and you might appoint him or her as "social director" for the workshop, or some similar honoring function.

Small Group Grope.   In larger groups, the following exercise can be used to break out into small groups for continuing work in the small group format. Obtain packages of small, colored, sticky dots, in five or more colors—one color for each small group. Have the group stand in rows or a circle, and place a colored dot on each person's forehead. Explain to the group that how this nonverbal exercise will establish the groups they are to work in. When done, ask the group to find all others with the same color dots. Participants must avoid using mirrors, eyeglasses, or writing notes. Without speaking, all groups must find each other. Participants might wish to share their experiences with the group.

Networking.   This exercise can be used in mixed groups where some people are already well acquainted and others are not. The intention is to physically show the network of association among team members, and it gets people up and moving around.

1. Have everyone stand and move into a space in the middle of the room.

2. Have each person place their hand on the shoulder of someone they know or have met before.

This process allows the facilitator and the group to see how associations are distributed among the team, and where relationships exist or need to be formed. If few people are connected, ask the members to move into the positions they want to take. Pay attention to the pattern that forms when this occurs—if people form isolated clumps, you might need team building to break down barriers among members. If everyone joins hands and forms a circle, your team might be well on its way toward a group identity.

Human Clock. The human clock shows the relationship of team members to their length of service in the organization. If facilitating within established teams or deeply connected organizations, it is interesting and useful to understand the depth of experience within the group. This is especially useful for external facilitators.

Have the group members form a circle to represent a clock, with each position indicating the relative tenure of team members in the organization. The newest member starts at the 1:00 o'clock position, and people position themselves around the circle until the member at 11:00 o'clock represents the longest tenure.

After the clock is formed, briefly facilitate discussion among the members about their experiences with the organization at the time they joined. This can serve as a type of history or evolution of the organization, and will raise interesting questions among the participants. Depending on the interest level and need for team building, this exercise can range from 5 to 30 minutes.

Telling Lies. This is a useful icebreaker when some evident tension in the group might be tied to relevant issues to be explored in the workshop. Ask the participants to each prepare three lies about their organization, and have them share them one at a time, in order. *Lies* are statements that they believe are not true, but might be expressions made by others in the company or institution. Write down the statements on the whiteboard (not permanently on pads!) and, when complete, have participants share what they notice about the "lies." This exercise allows participants to release frustrations and express the unspoken in a safe way. It enables participants to share humor about the shared conditions in which they all work, and to share exaggerated notions about their working environment—which might actually be closer to truth than to lies. Be careful with this exercise, since it will reveal more honesty than participants expect, and some debriefing might be required.

5

Team Design
Workshop Methods

Joint Application Design, planning workshops, design reviews, and Team Design commonly originate as a group of people committed to an outcome for a limited period. Successful work of this type does not just start with a meeting, however. As described by Michael Schrage (1995), "the reality is that most people *do* hate meetings…Yes, their colleagues and peers may be bright enough, but when everyone gets in the same room, the whole is less than the sum of its parts." He describes the typical "ecology" of meetings in the common situation where "the group is nothing more than a collection of individuals who happen to be sharing physical proximity and a common problem at a point in time" (p. 122).

Instead of a meeting, use a *workshop* instead. It may seem like only a semantic difference, but some distinction is necessary, given the context of meetings in the current workplace. The difference is not necessarily subtle. A *workshop* is a planned gathering with a purpose, a vigorous agenda, discrete goals, and the required participation of every attendee. It may not be *the* reason your team gets up and comes to work, but it's a lot more inviting than holding another ill-defined meeting.

Language and roles matter a lot in this work. The more structured the process appears, the more it is like a ceremony or a procedure. We are trained by years of attending school, religious practices, and official assemblies to behave differently when in a *purposeful* group. There are specific jobs for everyone to do. Each person is *needed* by the group as a whole. There are keys to participation that make all the difference in having a productive, creative, and satisfying experience when working as a group.

First, what are the basics you need to know? How should you start up, plan, and carry out a design workshop? This chapter presents the structure of the workshop, the things you must know to get started, and the general methods used to plan, design, and guide the Team Design workshop.

Planning the Workshop

What is the primary purpose of the workshop? What does the group want to accomplish? You may enter the workshop with a given notion of purpose, but getting true commitment requires that the group define and *own* its purpose. During the planning period, have team members contribute to the definition of the purpose. Ask them in interviews or planning meetings what they would add, or how they envision the purpose. This will involve the team members in thinking about their work together and how they will personally contribute. You might be surprised to find that the team members answer with a clarity surpassing the sponsors'. After all, they are the ones closest to the problem or product.

How should the format of the workshop be structured? Are you conducting a one-shot workshop with limited time to accomplish a wide range of activities, or a set of focused workshops that can be phased over a period of weeks? Force the team to choose among conflicting goals, if necessary. Are rapid results more important than thoroughness? Is a creative breakthrough solution important, or will just something that suffices do?

Workshops across the life cycle

What *type* of workshop will satisfy your goals and requirements? Chapter 1 presents 10 types of participatory workshops. Ten general processes for conducting facilitated workshops are defined. These are shown in Table 5.1, matched to the phases of the system development life cycle.

What do these different workshop processes mean to us as organizers or facilitators? When would you be required to work with these different workshops? How might you set out to facilitate or plan an effective session supporting these 10 processes? Would they be handled differently depending on the life-cycle phase in which they are conducted?

Workshop planning

Any workshop requires planning and coordination, and the perceived quality of the meeting will reflect the amount of advance preparation.

TABLE 5.1   Workshops across the Life Cycle

Life cycle phase	Type of workshop
Planning	Project planning Strategic planning (system or organizational) Process improvement Product planning Decision support
Requirements definition	Process analysis and redesign User or product requirements Decision support Selection of software package Make-or-buy decisions Application design or prototyping
Solution design	Application design or prototyping Decision support
Implementation	Application design or prototyping Decision support
Distribution	Process improvement Decision support (e.g., acceptance testing)

Plan on one week of preparation for a two-day workshop, and two weeks or more advance work for a week-long workshop. Longer workshops don't always require more planning than this, since a pattern of work is established during the first week, and less preparation is needed to keep the team moving.

The primary factors to consider in your planning revolve around the project as much as the product or system design goals. Because of this dependency on the project, it is best to work closely with the project manager during the preparation phase to understand his or her goals and dependencies. Design workshops must often support a major milestone as well as system deliverables. Review the project plan, schedule, and work breakdown structure (WBS) to understand the dependencies. For example, a Team Design workshop may be held to kick off the user requirements discussions with a customer. You would meet with the project manager and the customer representative, if possible, to review their plans and understand their schedules and goals. You would review the proposal and the basic requirements in it and any other documents. The project schedule would reveal the due dates and timeframes allowed for requirements and design deliverables. Working backward from the milestone dates for documents or other deliverables, you would build in enough time to complete the workshop, draft the deliverables, and conduct a review and finalize it in time for delivery. Even if you're working as a facilitator, you might not actually be responsible for the deliverable, but your workshop plan must enable the team to meet its commitments to the customer and the schedule.

If multiple analysis and design documents or prototypes are required, create a workshop strategy that brings the team together for discrete periods of time for each component or deliverable. Plan the workshops to conduct most of the content definition in the Team Design workshop setting, but give team members sufficient time to prepare, refine, and review your team's products.

Several significant planning considerations determine your workshop structure, duration, and style. These are described in the following.

Size of project: small, large-scale, or phased. Project size guides the breadth versus the depth of the workshop. With a smaller project, a single workshop may be all that's required, at least for each stage of the life cycle (analysis, design, and development). A large project might involve numerous stakeholders and more core team members, and workshops from three days to a week should be scheduled for the start-up period.

Complexity of design: simple, complex, or unknown. Complexity of design is based on several criteria: the difficulty of the requirements in relation to the experience of the team; the novelty of requirements and design, where new concepts and/or technologies are being used; and system complexity factors, such as the number of interrelated functions and the number of interfaces. For quick planning purposes, consider complexity as a rough guess based on the number and interrelatedness of requirements and the team's relative experience level in the area. Sometimes just chunking a project into several phases greatly reduces complexity, and each phase might be considered a simple design. If the design is considered simple, be cautious and plan the workshop as if it were of medium complexity. Many unknowns arise during design sessions that add to complexity and that are not foreseeable when discussing requirements among the team members individually. A design known to be complex forces a serious assessment of workshop duration and approach. Plan on spending at least twice the time in workshops for complex requirements, and even longer if they are both complex and unknown.

Project deadlines and milestones: near-term versus midterm. Deadlines and immovable deliverable milestones factor greatly into your planning. For near-term deadlines, the team will be pressured to conduct a rapid workshop, settle decisions by compromise, and cut corners on meeting requirements. Midterm deadlines are any milestones that are not under extreme pressure for immediate delivery. Due to the raised expectations often attending JAD-type workshops, don't be surprised if most workshops are designated to support near-term turnaround.

Number of stakeholders: few versus many. If only one or two user or stakeholder groups are attending the workshop, the processes you select to engage their participation can easily be tailored to their needs and level of experience. The more stakeholders involved in the workshop, the longer it might take to reach consensus on issues and the design approach. If more than one user group is directly involved in the workshop, consider adding sufficient time for each group to be educated and oriented to the work required in your session. Some users are more technically savvy than others—don't let the more experienced users drive the pace of the proceedings. All stakeholders are your customers, and all deserve to understand the impact of their decisions on the work and system design.

System interfaces: none, few, or many. *System interfaces* refer to the existing external applications that the process or system under design must interact with to produce the desired result. This factor relates closely to the complexity issue, as a stand-alone system will usually be less complex than a system interfacing with other applications. Existing systems typically surface unchangeable constraints around which your design must maneuver. In many cases, the system interfaces will not be known until all your participants are available in the workshop. Each interface brought into the design raises new or adjusted requirements. The temptation for a fast-paced design team is to leave these interface requirements undefined until a later time when further investigation can reveal the workable details. When this occurs, be aware of how specific interfaces to older applications or processes can cause problems, forcing your design to accept workarounds or unwieldy solutions which might be considered unacceptable to users when the full impact is known. The sooner these impacts are communicated to a participative design team, the more effectively agreements can be made toward the solution.

Technology risks: low versus high. High-technology risks in the requirements force the team to assess the risks and consider more alternative solutions than when implementing low-risk technology. When a project changes both business processes and computer-based applications, risks are higher than if just one "system" receives the primary focus of attention. Business process reengineering efforts that overhaul multiple systems and work processes are especially risky, and a design team must be pushed to explore the potential risks inherent in any solution proposed. When an entire organization changes technologies—such as the move among many product companies to incorporate the Internet or to produce a software package for a new platform—unknown risks are present. The design or workshop coordinator could integrate technology expert or consultant participants into the sessions at designated times to assist the team in working through the risk factors attendant with new technology.

A related technology risk is incurred when high-risk technologies—such as moving to a client-server environment or moving applications onto the Internet—are first implemented on a low-impact project. If the project is not high-impact or difficult enough, people in the organization will not herald the benefits of the new technology, since the same benefit could easily have been generated with a conventional technology. In other words, the new, high-risk technology will not appear to be the silver bullet hoped for by the developers. Traditionally, however, high-risk technologies are tested in low-impact situations so as not to invest too highly in a critical enterprise that might fail. Be aware of this interaction, and test risky technologies internally before recommending their use to management. When confident of a technology's value, recommend its use on a high-impact project. Be sure to firmly establish all the goals, agendas, and strategic outcomes for a project, both obvious and hidden, in order to account for them before finalizing technology decisions. Hidden project agendas can also kill technology ventures, as other groups invested in competing technologies can use the newly visible project as an opportunity to squelch its growth through rearranging organizational priorities, human resources, or funding.

Organizational impacts.   Finally, significant factors are often overlooked in the rush by the team to move into technical solutions and move forward on the design. *Organizational impact,* or the extent to which people's workgroups and jobs are changed, is a high-risk factor. The more organizational impact is involved, the more the team must evaluate potential change-management problems. If your planned system interferes with embedded work processes, or political organizations such as unions or government employees, you should plan to deal with the expected sensitive issues in advance, if at all possible. With multiple stakeholders, the organizational issues can become show stoppers, as disagreements can easily arise during discussion of solutions and design implementation. Organizational issues should be anticipated and raised during executive interviews, as management decisions will often have already had some bearing on the organization.

As you take these planning factors into account, consider the extent to which several other situations might impact the workshop setup. What is the extent of the design to be accomplished within the workshop itself? How much do you plan on producing during the workshop, and what deliverables will be produced offline later as a result of the information gathered? If deliverables will be prepared during the workshop, be prepared with an agenda and plan to gather inputs, organize materials, and enter the data within a workshop session. If much of the design will be created in participatory workshop sessions, be sure to include the appropriate customers, users, and reviewers in the workshops and plan for enough time to produce and critique competing designs.

Finally, evaluate the experience of the facilitator, especially if it is yourself. Is the situation compatible with your experience? If conducting a requirements workshop, have you or the assigned facilitator worked with requirements analysis sessions or the domain before? Or is your experience sufficient for the particular group and its potential degree of difficulty? Evaluate the capability of the cofacilitator also, if one is used. If the facilitator is fairly inexperienced (for example, five or fewer workshops experience) add more time for facilitator learning and for working through group issues.

Understanding the workshop environment

A brief treatment of the workshop environment will be useful to encourage thinking about the physical, political, and social dimensions surrounding the workshop. As with other sections, the intent here is not to instruct but to encourage thinking and reflection.

Experts and researchers ranging from Doyle and Straus (1976) to Holtzblatt and Beyer (1993) recommend gaining access to a dedicated space, your own room for working with the team. Many JAD workshops last anywhere from two weeks to eight weeks, with most in the one- to two-week range. The productivity and comfort of the team working together is significantly enhanced with a dedicated workspace. Extensive thinking, designing, and mocking up must be done in a place where the group memory can be maintained, at least through the course of the design period.

A "floating JAD" is not an effective way to manage a large project team. You could rent or lease a space for the project team, but you might be subject to numerous limitations on your use as well as additional expenses. Off-site workspaces are useful for groups attempting innovative or unique work that might be scrutinized too closely if conducted at home.

Some other considerations for the workshop environment follow.

Physical environment. Whether conducting JAD-type sessions or just intense integrated project teamwork, your team will require continual use of a dedicated workspace. You must be able to arrange the space in ways that support your team's interaction and access to tools. You must be able to rearrange tables and chairs and move projectors, screens, easels, and other equipment. Secure a space large enough for the working team, and outfit it with tables, chairs, and large whiteboards and easels. Be sure you have the ability to post (and leave) sheets of diagrams, drawings, lists and other items on the walls. This will allow customization of the space, and will allow all members to focus on the immediate work at hand and to pick up each day's proceedings where they left off in the previous session.

Support facilities are often necessary for intensive multiday workshops. Presentation equipment and supplies are essential, and specialized projectors for computer displays or multimedia presentations must be tested before use. Lunch and other breaks should be supplied by providing adequate refreshments and service. If lunch remains are not removed, it lends a less-than-professional air to the workshop by midafternoon. Other special needs should be handled in advance, such as video or phone teleconferencing or special guest arrivals.

Organizational environment.   Observe your organizational environment by reflecting for a few minutes. Think about the current organizational structure, the hierarchy or levels of management to which you belong. Think about the current procedures and attitudes for pushing process innovations such as team-building and design workshops. What steps must be taken to ensure access to team members, stakeholders, and—especially—customer or user representatives? If your customers and users are external, are you required to work through sales or marketing representatives? What involvement will sales or marketing require? Whose management must be involved, or at least informed?

Consider the organization and its processes as a whole. What is the current product development process and organizational readiness? What agreements, forms, permissions, schedules, and communications are required? Are there competing interests in the organization, and should they be informed, involved, or ignored? Are there organizational champions for the team approach? Are you missing any part of the organization that could be invaluable later on?

Organizational context.   The organizational context for the workshop is important to consider when planning to use new approaches for the design process. What makes more sense in your environment, a structured workshop (such as JAD) or a more creative approach of participatory design (direct codevelopment with users)? If your organization fits the business or systems contexts described in Chap. 3, has many internal customers, or is an information systems resource for a service corporation, the workshop approach will probably be more successful. On the other hand, if your organization fits the user or product contexts, has a designer-driven product process, or is a smaller company with more democratic management, a participatory approach might be the better way. Refer back to Chap. 1 for discussion of these approaches.

Management or user goals. Workshop planning must also consider the needs and goals of both management and the users, two constituencies that are often at odds with each other. Management goals often drive the JAD agenda, but user involvement can and should influence the system or process design. Conflicts can arise when management narrowly defines the scope for a design process, then users find that the scope doesn't support their goals or limits their effectiveness. The facilitator can be caught between conflicting interests, needing to satisfy the sponsors (usually in management) and wanting to create a workshop that is fair to the users and honors their contributions.

Resource commitments. Ensure that persons assigned to the workshop team are in place and that reasonable commitments are made for their involvement through the expected time period. Be sure people know their roles for participation in advance, and are prepared with any materials or documents required for their full participation. If observers, recorders, and support staff are required, define their expected involvement and obtain their commitment as well.

Support and logistics. *Support* can include anything else required to run the workshop smoothly. Be sure you have access to computers and display equipment as needed well in advance. Obtain support for presentation materials and participant supplies, and have extras of almost everything readily available. Other equipment and tools might include such meeting-support systems as interactive whiteboards, speakerphones, or videoteleconferencing equipment.

Logistics are those things that must be planned and arranged well before the session. Facilities, meeting and breakout rooms, rentals, and refreshments are typical arrangements requiring coordination in advance. A support person can substantially assist in coordinating logistics, which is especially important for larger workshops with numerous needs.

Sponsorship and team commitment

Sponsors were briefly discussed in Chap. 2 as the senior stakeholders who secure access to resources for the workshop, including people, money, and time. The sponsor is usually the executive directly responsible for the product area requiring development. A senior manager should be enrolled to serve as the sponsor for design workshops that affect numerous organizations or customers. Even for smaller-scale projects, having a sponsor for the workshop helps your team gain the time and resources to perform well. The sponsor's commitment provides organizational and political support, as well as the functional role of providing resources. The senior manager can handle questions of direction and issues generated by other managers and stakeholders. This ensures that the project and the workshops that support it have the management commitment required to survive the initial startup. Other managers often become sponsors of project-level workshops, and project or product leaders also sponsor design workshops. But the executive sponsor provides a critical support structure for any multistakeholder design process.

Meet with the sponsor early in your planning to understand what results are expected. In some cases it might be wise to communicate that requirements or specifications are not guaranteed; the outcomes of design workshops or JADs are not *engineered*. Remember that the purpose of having a team session is to ensure representation of differing needs and opinions and to gain consensus of approach. Especially if representing the information technology organization, you cannot manufacture the result.

Leadership, although a rare commodity in many organizations, remains necessary for the performance of design workshops. The team approach to design and development goes against the model of control many organizations attempt to use. When working with multiple stakeholders on a consensus-driven team, a team-level democracy in action emerges that requires supportive leadership.

Leadership is the ability to set new directions, to push for what's right, and to inspire others. As a facilitator, however, you are never in a position to compensate for missing leadership. The project leader should usually be the accountable party for the workshop. The facilitator can only facilitate, and should not make decisions on behalf of the project team. Leading the group workshops does not confer leadership—even if the group votes to make you the leader! Impartial action on behalf of the group is a primary facilitation function. Establishing oneself as a leader can destroy the balance of trust between the managers and the design team that is required to empower the members of the team. The facilitator's commitment must be to support the team in its goals, not to champion new goals in the organization. At least not on behalf of the design team!

Gaining commitment.   How can the team's committed support be obtained? Several simple actions can be taken by the managers involved:

- Gain the support of the top bosses, and have one of them give a pep talk to the team at the start of the workshop. This demonstrates the executive's interest in and support for the design team and the goals for the workshop.

- Have the executive or manager write or sign the initial memos requesting other managers to provide people for the workshop or project. This allows commitments to be formed among the managers.

- Have a committed project leader who communicates with the team and allows the team to work together. Project leaders who want to define the scope and actions themselves are no good in team workshops. A team must have the ability to discuss issues freely and to perform technically without being second-guessed or managed down by the team leader.

To create endorsement for the team, learn about and understand your sponsors. What do they expect from the workshop and the project? What are they willing to sign up to as an initial investment? Have they pulled you into their project, or are you enrolling them into yours? Who is your sponsor's customer? What do *they* want from the project? Are you accountable to your executive's customers? If your sponsor is a development manager, his or her customer is probably in a business function. Meet with your sponsor's customers, and have them work with your team or speak at your kickoff. Find out the expectations of the sponsor's customer and of the end customer. Do they have any preconceived notions? Do they fear the workshop is just to have them bless an already-designed solution?

Finally, notice the composition of your assigned project team. What are the goals of the individual team members? And determine the commitments and desires of your customers and users, whether they are on your larger team or not.

Workshop participants.   Workshops are more effective with a small number of knowledgeable and involved people. Psychologist George Miller's (1956) principle of "seven, plus or minus two" applies to the selection of productive group sizes as well as to other significant groupings. (The principle states, basically, that people can only process a limited amount of information at a given time—seven pieces of data, plus or minus two.) With more than nine members in a working group, it generally becomes difficult to assimilate the various contributions and to work cooperatively. Larger groups break out into smaller groups for the purpose of focused participation, as the larger group cannot maintain participation. Less involved or dominant people tend to withdraw in larger groups, thus defeating the purpose of a mixed-discipline participative group.

Workshops with 12 to 15 people are generally manageable, but with more than 20 participants the venue becomes more appropriate for a facilitated meeting rather than a productive design session. Some simple reasons for this recommendation include the following:

- It is difficult to gain consensus with a larger number of people.
- It is difficult to have everyone participate—the dominators tend to control discussions.
- It is harder to keep participants on track—too many other agendas are brought into the session.
- It is difficult to perform group design work without breaking into small groups.

There are exceptions to this general recommendation, of course. The workshop format chapters (Chaps. 6 to 10) discuss the various roles and subteams that might be used in design sessions. In many situations a larger group is naturally engaged, such as in requirements definition, strategic planning, or other management-level processes. Smaller teams tend to work in the more hands-on workshops for application design and decision making. If a larger group is required due to project scale or the need for representation of many organizations, the organizer can create smaller working groups of five to seven people as principal team units.

With any group size, the participants selected should be the best available for the job of team-based design work. Every person attending must be expected to participate, and their ability to cooperate can count as much as their technical knowledge and skills. In cases where specific skills and knowledge are required, consider using team-building practices (discussed in this chapter) to promote the evolution of a high-performance team. Team-building exercises can be used in the early workshop phases to establish teams and small groups for the purpose of working together effectively in a group of any size determined necessary.

Designing the workshop

Much of the work in planning involves thinking through the best approach to use in your case and gaining agreements to use that approach. However, the core of your planning is in designing the actual session or workshop process. The Team Design workshop provides a structured, flexible context for creative group work. A workshop can be put together from building blocks to fit its unique purpose. A step-by-step cookbook approach, which can work in traditional JAD, is not used or recommended. Team Design is intended to be *customized,* distinguishing it from other methodologies and problem-solving approaches. Its flexibility allows it to evolve with an organization's changing development and project management methods. Instead of steps and procedures, Team Design uses *formats* — guidelines appropriate for general types of design workshops. The formats are envisioned using *agendas* that break the workshop into common phases and suggest some component activities.

Using agendas and formats. Although it may seem obvious to establish and distribute an agenda for the workshop, many (or in my experience, most) meetings are held without specific agendas. Leaders often wait until the meeting to define the agenda, or have the team help to define it at the start of a meeting. Another advantage for using the workshop approach is that people expect preparation for a workshop. A defined agenda is required and expected. This does not inhibit creativity or limit problem solving — an agenda helps focus all members on the same goals.

The importance of agendas was succinctly expressed by Doyle and Straus (1976) in their classic guide to meeting management, *How to Make Meetings Work*.

> We can't emphasize enough: Everyone should know what to expect before coming to a meeting. You must be explicit about what's going to happen, how the meeting is going to be run, who is going to play what roles...If all participants receive a detailed meeting agenda at least a day (preferably a week) before the meeting, they will come prepared, and most of the common causes of confusion at the beginning of meetings will be avoided. Because most of the procedural questions will have been settled in advance, your meetings will be shorter and more effective (p. 201).

Creating agendas. Team Design agendas are based on the workshop format, which offers guidelines differentiated among the various workshops for front-end analysis, product design, decision making, and so on. The goal or phase of the development process determines the applicable format for the workshop. The format suggests an appropriate agenda for conducting essential workshop activities and exercises. The agenda is the road map you and the entire team will use to conduct the workshop.

Workshop agendas identify each major topic of discussion and define the timeframe allocated for the work. If workshop planning or a pre-JAD has been conducted, sufficient information should be available to build an effective agenda. In many cases, you might not have a lot of detail upon which to base the agenda, in which case the Team Design formats provide some guidance. Distribute the agenda to all participants prior to the workshop, and include advance copies of any process information or design products (for example, reports, screens,

Team Design Workshop Agenda
Project: Date: Room:
From: Start time: End time:
Attendees/team:
Purpose of workshop or meeting:
Facilitator: Please be prepared to:
Workshop activities:

Activity	Time	Person responsible
1. Introduction: Ground rules and procedures	8:15–8:45	Facilitator
2. Project overview	8:45–9:30	Project leader
3. Requirements discussion Review document in advance	9:30–10:15	Facilitator and project leader
Break	10:15–10:30	

Figure 5.1 Sample workshop agenda.

and diagrams) that will be used in the workshop. The basic elements of any agenda are described on the example form shown in Fig. 5.1.

Following the agenda.   Select an appropriate workshop format and create an initial agenda. Formats provide the template for an agenda—they are not the agendas themselves. The workshop activities support specific deliverables pursued at each point in the format. Be sure to ask workshop participants for their input to the agenda in advance of the session. Facilitators use several basic introduction activities for almost any workshop. An introduction with a brief explanation of purpose or an icebreaker exercise are typical, followed by activities that generate early group engagement and thinking.

Introduction.   Introductions can be handled by the organizer, facilitator, or participants. Be informal, yet purposeful, to indicate the pace and style you expect people to maintain. More formality will be expected in executive sessions—but, then, only at first. In any creative workshop, it is important to have everyone feel at ease and able to freely express themselves. Basic "meeting manners" guide the session introduction:

■ Introductions of group members are important, especially if customers are involved. Have people describe their work and their role on the team, since this is the place to establish some context for working together. This can be an icebreaker exercise, as well—have people answer several simple questions about themselves (college attended, favorite sport, last vacation spot, hobbies and interests) or introduce their neighbor.

- Write the agenda for the day on a whiteboard or newsprint, and review it with the team. There might have been changes to the agenda since its distribution, and these should be pointed out. Ask for comments or changes people would care to make. This is an early opportunity for contribution and agreement. Make changes to the board agenda, and then stick to it.

  Also review the full workshop agenda and discuss any input or feedback. If significant changes are made to the agenda, distribute a revised copy the same day.

- Discuss ground rules and the purpose of the workshop or meeting. Ground rules are a must and should always be presented at the first meeting of a new group. Ground rules can be preprepared by writing four or five of them on a sheet of newsprint—post it as a starting point. Have the group add the new rules they choose to work by. Refer to Chap. 4 for the treatment of ground rules.

The purpose of the workshop may appear obvious, but it should always be covered. Write down the purpose at the start as well—it may be redefined over the course of the workshop, which is not necessarily unproductive.

Getting the workshop started.   Once the basic introductions have been covered, you'll want to get the workshop moving. Help participants build a mental model of an effective workshop by providing structures that establish topic areas and boundaries for discussion. Within these boundaries, emphasize the freedom participants have within the discussion. To assist in this process, consider the following recommendations:

- Group together related areas of discussion. First bring up global topics that affect the course of the meeting or impact everyone in the room. The agenda or the process for conducting the workshop itself are typical global topics.

- Push involved group processes or significant design further out in the agenda. Allow the group time to learn to work together through activities in the initiating and scoping phases (as described in Chap. 6). *Initiating* activities prepare the team for deeper work by establishing the team identity. *Scoping* activities generate a common mental model of direction and of the bounds within which to work.

- Build in transitions and break points in the process.

Use the introduction period to create an atmosphere of collegiality—start to generate the momentum of working together immediately. Lessons from team-building work indicate that an effective way to start the group working as a team is to have them create a common theme, such as through creating a vision statement.

Before starting into a creative task such as visioning, first be sure people are comfortable with each other and in working together. This is not always as easy as it sounds—some groups settle in immediately, other groups never become a cohesive team. What can you do to make the difference?

Making It Happen

You've planned a series of workshop sessions specifically for a new project with a new team. You've discussed the plans with sponsors and project managers, have arranged for the meeting room, have interviewed the participants, and have written a preliminary agenda. Formats for the workshops have been selected (for example, Planning and Decision Making and Application Design) and new analysis and design tools have been considered for integration into the process. What could be missing?

Moving forward with a new team is not a matter of management directive, willpower, or even consensus. New teams take time to learn how to work together. People need time to become comfortable working with one another, and with a facilitator, even if facilitation is a revolving role taken on by all members. They require a space where cooperation can develop through natural work processes. Team building can provide the initial boost for the team in working together and building synergy.

Also, workshops are often effectively supported by computer-based meeting tools. While CASE and diagramming tools are considered part of the JAD orientation in design workshops, group-process tools can be employed in many workshop contexts. Consider using computer-based meeting or decision-support tools when involving remote participants or a highly mixed stakeholder group, and potential miscommunication or conflict should typically be avoided. These tools are also valuable for concurrent documentation of processes, and they can be operated by the recorder in conjunction with facilitation. Although not related to the team-building process, computer-based meeting tools can be valuable in moving the team forward at an accelerated rate.

Building the team

How do you get started on building a highly effective team? What are the best tools and processes available for establishing and working with new teams? And what challenges are presented when working with established teams that do not function cooperatively, or, in business parlance, are not "high-performance"?

Team building represents an important competence for the workshop facilitator, especially considering the organizational development implied in Team Design. Although much of the discipline of team organizational development is beyond the scope of design processes and workshops, the basics of team building are necessary and learnable. Every facilitator and organizer should adopt a favorite team-building approach as a method for initiating new groups of participants in the design workshop environment. Most facilitators will benefit immensely from gaining professional training and experience in team building, and the participants in groups they facilitate will benefit from learning to work cooperatively as team members.

For Team Design, team building can be said to be *the process of facilitating a group of participants in working together as a cooperative group with commonly held purposes and goals.* In short, it is evolving a team from a group of individuals. Chapter 4 presents numerous functions of *facilitation* that contribute to team development. However, a deeper understanding of team building contributes to the planning of processes and exercises for the Team Design workshop.

Several excellent team processes have been used and favored by different proponents since the recognition of teamwork as a critical organizational need in the late 1980s. Team development methods have been espoused from the separate disciplines of organizational development, professional training, quality management, and industrial/organizational psychology. Two approaches to team building are presented to cover two different classes of approaches your facilitation style might adopt: *The Team Handbook* (Scholtes 1988) from Joiner Associates and *Team Spirit* (Heermann 1997) from the Expanded Learning Institute.

The Team Handbook provides a cookbook of methods and guidelines for practitioners and participants. A team leader's handbook and participant materials can be purchased and employed by the practitioner "out of the box" for use with a technical team. *The Team Handbook* approach stems from quality management practices, and presents the quality philosophy of W. Edwards Deming as its foundation for team involvement. The implicit goal of *The Team Handbook* approach is to focus coordinated activity on problem solving for significant technical challenges, using the tools and techniques of quality management. As a teambuilding method, it is more technical than organizational, and presents a fairly businesslike view of the team as a highly purposeful organization. *The Team Handbook* does not, therefore, offer many selected techniques for engaging teams in reflective, personal, or emotional discussions. Its strengths are more inclined toward facilitating effective meetings, using quality improvement methods to gain insight into problems, and managing the group process effectively.

The team-development model supported by *The Team Handbook* is the well-known four-stage model introduced by Tuckman (1965):

1. *Forming.* The initial stage during which groups seek purpose and relevance. Social relationships are established, and the group initially begins to work with the leader.

2. *Storming.* Conflict begins to emerge between members as they recognize differences in goals and perspectives. Conflicts between members and leadership emerge as people struggle in defining control and direction.

3. *Norming.* Group members recognize commonalities and shared interests in the team and establish processes for communication. Conflict is replaced by more group harmony, and a sense of team cohesion arises.

4. *Performing.* Team members generate insights into the team's processes and work cooperatively through group problems. A team identity has formed, and members associate strongly with the group.

Team Spirit presents a holistic view of teams that integrates thinking from organizational, scientific, and spiritual foundations. The purpose of *Team Spirit* is to create a true bonding of group members before they can work cooperatively as a high-performance team. *Team Spirit* endorses a five-phase *spiral* as the model of team development, describing stages the team members must move through in becoming a team. This model of addressing critical team concerns in team building derives in part from Alan Drexler's (1988) Team Performance System, which uses a seven-stage model of team behavior. *Team Spirit* expands the typical view of the team purpose by allowing that teams are unified by a common theme of *service,* which becomes a core integrating value for all members. Service is described as *delighting customers and contributing to others,* which draws from studies of long-term high-performance teams. The five phases are envisioned to support a core theme of service. These phases are characterized in order as follows:

1. *Initiating.* Introducing and learning about team members and their interests, disclosing and sharing, and creating a common sense of belonging.

2. *Visioning.*   Developing a shared vision or purpose as a group, developing mutual interests, becoming closer through sharing ideas, and establishing a team presence.

3. *Claiming.*   Identifying and aligning with roles and goals available in the team, developing organizational support, and identifying competencies and personal goals.

4. *Celebrating.*   Bringing about team celebration through recognition of team and individual accomplishment, showing appreciation, and expressing positive regard.

5. *Letting Go.*   Allowing for constructive feedback among team members, providing disclosure and straightforward communication, and acknowledging completion of work.

Team Spirit identifies team introduction and common bonding in the first two phases of the five-phase dynamic. The first two phases of the spiral, Initiating and Visioning, apply to almost any type of meeting. For a workshop environment, these two phases can be made explicit by introducing them as agenda phases and selecting appropriate exercises. Initiating can include almost any exercises that orient team members and create a sense of belonging. Icebreakers, introductions, and small group disclosure exercises are effective in this phase of team building. Visioning activities in the agenda might include scoping, goal setting, or traditional visioning work to establish the shared vision for the team. Visioning work often results in mission statements and pictures or diagrams representing the purpose or goals.

Numerous activities in the Team Design scoping phase would apply in the Visioning phase of team building. However, the facilitator using a *Team Spirit* model would also observe that the five team-building phases operate continuously within all teams, and are not fixed phases that follow in lockstep. The model is used to understand where teams are located in the spiral, and the skilled facilitator works to encourage team movement to other phases as required.

The Claiming phase can occur at almost any time within team processes. Sometimes teams rush to the Claiming phase in order to settle power or role differences; in this case the team-building facilitator would ensure they had resolved the Visioning phase before moving forward, so that a well-defined shared vision could inform their role alignment. Claiming combines the functions of Storming and Norming from the traditional model, and can consume a great deal of the team's attention. Much of the actual knowledge work of design teams could be considered to occur as Claiming activity; facilitators might work to ensure that the team's goal progress does not move away from alignment with the shared vision.

Celebration and Letting Go are unique to the *Team Spirit* approach, and are often missing in other team-building models. Celebration allows the team to show true appreciation for the work they have accomplished, but also is necessary just to recognize and give tribute to the numerous occasions for acknowledgment. Celebration maintains the forward motion of the team and should be encouraged by facilitators during many points in a team's life together. Letting Go is a phase that encourages self-reflection and disclosure and allows the team to communicate things that are often left unspoken. By enabling people to express difficulty and provide feedback in a safe environment, team members are able to relieve themselves of difficult expression with others, freeing them up to recommit to the team's purpose.

Team building is a continuous process of facilitation, and cannot be localized to just the beginning stages of a group's work together. It is a way of working with groups to develop their capability to function cooperatively. The facilitator works as a coach more than as a leader, and models effective behavior for the team throughout workshops or other team meetings. Team-building activities are planned and show up more during the beginning of the group's work; as the team becomes more cohesive, members settle into roles and work together to support each other's team behaviors. The team-building process can then become more one of maintaining effective cooperation and focusing attention on improving team behaviors when required.

Meeting-support tools

Several classes of meeting-support tools can be distinguished, from simple presentation tools to real-time group conferencing systems. Any of these tools might prove useful in different workshop environments, and it is likely that you have already used some of these tools in facilitated sessions. Nonetheless, a brief discussion is given of each area to serve completeness of coverage.

Meeting-support tools include several categories of software and communications systems used for facilitation and cooperative work. New tools supporting interactive, online, and collaborative meetings show up continuously in the market, making facilitators work to maintain currency in the specialized systems available. In this section, tools are covered as general examples with their relative strengths and weaknesses as a class. To see specific information on available products, refer to the trade magazines and professional journals that frequently survey the offerings in this emerging field, and check the World Wide Web, where many vendors offer free product trials.

Meeting-support tools can include any of the following:

- Portable personal computers
- Presentation support
- Remote participation—teleconferencing
- Asynchronous collaboration—groupware
- Synchronous collaboration systems

Portable personal computers. Portable computers are ubiquitous and probably necessary, so they deserve mention as a meeting-support tool. Whether you use a notebook-sized PC or any other compact computer, the carry-on go-anywhere processor has become a staple of the development facilitator. Essential for notetaking, running CASE tools, or giving demonstrations, these PCs are just a given in the workshop environment. For extended sessions (over three days), provide an accessory monitor, a full-size mouse to replace the typically pitiful pointer on most notebooks, and possibly a full-size keyboard for the recorder. Using the smaller PCs without these accessories for over a week of continual use is ergonomically incorrect, engendering eye strain, ineffective pointing, and inefficient typing.

Presentation support. Don't make your team suffer through barely visible presentations or weak transparency drawings. Arrange for good presentation-support tools. If using a computer for presentation or demonstration, a display projector or monitor projection panel is necessary. Be certain the display can accommodate the resolution (and scanning frequency) of your computer's video adapter.

Single unit display projectors provide a much stronger and clearer overhead picture than using separate LCD-type display panels with overhead projectors. High-quality, high-power overhead projectors are necessary if using a monitor display panel.

Don't forget to include the basic overhead projector and transparencies as an alternative and highly interactive display, regardless of whether the presentations are computer-generated. Overhead transparencies allow substantial spontaneity, and people who might be uncomfortable with computers will appreciate their use. These tools are simple yet effective presentation support, portable and highly visible.

Remote participation and distributed development. If you aren't yet involved in a distributed development project, you probably will be in the near future. As a consultant, most of my projects in the most recent four-year period involved either an off-site client, a distant user group, or a remote development team. At large companies with internal efforts, such as General Electric, AT&T, and IBM, customers and user sites tend to be located in areas other than the large development centers. And if you've ever worked with small companies, you are well aware that you might often travel to customer locations for evaluation and installation. Development that takes place in multiple locations or involves planned activities directed from a central site and distributed across remote sites is *distributed development*. Rather than being an exception, distributed development has almost become the norm in many organizations, even if it is not acknowledged as such.

What are some of the characteristics of the distributed development project? A working description might include the following:

- Projects where design and development tasks are performed at more than one physical location, usually where geographical distance necessitates travel and special arrangements between the sites

- Projects where customer installation locations are located in several or numerous locations, and especially where the extent of technology used requires development and systems management at each location

- Projects where large portions or major functions of a development effort are performed by contractor companies or consultants remotely located or inaccessible to the project or corporate management

- Projects subject to any combination of these factors, a situation of increasing frequency

When is a project extended or distributed enough to be managed as distributed development? This is a fairly new area for formal observation, and as such, different guidelines emerge from distributed development project experiences, of which some are unique to the type of work performed and some are specific to an industry.

In consulting work arrangements, wherein corporate information systems are outsourced or developed by specialized consultant companies, distributed development projects are becoming the norm. Large corporations typically have multiple locations, often across continents, and are increasingly using information technology to support virtual interaction across the company. Companies such as AT&T, General Electric, major financial institutions, and major automakers are constantly upgrading their computing and communications infrastructure with the goal of using information technology to manage their businesses more effectively, to negate the effects of distance on their operations. With an extensive use of the Internet as a communications channel and even as a computing platform, corporations are in constant technological change and use consulting companies extensively. Whereas 5 to 10 years ago electronic mail was one of the few desktop communications technologies installed across corporate networks, these internal networks now integrate all desktop and IS applications within the intranet network. Consulting companies have been the beneficiaries of this opportunity for the most part, since they have experience in many such installations and in the networking and application technologies.

Distributed development projects have created a compelling need to support remote participation across one or more locations. It is not unusual for projects to require participation across five or more locations, as different development groups, managers, product groups, and customers have become spread out geographically in many companies. The challenge for the facilitator is to organize and moderate constructive workshops using remote communication tools, and to integrate the group contributions in a practical and useful form.

Some of the tools used to support distributed remote participation include the following:

- Teleconferencing
- Video-based conferencing
- Meeting-support systems
- Collaboration groupware

Teleconferencing.   If conducting a workshop with remote participants, be sure that the teleconferencing systems—telephone or video conferencing—are adequate for the workshop needs. Test the speakerphone or video conferencing system yourself in advance of the session to be familiar with any problems or inadequacies. Workshops with remote participants have unique challenges, often requiring some compromise to the agenda or process. At least ensure that the equipment doesn't present the biggest barrier to participation.

Remote participants in any design workshop will feel disconnected from the process even under the best of circumstances. Face it—nothing is better than working in person with the team. In many situations in current corporate environments, with knowledge workers and consultants geographically distributed, you will face the reality of including people in your session or meeting using telephone or video-based teleconferencing. Your job requires engaging their participation to maximize their contributions and the value of the team's time spent together. Whether remote participants use telephone conferencing, video teleconferencing, or even computer conferencing, many affordances available to in-person participants do not exist. Few situations are more distracting to cohesion and progress than including participants who cannot follow or contribute to the proceedings. If you choose to include remote participants, discuss the processes for their inclusion with them.

Problems with telephone conferencing. With telephone conferencing, the remote participant finds it difficult to follow the flow of conversations and decisions, as the visual cues from nonverbal behavior of the group situation are lacking. In an audio-only participation, listening is emphasized over speaking, as in-person participants forget to include the speakerphone listener. Also, the remote participant often cannot detect the appropriate times to break in with contributing statements or questions, since the visual protocols (such as eye contact and pointing) used as indicators for sharing the floor are absent. If diagrams or other visuals are drawn on a board, the remote participant will have difficulty visualizing these shared concepts.

Don't allow remote participants to take control of the meeting or to dominate discussions. If they cannot see the in-person team, they might not realize the alienating impact of a monologue, and it could easily be resented by group members who feel that their shared context is being disregarded.

Therefore, when including remote participants be sure to plan for their inclusion, and discuss their role with them and with the in-person team. If technical experts are to be included remotely, they might be given any materials that the team will be working with in advance. Give them specific periods on the agenda to raise issues of particular concern to them, and facilitate the discussion to ensure that their points are covered on the group memory or diagrammed processes. If their role is more observational, you might only need to refer to them from time to time to acknowledge that they are listening and involved as team members.

Video-based conferencing. Videoteleconferencing (VTC) addresses some of the problems found with telephone conferencing. It allows group members to see a credible likeness of one another, visual cues and meeting protocol can be more easily observed, and diagrams and brainstorming sessions can be viewed and understood in context. It provides a group context for the remote viewer, and enables a local group to more easily include the remote member. It also allows for a distributed team session when several groups of remote members must interact with the facilitated workshop. The ability to engage multiple remote subteams is one of the greatest strengths of the videoteleconference.

A videoteleconference session typically requires a facilitator to coordinate the focus of discussion and maintain the agenda. Typically, the facilitator is one of the members of the local or primary group, with remote members following the facilitator. If a VTC is used for training or presentations, the facilitator might lead the session from a remote location, with multiple viewers participating in groups. A major strength of the VTC is in engaging multiple subteams in one-way communication, such as a ceremonial presentation or a lecture followed by a moderated discussion. When participants must only attend to presented information, and do not expect to interact with more than a question or two, the VTC works well. When attempting true multidirectional collaboration, the VTC becomes more difficult.

Adapting to videoteleconferencing. Using the videoteleconference for team interaction can be awkward, and introduces problems of its own. The strength of including multiple remote participants also forces distraction on the local, or in-person, facilitated team. With VTC, all communication tends to be managed through the remote channel, which is perhaps the direct opposite of when telephone conferencing is used. Due to the intrusiveness of large video monitors and the protocol required in managing face-to-face remote communication, the local team tends to spend an inordinate amount of time interacting with and listening to remote participants as opposed to working among themselves. Whereas the team easily ignores speakerphone listeners, the local team is almost ignored by the presence of the VTC participants.

Technical problems inherent with VTC communication can distract or challenge facilitated workshops. The typical delay (with 1990s technology) of the video signal over telephone lines distracts the normal flow of conversation. Individuals cannot adapt to a pace of discussion when speakers' utterances are delayed in transmission—someone initiates a topic and a remote participant's delayed voice immediately breaks in, causing an unnatural pacing of conversation.

The other inherent problem is that of maintaining *grounding,* as described by Herbert Clark (1996). When people work together on any activity, including conversations and such simple actions as opening a door for another, subtle cues are introduced into their joint action that enable coordination. This common ground established during joint actions allows participants to recognize via joint evidence that they have accomplished their action. People demonstrate grounding in conversation by quickly interspersing acknowledgments during another's speaking (yes, I see, uh-huh), and speakers and listeners can quickly restore a lost position in conversation by referring obliquely to a point that was just raised. Interruptions and follow-up questions are commonly accepted as natural tactics in cooperative speech, as they are easily grounded in the participants' common experience. Grounding is also supported by gesture, pointing, and—especially—gaze and eye contact. By looking at the people we are speaking to, multiple roles and references to actions or agreement can be acknowledged quickly and powerfully just through the established grounding of common experience.

In VTC and other video-based communication, most of this grounding is removed or, at best, awkward. The speaking delays in the VTC make quick interjections almost impossible, and the simple interruptions of normal conversation become surreal games of tag, as each speaker starts to speak, then stops when another breaks in out of synch. Because there is no commonly held space that all parties share, gaze cues toward locations or other people are strangely misplaced. Finally, participants cannot make true eye contact, and even when attempts are made, no one has feedback evidence that eye contact was made. Therefore, VTC tools should be used when necessary, but not as a replacement for face-to-face meetings where conversation, creative discussion, or negotiations must take place.

Using videoteleconferencing. The videoteleconference is a fact of business life, and it is a cost-effective solution for meetings with stakeholders and customers at remote locations or where only minimal participation is required. With the preparation of a focused agenda, the VTC can be organized into the workshop as an integral discussion. Several practices learned from experience might be considered for facilitation with the VTC:

1. Before setting up the VTC session, plan the agenda with input from the remote participants. Review your plans with them and discuss their specific areas for contribution. Group together all areas where their participation is most useful, and give them the opportunity to close with the overall group at the conclusion of this period, if appropriate. If remote participants will be primarily observing the workshop during a period, discuss this in advance so all members know to expect less interaction during these times.

2. During the VTC period of the workshop, treat all remote members as if they were part of the in-person facilitated team. As a facilitator, guide the discussion and listen for misunderstandings. Clarification of comments and acting as traffic cop for the conversation might be necessary to maintain a balance of discussion among the different groups.

3. If more than one group is participating remotely, be sure the groups understand basic VTC protocol. Designate your workshop site as the host site; any other sites will maintain your site as the default view. Have each site hold the *mute* function during the pro-

ceedings, to prevent the VTC from shifting the monitor views to the noisiest site. As the facilitator, allow each remote site to respond to questions or discussion points in turn. Designate a leader at each site, and ask them one by one for any feedback.

4. Don't overuse the VTC document display during the session. This device is useful for presenting diagrams or visual information on paper over the VTC, using a special camera platform. It should be used very briefly in most workshops, since it has the effect of replacing the view of team members with a static view of a page, which quickly becomes tiresome for remote viewers. By focusing the group's attention on a static image, the session becomes a telephone conference in format. Also, team members lose patience during the time it takes to shift the equipment around to present the page. It might be more effective to have a recorder or assistant fax a well-drawn copy of diagrams to the remote sites while maintaining the visual face-to-face effect of the VTC.

5. Involving participants attending a face-to-face meeting is difficult enough at times, given the resignation many of us have about spending time in nonproductive meetings. When working with remote participants we face the double difficulty of facilitating an agenda with different groups separated by distance and, perhaps, culture and style. We've discussed ways to manage and understand telephone and video conferencing, and other ways will emerge when you observe and engage your teams.

Generally, remote VTC participation is a special form of face-to-face team engagement, not something atypical. However, the patience and courtesies required in these situations can wear down many team members in a purposeful workshop, impacting their creativity and productivity. Some tactics can be used with any such meeting. Break the remote meetings into sequential time segments and pursue specific issues, using an agenda. When conferencing with the remotes, stick to the agenda, and note new issues as they arise. Don't try to handle or resolve new issues or problems when they emerge in the session. That's what other sessions are scheduled for.

Meeting-support systems. *Meeting-support systems* are tools used by groups to work together on tasks, regardless of whether they are actually located together. Videoteleconferencing could be considered a meeting-support system, although it is not a *synchronous* collaboration system, as are most in this category. Almost any system that supports participants in capturing contributions, organizing meeting notes, and managing group activities in meetings can be included in this area. This class includes such tools as group support systems (GSSs), group decision support systems, shared whiteboards, and shared document systems, all of which enable a team to work together and see their contributions and responses from others at the same time. The synchronous collaboration enabled by these tools allows participants to work with each other at the same time, regardless of location.

Among the computer-based tools presented in Chap. 2 (applicable to JAD-type workshops) are communications and group interaction tools, the category of interest in this section. Tools in this class of groupware typically include group conferencing, decision support, and meeting management systems. Most of these systems are not typical *groupware*, referring to group information and networked communication, but are real-time group-support systems, a very different interpretation of groupware.

Some of these tools handle the problems of grounding inherent in the video-based systems by providing a common point of focus without the video channel. By displaying content and contributions instead of video images, participants can coordinate on the work at hand and avoid the distractions of the unnatural and formalized VTC. Among all the different types of group-support systems, the following tools are included or combined:

- *Electronic brainstorming.* Supports interactive brainstorming in a common database where contributions are visible and can be anonymous or attributed.

- *Electronic whiteboard.* Supports drawing, listing, and other freehand rendering on an electronic whiteboard, allowing all members to view the proceedings as they occur. Versions of this tool have been designed to allow multiple people to draw on a virtual whiteboard.

- *Group voting.* Supports multiple voting methods to obtain feedback on issues and proposals. Tools include agree/disagree, ordered ranking, multiple choice selection, allocation of points, and 10-point scale.

- *Surveys.* Tools to develop and broadcast surveys, allowing up to 100 questions. Analysis and filtering tools are available.

- *Evaluation of alternatives.* Group decision support tool, rates alternatives against weighted criteria that can be adjusted to explore variations of emphasis.

- *Categorizing and prioritizing.* Allows multiple inputs to be categorized by the group, and provides tools for assigning priorities to items or categories.

- *Group outlining and group documenting.* Group definition of topic outlines supports the construction of plans, proposals, and specifications. Group documentation tools support synchronous developing, editing, annotation, and review of a common document.

- *Issues and commenting.* Supports issue management and tracking of issue resolution and action.

Most of the meeting-support systems work best with a facilitator leading the multiple participants in the meeting and in the process of using the tools. IBM's *TeamFocus* and Ventana's *GroupSystems* tools require facilitation for effective use of both tool and group process. The *MeetingWorks* toolset from Enterprise Solutions provides a coordinated group meeting system requiring facilitation for its Chauffeur module. Other tools, usually those less sophisticated, recommend facilitation but do not require it as such. Recent research indicates that facilitation significantly improves group performance, process, and cohesion when used with GSS systems (Anson, Bostrom, and Wynne 1995; Niederman, Beise, and Beranek 1996). However, a number of concerns for relying on technology have been found with facilitators, who express concern for participant discomfort with the tools. The more technical facilitators tend to be more comfortable with the tools, and such facilitators are more likely to be involved in design workshops. Also, as GSS tools can restrict the flexibility of the meeting process, active facilitation serves to mitigate the participants' sense of restriction.

Networked collaboration groupware.   Networked collaboration groupware, such as shared database and e-mail communications, can integrate with the workshop environment with effective results. These groupware systems are typically used in an asynchronous manner, with work typically performed on an individual basis, as required while in one's office or away from the workshop. These groupware systems support collaboration by allowing participants to post information to shared documents, specialized databases, and tracking applications.

Networked collaboration groupware systems are quite diverse, and in this treatment include the following categories of asynchronous group communication:

- *Workgroup applications.*   Software applications designed for specific use by workgroups or distributed teams to share information in common databases. This category is typified by Lotus *Notes.*

- *Electronic mail.*   Packaged network-based electronic mail systems allowing individuals to compose, send, and receive messages. Typified by Microsoft *Mail* and extended by applications such as Novell's *GroupWise,* e-mail is usually included in complete groupware systems.

- *Group calendaring.* Calendaring systems assist teams in scheduling regular meetings and assigning blocks of time for workshops or ad hoc meeting periods. Typified by Microsoft *Schedule Plus* and included in Novell's *GroupWise.*

- *Information sharing.* Applications that allow threaded group discussions, allowing individuals to post topics and responses and to view and annotate multiple discussion databases. Typified by Lotus *Notes* and Netscape *Collabra.*

- *Workflow systems.* Considered networked and asynchronous, but not typically used in development workgroups, workflow systems automate the flow of routinized work products among work teams. Workflow tools often provide workflow design modules that can be used by design teams in designing workflows. Typified by Action Technologies *Action Workflow.*

- *Internet-based systems.* Certainly networked and asynchronous, the World Wide Web, Internet newsgroups, mailing lists, and bulletin boards are all useful information sources for workgroups. Not currently considered groupware as such, these systems represent foundation technologies that can be built upon for specialized uses.

Groupware tools have evolved extensively since most of the references cited in this book were published. Notice how the category of *groupware* has been become crowded over just a five-year period by these different types listed in the preceding. Groupware can play a significant role in bringing remote participants into the design space, and is useful in sustaining the group's design activity and momentum after the initial design sessions. By including groupware in this treatment, the intention is not to discuss all the systems considered to be in the groupware category. That would require its own volume, given the expansion of technology in this area with the evolution of e-mail and Internet applications.

Groupware can be considered to be any software system running on networked computers supporting large or small organizations with the ability to share information, thoughts, and conversations in ways that encourage group interaction instead of isolated individual contributions. With this definition, even pedestrian e-mail could be considered groupware, if used in a group manner. Let the software companies haggle over defining their tools for the marketplace—the technology evolves rapidly enough that to try to nail down a description is futile. For our purposes, let's look at the fact that in groupware all individuals on a team have access to each others' communications and idea products in electronic format. Intellectual contributions can be made to the group as a group identity, and responses from any group member are available and visible throughout the group. It supports asynchronous conversations among all team members at an individual's convenience.

Commonly used groupware products, such as e-mail and scheduling, will not be addressed further in this discussion as they don't contribute *unique* value to the group workshop process. Instead, two general categories of groupware are presented, as they support the specific work of team processes. One is the *groupware application and information sharing* concept, which might be used as the team database for sharing ideas, communications, and documents with all team members. The other category is the *meeting-support system,* a groupware type that allows team members to contribute to meeting proceedings electronically, supports a group memory for the workshop, and assists decision making.

The dust has not settled on the groupware market, and widely varying results are reported. Apparently, some organizations report enthusiastic and widespread use, and others have had trouble with user acceptance of groupware. Jonathan Grudin (1994) identifies eight problems for groupware developers, based on his study of a range of groupware systems in real-world use. If we consider that our context for groupware is either using it as a documentation and meeting-support tool in workshops or as a team database following the session, a few relevant recommendations derived from Grudin based on these concerns should be noted, as follows:

- Ensure that the groupware system does not require additional work from contributing users who may not receive direct benefits. For meeting-support systems, benefits are probably immediately visible during the workshop. For a follow-on team database, input and responses to the system must be very simple for all team members, or only those who benefit from the information will be active contributors to the database.

- Select and use groupware that does not disrupt tacit social processes or threaten political structures in the organization. This concern is more subtle, but more powerful, than the others. In this scenario, you would never know *why* a groupware system was rejected; it would just fall into nonuse after some trial period. A meeting-support system would probably not pose this problem. However, a groupware-based team database should be open and visible to management and stakeholders, and not subdivided into secret partitions where only parts of the team have access.

- Select and use highly flexible groupware that adapts to the ways your team will work. Many groupware systems will not accommodate the exceptions and improvisation that occur in teamwork. A groupware system for any purpose should allow the team members to design the processes, interactions, and databases that support their way of working. Anything less will fall out of favor once users find that it can't support their process view.

Using Basic Workshop Methods

Throughout your work as a facilitator or analyst you will encounter opportunities to provide service to team meetings in a more casual fashion, or without much advance notice for preparation. You might facilitate, or instead participate, improvise, or otherwise interact effectively as a contributor. In another scenario, you might be engaged in following a process for a Team Design workshop and have to respond to an unplanned need for problem solving or idea generation. You'll have to make something up at that moment, and will require a bag of tricks from which to draw.

Most experienced facilitators fill their bag with tricks over a period of years, trying new group methods and reusing the ones that work. Your tools for these impromptu meetings and situations can be gained from experience, or learned from the use of several basic methods that repeatedly emerge in many meetings. The following methods are described as basic skills and methods effective for most Team Design and many day-to-day meetings where you are called upon to support creative problem solving.

Scoping

When starting a system project, the boundaries of project scope should usually be established very early. Boundaries are set by customers to ensure that the work they support is not overextended or overbuilt, and boundaries are set by development management to ensure that a product is delivered within cost and schedule constraints. Project planning consists of many scope tradeoffs, and boundaries are set, redefined, and reset continually until a baseline scope is agreed upon.

Scoping is this process of defining boundaries for a project or system. To set the scope is to stake out the territory from which work will proceed, and to establish agreement within the group for appropriate areas of discussion. In project management, specifying the scope is fundamental to gaining control over the project. And in facilitation, you'll have the team carve out the scope of the project or system and reach consensus on its limits.

Scoping is done very early in the course of a workshop as a way of communicating the purpose of the session. Scoping the problem space or project provides a focus for the team, and gives the facilitator a means to keep discussions on track.

To effectively work with a team in defining the scope for a process, project, or design, it helps to have gained an understanding of the scope yourself. In your advance planning, identify the *current* scope from discussions with the project manager and other managers. If a strictly defined scope is imposed on the team, it may be useful to work through team issues regarding a mandated scope up front, within the first hour or so of the session. If any flexibility exists in the scope for either change or redefinition, the areas open for change should be clarified and presented to the team. At the very least, a design team is expected to identify issues from the requirements impacting the design and development.

When to use scoping.   Use scoping at the start of the technical discussion or when identifying the problem to be addressed. Have team members who understand the scope lead the discussion of project and workshop scope and facilitate understanding of the current boundaries.

How to use scoping.   Once the scope is described or understood, use a diagram of it during the technical session to manage issues and requirements that emerge. Use a scope diagram to bring discussions back to relevant topics when conversations diverge. Use it to ask team members to reflect on whether new issues fit into the scope or lie outside its bounds.

Scoping methods.   Draw a large circle on newsprint to represent the limits of the scope. Using input from team members, identify major topics that fit within the scope and write them inside the circle. Draw smaller ovals outside or intersecting with the scope circle to represent related functions that fit either outside the scope or have some interface with it. The simple diagram in Fig. 5.2 shows an example of the scoping diagram.

Function decomposition diagrams are also an effective method of representing the scope in more detail and of breaking down processes into a hierarchy of related functions. Function decomposition is part of a larger process analysis and is usually performed later in the technical session, when team members understand the problem area more fully.

Visioning

It's quite common to hear people speak about *setting a vision* or having a *vision* in the sense of a significant shared goal. In a more creative view, a *vision* appears as an initiating idea that defines a new

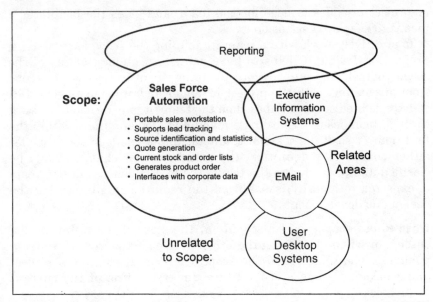

Figure 5.2 Simple scoping diagram.

direction, creates a new thing, or brings about a new way of doing business. Creative people and teams establish a vision as a reachable ideal, a possible destination to function as a focus for direction, inspiration, and guidance. Vision exercises are commonly used in executive retreats, process teams, and new product development groups. The practice has become so familiar to some that in some organizations that have ritualized visioning, nearly every line group or project team develops a vision or a mission statement.

When pushed down from top management without the benefit of cocreation by stakeholders, the vision process is sometimes ill-regarded. It has gained a mixed reputation over the years as a process for identifying and visualizing major goals, and like many creative group processes, it can be misused or fall victim to treatment as the latest management fad. As a process, visioning is both powerful and subject to concern, as it can be easily misunderstood or wrongly applied. For example, when a vision statement is imposed on nonparticipants or replaces true goal-setting, it can create dissension and distrust. And when overused by organizations (when your maintenance crews begin posting their vision statements in the closets, perhaps), the impact of major visions can be diminished.

As previously discussed in regard to agenda items, *visioning* is an effective process for generating a common direction among team members. Visioning is widely understood as a technique for eliciting creative thinking about the possibilities of a situation, where a group is led through a process for imagining possible accomplishment. As such, it's a powerful technique that can be used in many situations.

When to use visioning. Use a visioning process at the start of the group's "thinking" work, when the preliminaries are concluded and the team is wondering what their purpose might be. Use visioning at the start of a technical session if a scope is not yet defined. If a scope is to be enforced, you might still use it before the scoping process to allow team members to share their "blue sky" expressions about the possibilities of the product or system. Always hold visioning processes after some team initiating work, allowing members to become comfortable with their participation as team members first. Visioning can also be used effectively at different times throughout a workshop, especially at times when it appears that the group is not moving forward with creative ideas and needs a jump start.

How to use visioning. Use a visioning process as a way of generating group synergy at the start of the team's work together. Use visioning as a means of creating a group expression of purpose, motivation, and commitment. Use visioning to create the initial work toward a mission statement or a project or product vision.

Visioning methods. Several simple visioning methods can be used, as follows:

Future work stories. Have the group brainstorm their vision for work by projecting into the future 2 years, 5 years, 10 years, or further. Ask the group to reflect on a time when they were engaged in a high-performance team that brought success and satisfaction. Have them project this feeling into their future with their current project, and describe what's possible in their work in two or five years.

Have them think further out if the group is enjoying the visualization. If not, have them stop at five years. Have members describe their own visions out loud and write their descriptions down on newsprint and interactively discuss them with the group.

Shared vision: small groups. Have the participants break into small groups of two or three members each and brainstorm among themselves to develop their shared vision for their work. This works best when each small group is comprised of participants with similar jobs, so their shared vision can be true to life. After five to eight minutes, have each group share with the whole group, and work toward a common vision. Use newsprint and colored markers to have groups document their vision in words or drawings.

Team mandala. *Team Spirit* uses the exercise of the team mandala as a way of bringing a common visual focus to the team. A *mandala* is a symbol or group of visual symbols, usually arranged in a circle, that pictorially describes the essence of a visualized subject. It is also used to visually identify the team or enterprise *mission*. It is like a coat of arms, in that it becomes a representation.

This exercise should be used with teams that have worked together for some period of time before the session (*intact* teams). *Team Spirit* groups report how their mandalas become powerful symbols for their teams, and at least one team has used the mandala as a symbol for its product. (Consider it as "splash screen" or Web site graphical material, at the very least!)

Team members break into small groups to create the team mandala, which is "a visual representation of the team's distinctive core values and vision." Groups are asked to consider their relationship to the team from the perspective of customer service as well as of support for each other. The mandala is to capture several visualizations, from brainstorming the following concepts:

1. Brainstorm the essence of the team's work together in serving customers, and create an image of customer service—that is, what is the team's reason for being?

2. Brainstorm the essence of the team's work together in supporting and serving each other, and create an image of mutual support.

3. Bring the two images together as a unified image, and create the team mandala. Share each of these with the full group for about 20 minutes.

Envisioning the ideal system. This exercise has frequently been used with teams in system-design workshops, particularly at the beginning of requirements definition or planning sessions. Have the group brainstorm, no holds barred, the elements of the ideal system given unlimited time, money, and (to some extent) technology. Accept all ideas, and list them on the newsprint. Encourage the team to build on one another's ideas to create the system of their dreams, that solves all their problems, and redefines their work. This vision is often used as a touchstone, or reference point, for their actual requirements. A scaled-down version of this exercise can be used within requirements-gathering sessions, as a way of gathering and discussing all potential ideas for requirements planning. As a facilitator, look around for other visioning exercises you might use in different situations. Visioning sessions are a core function of team building, and they have a useful function in development and design teams.

Goal setting

Goal setting is a process of leading the team members in defining and agreeing upon their goals as a group. It is used to create a shared commitment to goals by defining them as a group. It can also be used to provide direction for the workshop and the team. Although in principle this is a very simple process, it can become one of the most involved sessions in a workshop. Team members quickly understand that they are establishing and committing to *their* goals and plans, and once the ownership of the goals is realized, the results are typically taken quite seriously.

To start, goal setting involves elicitation of the team's definition of *goals,* so that all participants agree on the level or context of goals. In other words, are their goals to be project, system or product, or organizational or team goals? Goal setting starts by laying out the rules of the game, identifying the domain of the goals and how goals should be described. A good rule of thumb is that goals should be short, specific, and measurable. Give an example of a well-formed goal meeting these criteria, such as "Provide all cost proposals to customers within one working day of the request."

After describing the process, the most important function of the facilitator is to listen, rather than guide. Listen for how goals are expressed, and provide assistance in defining goals if required. Make sure all participants have a chance to participate, and call on members who seem to be shut out or are not engaged.

When to use goal setting. Set goals at the start of the session, before technical discussions but after visioning exercises (if used). Use goal exercises during the workshop to refer back to established team goals if the team loses direction or focus.

How to use goal setting. Use goal setting as a means of generating buy-in and creating group energy around tasks. Goal setting can be used for any group, even if all members are new to the team. It can be used instead of visioning for workshops where visioning processes might not be well accepted.

Goal setting methods

Facilitating dialogue and discussion. The simplest way to create goals is to facilitate an open discussion about the goals of the team. If needed, identify different domains or categories of goals if they appear to be mixed across project and product. The dialogue process described in Senge's (1990, 1994) *Fifth Discipline* books is an excellent way to engage the group members fully in discussing their goals and values related to goals.

Brainstorming and prioritizing. A more structured method involves brainstorming for about 10 to 15 minutes on the *possible* goals to which members wish to commit. Use any of the variations of brainstorming as appropriate, such as full group or individual contributions around the room. After exhausting the team's possible goals, categorize the goals into groups, if appropriate, and have the group prioritize goals within each group. (Grouping keeps the ranking of goals relevant to the category, so that significant goals in different categories aren't being compared inappropriately.)

Goal setting exercise. Start with a problem statement or the vision. For system or project goals, also consider using the scope diagram. Have the group contribute goal ideas based on supporting the problem statement, vision, or scope.

Have the group identify the top *business* goals related to the statements. Have them identify the top *project* goals. Then start identifying product or system goals. Brainstorm the goal ideas first, and refine the wording later. Use a *model goal* as an example for refinement and clarification. Categorize related goals, and narrow each group down to five to ten. A final step is to rank the goals within each category.

Interactive lists

Interactive lists are simply a catch-all for continuously facilitating group ideas and contributions by listing all issues, ideas, and concepts that arise on newsprint or boards. The purpose of list keeping is to maintain a visible shared group memory of all important communications. This also assists the team in categorizing topics for discussion, managing emerging issues, and handling out-of-scope topics.

When to use interactive lists. Lists are interactively maintained with the group by the facilitator throughout the workshop or other sessions. It is a continuous activity that starts with the earliest discussions and exercises and continues through all sessions. The activity can be passed to others, and typically is supported by other members during the session.

How to use interactive lists. Use interactive lists to capture ideas as they occur. List discussion topics, items that emerge in discussion, ideas and results from all exercises, and all other contributions that might be shared by the team. List items during their expression, and refer back to specific lists throughout the session. The facilitator's job is to make sure items are handled during the sessions and not ignored.

Interactive list methods. It is something of a stretch to identify *methods* of interactive listing. Instead, consider the different areas where lists are appropriately used. If working with mostly nontechnical participants, use interactive lists during early discussions to elucidate variations in the technical discussion. Separate requirements, processes, and design items into their own lists so participants can begin to sort out the distinctions for themselves using their own inputs as examples. This is much more effective than defining the differences and expecting people to remember and classify their discussions accordingly.

Other interactive lists maintained in workshops include the following meeting-management lists:

- *Policy issues.* Policy, organizational, or business-related issues that must be handled outside the proceedings.

- *Parking lot.* A list created as a holding place for ideas that don't fit a current direction or list.

- *Out of scope.* A list for ideas that don't fit the designated scope but may have utility and value for other discussions or related projects.

- *Ground rules.* This list remains active throughout the workshop, as new ones might be added as required at any time during a session.

Brainstorming

Brainstorming is probably the single most used and misused group-work technique. Developed by advertising visionary Alex Osborn more than half a century ago, it has been used in every type of business group process since. Numerous variations of brainstorming have been created, and it is a technique that can be combined with many others as a step in a larger idea-generation process. Brainstorming fosters creativity in groups, and requires participation by the entire team, making it an effective way to get the whole team involved. Use brainstorming to generate a large number of ideas in a short period of time, and to expand the thinking of your group to include all of the dimensions of a problem or solution.

When to use brainstorming. Brainstorming can potentially be used during any group process, if the situation calls for it. Use it in the early phases of any project or Team Design processes for requirements and design problems. It can also be used throughout any project as a tool for generating alternatives and problem solving.

How to use brainstorming. Use brainstorming for generating or elaborating requirements with customers or users, or further downstream in analysis while generating scenarios for use in validating requirements. Use brainstorming in the design phases to generate creative ideas and alternatives. Project managers can use it throughout the life cycle of a project to involve a team in creatively participating in generating alternatives for problem solving.

Simple brainstorming methods.   Basic brainstorming is simple, and only requires following a few guidelines to be extremely effective. Probably anyone interested in reading a book such as this one has participated or led many brainstorming sessions, but there is always more to learn from other practitioners. Some of the basic guidelines include the following:

- Set a topic for the session and establish guidelines for the team to follow.
- Set a time limit.
- Encourage contributions from everyone, and call on people if they don't participate.
- List all contributions as they are offered on an easel pad or whiteboard. Have the recorder note all items so nothing is lost.
- Encourage everyone to freewheel. Allow no discussion of topics, allow no judgments from any members. Encourage the teams to build upon ideas generated by others.

Round Robin.   The Round Robin technique is most effective with a smaller group, from 5 to 15 people. Round Robin is useful for creating ideas and organizing them for use in product or system requirements, design, or planning. It involves gathering input from every member of the team, one at a time, until ideas are apparently exhausted. The steps are simple:

1. State the purpose of the brainstorming session, and describe how the process will be conducted.
2. Solicit brainstorming inputs from the group one person at a time. Continue the process until no further inputs are forthcoming.
3. As the facilitator, capture all ideas on the board or easel charts. After receiving all ideas from the group, clarify any that might require it.
4. Create groups from the ideas based on categories suggested by the team members. Have them generate the names and assign ideas to the groups.
5. Finally, have the team rank the ideas for further organization, either within groups (if many ideas) or across all groups (if fewer than 30 altogether). Use a group voting process for ranking.

Nominal Group Technique. The Nominal Group Technique (NGT) is also most effective with a small group, as it is more elaborate than simple brainstorming. It is a more structured form of brainstorming in which all participants have an equal influence on the results of ideas generated or priorities determined. Since participants' inputs are written and then presented in an ordered manner, authority or personal influence on the process is lessened. NGT works well for those who are more comfortable with thinking a problem through thoroughly and are perhaps not as participative in group discussions.

The NGT process is used effectively for difficult problems, not those that can be easily settled or discussed through more conventional brainstorming. NGT is recommended for more narrowly focused problems, and not for "blue sky" brainstorming with a wider scope. It is useful for identifying the group's priorities without the influence of discussion or personality, and provides the team or session leaders information on the critical variables of a problem. NGT allows the workshop leader to assemble the individual responses and present them in a nonbiased manner to the whole group, where they can be organized or prioritized. The steps in the NGT process are as follows:

1. State the purpose of the session and describe the NGT process for group idea generation. Identify the problem to be discussed, or pose a stimulus question for the group.

2. Solicit silent input from the group. Provide index cards or small paper pads for writing down ideas. Allow the group a fixed time period, 5 or 10 minutes, to compose their thoughts and write down ideas.

3. Participants offer their idea suggestions to the facilitator one person at a time around the table. Each participant is asked to read the next idea, unless their idea has been suggested by a previous participant, in which case they pass. This continues until all ideas are used or exhausted.

4. The leader captures ideas on the board and facilitates discussion. Each idea is briefly discussed in the order in which it was written on the board, and is clarified by the originator. The facilitator will move through the list from the top to clarify the suggestions and ensure that all participants understand the ideas.

5. Once it's clear that all members understand the ideas, they can be grouped into categories, especially if more than 30 to 40 ideas are generated. It is not uncommon for NGT to generate over 100 unique ideas, making it a powerful tool for idea quantity.

6. Grouped or not, the team ranks the ideas in a simple voting process. The NGT process usually uses written voting—members

write their top five ideas from the board in order on another index card. Tallies are organized, and the ideas with the most top votes are sorted and written on the board.

Several variations of the NGT process are documented. Higgins (1994*b*) notes the Mitsubishi Brainstorming process, a Japanese variation of NGT. This method was developed to elicit full group participation and to lessen the domination of any particular team member. Members are given plenty of time to generate ideas, including a warm-up period, totaling about 15 minutes or longer. When all are done writing, volunteers read their ideas aloud. Other team members are encouraged to build on the ideas that precede theirs. For the next hour or longer, team members explain and discuss their ideas in some detail among the team. The facilitator draws what's termed an *idea map* on the board or newsprint to illustrate the group's ideas. The visual representation of ideas stimulates further idea generation and discussion, and provides a useful organization and visualization of the ideas and their relationships to each other. In this way, the facilitator works more as the team's scribe in this process, rather than as a structured discussion leader.

Crawford Slip Technique. The Crawford Slip Technique works well with large groups of 20 or more participants and generates a large number of ideas in a short period of time (30 minutes or so). This is a *noninteractive approach,* and does not allow for group discussion or group synergism. The Crawford Slip Technique does use the power of the group to reach consensus, in that the ideas indicated most often become the group's consensus. The steps in this process are as follows:

1. State the purpose of the session and identify the focus problems for the session. These target or focus statements are selected in advance of the group session. One approach to Crawford Slip has a central problem area identified for the group, and several questions or issues derived from it are used as targets. For example, the problem area might be: *reengineering the product release process.* Target questions or statements might be: *What works best from our current release process? What areas could be improved? What roles or organizations should be involved more? Less? If you could redo the process from the ground up, what would you do? What incentives might we use to reinforce improvement of the process?*

2. Solicit silent input from the group by having all participants write their answers to each target question on separate slips of paper or index cards. Participants write quickly, but provide enough detail

to distinguish the idea fully. All responses are submitted to the facilitator.

3. After completing their suggestions, participants typically leave the room or take a break from the proceedings. All inputs are compiled by the facilitator, usually with assistance. Ideas are sorted into meaningful categories and are assembled into a report or presentation of the results.

4. Typically, the ideas with the highest frequency of response become the group consensus. Within each category, the ideas most often mentioned become the top-ranked ideas with the most promise of support. Ideas that follow are listed, but may be ranked as with lesser group support.

Storyboarding. Storyboarding is a more advanced method, originally developed by Walt Disney in 1928 as a way of creating new animations. Storyboarding literally was designed to generate the story line, characterizations, and animation details across a series of boards, allowing a team of collaborators to work with the entire story and sequences as a whole. It's a tailor-made process for facilitation, as it requires a group guide to keep track of the storyboarding process and the threads of story-line development, as well as to maintain group communications throughout the exercise. Storyboarding also requires active participation from all team members, and is a hands-on experience for everyone involved, not just those working the boards.

As in traditional brainstorming methods, the overall concept is determined and the central idea for storyboarding is proposed with only minimal discussion. The ground rules are the same as with brainstorming—any ideas are acceptable, no criticism of ideas, a time limit is set, and building on others' ideas is encouraged. The facilitator keeps track of ideas, items, and issues and helps guide the process. An initial board is drawn with colored markers and newsprint or special large cards on the wall to illustrate a starting point for the process. If another starting point is desired, allow others to draw out their ideas and place them on the wall. Facilitation is used to move the process forward by keeping the group generating a flow of ideas from the initial idea, stimulating the team to think of different ways to connect boards and to create new ones along the lines of the envisioned process. Storyboarding is demanding for the facilitator and the team, but is one of the most effective methods for creating ideas along the lines of a scenario or task. By making all representations of the process or system visual, and by drawing in users, interactions, and other tools used in the process, a powerful simulation of the envisioned system or process becomes real to all participants. When done, the team can read the story of the system and visualize an effective sequence of interactions, and can see where functions are missing or are not well described.

Storyboarding can proceed from a disciplined, procedural orientation with extensive detail or it can be conducted as a more informal idea generation process. Traditional (Disney-style) storyboarding has four major phases, providing a discipline for using the technique:

1. *Planning board.* This board becomes the framework and plan for the storyboard process; it lays out the basic ideas involved in the scenario or the steps needed for the desired result.

2. *Idea board.* Ideas initiated on the planning board are expanded, and topics are added to the boards using wide-open brainstorming and associating ideas across the boards. Without adding structure, the idea board generates numerous specific concepts that can be organized into patterns in the next phase. Both words and pictures can be used to express ideas on the boards—words are grouped according to loosely defined concepts or categories, and pictures are drawn to describe interactions, system or user interfaces, and tasks or processes.

3. *Organization board.* After the idea board has been exhausted, or at least completed for the session, the organization board is used to place actions and outcomes to the ideas. For each board or major topic heading, ask the following questions: *What, Why, Who, Where,* and *When?* This is deliberately a nontraditional order for the five Ws, as it makes no sense to continue with *who, where,* and *when* if you cannot answer *what* and *why.* Find the definition and purpose of the concept first, then assign actions.

4. *Communication board.* This board is recommended as the final step. Develop a communication plan to inform the organizations requiring your deliverables of the actions, products, and intentions developed through the storyboarding exercise. Usually this will have been discussed to some extent up front with the team during the initial (Initiating) phase of the workshop. Revisit the required communications again, following the storyboarding; new stakeholders and organizations may have come into play, requiring a revised communications plan.

The team creates the storyboard by writing ideas on at least two sizes of cards, which are pinned or taped to the wall. Large cards are used to title the headers; smaller index size cards can be used to describe the *subbers,* or items that belong to the category described by a header. The facilitator organizes the materials, presents the process, and keeps the flow of ideas moving. Participants can pin their own cards to the wall during the discussion, or (traditionally) a *pinner* volunteers to stick the cards in the appropriate positions for the team.

Start with a large card and write the topic for brainstorming clearly and concisely. This is the focus for all contributions to the storyboard—and although the topic might be decided in advance, it's always appropriate to have the group discuss the topic and reword or change it. Team ownership of the process is essential to quality work in any group creativity session.

The topic card gets pinned to the wall as the first step, and brainstorming continues to develop the headers that follow as the main categories or groupings of items for the storyboard. Headers can follow a sequential order (as in an actual story) or they can be defined at random as they are invented. In the example shown in Fig. 5.3, headers describe the different categories of games that might be created for an Internet-based game available on the World Wide Web. In this example, the header categories are broken down through brainstorming into the various types of games and attributes of those games that belong to each header category.

As ideas are contributed to the storyboard, the facilitator and pinner must continually reorganize headers and subbers so the overall scheme makes sense. Participants will usually indicate how items should be organized, and will identify the best home for their ideas during the process. When complete, a storyboard will usually have from 6 to 10 headers and any number of subber items. The group can prioritize headers if the number becomes too large and unwieldy. In addition, a *miscellaneous* header is often positioned near the topic to allow for contributions that don't fit into any category at the time. This allows the group to continue forward without forcing a decision

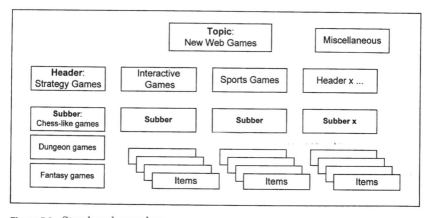

Figure 5.3 Storyboard procedure.

regarding the fit of an offbeat item. As the process continues, the miscellaneous items sometimes fit into new categories or are dropped.

This process for storyboarding is fully described in Higgins (1994*b*) and other sources. Using the full storyboarding process generates a higher quality and volume of ideas than just free-for-all brainstorming. Although it might take from an hour to three hours to work through a full storyboard, the completed product is useful and defines a full process, solution, or product outline. More informal, less disciplined storyboarding processes can also be used to generate scenarios and design concepts for products and systems.

Informal storyboarding. A quick and dirty informal storyboarding process can be used when less time is available to the participants but an active brainstorming method like storyboarding is called for. Sticky notes on a whiteboard can be used as a fast and easy posting technique to list topic headers, but index cards on the wall work just as well. Have participants work either as a group or as individuals to brainstorm ideas on notes or cards, depending on the nature of the group and its personalities. Have participants then post ideas on the board themselves. Only minimal discussion occurs during the period. After the ideas are posted randomly on the board, have the group create categories and rearrange the ideas so they fit the groupings. Most of this idea invention is done in relative silence, and only after all the ideas are posted does discussion start. The following steps summarize this process.

Informal storyboarding steps

1. Identify the subject or theme for focus with the group.
2. Brainstorm ideas with the group or as individuals.
3. Capture group ideas on a flip chart or sticky notes. For individuals, have them write ideas down on sticky notes or index cards.
4. Randomly place the ideas on a wall or whiteboard.
5. Direct the entire group to sort the cards into groupings without discussion.
6. Discuss and prioritize the organized storyboard, if required.

Headers are developed after the fact for each grouping of cards, and the group finishes with a storyboard. As the facilitator, look for common ideas and themes and point these out to the group as they work through the final steps. The entire process can be performed in under half an hour for a six-header storyboard. For more complex problems, or a more involved creative group, the process can take an hour or more.

Enhancing brainstorming. Easy access to the Word Wide Web has introduced new ways of extending the scope of brainstorming. As part of the preparation for a creative workshop session, research some of the topic areas of interest using popular search engines available on the Web. Try different combinations of search terms to retrieve 5 to 10 pages of Web sites that directly or indirectly deal with your topics. For example, if your design session will be focusing on internal Help Desk functions, you might search on *support services, computer support, Help Desk software,* and so forth to generate a variety of responses. Print out the pages with descriptions of the sites to hand out as part of the brainstorming.

A creative facilitator has described his use of this approach with workshops. Following brainstorming exercises, the group is broken into pairs. Each pair is given two or three pages of the Web sites and descriptions to generate even further new ideas. Providing PCs with Internet access turns this into an even deeper creative exercise, as the pairs can locate the various Web sites directly and discover numerous approaches beyond their original ideas.

Storytelling

Storytelling is the most ancient method, a process of creative invention with centuries of tradition and history. Inspired stories create a sense of belonging, appreciation, and empathy within a group. Stories reveal personal values, history, context, and identity through the disclosure of the storyteller's experience. Team-building processes use personal stories as a basic means of initiating, or bringing the group together in an experience of understanding. Stories create trust and respect among members in a session and, in a practical way, bring forward new ideas from past experiences.

When you think of *stories,* what's your impression? Many of us might think back to novels or familiar tales we've heard over the years. Others might have the notion that stories are not quite relevant to the work at hand. Thomas Erickson (1996) discusses the usefulness of stories in design work at Apple Computer:

> The collection and generation of stories happen most during the early stages of design and serve as a precursor to more formal analyses. However, stories are useful even after the initial fuzzy knowledge has been codified into problem definitions, design principles, lists of user needs, information flow diagrams, prototypes, and other, more formal design representations. Once the early stage of design is complete, stories become important as mechanisms for communicating with the organization (p. 34).

Stories elicit experience and wisdom from the team, and can be brought into creative work, design and analysis, and facilitated workshops in several ways. Near the start of a session, stories can be sought from the team for initiating, as part of discussing personal background and experience in an area. As the facilitator, be sure to have several stories available for the telling just to start the process rolling. When introducing yourself, have a brief story about facilitating to give some advance notice about your style or way of working with the group. With a little humor mixed in, stories go a long way toward putting a group at ease with a facilitator or moderator.

During introductions, team members will usually say a few words about their background or interests as a way of sharing themselves with the team. This common initiating practice allows new members to provide some context for later contribution, and allows team members to understand one another and the sources of differing viewpoints. During introductions, have each member tell a brief story about something unique, personal, or applicable to the job at hand. Whatever the type of story, have each member tell one in the same category of experience.

During a workshop session, stories can be used to generate ideas or interest in special areas of discussion or problem solving. They can also be used to initiate a conducive team environment, loosen people up, and establish relationships. And they are the source of useful design information from a user's undiluted perspective. Erickson describes their use as part of design discussions:

> I almost always begin a design by talking with users. Initially my goal is simply to collect people's stories. I believe that the stories people tell about what they do and how they do it contain information essential to designing good interfaces. Stories reveal what people like about their work, what they hate about it, what works well, what sorts of things are real problems. But although stories can contain a lot of valuable information, I believe that the process of collecting stories—rather than the stories' content—is the most valuable contribution to design."

Sharing of relevant experiences is probably the simplest form of storytelling, and is a valid way to introduce personal experience and lessons learned into a session. Other methods for storytelling support a more disciplined perspective. Stories of personal experience can be used to illustrate the effectiveness of a technique or success of an approach proposed for the team or project. Structured stories from the team can build scenarios for testing out problem-solving concepts and product ideas.

Diagramming

Diagrams are perhaps the most widely used communications tool in requirements and design specifications, yet they can also be used throughout the entire development cycle. Diagramming is a skill that draws not on drawing talent but on abstraction and representation. Adapting the representation to the communications need is the skill required for Team Design work. Diagrams can establish the boundaries of discussion for a process, project, or design, as in scoping or context diagrams. Diagrams can define the structures of systems, hardware, software, and networks. They can effectively describe tasks and roles in an organization and the flow of information in organizational processes. Different diagrams are used in defining low-level data flow, software module structure, and database designs. A new type of diagram can be adapted or invented for almost any purpose.

Diagramming is appropriate at almost any point in a Team Design workshop or design session. At the beginning of the session, diagrams set the scope and communicate the big picture for the design. During the session, diagrams can describe the requirements for information use and flow, design structures, and use of data across systems and modules. When developing the final deliverables as products from the Team Design workshop, diagrams started in the session can be refined and submitted as part of the final definition of a process or product design.

This section describes general diagram types available for facilitation and group definition, which might be used by any facilitator almost anywhere in the workshop proceedings. Specific methods for diagramming are presented in Chaps. 7 to 9 for the specialized practices of business process analysis, requirements definition, and application design. Three basic methods are described in this section:

- Pictorials
- Flowcharting
- Simple hierarchies

Pictorials. A *pictorial* is simply a drawing, a sketch, a representation of an idea in visual terms. Especially with user teams or nontechnical groups, using drawings instead of standard diagramming methods is an inviting way to gain participation. A pictorial is understandable by every team member, and does not require a legend or technical background for readability. It is perhaps the least intimidating form of communication a facilitator can adapt; words can be misread and misunderstood, yet give the impression that understanding has taken place. With pictorials, if a concept is not understood, participants feel free to ask for clarification and might offer pictorial notions to improve the diagram.

Pictorial diagrams can follow the flow of a story or discussion by drawing out concepts and showing their connectedness through visual relationships. Pictorials are excellent for showing the flow of tasks or scenarios where a simple process is discussed and must be described so the team members can all focus on the same representation. Pictorials, although simple and descriptive, are not as portable as words. Pictures must be redrawn from the board if they are to be reused in a document after the session. Pictorials can be rendered using a software drawing package, with the resulting drawing appearing similar to that shown in Fig. 5.4. If a scanning whiteboard is used in your session, the actual drawing from the board can be generated on paper and redrawn or scanned at a later time. The technology of drawing is fairly simple, and should not be considered a hindrance.

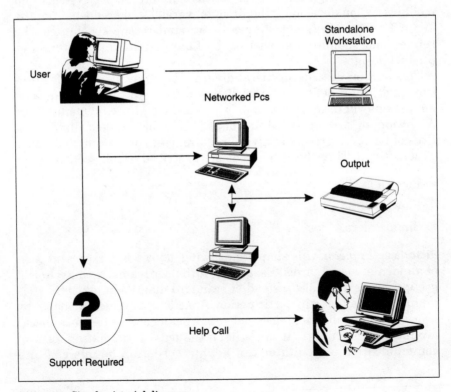

Figure 5.4 Simple pictorial diagram.

Flowcharting. Flowcharts—aren't they used for computer programming? Actually, they serve a better purpose as a problem-solving tool for identifying problem areas in a process or task or for analyzing the causes of ineffective performance. They are a general tool used more now for diagramming process relationships than for programming. Originally designed as a tool for describing program flow (input, process, and output), flowchart symbols and diagramming methods are more commonly found as high-level process diagrams and workflow representations. The flowchart is one of the simplest and most powerful diagramming methods, and can easily be adapted to diagram process problems as they arise in design workshops. As a facilitator, knowing and using the basics of this tool can fulfill at least half the requirements for process definition in a simple workshop. For specialized methods of diagramming processes, refer to the Team Design formats in Chaps. 7 to 9 for applications in process definition and application design.

Flowcharts support group analysis of processes and tasks by revealing the sequences of a process in a step-by-step manner. Analysis using the flowchart technique leads to improving or streamlining the process, identifying steps to measure, and identifying steps that do not contribute to the business value of the process. By analyzing the flowchart, the team can recognize and discuss the redundant steps, unnecessary activities, and complicated paths revealed. Hidden decision points are shown in a process flowchart, and a view of the complete process takes shape as the team works through the analysis.

Flowcharts can be used as part of a business process requirements definition, user requirements for a new system (and its redesign processes), or for educating users and others in standard task procedures. A baseline of a current business process can be communicated with a flowchart, and a process redesign can be compared with the baseline to show improvements or recommended changes.

Over the years numerous symbols have been added to the flowchart technique, but for informal (nonprogramming) usage, only a few symbols are ever used. The six symbols shown in Fig. 5.5 are about the only ones needed to get by with simple flowcharts. The example in Fig. 5.6 shows the input and output (same symbol), process, decision, and flow line. These four symbols can serve most of the simple flowcharting requirements in the workshop setting.

To draw a basic flowchart as a facilitator, discuss the process to be diagrammed to some extent in advance of drawing. Identify the activity experts from the user or owner groups, if more than one group is involved. Discuss the scope of the process—determine whether it makes sense to diagram the entire process or to break it up into composite tasks and diagram them one at a time. Draw out suggestions

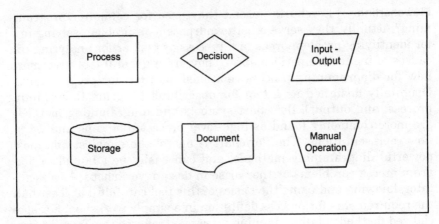

Figure 5.5   Flowchart symbols.

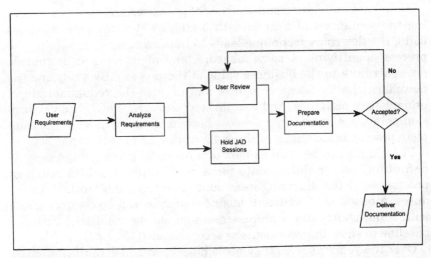

Figure 5.6   Simple flowchart.

from the team, and identify any organizational structure that should be defined for the process flow. Once the scope for analysis is determined, write a label for the flow diagram on the board, and ask for the initial inputs to the process.

The primary input, or *trigger,* is the activity or event that initiates the process in the real world that the flow represents. Draw an input symbol on the far left of the board and give it an unambiguous label. If a large process is defined (more than 15 process steps) use numbers to specify the symbols, or just remember to add them later when the chart is formalized in a diagramming tool and printed. Define the step that occurs following the trigger event, and label it as the first step in the process. Draw a flow line to the process symbol with a single arrowhead indicating the direction of flow.

The discussion may continue rapidly from this point—don't be concerned about getting the diagram perfect. Several iterations are usually required to refine the flowchart, some of which are done with the group and, usually, another when drawing the diagram in the tool. Continue gathering process steps and diagramming their flow logic from left to right, indicating the relative sequence. If steps are conducted in parallel, draw forked lines from a process symbol to two or more process steps that could occur simultaneously. If a decision, handoff, or approval is required in the flow, draw the decision diamond and indicate the decision logic in simple terms. At the conclusion of the process, you will typically draw at least one output symbol. Multiple outputs are also possible, and these should be shown as results from their own development sequences. A finished chart shows all steps at the same task level (for example, all steps are high-level activities, or all are detailed steps) to complete a process from start to finish.

When drawing flowcharts it's not as important to use a strict methodology as it is to just be consistent. Drawing flow lines with a single arrowhead is a good convention to show a specific direction of action, but if you prefer to use bidirectional arrows (with arrowheads on each end) be consistent and use them wherever they apply. Using the storage symbol as a convenience representing any current online data source is useful, as is showing strictly manual processes with the special manual operation symbol. Invent new symbols or new uses for symbols if the need arises—the purpose of flowcharting is to communicate, and if the team or its facilitator requires a new tool to express an idea, don't let convention or technique interfere.

Flowcharts quickly become a workshop staple for describing time-sequenced processes or task workflows. When defining business processes, other methods are better used, but as processes are decomposed into their subprocesses, flowcharts illustrate the user level of manual tasks and work processes. Dependencies among functions are naturally shown by the use of single direction flow lines and defining decision points in a process. Input and output dependencies are shown by the use of symbols, reflecting an end-to-end sequence of actions that starts with a defined input and concludes with one or more outputs.

Roles and organizations can be described within flowcharts by segmenting the chart into rows or columns corresponding to organizations in the business, or by using color coding to identify the roles or departments responsible for an activity. The Process Mapping technique discussed in Chap. 7 is essentially such a flowchart with organizational segmentation used to show responsibility and hand-offs in a business process. To define a process to this level of detail requires the involvement of users or experts in the activities discussed. Even with expert involvement, disagreements commonly arise regarding how a process should be represented, especially when users and their managers discuss the process separately. The *point of view* of a process diagram should be noted during the analysis. Users might reveal the set of steps actually used to perform a task, while their managers might describe how the task is *supposed* to be performed, according to rules. Discrepancies between these perspectives reveals problems with the task or process itself that can be surfaced for evaluation.

The example flowchart in Fig. 5.6 shows a simple task-oriented workflow for developing requirements documentation. A simple workflow is illustrated, with *user requirements* as the existing input to the flow. Several processes are applied to it along the path. Parallel activities are shown with *user review* and ongoing *JAD sessions,* with the activities merging into *preparing documentation.* Following the decision point of whether to *accept* the product or not, the final output is *delivered documentation.* A document symbol could also have been used here, but that might limit the imagination of the chart's users, who could opt for prototypes or online documentation as well as for a paper document. In this way, the more general symbols leave more options available to the team in the design process. Not every element should or can be defined in detail, and techniques like the simple flowchart allow for further definition to improve a process.

Simple hierarchy. A *hierarchy* describes the natural organization of items related by grouping or belonging. Whereas flowcharts show temporal or dependency relationships, hierarchies express the functional relationships or ownership among groups. Like a family tree or an organization chart, the hierarchy is used so extensively as a diagram type that we don't notice its effectiveness. It is easily understood, and it makes immediate sense to people. As a facilitator, you won't have to train the team to read a diagram or to draw with unique symbols to use the hierarchy. The skill to learn is merely recognizing where to best employ hierarchies for the team members to communicate their ideas.

Several types of hierarchies can be used in Team Design and other development sessions. The following types are often used in business requirements and system design:

- *Function decomposition.* Shows the related functions in a process.

- *Concept hierarchy.* Shows how concepts are related and broken down into elements.

- *System hierarchy.* Breaks down related system components in a treelike format.

- *Organizational hierarchy.* Defines the relationships of roles or persons in an organization.

- *Work breakdown structure.* Defines the composite activities of a large project.

In addition, hierarchies show up in specific design methods where the technique is naturally applied:

- *User interface or screen layout.* Shows the composition of the data entry screens in the user interface.

- *Object model or class hierarchy.* Shows the breakdown of classes and objects available in a class library for object-oriented systems.

- *Software module structure.* Shows the relationship of designed modules in a hierarchical diagram on a structure chart.

Not all these methods are described in this chapter, but all are worth understanding for potential use in design work.

The example in Fig. 5.7 shows a simple concept hierarchy describ-

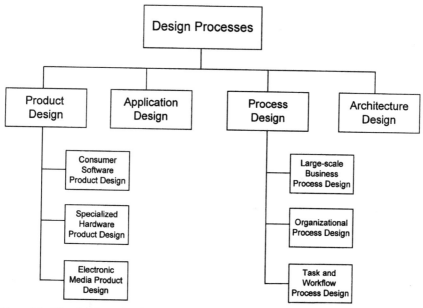

Figure 5.7 Simple hierarchy diagram.

ing the components of the domain of *design processes*. The parent concept identifies the domain, and the next level below specifies four types of design processes covered in this book. Under two of these concepts appear a small set of design areas. This breakdown would be continued by listing the design activities appropriate to the types of product or process design in the lowest-level boxes.

As a facilitator, your conversation to develop the conceptual hierarchy might go something like this: "Let's look at design processes in some detail then, and draw out a concept diagram to identify all the areas of design we know something about. What are the major areas of design we could focus on (design of products, applications, processes, and architecture)? Do these areas reflect our industry and our understanding? Are there any others we could add (such as documentation, networks, and workflow)? Which of these should be placed at the top level and which are components? Let's break it down further—think about the problem as if we were to develop a training course or textbook on all areas of design. What's next? Let's take product design—what types of products require unique, independent processes? (Software, hardware, multimedia...) How can we specify those product types?"

Engage the team members in a thinking conversation about their problems, concepts, or functions. Use a brainstorming approach, writing down everything suggested and rearranging it later. Or use a more structured approach, challenging the team to think through the problem in sequence. The hierarchy method is nothing if not flexible.

Specific hierarchy definition methods are also described in Chap. 9, which covers the Team Design format Application Design.

6

Team Design
Process Formats

*Design is always already happening. We
don't offer a magic solution, but an
orientation that leads to asking significant
questions. Design always proceeds, with or
without articulated theory, but we can work
to improve its course and its results.*

WINOGRAD AND FLORES
Understanding Computers and Cognition

When setting out to fulfill the demands of a project requiring new
design, collaboration, or decision making, you confront a pattern of
history. Up against the notions, behaviors, and ideas of the prevailing
culture, you're tempted to consider that what worked in the past will
support your project today. If considering this line of reasoning, be
honest with your corporate history—how successful were the process
and methods of design in the recent past? When projects were concluded, did your team ever review the practices and design methods
used and evaluate what worked well and what didn't? After the glow
and hard work from making your product release date has subsided,
it's difficult to recall the sometimes torturous processes imposed on
the team while creating and recreating the product design.

When months separate the product's delivery from its design activities, who remembers how well your processes worked? Without adopting the rigor of the Software Engineering Institute (SEI) Capability
Maturity Model, the original details of your design process are probably fuzzy, perhaps even idealized. If typical, you started with a group
of assigned people in a room with a project manager or boss describing the project and your roles. Expectations regarding team ability

were high, and you might even have felt you had a clearly defined role on the project. Perhaps senior team members took the lead, and initiated requirements analysis. Later on, you were asked to participate in "design meetings." Things got drawn on the board, ideas were tossed around, some of it was written down. If a more disciplined process was used, perhaps you used a CASE tool to document the proceedings. Somewhere along the line, things got cleaned up, organized into a workable order, and a *design* emerged.

Throughout the design (specification) and development (coding and testing) processes, you might have considered better ways to create a software procedure or to improve the user interface. Others were adding their improvements and improvisations along the way, and possibly the design improvements were coordinated. One thing was for sure throughout the process—*design was always already happening*. It's not that we don't perform design well—we emerge with good design sometimes, in spite of the process. But all too often, the process itself impedes our ability to create or contribute to an excellent design. As the time allotted for design fades away, the internal design process—your thinking about what you're building—continues. Design is already happening—it is imaginative and pervasive.

Design becomes formalized by the need to work in teams, or at least in multiple partnerships. By the nature of the complexity and expense of product and software systems development, many parties are brought into the group to contribute and to represent the factions of the business. The team itself is a given, but our interactions within the team are not. Our ability to coordinate and communicate the concepts and details throughout complex designing is not fixed. There are numerous approaches to address team development processes— Team Design is but one.

What does the Team Design process address that can't be done as well using traditional or current design methods? For one, most current methods do not adequately address the team development or organizational issues. Technical concerns such as requirements, design, and development processes are separated from what might be considered human resources or organizational development. Without a framework for understanding the impact of organizational concerns on software projects, this problem is likely to continue in most organizations. Team Design *contexts* (Chap. 3) address the different organizational and system backgrounds encountered across the range of work environments, from management and operational to product development to academic or research. The contexts of business, user, system, and product reach across industries and organizations, and might also be applicable in unforeseen environments not explicitly addressed.

Contemporary analysis and design methods do not provide a general means for conducting these processes in a team arrangement. Analysis methods such as structured analysis, business process mapping, and systems thinking approaches do not supply guidelines for managing analysis in a team setting. Traditional and modern design methods also provide little support to the team practitioner. From CASE and structured application design to object-oriented design and the various development approaches, teams are left to figure out the best usage, roles, and coordination for themselves. The typical team processes currently in favor include design meetings, cross-functional team meetings, and, of course, JAD workshops. However, many JADs are hampered by either of two extremes: the information technologists driving the use of structured methods that are not understood by users, or the user organization driving the session with inefficient hand-holding JADs that cannot work through the analysis in enough depth to satisfy technical requirements. In either case, both user organizations and development teams must also have access to facilitators and a working JAD process to enable the coordination of design work. The Team Design *formats* address these issues by providing a fairly exhaustive framework of analysis and design methods in several major project areas. The formats can be used by novice workshop organizers to check available methods and build appropriate agendas. Experienced facilitators can use the formats as checklists and methodology guides for conducting workshops with a richer source of methods.

Finally, most development organizations tend to use design methods they already know and are comfortable using, and do not change unless a motivating need exists. Common difficulties such as requirements churn and articulating a design do not qualify as motivating needs, since these problems are, in fact, the status quo. Two reasons for *not* using different methods often arise: (1) if my team already has trouble establishing requirements and the design for a new product, introducing new methods will only add to the trouble; and (2) we're supposed to be the experts in this stuff, and if we don't already know a method we're not going to risk looking stupid while we learn a new one that's not proven! In other words, if the status quo doesn't work well, but it's what the organization expects, then why go through the trouble to change? Most of the methods discussed throughout the formats are well known, proven, already established in current procedures. The difference in Team Design is that the methods are integrated into a flexible coordinated process; they gain a synergy when used together. Also, the methods are described for use as team procedures, not as procedures for individual practitioners. Therefore, development teams should be able to pick up the formats from their current knowledge base of methods, and add to their toolkits by selecting the appropriate methods from the formats as required by their projects.

Development Teams—A Case Study

Curtis, Krasner, and Iscoe (1988) discovered when investigating numerous large software projects that competent design work must be performed as a team. However, software project teams do not always behave as if this were the case. Of the many things that can and do go wrong in development projects, three significant problems emerged:

- Application domain knowledge is inconsistent, and typically weak, among team members.

- Requirements are not well defined, and constantly fluctuate and conflict.

- Communication and coordination breakdowns are frequent and extremely counterproductive.

These problems were identified as the primary cause for typical software project breakdowns, such as schedule and cost overruns, poor design, and unmet requirements.

The domain knowledge shortfall is a normal problem among developers. Developers don't have background in all application domains, and cannot be expected to understand every domain. A fairly steep learning curve exists for developers on most projects where a new application domain is undertaken. Curtis and his team found that specification mistakes occurred due to the lack of domain knowledge. For example, if a project team had developed software for overnight package delivery services, they would not have the domain knowledge to tackle an air traffic control system.

In successful or extraordinary projects, the consistent underlying factor was the presence of exceptional system designers with background or learning in the domain, and with understanding of both customers and developers. These individuals were, in all cases, considered *designers,* not programmers. They were *interdisciplinary* in educational background and experience, not technical specialists. The other contributing factor was that they were skilled at communicating a technical vision to the project team.

Problems with fluctuating and conflicting requirements were identified as the second major factor. Customers misunderstand the trade-offs during the requirements analysis process, and do not readily understand how new requirements might impact many others already identified and considered to be part of the emerging set. In large organizations with both internal stakeholder groups and product customers, internal customer departments, such as marketing or sales, might levy requirements that differ with the external customers'. These conflicts are not easily remedied (and the internal customers usually win out since they are closer to the development team). Finally, if a large design team is involved on a project, different parts of the team might design different parts of the system. As requirements change between the different teams, understanding or communication of the impacts does not easily take place. Without a process for managing requirements, these problems can eventually overwhelm the project.

From months of observation, interview, discussion, and analysis, Curtis and associates uncovered the root causes of significant common problems plaguing software development. Their work produced insights for improving the process. They suggest leveraging the possibilities revealed to customers through the requirements process.

Suggestions for addressing the requirements problems include the following proposals:

- Early prototypes of the system should be developed and provided to customers for feedback. Prototypes should be comprehensive enough to surface problems at an early phase in development. By working with an interactive model of the requirements through a prototype, customers and developers quickly see the results of the requirements as they are developing. Inconsistencies and conflicts in the interpretations of the requirements domain will be exposed, and remedies are much less costly during the requirements phase.

- Requirements should not be baselined until the development team has a significant understanding of the application domain. *Baselining* is the act of freezing a specification and initiating change control from that point forward. Premature baselining leads to inadequate interpretation of the requirements and their impact. By holding off baselining, requirements can be allowed to evolve during a planned design phase as part of the process. Baselining can be done when the team and customer are prepared to accept a necessary and sufficient degree of domain understanding.

- Some part of the system must be built before other requirements are revealed. As the development team encounters and solves basic architectural and development problems early in development, new requirements and improved ways of handling existing requirements emerge. A flexible process that plans for this occurrence manages requirements more effectively than a traditional rigid methodology.

Curtis and company addressed the factors of communication and coordination breakdowns in the development process. Traditional development teams operate within organizations where communication links among members are often remote or infrequent. Departments are organized to support organizational efficiency, while teams cross these boundaries. Team members are often not aligned with one another. Therefore, technical documents (such as specifications and requirements) are weak when used by themselves to communicate a complete design. They are not understandable to all team members, and are often written from the perspective of just part of the team.

Effective development-team communication starts with an *accepted shared representation,* which is not easily achieved through documents. This shared understanding among team members is required as a point of departure. Stakeholders must clarify what is meant, discuss the implications, and settle differences before communication has really happened. Documentation is typically used as the main source of communication between successive teams in a process (marketing, project management, requirements, testing, and others). By itself, it is usually an inadequate base for the implementation of a large set of requirements. Communication among individuals from all parts of the organization is necessary to overcome the coordination problems that will occur. Curtis reminds us that it is critical to have people on the team who span organization boundaries and serve as information coordinators.

Finally, Curtis proposed three capabilities that enable the development environment to support more effective requirements management:

- Knowledge sharing and integration
- Change facilitation
- Broad communication and coordination

Team Design addresses these needs through the mechanisms of the workshop and team structure. Although most of the Team Design approach integrates or assumes the use of team workshops, the facilitated workshop is not the essential part of the process—the coordinated *team* is. These two basic structures support Curtis' three recommendations by: (1) providing an environment for sharing knowledge among team members and integrating learning, (2) providing for a team structure that can be oriented toward rapid change as needed, and (3) creating the communication framework through a team structure that supports coordination. The shared representations necessary for learning and for organization of knowledge come about through team interactions, often just in dyads or small groups, but results are eventually shared as common learning within the team. Facilitation during workshops provides modeling of communication and provides a grounding for team members to easily communicate with one another.

Finally, the development approaches discussed by Curtis are addressed by the Team Design formats, which provide frameworks for design and development activities across different organizations and project types. Their recommendations for requirements definition include prototyping, iteration, and user involvement, all essential components of the Requirements Definition format. Although teams can use facilitated workshops and still encounter difficulties, the opportunities for miscommunication are minimized, and the active coordination of work among team members minimizes the "hiding" of information.

Using the Team Design Formats

Team Design formats offer guides for the practice of design techniques. These are not intended to be cookbook, theoretical, or directive, but organized *best practices* based on experience and research. The formats offer design practitioners flexible, adaptable guidelines for design work processes. Additionally, the context guidelines from Chap. 3 support adapting the formats to fit the appropriate organizational contexts or corporate cultural considerations.

Several categories of workshops are defined according to their specific design goals. Each format provides a structure to follow which includes:

- A baseline agenda to use as a starting point
- A set of group activities to generate the deliverables for the workshop
- Descriptions of practices for using the appropriate development methods

The formats are described in the front of each section, providing an overall framework or agenda for organizing workshops or development processes. Formats provide a structure for a facilitator or project manager to organize, prepare, and conduct the workshops and other activities necessary to produce deliverables using the Team Design approach. Like outlines for meeting agendas, they guide the formation of the formal agenda used to prepare the participants for the workshop. Unlike meeting agendas, the formats guide the facilitator or organizer in evaluating a course of action and in selecting appropriate tools for the workshop.

The formats organize a full set of practices that might be conducted as part of a development project. Five formats are defined, incorporating analysis, design, planning, and decision making. Three of these involve systems analysis and design, and the others cover planning and decision processes. Each format defines a full life cycle for the activity, so that either a full-spectrum workshop or a series of partial workshops might be used in an organization. The five Team Design formats include the following:

- *Business Process Design.* A *front-end* process that integrates the life cycle of activities used to identify, analyze, and redesign business processes. This format supports a team in starting with an objective and completing with a redesigned business process.

- *Requirements Definition.* Another front-end format, it pulls together the life cycle of requirements analysis activities into a unified process. This format supports teams in evaluating the initial business requirements and working through to completion of a requirements definition. This can be considered the *design* of requirements.

- *Application Design.* This format integrates application analysis and design activities into a team workshop format. From a foundation of JAD, group design practices, and systems analysis, the Application Design format supports development teams in working from their requirements to the point of development. Unlike the other formats, Application Design integrates a front-end format as an input—either requirements or process design.

- *Team Planning.* Planning is typically a front-end activity, but this format can be used during workshops for almost any other purpose. Team Planning supports group planning activities for strategic planning workshops, project planning and scheduling, and business planning.

- *Decision Making.* The Decision Making format supports team-based decision processes, any of which might be used at any point in a business or product cycle. This format can be used at any point within development, or in nondevelopment decisions. Decision Making can be used as a set of coordinated techniques following the same design cycle as the other formats, but in a much shorter time period.

The three analysis and design formats can be used independently or together. Some projects might only designate a team process for business process redesign or requirements, and not application design, so the formats for these processes could be used independently. Other development teams might use team processes throughout the life cycle, and might use the formats together in one of the following ways:

- *Sequentially,* where business process redesign is conducted first, followed by requirements definition, then by application design. This approach might be used where different teams are responsible for each phase of work, such as in long-term projects or for large reengineering projects.

- *Cumulatively,* where each successive process builds on the results and products of the one before it. This approach is recommended when a single development project team or a cross-functional integrated team is responsible for the entire project. Synergy is gained across the formats by using the same methods across phases of work. A typical team might define system requirements as part of the business process design, and would share methods from both formats. Likewise, requirements methods would lead into developing the applications.

- Planning and decision-making formats might be incorporated into any of these approaches. Most projects will require a planning phase, and many will require formal decision processes and priority setting. The planning and decision formats can be introduced within any of the analysis and design processes.

See Fig. 6.1 for a visual representation of how the Team Design formats relate across the general development life cycle. Although there

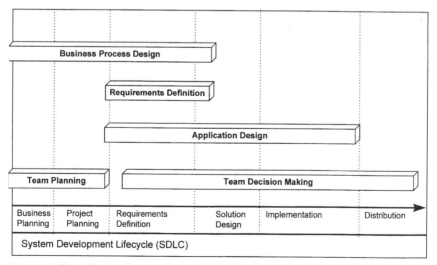

Figure 6.1 Team Design format relationships.

is significant overlap among the analysis and design formats, these can be adapted as described in the preceding, and so are not dependent on one another. However, when using more than one format across a project, the overlap in design methods allows your team to adapt the methods where they best fit in the project's situation. Therefore, if process analysis is performed in Business Process Design, it stands throughout Requirements Definition or Application Design.

In the Business Process Design format, several systems analysis methods are used to construct the process models that represent the business process. These methods are described under the business process area, but are also at home in the formats for requirements definition and application design. Since business process analysis is often conducted as part of the overall system design, Business Process Design is initially used for developing a workshop plan or team agendas. As a facilitator or analyst, note that many of these methods can be used across formats, and they might be well-suited for your environment under a different format. However, to avoid redundancy the methods are described in detail in the first format where they are most applicable.

To familiarize the practitioner with reading the formats, example activities in a model format are shown in Table 6.1. Three columns in each table list the following:

- *Design phases.* Phases of design (shown as the italic listings) are indicated for each major set of agenda activities. The phases correspond to the Team Design cycle described in the following section. Formats typically show three or more agenda activities within each design phase, such as shown under *Initiating.*

- *Methods.* Methods are associated with activities within a phase, but in this model are shown as examples of common techniques. The methods indicate recommended or typical design methods used by teams to perform the activities in each phase.

- *Inputs and outputs.* Inputs (in) are required or recommended deliverables or conditions to enable a given activity. *Outputs* (out) are recommended products developed as a result of completing an activity.

The Team Design formats are designed to be used as both agendas and guidelines for creating and conducting workshops, design meetings, and other facilitated sessions. If you have worked with effective meeting agendas, some consistent activities will look familiar. Some work is necessary before the workshop to plan the session, and during this period facilitators and participants share their initial ideas about the purpose and style of the workshop.

TABLE 6.1 Model Team Design Format

Agenda activities	Methods	Inputs and outputs
Planning: Preworkshop		
Advance planning for workshop	Project planning, team planning, workshop planning	In: Business case, schedules
		Out: Workshop plan (initial)
Preparation for workshop	Team and workshop planning, coordination, interviewing and surveys, discussion	In: Workshop plan (initial)
		Out: Workshop plan (final)
Initiating: Workshop		
Welcome	Agenda, ground rules	In: Workshop plan
		Out: Agenda
Team building	Warm-ups, introductions, exercises	In: Agenda
		Out: Team identity
The workshop process	Agenda, discussion	In: Workshop plan, agenda
		Out: Project goals
Scoping: Identification	Brainstorming, scoping diagrams	In: Mission statement, project goals
		Out: Purposes
Visualizing: Analysis	Brainstorming, system diagrams	In: Purposes, scope
		Out: System or process vision
Usage: Application	Scenarios, prototypes	In: System or process vision
		Out: Scenarios, prototype
Packaging: Completion	Design diagrams, mapping, final documentation	In: Scenarios, prototype
		Out: Design package
Validating: Evaluation	Design evaluation, test planning	In: Prototype, design package
		Out: Validated design

The Team Design cycle

The phases of the Team Design cycle apply consistently across all formats. The phases provide a useful model for coordinating a team in participating with a *direction* of design, without dictating the design process and tools. The phases shown in the model format reveal a full extended set of activities, representing an end-to-end design process.

All phases will not always be used in planned workshops. A typical design project might only adopt two or three phases for workshops. Even though a team workshop approach can be used throughout the design cycle, and even a development life cycle for some functions, this will not always be possible. Many organizations will start with scoping and visualizing workshops and have individual designers and small groups continue with the design work from that point forward. In some organizations, Team Design processes might start off by being used for front-end analysis only; as practitioners become familiar with their use, they will grow into use for the full design cycle.

Six phases, which are applicable in most of the formats, are shown in the full design cycle. *Initiating* should always be planned for all new teams and new projects, and considered for projects where new team members are added over time. Initiating provides the opportunity to build team relationships and group synergy, and it cannot be underestimated as a productivity booster. *Validating* is a recommended phase for evaluating the products of *design* formats (business process, requirements, and application design) but is not typically used in planning or decision-making contexts. These phases are described as follows:

- *Initiating.*   Kicking off the workshop with team-building and team assimilation processes. Formal initiating is typically used only at the beginning of a series of workshops, or with new teams only. Informal initiating processes can occur whenever the need arises for reinforcing team relationships.

- *Scoping.*   Identification of scope and process. In most formats, scoping involves identifying the components and boundaries of the problem or requirements addressed by the design. Scoping often entails defining current processes and data, gathering basic information, and setting goals and objectives.

- *Visualizing.*   Analysis and envisionment of the process. This phase bridges the design from the current analysis to the new requirements or vision. Visualizing expresses the design in terms of the vision for the new system. Numerous front-end analysis methods are used in visualizing to enable teams to construct appropriate design models.

- *Usage.* Application of the process in context. Usage addresses the process of designing a system for its context of use within organizations, by users. Usage integrates operational models, scenarios and use cases, and prototypes in order to surface issues, test assumptions and iterate the design within an identifiable context.

- *Packaging.* Completion of the design process. Packaging is the phase where a design model or specification is produced from the analyses, iteration of design, and learning of the prior phases. Packaging generates the deliverables typically used by customers or developers outside of the design team.

- *Validating.* Evaluation of the design and process. Validating is a phase recommended for review and evaluation, which is typically used in analysis and design formats, but not for planning and decision making. Evaluation is built into the usage phase, but in a more informal process of obtaining feedback from users on the emerging design model. Validating is a more formal testing of the design *package.*

Each format chapter describes its applications of the scoping, visualizing, usage, and packaging phases in sufficient detail for practitioners to adapt them to their development projects. Within these phases, each format provides recommendations for methods best suited for the deliverables and activities in that format. The methods and tools are recommendations only, and are provided from the background of research and experience. However, practitioners have their favorite approaches and tried-and-true methods. Once the relationships among design activities and deliverables has been understood, practitioners can integrate their own preferred methods and tools into the structure. The model Team Design format (Table 6.1) also shows the use of a preworkshop period with two basic activities. This is not actually a phase of Team Design, as it is a preparation period for facilitators and organizers to assemble the team, gather information, plan for the project and workshops, and lay the groundwork for the process. This preworkshop period is consistently used across all formats, and does not vary by format. Therefore, it will be described once in this section and assumed for the other format descriptions. The initiating phase is similar, in that it is consistent across all formats, and does not vary in structure. However, each team and organization will be different, and a huge variety of exercises and activities can be used in the initiating phase.

Planning: Preworkshop. The preworkshop is used as the planning period for the workshop organizer, the facilitator, and the project manager to plan and prepare for the sessions. Guidelines for planning

TABLE 6.2   Team Design: Preworkshop planning

Planning: Preworkshop	Methods	Inputs and outputs
Advance planning for workshop	Project planning, team planning, workshop planning	In: Business case, schedules Out: Workshop plan (initial)
Preparation for workshop	Team and workshop planning, coordination, interviewing and surveys, discussion	In: Workshop plan (initial) Out: Workshop plan (final)

are discussed in Chap. 5; basically, the idea is to set aside enough time in the preworkshop period to adequately prepare for the workshop. For a two-day workshop, a week or more of advance work might be required to ensure that the workshop is well planned and productive. Also, participating team members must have enough advance time to digest advance information and make preparations to be capable of collaborating in the workshop.

Advance planning for the workshop starts with the project and workshop planning factors discussed in Chap. 5. These activities involve the general methods shown in Table 6.2, including project, team, and workshop planning. For a new project or a new workshop series, the first inputs to planning will likely be a project description or business case and any schedules that have been prepared. The essential output for the workshop will be the workshop plan, which includes project and team planning relevant to the workshop.

Preparation for the workshop might require continued planning, with participation of sponsors or management and discussions and interviews with participants. The methods for preparation can include any activity necessary to establish the groundwork for the workshop. This activity includes coordinating with stakeholders, discussing roles and participation with the entire team, and gathering information required to better understand the processes or systems to be designed. Interviews are used in advance to gather specific detailed information from participants and nonattending stakeholders. Surveys can be used as a means of tapping into the larger organization and gathering feedback on a number of issues relevant to the workshop. The initial workshop plan is the primary input, and the revised and final workshop plan is the output.

The initiating phase starts the workshop, and integrates all of the introductory sessions and most of the team-building processes. Initiating is used at the start of all projects and series of workshops; even if it is not recognized or explicitly used, an initiating period of some sort mediates the integration of individuals into a working group. A mini-initiating session should be held at the start of every new meeting as well, to check in with participants, obtain feedback about the process, and take informal measures of perceived progress.

Team building activities follow the welcoming, and these can take the form of many different approaches and exercises. The goal or output of this activity is a group with a team identity, ready to work together over the project or, at least, the workshop period. Introductions are typically made, and warm-ups and small group exercises are used for members to learn about each other. If the facilitator uses a team-building method, such as *Team Spirit* (Heermann 1997) or methods from the *Team Handbook* (Scholtes 1988), they would be started at this point.

Finally, the workshop process activity provides the opportunity to discuss the workshop agenda, and consensus can be reached on agenda topics, ground rules, and scheduled items. Discussions are held with the team to craft policies and agreements for working together, and any facilitation rules are brought forth and discussed. The goals for the project can be discussed openly, and agreements and proposals affecting the workshop and project can be mediated before working too far into the process. The output shown for this activity in Table 6.3 is *project goals,* but these are goals that have been shared, discussed, and understood among the team. The most important output is a cohesive working team capable of conducting intensive analysis and design work in a workshop setting.

Although a specific phase is not granted for concluding the sessions, wrapping up a single session or a workshop series is serious business. The facilitator must be sure to use the last remaining goodwill and energy of the group to obtain commitments on actions and follow-up. A workshop might appear to be successful due to the enthusiasm, forward progress, and output of workshop deliverables. But if the actions agreed to in the workshop are not secured and followed through, the results will not come forth. The *welcome* activity starts

TABLE 6.3   Team Design: Initiating Phase

Initiating: Workshop	Methods	Inputs and outputs
Welcome	Agenda, ground rules	In: Workshop plan Out: Agenda
Team building	Introductions, Team Spirit, Team Handbook, warm-ups, exercises	In: Agenda Out: Team identity
The workshop process	Agenda, discussion	In: Workshop plan, agenda Out: Project goals

the session, with the facilitator discussing the agenda and the ground rules. A warm-up exercise is sometimes used as a team builder, but with design sessions, people are usually ready to work very early on in the workshop.

The other design cycle phases of the workshop are described in depth in each of the formats, and they share much in common with one another. Therefore, in each chapter covering the following formats, the methods and techniques used are described only once, in the first format where they are used. The other commonality is that deliverables are similar in form and intent among the formats—three of the formats deliver a design product in the packaging phase, and the other two deliver plans or decisions, which are also similar in their requirement for follow-up action.

Design methods and deliverables. Multiple deliverables are indicated in each format, with both methods and inputs and outputs indicating guidelines for selecting methods and the dependencies between phases. As guidelines for teams, the methods described for each activity are recommended from experience and research, and these methods have been found to work in the various organizational contexts and development environments described throughout. Other methods can be used by teams with the formats—they are descriptive more than prescriptive. The key to the process is more in the format framework than in the specific methods themselves. As in analysis or programming, an effective framework that works is better than just a list of methods or practices. Structured analysis requires the framework of the function hierarchy, and object-oriented C++ programs would be unworkable without the initially defined framework of classes. As in programming, the *methods* are often defined by the creative practitioner.

Not every deliverable must be produced in its logical entirety, as is sometimes considered desirable in other approaches. Deliverables are initiated in the workshops, designed with participation from the team, and used to gain agreement and understanding. Analysis diagrams can be started within a workshop and completed by analysts outside the team environment. Some deliverables need not be finished within the format itself, such as prototyping, which continues from front-end analysis to design. Prototypes can be built to demonstrate user interface concepts or partial functions, and might never be fully completed during the workshop period. Design documents and CASE diagrams can be completed as individual activities, but should never be exhaustively developed within the workshop.

Zahniser (1993) discusses the operational use of the *90-90 rule* in design work, which supports the recognition that deliverables are not always completed in the workshop. The 90-90 rule describes the situation wherein the first 90 percent of a system effort requires 90 percent of the time, and the remaining work requires the other 90 percent of the time. This principle should be a familiar perspective to any veteran of large systems projects, and serves to illustrate that exhaustive work toward any deliverable erodes productivity at some point. Zahniser points out that the 90-90 principle operates in any system that involves learning, and addresses the need for team learning in the *Design by Walking Around* (DBWA) approach. DBWA uses multiple design views developed using numerous methods—from context and function diagrams to ERDs and prototypes—and iterates among the views during design with an active intention to learn from each view and incorporate the learning into the other design views.

Therefore, while common sense might appear to support developing complete deliverables, experience shows the effectiveness of partial designs. The Team Design cycle allows analysts and designers to produce partial design deliverables, developing complementary views of a design within a workshop. Iteration of the design products is largely conducted outside the workshop, by analysts taking the design products to the next level of detail. But even without this extra level of detail, partial design deliverables can still be brought into the next Team Design phase, as long as they are continually advanced as the team learns more in the following phase.

Design cycle and design language.   The Team Design formats show a *cycle* of activities, with deliverables from one activity serving as inputs for the next. This provides allowance for revision in the next activity, including additions that could not have been envisioned in the preceding phase. Software design is highly iterative—Team Design accounts for this by supporting iteration from one phase in the format (scoping) to the next (visualizing), and by building on the products of the previous phases. This process is built into the workshop approach, and can be leveraged by the team for faster throughput of design work.

Design cycles are evident in most published methodologies, although few of them describe their methods as integrating a cycle of design activities. Most process management or development methodologies describe *phases* or *stages,* but do not map these to a consistent set of similar actions used in most analysis and design work. A recent effort to document cycles of design by Rheinfrank and Evenson (1996) describes the steps identified in the development of what they term *design languages.* Design languages are used by the designers with participants in any domain of design, including product design, architecture, or city planning. Unlike the design cycle described for use in team coordination, design languages are evolutionary, embedded within the cultures of their use, and are typically not revealed. To the extent that they are understood, design languages are highly useful—to the extent that they are undisclosed, they can grow outdated and suppress innovation within an organization or industry. As explained by Rheinfrank and Evenson:

> This habit is particularly dangerous in a time of accelerating change. A business might be in the habit of using a language that no longer allows it to produce products that make sense to customers; thus, it becomes particularly vulnerable to a competitor whose product line suddenly addresses a more appropriate set of needs (p. 70).

The design language process as revealed by Rheinfrank and Evenson involves five steps, discussed briefly here so that correspondences might be made to the Team Design cycle:

1. *Characterization.*   Characterization reveals the underlying assumptions and traditions of the design process. By surfacing assumptions about design and users, designers can bring forward alternatives and create space for new possibilities to arise outside of the traditional design.

2. *Reregistration.*   This activity creates the new working set of assumptions to guide the design process forward. Tasks such as market and field studies and user analysis assist designers in understanding the new set of operating principles to enable creative openings and to guide future design.

    "Results are best when customers, users, engineers, salespeople, and executives can all participate in this reregistration process, since each brings unique and relevant domains of knowledge and experience" (p. 77).

3. *Development and demonstration.*   This activity is described in terms of *developing* the appropriate design language for design work. Development constructs the elements of design to be employed in a design process, through techniques such as scenarios and prototypes. Demonstration provides the space and designed objects for interaction of participants with these new elements.

4. *Evaluation.*   Evaluation provides the opportunity to place the demonstration artifacts in a context of use and get feedback from interaction. Both formal (usability evaluation) and informal (comments on a prototype) processes qualify as evaluation.

5. *Evolution.*   Evolution enables the design language to be modified and extended through learning and continual evaluation.

Evolution allows the design language to change as needed when the business and the context of products change.

The first two steps, *characterization* and *reregistration,* are embodied roughly across *scoping* and *visualizing.* Scoping surfaces design assumptions in the analysis and design formats. Visualizing creates the new set of assumptions and idealized approaches to be incorporated into the design process.

Development and demonstration are represented in Team Design's *usage* phase, as the scenarios and prototypes are created and iterated in the context of understanding of their *use. Evaluation* is found across *usage* and *packaging,* with immediate user feedback and contextual evaluations provided in the usage phase, and more formal evaluation and test planning managed in packaging. A validation phase is specifically provided in the system analysis and design formats, for the formal evaluation of processes and system artifacts. *Evolution* is accommodated in the *validation* phase, but only in the form of design process evaluation as a post mortem for the team. Evolution will probably be driven more by the *users* of Team Design than by methods included for its evolution.

Rheinfrank and Evenson provided one of the first assessments of design languages in their use of the term, and identified the characteristics of general design processes. Essentially, design languages allow new design approaches to become institutionalized in use by a group. The awareness of design language also enables the resulting process to evolve and not become locked in past the point of relevance. Probably the more difficult aspect of integrating new design methods is identifying when they no longer serve their purpose effectively. As Team Design methods might represent a departure for many organizations interested in adopting new approaches to system design, these methods are not presented as rules. Team Design is intentionally flexible, allowing project managers and facilitators to draw from various system design methods as building blocks of a customized design language, a metadesign approach to constructing an effective tailored methodology for the organization.

7

Designing
Business Processes

Reengineering and redesign of business processes have flooded the business book market and made careers for management consultants over the last five years. Whether their management approaches are valid or not, most of them point to the need to evaluate and redesign the basic structure of business processes. The point that remains, regardless of reengineering, is that organizations must constantly evaluate and improve their processes and systems to remain competitive.

Business process design is addressed first in this chapter not because it's a popular topic of interest to business, but due to its necessity as the initial analysis task in information system development. Redesign of business processes must be conceived as the *essential* first phase of any substantial development effort. Not every process must be redesigned radically, as in reengineering, but every process touched by automation or new work requirements must be considered fair game for redesign. Without undertaking the attitude of business process change with the opportunity for new system work, your best system plans are just paving over cowpaths. The first area of concern for a requirements, product, or system team is to review the underlying process that the business relies upon.

Take a look at your current projects in this light. For an accounting process, this might not be such a big deal. For a customer service system, however, the underlying process might be critical to your future success. If your business is moving from a problem-oriented customer service process to a customer-oriented support process, a whole new way of doing business might be designed, changing not only data systems but personnel requirements, organizations, product literature, and every communication that touches a potential customer. Failing to take a strategic business perspective and missing the rare opportunity to create a better process will diminish competitiveness and growth. The business process design approach is primary, and should be integrated to some extent into every workshop where your team is starting fresh. The rest of this section is devoted to methods on how you might do this in your own workshops and development processes.

Process design *should* always be part of business reengineering, and it can also become a state of mind for rethinking business effectiveness. *Reengineering* was originally conceived by Hammer and Champy (1993) as "the fundamental rethinking and radical redesign of business processes to achieve dramatic improvements in critical contemporary measures of performance, such as cost, quality, service, and speed." When Hammer and other reengineering experts discuss business processes, their focus is different than that of a layperson or a typical operations-level manager. Hammer and Champy point out that managers tend to focus on tasks, jobs, people, and structures, and are not naturally oriented toward processes. Business processes represent a complete set of actions that support recurring and consistent transactions, initiated by a customer request or other input and producing an output that is of value to a customer. A business process is composed of jobs, individual tasks, and structures, but is not typically owned by a single organization. Usually, a business process cuts across many functions.

Business process reengineering enjoyed too much publicity for a time, was overly used and misused, and in its public misuse became a euphemism for cost-based restructuring and layoffs. Remember that reengineering was explicitly never intended or designed as a cost-performance or resource-management approach. Reengineering is about creating competitive value through redesign of business processes. Good people with required skills are essential to any business process, and in the approaches discussed in this chapter, these people are typically in the user community, one of your most valuable groups of stakeholders. Davenport (1996) clarifies these issues in an article published on the Internet by the magazine *Fast Company:*

> The most profound lesson of reengineering was never reengineering, but business processes. Processes are how we work. Any company that ignores its business processes or fails to improve them risks its future. That said, companies can use many different approaches to process improvement without ever embarking on a high-risk reengineering project.

This chapter describes a format for teams to perform business process design, whether for redefining core processes, large-scale reengineering, or preliminary system analysis. The format allows for a high degree of flexibility, and your team must determine the extent to which design methods are applied. The message of Team Design is that facilitating a cross-functional team in applying the best appropriate methods enables successful business process design.

Business Process Analysis and Design

Many methodologies have emerged to deal with business process issues. Some techniques were devised specifically for process analysis and workflow, and others already in use have been adapted for business process problems.

The basic model for this format relies on *systems analysis,* a set of mature tools and problem-solving methods useful for analyzing complex systems. Business processes are systems, whether they were designed that way or not. As such, they are amenable to analysis using a number of well-accepted methods. A business process approach does not make the assumption of information technology applications throughout the analysis and design. Instead, a pure process perspective is used, somewhat independent of specific technologies. Software tools and information technology will always be encountered in the journey of design; however, it distracts from our purpose to always think in terms of system solutions. If the purpose is to design or redesign the best-fitting business process for a given business problem, the process is evaluated as coordinated work that supports the business. Introducing information technology too early in the game makes the team vulnerable to jumping to solutions, or to fixing problems with the company's favorite system before the *process* is well understood or well designed.

Finally, even the business process perspective can be abstracted too far, and a cookbook approach cannot be used with much success. Throughout this section the emphasis is placed on the *knowledge of users* and the people involved in the work processes. John Seely Brown, director of Xerox PARC, discusses this concept in an article coauthored with Estee Solomon Gray (1996):

> Processes don't work, people do. Look closely at the inner workings of any company and you'll discover gaps between official work processes—the "ideal" flows of tasks and procedures—and the real-world practices behind how things actually get done. These gaps are not problems that need fixing; they're opportunities that deserve leveraging. The real genius of organizations is the informal, impromptu, often inspired ways that real people solve real problems in ways that formal processes can't anticipate. When you're competing on knowledge, the name of the game is improvisation, not standardization.

Consider this advice when pursuing business process design. Although guidelines and structured methods are discussed in the rest of the chapter, business process work requires creative thinking and a whole-systems viewpoint. Use the chapter as a resource for knowledge and become familiar with several methods that apply to your organization's style. Workshops or unstructured Team Design meetings can both be used; the key is to allow the team to bring its knowledge and creativity to bear on the challenge of redesigning business processes. In the same way that jazz musicians can improvise *because* they know the fundamentals, find the comfort level in your own fundamental methods, and improvise from what already works well.

Workshops for business process design

Business process analysis and design is well suited to workshop work. The team approach is almost mandatory—a large number of stakeholders are often affected by process change, influential managers may have much at stake in process redesign, and the product of the process design might impact numerous downstream functions in the business. The Team Design workshop invites participation and provides methods for engaging in this work. The stages shown in Fig. 7.1 reflect the most general passages of team development work in business process design.

Starting with the initiation stage, the Business Process Design format begins with session planning and workshop kickoff:

- *Preworkshop.* Advance planning and preparation to understand the requirements for the analysis and design effort and to prepare for the workshop.
- *Workshop format.* The basic introduction of the workshop to participants. Establishing a team, setting a vision, agreement on approaches, and scoping the effort.

The following stages follow the basic Team Design model shown in Fig. 7.1:

- *Current process analysis.* Understanding the current business process; analyzing the process and defining its characteristics.
- *Business vision.* Identifying the business value of the process.
- *Process scenarios.* Designing the new business process as a system; team development of business process scenarios.
- *Process design.* Designing the business process as a prototype.
- *Process evaluation.* Evaluating the pilot and refining the design.

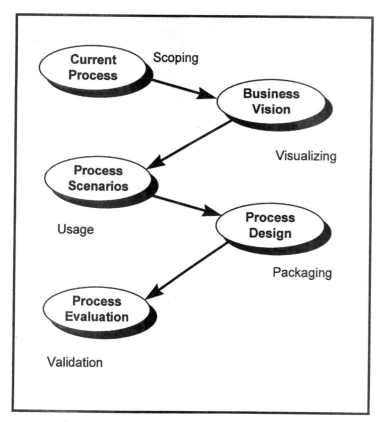

Figure 7.1 Stages in the Business Process Design Format.

Format: Business Process Design

A structure for business process design is implemented by following the format shown in Table 7.1. This format represents the full spectrum of activities that might be conducted for business process analysis and design, and is intentionally comprehensive to allow the practitioner to consider each step as a potential approach. The format can be tailored when planning a workshop, as a guideline for adapting the best methods for the particular team and the workshop goals.

The sections of the format represent the phases of work and actions in business process design. Each phase (in italics) encompasses a set of recommended activities. Each activity (on its own row) has associated *methods* for conducting the activity, and specified inputs and outputs. *Inputs* are requirements, documents, or conditions that must be met to effectively conduct the activity. *Outputs* are products, documents, or conditions created by completing an activity.

TABLE 7.1   **Business Process Design Format**

Agenda activities	Methods	Inputs and outputs
Scoping: Process Context		
Exploring the purpose	Dialogue, brainstorming methods, Breakthrough Thinking	In: Project goals Out: Purposes, mission statement
Defining the scope	Scoping diagram, context diagram	In: Purpose, initial scope Out: Scope definition
Goals for process change	Brainstorming, purposes hierarchy, goal setting	In: Scope definition Out: Process goals
Understanding the current process	Context diagram, physical process model, process mapping	In: Scope definition, process goals Out: Scope, Process diagrams
Visualizing: Business Vision		
Identifying process relationships	Process information flow model, relationship mapping, quality management tools	In: Scope, process diagrams Out: Process models, process relationships, lists
Identifying process opportunities	Value analysis, benchmarking analysis	In: Process relationships and models Out: Process vision
Process design requirements	Breakthrough Thinking methods, brainstorming methods	In: Process models, process vision Out: Process models, initial requirements
Usage: Process Scenarios		
Developing process scenarios	Scenario analysis, scenario design methods, process mapping	In: Initial requirements, process models Out: Process scenarios
Selecting scenarios	Scenario design methods, process mapping	In: Process scenarios Out: Detailed scenario
Documenting scenario design	Scenario design methods, storyboarding, process mapping	In: Detailed scenario Out: Process candidates, scenario process design, process requirements

TABLE 7.1   Business Process Design Format (*Continued*)

Agenda activities	Methods	Inputs and outputs
Packaging: Process Design		
Charting the new process	Process mapping, simple prototyping	In: Process candidates, scenario process design, process requirements Out: Primary process model, simple prototype
Demonstrating the process	Process mapping, interactive prototyping	In: Primary process model, simple prototype Out: Process design proposal
Designing the process	Interactive prototyping, process definition, workflow modeling	In: Process design proposal Out: Process requirements and design, system or process prototype
Validating: Process Evaluation		
Process prototype evaluation	Interactive prototyping Process evaluation planning Prototype evaluation	In: System or process prototype, defined process Out: Evaluated process prototype, evaluation plan

Analyzing and designing business processes

From the traditional perspective of systems or process analysis, a thorough analysis of all functions comprising a system is performed as the first phase of work. In our development life cycle, the *requirements definition* phase contains the activity of *requirements analysis*. Traditional approaches recommend various analysis methods for identifying all important constituents of a process before decisions are made to modify them or design new ones. Analysis has a time-honored place in education, business, and science.

Analysis methods abound in the business and research literature, and methods go in and out of style depending on current fads and publications. As business process reengineering advanced in the mid-1990s, process mapping and comparative benchmarking (*As-is* versus *To-be*) approaches gained in usage, even though these methods had enjoyed years of previous but more limited deployment. Object-oriented analysis gained some favor as a general modeling approach due to the increased usage of object-oriented programming in current systems technologies. However, attempts to generalize object-oriented methods to business processes have not caught on, due to several factors: the diagrams are not readable by laypersons (method complexity), the methods focus on data and not end-to-end processes, and no standard methods are accepted for object-oriented analysis. This chapter covers some of the more prevalent methods, but the reader should be skeptical of adopting any new method until experience has shown its value.

Taking a customer-centric point of view, three considerations arise when selecting a method for business process analysis, especially for use in a workshop:

- Is the method easy to teach and use with a cross-functional group of participants? Does it lend itself to the goals of the workshop, and can all participants pick up its usage quickly? Or is it something the IT staff will use (in the name of "standards") to intimidate the user participants?

- Will the readers of documents resulting from the workshop be able to understand the process and communicate effectively with the process designers? Will the user's management and appropriate executives see the value of process design proposals?

- Will the method communicate effectively to the implementers of the process? Will the downstream customers (IT, systems engineering, and administration) be able to use your process diagrams as their reference for pursuing the proposal?

The precision of the method, its ability to integrate with other methods, or its ability to handle complexity recede in comparison to these criteria. The purpose of the workshop is to engage the thoughts and wisdom of the entire team, not to achieve a technically elegant solution with details veiled by flow arrows and new symbologies. A preliminary model that everyone understands is better than a fully modeled process design that only the IT staff fully understands. Workshops and design sessions are held to build trust and to integrate the process knowledge of the entire team. Use the methods that gain cooperation, maintain trust, and build a solution that the whole team can support.

Regardless of the method used, pursuing too much analysis is counterproductive. Remember that your goal as a team is to arrive at a *design,* which means building the best-fit solution, not spelling out all the problems in the existing process. Analysis of current processes, using process-flow diagrams and decomposition, suffers a mixed profile in the literature. Hammer and Stanton (1994) advise against analysis beyond understanding in reengineering work:

> Unde standing your processes is an essential first step in reengineering, but an analysis of those processes is a destructive waste of time. You must place strict limits, both on the time you take to develop this understanding and on the length of the description you create.

Hammer further suggests the reason for overanalysis:

> The longer we analyze the current ways of operating, the further we fend off that awesome day when we will actually have to change something. Analysis thus becomes a defensive maneuver to avoid making fundamental change (p. 19).

In *Breakthrough Thinking,* Nadler and Hibino (1994) propose the *Limited Information Collection* principle, in which only enough information is collected to serve the team's understanding of the problem. The objective of their principle is to focus on the meaning of the information and not collect data for its own sake. They indicate that "too much information obscures important issues and does not help make the most effective decisions."

A class of process analysis methods models existing business processes using what's called the *As-is* model and designs new processes as represented by a proposed *To-be* process. Two popular methodologies for this analysis are process mapping and the IDEF diagramming methods, both of which call for some representation of current processes using diagrams. Even proponents of these schools of thinking recommend against spending excessive time modeling "as-is," or current, business processes. What becomes excessive varies depending on the size and complexity of the process, but a definite point of agreement is that the majority of the time and creative effort should be spent on designing the new process.

Even considering all this sage advice, it's worth investigating your situation carefully to discern the level of analysis that you might require. Not every current process is simple enough to break down and understand in even a day. Manufacturing, engineering, and other technical processes can be very complex. Administrative processes might have numerous components that have been cobbled onto the original process, making up a spaghetti-like process that can take some time to unravel with clarity. And if you are working as the facilitator of the process analysis, it's important to give all the team members enough time to understand the process so that users, managers, or technical staff are not left with insufficient understanding while the majority of the group moves on. One saving grace of using a Team Design workshop process for analysis and design is that in a workshop your participants will sit still for analysis for only a limited period of time before insisting on progress on the real product, which is a new process. Build the time limitations for analysis into your agenda, and the team will get the hint. Pursue analysis to the point of understanding—but not much further, or you risk having the team become comfortable with the inherent logic of the old process. The momentum for change can be fragile, and organizations tend to be conservative about major process changes. Extended analysis might soon lead to justifications for keeping the old process. The well-designed workshop will prevent this from occurring.

Leading business process design

Business process analysis and design require a different set of skills than are usually found among the information technologists. Facilitating business process work demands a mix of skills and personal attributes not expected for JAD sessions and facilitated meetings. A strong general understanding of business management and concepts coupled with experience in the realities of business environments provides a useful foundation. A deep background in one or several industries, as well as knowledge of standards and operational procedures in these industries, is probably an elementary position for a process design facilitator. Just as in systems analysis and design, the facilitator must understand the methodologies and the format of deliverables to be produced. And an experienced sensibility for business decision making, organizational behavior, and management group dynamics will be critical for long-term facilitation of reengineering teams.

Leadership *and* facilitation are required to advance business process work. The workshop leader must maintain a balance between facilitating of the team and motivating, energizing, and pushing the group to break down barriers to ideas and unlock new ways of thinking.

Technology is not as critical in this stage as the value of rethinking the process. Computer and software technologies will be as much constraining forces as enablers. The enabling value of integrated databases, networking, desktop software, e-mail, and groupware tools might generate a sense of positive and effusive communication. However, the availability of specific technologies, the team's understanding of them, and assumptions about technological directions will greatly influence the way business processes are designed.

The facilitator might be more of a leader in this design role than with other formats. By taking the middle ground, facilitators will understand the environment and all the variables as they are raised in the workshops. They will then be well positioned to make recommendations and to consult on process and staffing issues.

Other roles are required to effect the considerable change envisioned in business process design. The project manager must be experienced and considered as senior. He or she will be accountable for the results of the effort, and will require all the tools and support available. A technical team must be available to support prototyping the application software and the new procedures and organizational changes in the new process. This subteam will make decisions and tradeoffs among components of the ideal process and the realistic capabilities and affordances of the organization. Technical roles should be assigned to both process owners and process users, so that tradeoffs and tools are appropriate and designed for the real tasks in the work process.

Managing and directing cultural change is a challenge for business process redesign or reengineering. Senior management must be fully on board with the program, to the point of being the project champion for the organization. Anything less than top-level support will be insufficient, as major business processes cut across multiple organizations and stir up many unpredictable defenses among those benefiting from the status quo. Irrational opposition to the project will often emerge—and often due to senior management's unwillingness to fully commit to the effort.

Process workshop facilitators and leaders might do well to adopt a profile of skills suggested by management consultants, such as Davenport and Hammer, for managing reengineering efforts. Even as a facilitator, some of the skills associated with reengineering are necessary for understanding the direction to move the group when the team is lacking tools or direction or progress breaks down. Among the characteristics are the following:

Process and systems thinking

- The ability to think and communicate a holistic systems view of the business and its processes; being able to conceptualize the integration of processes into the enterprise
- Understanding the process orientation and the concepts of reengineering, workflow, and organizational structure
- The ability to identify problems (bottlenecks or disconnects) with current processes and to communicate these without attributing blame or causing dissension
- Knowledge of current technologies and tools and the ability to understand and communicate how automation and infrastructure support new processes
- Skill in project management, planning, and coordination

Creativity and design skills

- The ability to think "out of the box," to challenge perspectives, to invent new ways of looking at problems
- Analysis, or the skill of quickly sizing up problems or abstractions and decomposing (analyzing) into understandable components
- The ability to design new ways of performing tasks and of envisioning and communicating new methods for creating value

Personal and interpersonal

- The ability to see beyond personal and organizational factors, to encompass the whole picture and the larger group
- The ability to work as a team member or as a team builder
- Enthusiasm, restlessness, persistence, and optimism for the task
- Flexibility, adaptability, and tolerance for ambiguity
- Tact and precision in communication with others; the ability to listen to anybody, closely and carefully
- The ability to take the lead when needed and to sit out and listen when required
- The ability to encourage, teach, and allow others to make decisions and explore opportunities

In short, facilitation of business process work is not for the faint-hearted, and it is not the best forum for the sensitive, "warm and fuzzy" facilitator. It is energetic, concentrated, and difficult, requiring more leadership capability than the other Team Design formats. This said, the scope of the work is its own reward—facilitators with experience in application design and decision making might invite the opportunities and challenges of the business process redesign project.

Team Process Analysis Cycle

Process analysis is performed to support a goal other than the results of analysis. The team members should clearly identify their goal for analysis during the scoping of the process and the workshop itself. The goal might be to understand the process to better redesign it, to reveal problems in the process to make specific improvements, or to benchmark a successful process as a model to adapt to other processes. The goal is *not* to model the process in detail.

One of the first things to determine with a process that might span multiple business units is the appropriate scope of the problem. Look at the context of the problem and the design goal. How is the process to be deployed—across the corporation, geographically, organizationally, or functionally? The context of the new design will determine the level of analysis for the current process.

Of course, one of the primary considerations is the degree of automation involved. If a manual or partially automated process is slated for a major automation investment, a different approach is taken than if a currently automated process is redesigned. It is usually easier to design, since few dependencies on expensive systems will already be in place. Process analysis for automation must capture certain critical elements, such as customer uses and requirements for the process outcome, use of information and its required flow, and data as used and envisioned.

Automating a process does not always require extensive analysis of the current process. Since all functions of the current process are likely to change with the automation, the team might be free to explore more options and have fewer imposed constraints. Therefore, the functions of the current process need only be understood, and not specified in detail. The detail will likely never be used in the automation design, and system developers will not be interested in the history or logic of the manual process. Save those details for amusement a few years after implementation, when people ask how things were done before. Of course, if automation doesn't go well, the history and logic of the manual process will be brought back up quickly anyway!

Just remember that the goal is a good design, not an excellent analysis. If the goal is to analyze the current process in order to measure it, chances are the process is ineffective as it is, and extensive measurement will not be required. Ask the customers for feedback, those who use the outcome of the process you want to measure. They will tell you if the process is broken, and how you could fix it.

Customer interactions with the business process are crucial to understanding it, and should always be identified and highlighted on any analysis diagram or documentation. The most important aspects of a process redesign are in satisfying customers through the fulfillment of a customer-facing process. When taking on customer-facing processes, the team must invite or, at least, integrate the customer into the proceedings. Depending on the relationship, customers can become full-time team members, especially with government organizations. When planning, consider the best points at which to involve your customer representatives in the various process design tasks.

Is everything in the business a business process? In the zeal of reengineering, many analysts and consultants take such a process-centric perspective that other activities or problems in the business are diminished. This is a natural approach for consultants when the customer appears to be buying process work. However, business processes are fairly abstract, and in the real world a process becomes a coordinated set of activities performed by people in their daily work. Business processes might consist of functions and information when described on paper, but are composed of tasks, job roles, customers, and specific assignments when put into practice.

The details of human work practices—job and task design—must not be overlooked in process analysis and design, regardless of the level of automation. Current work practices serve the organization in highly valuable ways that cannot be easily observed through simple task analysis. People will have organized themselves in informal ways that bring knowledge and value to the organization, and much of this knowledge and learning can be lost when making sweeping changes to work practices. A social scientist on the design team might evaluate the human value of the current process by observing and evaluating the informal networks, conversational venues, and learning approaches used by people currently performing the practice of the work considered for redesign.

Organizational psychologists have been involved with group and team dynamics, training, and organizational planning. More recently, anthropologists and sociologists use ethnographic methods for observing and studying work practices as they occur in their natural environment of work. As explained by Hughes, King, Rodden, and Andersen (1995), many traditional analyses conducted in the service of process and systems design are engineering-based, and do not reflect the real work environment activities. "The result...is that essential aspects of the socially organized character of the domain concerned are obscured or, worse, misrepresented." Ethnographic methods have evolved from strictly research usage, and have been used recently in system design, particularly in requirements elicitation by informing designers of the real-world characteristics of the work process. In highly complex work where ethnography has been used, such as air traffic control, extensive knowledge of the work has been gained that would not be available with other methods. References are made throughout the bibliography sources to the use of ethnographic methods for analysis and design work in software development, process design, and collaborative systems design.

The Workshop Approach.   When using a Team Design *workshop,* a preliminary phase is added to the workshop plan. *Initiating* is used for teambuilding and to support the kickoff, and can be treated as a team-building phase. Each major workshop or new project team should have the opportunity for team integration fostered by this phase. Chapter 5 discusses workshop and team-building processes, and Chap. 6 describes the integration of team-building activities into planning and the formats.

Process analysis in advance of the workshop

As a facilitator, you might not be required to pursue process analysis in advance of the workshop; in fact, you could argue that it will bias your objectivity by accumulating too much detailed knowledge. As a consultant or organizer, this advance work will be common practice, and the information gathered and interpretations made must feed into the design workshop.

Especially if pursuing process automation, your understanding of the overall process, its strengths and weaknesses, and any existing automation will be necessary. Evaluate the process as a start-to-finish flow of work, and identify triggers that kick off activities, stoppages of workflow, and points of completion and handoff to other processes.

Initial interviews should be held with management owners of the process, and managers who will hold responsibility for the new process or automated system. Identify their goals, management drivers, strategy, and related objectives for the business process. Conduct interviews with key individuals and small groups to gain multiple perspectives on the process. Talk to key user representatives and their managers, and hold interviews with their customers, if possible. Hold these interviews before interviewing the users in the trenches, since you'll need clearance to get free access to people in the first place, and you'll want to know the official story of the process first. Interviews should not last more than half an hour, up to an hour only if your subject is truly engaged in the topic. Your efficient and courteous use of others' time will be appreciated. And you'll notice after interviewing more than four or five participants that common themes and similar areas are discussed. Regardless of the amount of time spent in each interview, your coverage of a fair sample of participants, stakeholders, and managers is key. Focus on open-ended questions that draw out elaboration, such as the following:

- How would you describe the business processes of interest? What are the goals of the business related to this process?

- What will redesigning the process achieve? What problems should the design team address? What would a successful redesign look like to you?

- In the current process, what works and what doesn't work? Why do you think so?

- Who owns the current process, and who should own the new process? How should the user's jobs be changed to work better with the new process?

- What are the key performance indicators or metrics for the process? What are the drivers—customer satisfaction, cost, efficiency, value, or sustainable growth?

- How should the process best be automated, in your opinion? What tools should be available for users of the new process?

Following the manager- or representative-level interviews, arrange interviews or discussion sessions with different process or application users across a range of task roles. A *contextual* interview approach is an appropriate method for eliciting real-life discussions of jobs and tasks as they are actually performed. Have some of the users walk you through a scenario or simple example of their tasks using the current application or process. Ask questions to understand the exceptions and workarounds to the standardized process used in their work. Questions appropriate to understanding business processes at the task level include the following:

- What is the primary job or process you perform? What other tasks do you perform that are secondary to this one or that you have picked up through your expertise?

- What are the different computer applications used in your job? How often do you use each one? Which is the most critical to the outcome of your job, and why?

- In your most critical task, can you describe for me the different steps required to perform the task from start to finish? Are all of these steps normally performed? Why or why not?

- Are unnecessary steps required in your work, such as entering data more than once or entering data that's not really needed by anybody? Why do you think this is the case?

- What causes the most time delays in your job? What could be done with information before it gets to you to make your job easier or faster?

- Of all the computer software you use at work or at home, what products or tools do you like to use best? Why—what features or capabilities do they offer?

Work to uncover problems and frustrations as people describe their current processes. Elicit their ideas and suggestions for improving or fixing the overall process. Discuss their requirements, vision, wishes for automation, or any new application proposals. Ask what the *ideal* system would be, what capabilities would make their job easier, more productive, or more enjoyable.

During the interview sessions, ask for copies of currently used forms and reports. Print any online reports and make notes as necessary. Be sure the data shown on the forms and reports is representative of the process. During the interview process, determine the process-critical information and identify any useless information. Also identify missing information that will assist in improving the process when it becomes available to the new application.

Process analysis in the workshop

Analyzing process information in your own office with your notes, source materials, and references is a tempting proposition. In relative isolation it's a much cleaner exercise to plod through the process variables and draw elegant diagrams describing "how it is" and "how it will be." This is also the method most analysts choose, and for good reason—you avoid conflict, messy disagreement, and alternative opinions. Which is exactly why new business processes should *not* be created in this way.

As inviting as it is, the risks are too great. A revised large-scale business process affects everybody in the organization, not just the managers and users in that process or the affected organizations. Cooperation and buy-in from the other organizations are essential to acceptance of the process. You will also find that the knowledge and insight of the hands-on users in the "process community" are necessary to design a full-featured process that makes sense to the stakeholders. The workshop approach is justified by the participation, team creativity, and buy-in generated from the active inclusion of stakeholders and organizational representatives.

So you've got the team together, what do you do next? Start with what they know and understand by analyzing the current process.

Rapid current process analysis.   Start by moving the group members through their comfort zone using a rapid analysis of the current business process. Since it's familiar territory, everyone on the team will be able to contribute something of value, leading to fast engagement of their attention and teamwork. Keep the process moving quickly— don't allow the group to make a career out of breaking down the current process.

The basic approach in a current process analysis starts by identifying both *organizations* and *systems* that support the process. Identifying organizations leads to analyzing the users and their roles, tasks, and flow of information. Identifying systems supports analysis of data, input and output, and upstream and downstream systems. As a team, diagram the most important of these procedures and elements, and collaboratively build a model of the process. This model should reveal redundant activities (if they exist), ineffective use of systems and people, and any obvious problems in the process.

However, most processes do not contain *obvious* problems (or they would have been fixed by now). Process problems are not easily detected from modeling just the subject process in isolation—problems emerge more from the relationship of the process to new business goals, or to other systems in the business where data or customers are handled differently. The single process is not the problem, but the interaction of an old process with new requirements could be the problem.

The rapid process analysis aims to uncover the basic conflicts in the old process, which often requires a ground-up redesign of the process, as opposed to process improvement. To get to the basic conflicts, work both top-down and bottom-up. Start with a top-down view by diagramming the process as currently understood, and list or note the goals and outputs of the process. Identify any quality and performance criteria, and note on the diagram wherever these requirements fail in the process.

Then move to a bottom-up view. One way of identifying activity-level problems that are critical to process performance is to focus on the impact to the customer. Whether the process supports an internal or external customer, it will only exist to satisfy the requirements of some customers who depend on it for value. Have the team identify the customers in the process, and show them prominently on the diagram. Ask the team to identify all the *customer-facing* activities in the process. These are all the points at which the performers in the current process have contact with any customer, directly or indirectly, through communications media, or by responding to requests or submitted forms. Especially if an output to the customer is required from the process, these points are the key to process breakthroughs.

Several methods for process analysis and diagramming are described in this section, any of which will support a rapid analysis exercise. The best method for use in a Team Design workshop is one you are already skilled at using. If they are not familiar, use a basic flowchart or process-mapping approach, due to their simplicity and ease of adaptation to any unique requirements of your project.

Team business process design.   Start with a description of the current business process, using the diagram from the previous activity as a model. Analytically tear apart the current process, inviting participation by using both analysis and creative ideation exercises.

One way to initiate new thinking about the old process is to investigate variations of the process—for example, by having the group break into subteams assigned to produce three new variations of their section of the process diagram. During this exercise, list the following characteristics of the current process:

- Different user roles and valuable competencies in the process
- Tools used by different users
- Good aspects of the process—things to keep
- Problems in the process—things to revise

Holtzblatt and Beyer (1993) address the issues of work redesign from the perspective of *contextual inquiry,* a methodology for deeply investigating and understanding user work processes. They describe some of the questions this methodology seeks to resolve, as well as their approach for process modeling and design.

> Working with specific customers gives the team an understanding of the work of those customers. However, we want an innovative design that transforms work in new ways and is useful to all our customers. How do we invent such a transformation? How do we ensure we have transformed the work usefully? (p. 94).

Holtzblatt and Beyer discuss how every system changes the work for the community of users for which it's directed. Their recommendation is to "design the effect you want your system to have explicitly."

> We make this conversation explicit through abstract work models. We gather all the same kind of models together: all the flow models, all the physical models, and the sequence models that address each task....Anything the team chooses not to represent will not be supported by the system. This abstraction allows us to meet the needs of a whole market by building on what we have discovered from individuals (p. 96).

Many process design methods can be used of course, but the goal of this section is to assist you in moving your team forward, not necessarily in working a certain process method in full precision or in building the perfect model. When starting the design phase of business process redesign, first impressions are powerful. The basic concepts the group falls into agreement with will eventually guide the new process. It's difficult to scrap a foundation built on team agreement, even when competent new thinking about the process persuades a revisiting of your work. Because of this phenomenon at the start of a design, consider using several divergent methods at a fairly shallow level rather than one or two approaches in depth. The discussion of scoping methods that follows addresses ways of creating a number of related models appropriate during the initial definition of the process scope and purpose.

TABLE 7.2   Business Process Design: Scoping Phase

Scoping: Process context	Methods	Inputs and outputs
Exploring the purpose	Dialogue Brainstorming methods Purposes hierarchy	In: Mission statement, project goals Out: Purposes
Defining the scope	Scoping diagram Context diagram	In: Purpose, initial scope Out: Scope definition
Goals for process change	Brainstorming methods Breakthrough Thinking methods Goal setting	In: Scope definition Out: Process goals
Understanding the current process	Context diagram Physical process model Process mapping	In: Scope definition, process goals Out: Scope, process diagrams

Scoping: Process context

Scoping activities require the group to discuss the purposes and goals of the process, and to come to agreement about the extent and limits of the effort. Often, project scope is determined through project planning; process scoping is conducted up front to better understand the business problem and the context of work to be performed, both in workshops and in support of the project. The scoping phase structure is shown in Table 7.2.

Exploring the purpose.   Business process design requires the team to define and evaluate the purposes of every function and task in the scope. Exploring the purpose of the process and its support systems allows identification of all the goals, assumptions, and opportunities of the process design up front. The group's involvement in exploring the purpose enables the healthy questioning and breaking apart of operating assumptions and policies that underpin the process.

This step is built into the agenda as an early activity, and provides a different context than other analysis processes that assume a given purpose. Having an agreed purpose is necessary before any relevant envisioning for the new process can emerge from the team. Some of the more "practical" team members might balk at revisiting what they consider a given purpose. However, team definition of the purpose gains agreement on the scope and guides the team's direction.

The facilitator can use several methods to engage the team in investigating purposes. This critical first step sets the scope and style for all future work together, and team relationships are solidified with these initial exploratory exercises. In reengineering projects, a defined scope or process is typically specified for the team's focus, and the team starts with inputs provided by management or research teams. These inputs are the starting point for serious defining of purposes, but are not the purpose as such. The methods discussed in the following sections provide some ideas for pursuing the purpose to achieve a shared understanding of process goals and purposes among the team members.

Brainstorming methods. Brainstorming methods can easily be used in team definition of purposes. Use a facilitated brainstorming method such as Round Robin to engage the team in considering the various purposes of the business process to be defined or redesigned. This is the first step in scoping, and helps define direction of the effort to follow, so it's worth considering all the possible purposes of the process within the business. The Round Robin method (as also described in Chap. 5) follows:

1. State the purpose of the brainstorming session (to identify the purposes of the system), and describe how the session will be conducted.

2. Solicit brainstorming inputs from the group, one person at a time. Continue the process until no further inputs are forthcoming.

3. Capture all ideas on the board or easel charts. After receiving all ideas from the group, clarify any that might require it.

4. Create groups from the ideas based on categories suggested by the team members. Have them generate the names and assign ideas to the groups.

5. Finally, have the team rank the ideas for further organization, either within groups (if many ideas) or across all groups (if fewer than 30 altogether). Use a group voting process for ranking.

Breakthrough Thinking.® The Breakthrough Thinking approach utilizes the *purposes principle,* a way of looking at the "problem space" to clarify the scope and purposes for a project. The purposes principle is based on the assumption that much effort can be saved if the initial purpose is defined precisely. Many technology-based solutions have been forced upon organizations to solve problems that were not well thought out. Nadler and Hibino (1994) point out ways to avoid these potential traps of overanalysis and "technology push":

> The purposes principle gives you a mechanism for seizing the opportunity to transform a problem into productive change. It provides a mechanism to avoid working on the wrong problem. But obstacles steeped in historical methods of problem-solving must be overcome. People tend to accept a problem as presented to them and, in doing so, almost assuredly eliminate the opportunity for a breakthrough solution. Accepting the

problem as given often leads to an "obvious solution," which is *not* a breakthrough, but which frequently gives rise to other problems. A *purposes* orientation helps you avoid being sold a solution to the wrong problem (p. 132).

The steps in building a purposes hierarchy using the purposes principle are as follows (adapted from Nadler and Hibino, 1994):

1. *Identify the stakeholders.* Locate the people your team must count on to learn about the domain, and their needs and purposes. Relying on those who know is a consistent recommendation in teamwork methods.

2. *Expand the purposes.* Ask questions of the stakeholders (and team) to challenge the problem as it was first presented. Ask people to describe the true nature of the business, to propose the purpose behind the obvious. Ask about your customers, and their customers, *why we're here.* Push the team to think about the real problem.

3. *Construct a set (or hierarchy) of purposes.* Nadler and Hibino suggest beginning with the *perceived need* of the group, such as "to develop a customer service system." Start building an array of purposes from this point, expanding the scope of each statement slightly until you arrive at a series of purposes (or functions). These should be worded very briefly with a verb and subject, and ordered in a hierarchy of *scope.* They suggest building purposes well beyond the possible solutions. For example:

   - To develop a customer service system
   - To support customers in solving product problems
   - To enable complete productive use of our products
   - To fully serve our customers
   - To support a better life for our customers and employees

4. *Establish criteria for selecting the primary purpose.* The criteria allow the team to focus on the appropriate purpose. Investigate the criteria for selection based on organizational needs and resources. These are constraining factors, and might include budget limits, timelines, human resource availability, and other resources.

5. *Select the focus purpose.* The criteria are applied to the largest scope purpose statement, and follow down the line until a purpose statement passes. This purpose is described as an *opportunity,* not just a problem to solve. Multiple purpose statements can be selected, if the increments of scope are fairly narrow.

6. *Define any measures of success or purpose objectives.* As you

reach this point, the exercise moves you into defining the target purpose and identifying measures of success, with measurable objectives for accomplishment. Objectives with critical success factors provide targets for realistic effort and planning.

The purposes hierarchy effectively moves the team members into thinking broadly about their reason for being, and evokes an expanded view of what's called the *problem space,* the dimensions of the problem or opportunity. Because its six steps generate objectives and success measures, it also handles the next two activities in the format, *defining the scope* and *goals for process change.*

The purposes principle exercise can involve the group for anywhere from two hours to two days. An entire workshop can be built around just exploring the purpose in this way, and for missions the business depends on, the time can be well spent. The world-class financial institution Visa International spent a year developing a purposes and principles statement—serious organizations take this work seriously. For the average business process, the purpose of the process leads into scope definition.

Defining the scope. Defining the process scope can be accomplished using one or more of the techniques described in Chap. 5, including the scoping and context diagrams. These diagramming methods are useful during the beginning stages of process analysis and design, when the team is gaining a common understanding of the domain.

Facilitators might start with the purposes hierarchy exercise to gain buy-in and direction, and to create a conducive creative thinking environment for the possibilities of process design. Developing analysis diagrams too early in the process leads to constraining ideas and narrowing the scope and purpose, closing off solutions before they ever get a chance to evolve. The purposes hierarchy exercise leads to rethinking the process and scope from multiple perspectives before the scope is finally locked in.

The team defines the scope using various tools to elicit the various perspectives. The facilitator can start with the purpose, and lead the team in diagramming the components and relationships that arise from that purpose. The scoping diagram from Chap. 5 (Fig. 5.2) provides a practical way to draw viewpoints from the group, and to work with an evolving scope throughout the workshop. The context diagram can be used as the next logical step, a more descriptive diagram that captures the various actions, dependencies, and work products driving the process. As the scope becomes further defined, a process hierarchy diagram supports a formal specifying of functions, their names and relationships.

If your team is using a BPR methodology, other approaches might be used to move into the next phase of work. For example, in Davenport's (1993) approach a process vision is derived from business strategy, with a strong emphasis on customer input into the process vision. Customer inputs take on different roles depending on the organizational context, but their usefulness is unquestioned. Customer inputs should always be part of the context diagram, for example. The process vision becomes organized into process objectives (change and performance targets and customer requirements) and process attributes (process operation and information). Davenport's visioning process fits directly into the next activity, *goals for process change,* and leads as well into the Team Design visualizing phase. Look at your own methodologies to determine how they might fit into the facilitated team process in a similar way.

Context diagram. A context diagram can also be used as a starting point for the new process, just to get the group thinking in a common direction. The context diagram describes the environment in which the new process will fit, hence its name. This is different from the context diagram you might remember from dataflow diagramming, in that it shows only the context but does not decompose into constituent functions.

The purpose of the context diagram is to communicate the organizational and policy functions in the environment of the business process. Context diagrams can be utilized as representations of work procedures, customer relationships, internal process events, expectations and directives, and management or informal work requirements. Using a context diagram the team can communicate the impact of process redesign alternatives, using a common model as a baseline. At a very high level, the team can identify how impacts to one organization, role, or function can modify work processes, deliverables, or customer expectations.

The context diagram shown in Fig. 7.2 is similar to the scoping diagram process, but more information is added to the model. In this use of a context diagram, the process to be redesigned is the overall process of product support. The environment of product support encompasses the three business functions that interact to provide support to customers (users). Transactions are shown by labeled unidirectional arrows, as between users and the help desk. The basic help desk process is described by the steps listed, and exceptions and relationships with engineering (to report system bugs) and system administration (to handle immediate fixes) are documented. A context diagram such as this provides a useful overview of the process, and generates the common understanding of a business process from which to work.

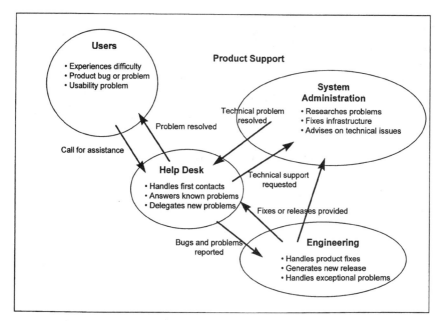

Figure 7.2   Context diagram.

The context diagram is a useful method for all four organizational contexts (business, systems, user, and product). As the team's definition of development context, the context diagram can portray the values or point of view of the team. In the example in Fig. 7.2, a user-centric perspective of the process is illustrated. The user and product contexts focus primarily on these aspects of use. A systems context might focus on the support systems used and data passed from each entity. A business context might add organization and manager names, or performance measures. Selection of the entities shown on the diagram illustrates the primary subjects of analysis, and transactions depicted reflect the team's top considerations for the design. Remember that process representations such as this are not "true" or necessarily accurate. They are useful interpretations of the focus and the affordances of analysis and design; that is, they show what we want to redesign and what's *allowable* in the scope to support our work. This and the other tools in this section support a common understanding that allows the team to work more deeply into the design problem.

Goals for process change.   Many of the goals for process change will have been identified through the purposes hierarchy exercise and scoping discussions, and from the initial direction for process change from management. However, if the goals are documented too early in the process analysis, they could limit the scope of inquiry. The team should not lock down its analysis too early, and revisiting goals as a *subset* of purposes can give the team time to learn and think. The goals for process change define the required targets and business opportunities available in the process redesign. This exercise asks the question "What should our goals look like given our purpose?" Unlike measurable business objectives, these goals should be more high-level statements of direction, defining needed changes, customer-related goals, and aspects of the current process to retain. These goals comprise the type of statement that might be handed to an executive to describe the purpose of the team.

The workshop methods described in Chap. 5 indicate several paths to generating goals with the group. Any of these might be effectively used, and combinations of the methods can lead to deeper inquiry. The following methods are typically involved:

- The *dialogue* approach (from Senge) can be used with teams that want to seriously engage multiple perspectives within a larger cross-functional team.

- Brainstorming and prioritizing goals is a more structured method to elicit all the *possible* team goals. Variations of brainstorming can be used as described in Chap. 5. If appropriate, the team might group or prioritize the goals.

- Goal-setting exercises, developing goals by following a structured exercise, starting from the problem statement or the vision.

As goals are defined, clarify with the group about whether some goals are actually purposes, business objectives, milestones, or visions. Goals are more useful when they are described at the same level of generality, with similar expression of detail. When a few good examples (as agreed to by the team) have been established, use these examples to guide the discussion and definition of the other goals.

Understanding the current process. The last step in scoping analyzes the current business process to an initial level of understanding. Workshop time is not used to analyze the process to extensive depth, but to map out the process in a team environment to build a shared understanding of the business process before engaging in redesign.

Two approaches might be taken by the team at this point. A level of shared understanding might be created by rapidly developing current process diagrams, using one or more methods of description. During this approach, the current process is analyzed only to the level of necessary understanding, which varies depending on the complexity of the process and the project needs. Scoping and context models used in the previous steps contribute to this understanding of the business process, and perhaps only minimal additional analysis is called for. Physical process diagrams and current process models are useful for this approach.

The second approach is to pursue a deeper analysis of current processes, using multiple methods to represent the different views and constituents of the process. Physical, workflow, and business-function models might be developed in this approach. A representative view of the current process, *horizontal process mapping,* can be taught to the team and used throughout the workshops. In this modeling approach, a sequenced mapping of the current business process is developed. An as-is model, representing the current process, can be developed and later compared to to-be process design models. For complex processes with numerous systems, tasks, interfaces, and other process relationships, this more extensive analysis provides a broad view of the process that facilitates redesign of all these components.

The following sections describe these modeling methods, all of which can be used during scoping, visualizing, and throughout the business process design. In following chapters, these methods will be referenced back to this section, rather than repeating the method description for a different use.

Physical process models.   When speaking of processes in a mixed group, each member will initially form a different mental picture of "the process." One of the most basic methods for creating a common understanding of process is to build a model representing the physical components of a defined area in the organization. Some people prefer working on a more concrete level than dealing with more abstract processes, such as information flow. By defining the physical components of a given process, those preferring the concrete orientation have a baseline of the process mechanics to which they can refer throughout the analysis. Of course, it's also a useful, if not essential, approach to constructing the model of the current infrastructure and physical systems supporting the current process, as well as any to be designed. The business and user contexts should typically create a physical process model to share a common understanding of the process infrastructure. Those working in the systems context might always develop such a model, albeit a strongly technical version. The product context might not use physical models at all.

Internal systems and infrastructure supporting the process are represented using physical process models. These diagrams describe the physical office or work environment with the equipment, networks, and machines used to support the process. Physical models can define an excessive amount of detail—try to scope the amount of resolution required to address your problem. If the physical layout of offices and shared equipment such as printers and copiers is not important to your design problem, they could be left out of the physical model. On the other hand, if proposing significant changes in the design of work, anything impacted by the design should be included. For example, if the new process requires scanning documents into computer-readable files, the proposed location of scanners in the office layout is important.

A physical process model is presented in Fig. 7.3, showing a systems context view of the physical structure of a process. Four office locations are illustrated, showing the critical components for the product-support design problem started in the context diagram (Fig. 7.2). The computer and networking infrastructure is shown (again at a high level in this example) as the basis for understanding the availability of existing supporting systems and possible technical solutions. If the product-support system is to be analyzed and redesigned, understanding the infrastructure might lead to the best ideas for the new process. For example, the current process requires that phone calls arriving at the help desk be logged and passed on to support specialists. Exceptional problems require a service specialist to remedy the problem at the customer site. The physical model enables a technological solution allowing customers to report problems and receive support directly through the network, using electronic communications and remote access.

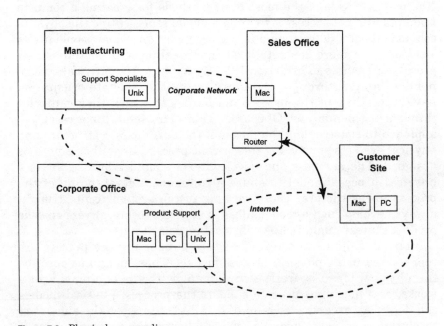

Figure 7.3 Physical process diagram.

Physical models might also be developed to show the physical flow of work around offices, plants, and locations. The point of view of the diagram is the critical distinction of this view, that of representing how systems, work, or processes are currently carried out in the physical world, with a minimum of abstraction. This diagramming approach is not always needed during an analysis, but becomes useful when the team evaluates the effectiveness of current procedures and discusses how work is currently carried out, including associated systems and infrastructure.

Horizontal process mapping.   Horizontal process mapping creates a highly readable visualization of the business process. Many variations of the process map are found, but the basic idea is simple. The horizontal process map captures the activities of the process *across* the organizations or business functions that contribute to the defined process. Anything or any group that provides an input or uses an output along the chain of events is shown as a flow from left to right. Without regard to organizational hierarchy, the horizontal process maps define a neutral view of the process that can usually evoke agreement from a heterogeneous team of managers and users.

The simplest horizontal mapping method is the *process flow diagram,* as previously described with the task sequential diagram and the different flowcharts. Although these simple methods are excellent for making progress in understanding a process or performing initial analysis, they do not provide the precision or information available using other techniques. A more expressive set of tools for defining process information are the process maps developed by the Rummler-Brache Group (1989).

The Rummler-Brache methodology for process management emphasizes a cross-functional horizontal mapping approach. Using three types of diagram structures, the Rummler-Brache business process modeling approach fits the requirements for designing all but the most complex enterprise processes. The diagrams include the following:

- *Relationship map.*   The model of current organizational relationships, using a customer-supplier chain.

- *Is-map.*   The as-is model of the current business process, developed to understand the way things are done today.

- *Should-map.*   The new process model, which takes shape over iterations of process design.

Each of these three constructs provides value, but for the most effective application, all should be used together as a process design methodology. The three diagram types are generally used in sequence, with the relationship map and is-map used first to describe the current business processes, organizations, and constraints. The should-map encompasses the redesign of the process.

While these analysis methods can be used as part of a process reengineering effort, they have been designed more specifically for process *improvement*. Big gains in productivity and effectiveness can be made using the disciplined methods of process mapping, even with a process improvement scope. If tackling a reengineering project, these diagram types can be used to document the analysis and design conducted. Remember from the sections on reengineering, though, that a more radically oriented approach must be taken for a total redesign. Some methodologists argue that spending time analyzing the current state of affairs distracts the team from conducting a clean-sheet approach to the process. These are factors your team must determine, based on project goals and the extent to which deeply engrained problems or issues exist in the business process.

When working with a team using these methods, an important concept to communicate is how the process or organization works together as a *system*. As with end-to-end processes, an organizational system moves forward when a trigger event kicks off a chain of internal events. The entire organization interacts as necessary to coordinate the production of an output of value to the (usually external) customer. Thinking in terms of a holistic system supports the reasoning required to design an effective new process that takes full advantage of the competencies of the business.

For each of these mapping methods, the same type of analysis and diagramming process is used. A cross-functional approach is taken, as opposed to a strictly linear flow through the steps. That is, organizational functions are shown for each diagram, showing any level of the organization as appropriate for the map. Although an abstract process flow is diagrammed, the map can show how information, activities, and materials flow through the process as a system. And, since it is a systems approach, the inputs, outputs, actions, and decisions are integrated into the flow. Standard flowcharting symbols are used, and activities and most flow arrows are labeled.

The relationship map starts off the process analysis from the organizational perspective. The scope of the process and the business problem (or *critical business issue*) is identified in advance of relationship mapping. The mapping process begins by identifying and diagramming the functional organizations of the business, independently of the process itself. Organizations and their functions are arranged on the diagram space, and then relationships are indicated. The relationships are flow lines drawn among the organizations, reflecting the customer-supplier relationship between them. For example, between design and manufacturing the relationship (or output handed off to manufacturing) might be *completed design.* Relationships show the dependencies and deliverables among organizations only at this very high level.

Process mapping continues with the is-map, or the current business process as described by the team. *Is-map* is Rummler-Brache's term for the process *analysis,* in which current business activities are analyzed in a start-to-finish manner, to be used as a baseline for process design. The flow of activities is represented on the horizontal map from input to output, identifying relationships to organizations and systems. Typical activity completion times are often defined, to be used as a metric in evaluating the redesign. During the first rough cuts of the diagram, *disconnects* in the process are identified, where delays or miscommunications occur. A value-added activity analysis is performed to identify where undesired redundancy occurs or where activities do not provide business value. The is-map is typically defined by the team, reviewed by different specialists outside of the team setting, and revised through an iterative cycle until a model is described that gains general agreement.

The *should-map* completes the cycle of analysis and design by defining the new activities replacing or revising the current process. Identical diagramming methods are used in defining the should-map, providing readability among all the diagram types. The should-map is built in iterations over a period of time, using scenarios and team exercises to review the effectiveness and robustness of the model against possible business conditions. A typical process design cycle might require up to 10 iterations or revisions of the model, testing each change against scenarios reflecting critical business possibilities. The following sections describe how the diagrams are constructed in their use as process models.

Relationship map. The *relationship map* provides the organizational process view of interactions occurring among business functions. To develop the relationship map, first refer to the scope diagram, affinity or other charts, and discuss the scope of the process to be defined. A set of current organizational charts will also be useful, to correctly identify departments in the organization. Establish agreement on the bounds or scope of the process, and draw out the participating departments in the process. Use a simple rectangular box to represent the organization or business function, and identify several that have a known significant relationship.

Adopting the systems perspective, evaluate the organizations involved in this process and identify the key events or triggers that put the process in motion. Usually, the event is in the form of an

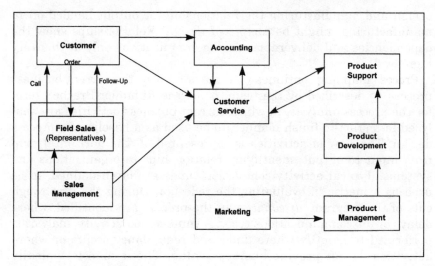

Figure 7.4   Relationship map.

external requirement or customer request, requiring some response
from the business. This can be considered to be an external entity or
it could be an internal function. Draw a box to represent this entity
and have the team consider its input into the organizational system.
Draw a flow line between the entity and the first function with which
it interacts. Label the flow line to identify the event or requirement
indicated by the entity. The example diagram in Fig. 7.4 shows this
entity as the customer and the interacting events as *sales call* and
order. (Typically, *order* would be the only event required to be shown,
since it is the trigger.)

Lay out the other organizational functions on the diagram. Use the
organization chart to identify and name the functions, and to understand current reporting relationships (which, although not critical for
process flow, are necessary for understanding political and management influences on the process). Review the functions with the team,
and identify the products, deliverables, or outputs developed by each
function for use by its customer function.

Walk through the steps of the normal process following the flow of
the input (order) through the various organizational functions.
Consider how each function deals with the information or input as it
arrives and adds value to the process before sending it through the
systems as an output. Trace the flow of this single input through the
system until arriving at the natural product or output of the process.
Identify and show other major inputs along the path as needed, such
as administrative information, payment, or service requests, as
shown in the example.

Rummler-Brache recommend diagramming an initial draft of the relationship map to draw out the majority of the functions and their key relationships. They suggest making the diagram more readable by cleaning up the draft to show the left-to-right flow of the inputs and outputs, and to reposition boxes to minimize clutter and line crossing. Grouping functions into primary and support functions across the diagram is also recommended as a way of separating the important information from the more peripheral.

As with the other diagramming methods, the suggested follow-up procedure is to quickly review the diagram with others in the team and outside as necessary, gaining additional feedback on its effectiveness and accuracy. Revise the diagram at least once—multiple revisions, if done quickly, do not distract from progress. You will be surprised at what was missed in the first draft. Iterations are necessary to develop a more true model of the process.

Current process map. The *is-map* is the next step in the process-mapping methodology. Where the relationship map shows the network of organizational dependencies, the is-map represents the current process flow. The is-map and should-map methods were derived from the quality management viewpoint, and using this "before and after" approach is recommended as a means of identifying quality issues and recommending improvements. The is-map method shows flaws in the current process, called *disconnects,* and enables the team to evaluate productivity and cycle time.

The relationship map provides a useful mechanism for starting the is-map, but is not necessary. The is-map can be developed as an independent diagram by engaging the team directly in analyzing the current process. The minimal source information for the is-map includes a statement of scope and identification of the process from which to start. Several is-maps can be developed by the team if a larger scope is undertaken, one for each specific process that has a defined flow from inputs to output.

The is-map is built like a flowchart, with organizational dependencies indicated by horizontal lines across the chart. Although the diagram models cross-functional processes, the functions are clearly shown as a way to identify responsibility and workflow. Refer to the example in Fig. 7.5, where the is-map shows a simple process flow for soliciting customer feedback. The figure shows all the organizations touched by the process, even those that are not directly involved for this process flow. Organizational functions are included for the purpose of analysis, allowing the team to discuss and determine whether they have involvement or not. If the process flow is expanded during analysis, the other organizations might show involvement as the team expands the scope. When developing the should-map, if these

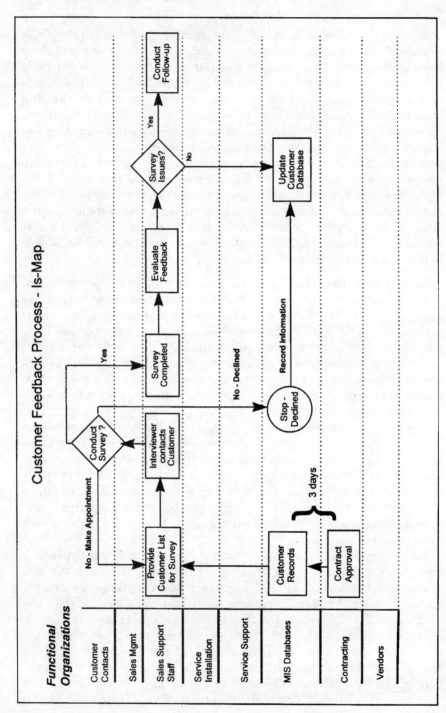

Customer Feedback Process - Is-Map

Figure 7.5 Is-map.

organizations become involved in the new process, it is useful to show their lack of involvement in the current process.

The is-map shows system disconnects, which are problems or flaws identified in the process flow. Disconnects are considered to be the sources of dissatisfaction or unacceptable performance in cycle time, cost or performance value, or product quality. These are flaws internal to the process itself. Disconnects are discovered by analyzing the inputs, outputs, and internal logic of the process. For inputs and outputs to the flow, the team is asked to find the following:

- Missing inputs or outputs
- Substandard inputs or outputs
- Late (or too early) inputs or outputs
- Inputs or outputs that do not add value

Within the process flow itself, the logic of the steps is ruthlessly evaluated. Everything about the process is questioned:

- Are all the existing steps required? Why or why not? What would happen if we changed the way we conducted any of the steps?
- Are any of the steps redundant, or is value duplicated by accident or by design?
- Are the steps logical? Could the process be simply reorganized to flow more smoothly? Do all the sequences of steps make sense? Could they be automated today?
- Is there anything missing from any steps in the flow? Should something be added?
- Where does the process hang up? What types of bottlenecks typically occur? Where does the customer wait, or what paper flows or material lead times cause delays?

Finally, have the team evaluate disconnects in the process *execution,* or its management effectiveness. Are all the steps in the process managed or performed efficiently by the staff involved? Are workers overloaded, or are the steps carried out by part-timers? Evaluate the impact of organizational and resource conditions on the process. Often, exceptions in the process caused by resource issues lead to overall process ineffectiveness. A well-designed process should not be scrapped due to resource management problems.

The goal of the is-map is to describe the process in just enough detail to identify problems, disconnects, and redundancies in the process flow. The overall goal is to redesign the process, however, and this endgoal must be kept in sight while conducting current process analysis. Sometimes the problems in a process are not clear—but you would probably not select a process that didn't call for significant improvement. Finally, the process itself might be completely redesigned as part of reengineering or automation. The very purpose of the process should be reevaluated, and the foundation for the process might change drastically. Consider the should-map shown in the next section, where planned automation so considerably modifies the process that it might not be recognizable as the evolution of the same process.

Process redesign map. The should-map continues the natural evolution of the process design. It is the team's concept of the redesigned process flow, following the analysis of the is-map and the development of a relationship map. The should-map, as shown in Fig. 7.6, diagrams the recommended process improvements and shows the change's impact on performance measures. If a total redesign or reengineering approach was taken, the should-map shows at a glance the entire new process, which can easily be compared to the existing process described by the is-map. Developing the should-map, the to-be process, is the major work effort of the process design team when using this methodology.

Rummler-Brache offer few documented guidelines for developing the should-map. This could be due to the nature of design work itself, as opposed to analysis. As our discussion has pointed out previously, *analysis* is fairly straightforward. Analysis proceeds from what's given, from a well-understood baseline. Design is creative, risky, and challenging. It requires making choices about work processes and technologies, and necessitates expensive change. Design steps into the unknown, it's a prediction that the new way will be better. Design cannot be performed in a step-by-step manner. A good design is born from assembling the right team members and preparing the conditions for them to create.

The should-map documents the decisions and ideas generated during design. Although it might start from reworking the is-map, this is not necessarily the best way. Two approaches are typical: the team can incrementally modify the is-map to show the preferred new process steps, or take a *clean-sheet* approach, creating an entirely new cross-functional process map.

When developing the should-map, address the goals and assumptions of the new process. Identify the quantitative and qualitative goals of the new process from the business requirements. List all assumptions that affect the process design, such as the usage and type of automation support. Use one of the other process design methods to draw the team's previous work into the design. Consider using one of the following as a basis for design input:

Customer Feedback Process - Should-Map

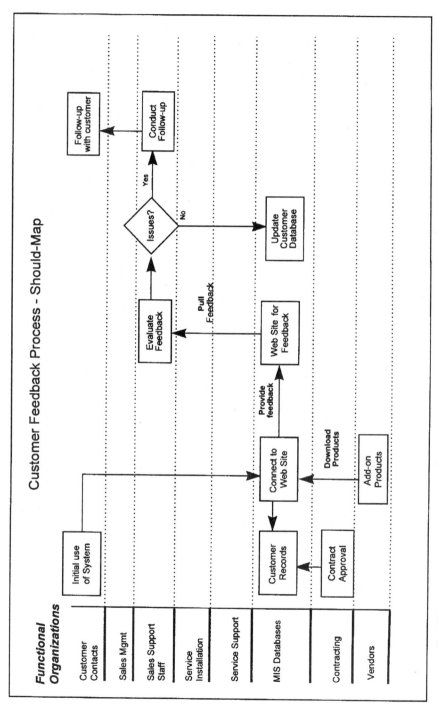

Figure 7.6   Should-map.

261

- Affinity diagram
- Information flow model
- Physical process model

The actual should-map is diagrammed more as an outcome of creative thinking and discussion, not as an analytical exercise. Process design is not necessarily accomplished by evaluating the is-map steps and disconnects and addressing solutions for each microlevel problem identified. Design is more holistic, and requires a view that encompasses the sources and reasons for *all* the disconnects. Design must question the very *existence* of the process (such as is done in the Breakthrough Thinking method). As the team progresses and discusses potential solutions, the resulting map is drawn to show the new flow as it emerges. A master should-map flow can be drawn on the boards or placed on the wall so all members can see it and participate, or it might be drawn in pieces, and be creatively assembled during a whole-group exercise.

As a facilitator or organizer, your job is more to prepare the environment for the team to create than it is to lead the design process. Prepare the environment by providing the physical and organizational conditions to support creativity, and by recommending design methods and creative thinking exercises. You want the team to break away from the herd mentality that often overcomes groups and to discover effective breakthrough solutions by working together under optimal circumstances.

To prepare the team for design in the workshop, have participants break into smaller groups and either assign or choose a subprocess or have each team address parts of the overall process. Sometimes it's easier to produce breakthrough ideas when focusing on just one part of the problem instead of the entire view. Bring the teams together to share their ideas and to extract the most useful parts of the emerging designs.

In summary, the should-map represents the new design in its initial form. Any new design must progress through iterations of evaluation, further ideation, and contribution by team experts and specialists. The should-map becomes the proposal and road map for implementation of the new process, requiring much additional detail to be added to this design model. But the design model continues to be refined, and becomes the model for a pilot process prototype or testbed. The should-map becomes the map of the new process when the pilot process is implemented, evaluated, and approved. This set of activities represents the basic approach to moving the design through to completion using the is-map and should-map methods.

Visualizing: Business vision

The visualizing phase of process design allows the team to expand the inquiry deeper into the requirements, problems, and conditions of the process. In visualizing, the team members also evaluate the degree of freedom and possibility they have for design. Although still an analysis activity, visualizing provides an opportunity to explore the options and interpretations of the problem area.

Visualizing begins the creation of new ideas and requirements for the process redesign. The visualizing phase of process design studies the relationships within and between processes, and uncovers business opportunities for advantage and effectiveness in the emerging new process. Table 7.3 shows methods and tools for visualizing the process design and defining process requirements.

This phase initiates the discovery and creation of business value for the process. Relationships between customers and the business, internal and external interfaces with the process, and customer-facing activities are investigated for improvements and breakthroughs. Visualizing the benefits of the process reveals new opportunities for customer interaction, creation of new products and other sources of value, and other discoveries. System and process requirements are derived from these team analyses as a method of capturing business value and planning for new directions.

As a business process analysis, the visualizing phase creates process diagrams and models of new relationships, and leads to a process vision. These analysis products are used in the usage and packaging phases to design the new process. They are used to generate an initial requirements document as the output of the visualizing phase.

TABLE 7.3   Business Process Design: Visualizing Phase

Visualizing: Business vision	Methods	Inputs and Outputs
Identifying process relationships	Process information flow model	In: Scope, process diagrams
	Relationship mapping Quality management tools	Out: Process models, process relationships, lists
Identifying process opportunities	Value analysis	In: Process relationships and models
	Benchmarking analysis	Out: Process vision
Process design requirements	Breakthrough Thinking	In: Process models, process vision
	Brainstorming methods	Out: Process models, initial requirements

Identifying process relationships. Within any business process a deep network of relationships evolves over the years of its use—relationships among members and roles in the organizations, between customers and managers, between management and line staff, among systems contributing to the process, between other organizations inside and external to the business, and between suppliers and the business. Any given process might reveal all these relationships, especially if it is a customer-facing process.

Using the process vision and various process diagrams from scoping, the team works through the discovery of relationships in the organization that impact the process. Particularly with regard to the process redesign, these relationships must be identified and understood. Disregarding their effects in the redesigned process can lead to difficulties in implementation, lack of user acceptance, and subtle forms of process sabotage.

Relationship is a general term, and a process design team might find multiple perspectives from which to analyze business process relationships. Numerous methods are available and commonly used in analyzing and portraying the strategic, business, functional, organizational, and information relationships inherent in the current process. By virtue of understanding these relationships, they are made explicit and available to the process redesign.

The following methods are recommended in this activity, most of which are rather accessible to most multidisciplinary design teams. These methods apply to some of the various relationships as described:

- *Process information flow model.* Applies to information usage and work process relationships.

- *Relationship mapping.* Applies to organizational and customer relationships.

- *Quality management tools.* Applies to strategic, business, functional, and task relationships.

Process information flow model. Process information flow models represent a more detailed look at the process, from the perspective of communication and the transmission of information. When improving or redesigning a process, the information flow shows how messages are currently passed along through various roles in the organization. Highly descriptive information flow diagrams can become quite complicated, so often these models are broken down into subprocesses where the interactions among six to eight roles are illustrated.

This modeling approach is pursued once consensus has been reached on a recommended or selected process for design. It is not a method that can always be completed within the confines of the team workshop. Sometimes, to collect useful data about how information flows throughout a process, a quick field evaluation must be conducted, involving interview and task observation. If your team members are fairly confident about their knowledge of actual information flow, the team might define the initial flow model in the workshop. At this level, the process model should also identify activities (ongoing actions that support the process) and tasks (well-defined step-by-step procedures), since these daily operations generate the most significant information of interest to the process. Defining ad hoc communications and information flow might be of some interest, perhaps to understand where distractions and breakdowns occur in the process.

At this level of process, we are not interested in the detailed information as referred to by *information systems*. Process information flow evaluates the communications that fulfill the requirements of roles in the business, as normally performed, and across the entire scope of work. By analyzing work processes from this angle, another source of process design information emerges, one that shows the significant communications required of a process and the way information formally and informally flows through the various roles. Information requirements are reduced to their essentials, and opportunities arise for redesign of work process and communications tools.

Extensive related detail is expressed through using information flow modeling methods, such as:

- How information is collected in the process
- How the roles in a process reformat the information
- Official and informal paths of distribution and dissemination
- How information is used by other roles
- Common tools used to handle communication of information

The process information flow model is adaptable to any of the organizational contexts, and is especially useful in the business and user contexts, where the models can become detailed diagrams showing areas for redesign opportunity as illustrated in Fig. 7.7. They might be used in the systems context to identify how manual information-based processes will be automated with communications software and networks. In the product context, generic processes can be modeled to show how the product concept will address current customer problems. Information flow diagrams verge on becoming workflow models, which identify the *sequence* of information usage as well as the roles and relationships. Workflow modeling might be more useful in the *design* stage of process redesign. Workflow design is an intensive

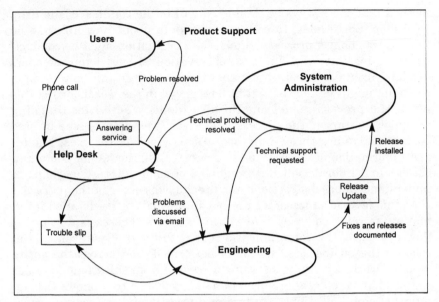

Figure 7.7   Process information flow diagram.

design method requiring an understanding of process information
and a foundation of systems, infrastructure, and physical process
knowledge. For the extent of effort required to produce workflow models, the effort is better directed toward the design work of building
the new process, and not mapping the current workflow. Of course,
aspects of the current process will always surface, and these components will be employed in the new process. However, extensive knowledge of the current workflow is not required to produce a good design
for the new process. Therefore, it is described later in this chapter as
a means of process design, rather than a current analysis method.

Quality management—business tools.   The *Total Quality Management*
(TQM) movement, inspired by the successes of the Japanese quality
approaches developed by W.E. Deming, infused quality methods into
business practice throughout North American organizations in the
last decade. Quality management applications to process analysis and
design offer a proven set of tools and a rational methodology for
process improvement.

TQM is known for its emphasis on continual process improvement,
and of course is strongly focused on processes. As opposed to reengineering approaches that espouse radical breaks from current processes, TQM approaches are grounded in *kaizen,* the notion that continuous incremental improvements lead to significant process advantage.

Practitioners have noted that whereas business process reengineering is always initiated from the top down, with executive planning and consultants leading the redesign effort, TQM is inspired from those working in the process, from the bottom up. TQM appears more democratic in this way, allowing good process ideas to become proposals and solutions. Many process consultants agree that there's room for both approaches in organizations, that they are not only compatible but necessary. After all, once a reengineering redesign has been implemented, who better to improve and fine-tune the process than the managers and users of the new process and system?

Historically, seven quality control tools were taught by quality advocates, most of which were readily adopted by North American corporations and government organizations in some part through the latter 1980s. These tools have found their way into nearly every course and seminar on TQM, and from there have become commonly used in many business analysis applications. Since these tools are thoroughly discussed in the literature of the quality disciplines, they are not described here in detail. Of the seven tools, the ones most applicable to Team Design workshop formats include the following:

Affinity diagram. *Affinity diagrams* are flexibly structured charts composed of the ideas, concepts, and issues gathered from interviews or brainstorming. Affinity diagrams are useful in the front-end analysis of information gathered from customers and users, and provide a method for the team to contribute to a shared set of concepts for requirements or design. A rough cognitive mapping of concepts is built by the team as a group participation exercise, making this tool especially adaptable in workshops. Using a facilitator, concepts derived from interview or brainstorming notes are written on sticky notes or index cards.

The facilitator guides the process, starting with a written concept and posting it on a whiteboard or wall. Participants are asked to look through their notes or concepts and select any items that appear conceptually similar. Ideas that relate to the initial one are posted beside or below it. Categories take shape as the facilitator works through the concept notes. Items are moved around from group to group as new categories emerge. Titles for the categories are generated only toward the end of the session. Category titles emerge from the groups as obvious identifying labels, or perhaps from one of the items posted in the group. Figure 7.8 shows an example of how an affinity diagram is organized during the process of selecting concepts and organizing categories. The affinity diagram approach is similar to *conceptual mapping* or *cluster analysis,* two other techniques used in cognitive psychology to capture concepts and discover natural patterns of organization.

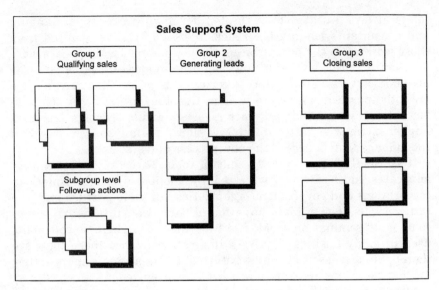

Figure 7.8 Affinity diagram.

An organized set of grouped concepts takes shape on the board, reflecting the team's shared views on how the functions and concepts of the system or process best fit with one another. The set of groupings in the diagram can be captured on newsprint, a CASE tool, or a drawing tool for further use in requirements analysis or design documentation. The *natural patterns of organization* that evolve during this process have value in requirements and design due to their direct correspondence with interviews or feedback from users. This lends the affinity diagram an *ecological* validity, as they are derived from the experiences and relationships understood by the cross-functional group, and are not analytical abstractions.

Although the affinity diagram is described in this section, it is recommended for use in the Requirements Definition format as well. After using the technique in a workshop or two, it will be readily adopted by the team and facilitators as a useful and rapid approach to organizing concepts and building a shared model of the design and priority requirements.

Cause and effect diagram. Of the quality control methods, the *cause and effect diagram* or *fishbone chart* developed by K. Ishikawa provides the most value for the time spent on its use as a workshop tool. Unlike the other tools listed following, the fishbone chart can be drawn as a facilitated exercise, allowing for group input into the cause and effect problem solving it supports. This is more of an analytical technique, useful for breaking out the components of a problem to better understand the origins and behavior of a systematic problem. This method is particularly useful when direct causes of errors or dysfunction in a system are not easily localized, and where multiple causes might interact with a problem. As a visual method, it's also noteworthy as a tool for identifying opportunities for solutions that might be missed with group brainstorming or more structured analysis tools.

Note in Fig. 7.9 how the fishbone chart is drawn, with branches for four distinct domains of interaction: *people, procedures, equipment,* and *environment.* These four branches are recommended for groups using this method as a starting point for identifying appropriate objects and actions contributing to the problem or available in the opportunity. The problem statement or goal state is shown in the far right, following the arrow that points to the effect. Facilitators often use the fishbone diagram as part of brainstorming processes to generate new ways of seeing the problem or condition.

The other commonly presented analysis diagrams used in TQM for quality control do not lend themselves to the workshop format of analysis and design. These include histograms, run charts, and control charts, which are used more as data collection and analysis tools, which require data collection and are time-consuming to prepare. In some cases they will be useful as tools for presenting findings to the team or in published analysis reports. In keeping the focus on tools supporting *design,* however, these highly analytical methods are not emphasized here.

Quality management practice also recommends seven *management and planning* tools. Several of these tools evolved for use in nonmanufacturing work environments, and have found application in systems

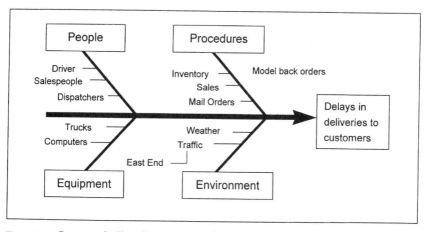

Figure 7.9 Cause and effect diagram.

development management. The first one listed, in particular, can be used for a variety of purposes in design workshops.

Hierarchy diagram.   Hierarchies are a useful construct found in almost every Team Design format. Hierarchies are used in different applications for representing system structure, organizations, process decomposition, data, or anything that can be visualized as a parent-child decomposition. Hierarchies have been used in analysis and design for system structure, software modules, project work breakdown structures (WBSs), and requirements charts. Hierarchy diagrams can be drawn as top-down trees, left-to-right webs, and even combinations of both directions, such as in the WBS.

A typical hierarchy diagram described in more detail in the Requirements Definition format is the function hierarchy. A *function hierarchy* shows the breakdown of a business process into its constituent functions, shown in a parent-child relationship. Variations of hierarchies can be applied as needed by experienced analysts or facilitators to class or object models, customer attributes, systems and components, and other breakdowns as required. A basic example of a hierarchy diagram is shown in Fig. 7.10. This shows a process hierarchy, or a breakdown of business processes from the scope, at the top level. (For purposes of the distinction, a process is an ongoing, continuous business activity composed of functions, which are tasks or procedures that have a start and a finish.)

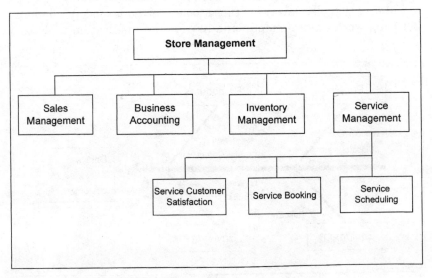

Figure 7.10 Hierarchy diagram.

A process hierarchy is another method for identifying and relating business processes within an easily understood representation. The key to building the process hierarchy is keeping the group's thinking aligned at the right level of representation. It's common for a mixed group of team members to mix abstractions such as process and function. Define your terms with the group before working through the model and identifying processes. Although the hierarchy diagram is used extensively in systems analysis work, not every use of it must be analytical. If the purpose is to develop an analytically correct model, ask the group to question ambiguous processes as they are described, to see if they meet the definition. If the purpose is to evoke brainstorming from the group, don't be concerned about the quality of definition—just keep the group generating ideas, and sort out the good ones later.

Matrix diagrams. Matrixes and tables are useful methods for showing relationships between two or more dimensions of information across a table of rows and columns. They provide the ability to display an immense amount of information in a compact area, by virtue of the relationships described in its structural organization.

A *table* is a simple structure with at least a single group of categorized concepts with items, examples, or lists below each heading label. Tables are used in process analysis as mechanisms for describing process elements and actions, to show priorities, and to efficiently document findings and organize concepts.

A *matrix* is a type of table, but is able to organize considerably more complex information. An example might be the work breakdown structure (WBS), which becomes a complex matrix when used to define a chart of accounts for a project. Matrixes can be used in plotting the variables comprising a complex decision. Other types of matrixes used in analysis include the quality function deployment (QFD) matrix known as the *house of quality*. The system matrix described in *Breakthrough Thinking* (Nadler and Hibino 1994) provides an excellent tool for organizing multiple process variables in a single visual format, allowing the team to discover useful patterns and to identify missing critical functions. The system matrix is presented in Chap. 8, under the Requirements Definition format.

Check sheets. *Check sheets* are simply tools developed to collect and compare data using a standard reference list of data points. Check sheets are useful for team members to use to conduct independent assessments or surveys outside of the workshop. Information collected can be collated and compared, to be discussed within the team. The Team Design format tables found at the beginning of each section are examples of complex check sheets.

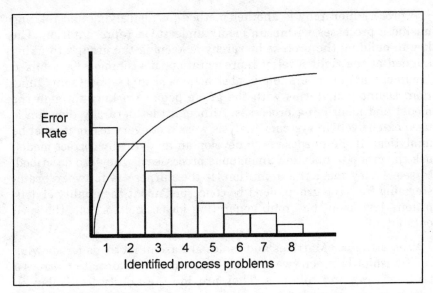

Error
Rate

1 2 3 4 5 6 7 8
Identified process problems

Figure 7.11   Pareto chart.

Pareto chart. The *Pareto chart* is useful as a tool for presenting the results of information about a problem or making decisions for exploiting a process opportunity. Paretos show the relative importance of problems or situations using a vertical bar chart format, as seen in Fig. 7.11. The bars represent percentages of identified problem responsibility, descending from left to right so the highest bars show the highest responsibility for a problem or opportunity. The Pareto is especially useful for focusing on the few problems that cause the highest percentage of errors, or those areas that account for fewer problems and are not worth dealing with. Cumulative percentages are described using an overlay graph line showing the rate of responsibility or coverage of the bars.

Scatter plot. The *scatter plot diagram*, like the Pareto, is taken from statistical process control. They can be used as a visual approach to diagram the relationship between two sets of data plotted on an *x, y* axis as seen in Fig. 7.12. The scatter plot can show the strength of a relationship between the two axes, which might represent a cause and effect situation or just a perceived correlation. Scatter plots are most often used in reporting results of analysis, and are not typically generated in group sessions. Facilitators experienced in TQM methods might use the scatter plot informally to demonstrate concepts or relate findings to the team.

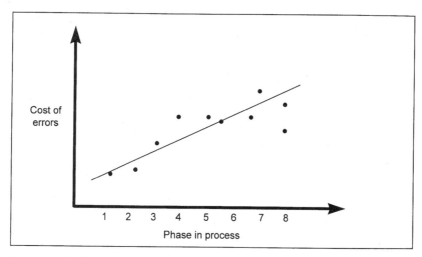

Figure 7.12 Scatter plot diagram.

Identifying process opportunities. Visualizing pursues the business value available in the process, which means different things to each organization and to each team. Process opportunities are the possible advantages, efficiencies, and organizations that evolve from envisioning a better process design. Identifying process opportunities provides methods for the team to evaluate the possible business advantages in the process. This activity also supports investigating similar processes to discover value-creating processes that might be integrated into the design.

Two business analysis methods often used in process reengineering efforts are described here, *value analysis* and *benchmarking*. Although numerous other business analysis methods are in use, different types of businesses will adopt different analysis tools for discovering and evaluating areas for improvement and efficiency. Organizational analysis, industrial engineering methods, manufacturing process analysis and financial analysis are all possible methodologies for identifying opportunities to enhance business value.

Business analysis methods. Several contemporary analysis methods are strictly designed for business analysis—these are techniques used to exploit the business value of the process or business operations. These methods are not oriented toward information system or process design, but are used to evaluate the value, purpose, and business metrics for a process. Therefore, they might be considered a first step in the definition of processes for automation.

Value analysis. *Value analysis* comprises a family of methods used in the analysis of business processes from a business value perspective. Value analysis originated as a cost management method, and has evolved as a product development approach used to analyze the logical components of a business process to evaluate the capability it provides the business. The full value analysis process (Halé 1995) produces a formal model of the business process, and is an alternative process analysis methodology. The formal model starts with business objectives, describes business processes and components, and specifies required capabilities. A value analysis results in a formal specification for information systems supporting the process design. Three diagrams are produced in value analysis:

- *Value-added diagram.*   Represents the business value of a process (or capability).

- *Concept diagram.*   Represents the results of the concept analysis.

- *Event diagram.*   Describes entities and their state changes through the process.

Value chain analysis. *Value chain analysis* (Porter 1985) is a type of end-to-end process analysis that assesses the business value of components in the *value chain*. Value chain analysis is used in cost management or to evaluate cycle time. The value chain is simply the total sequence of activities required to produce a defined output. Value chain analysis is performed like a task analysis of the chain of activities. It is an opportunistic approach, in that the exercise of analysis is performed to identify opportunities to improve measured values. Each step in the process is analyzed against metrics of completion time, function cost, contributive value, or quality. Value chain analysis is a popular reengineering technique, even though it is not a technique described in the major reengineering texts. It is often used in conjunction with benchmarking, as an exercise in measuring the potential business value of redesigning the process and evaluating the process against a known benchmark of effectiveness.

The value chain can include all the steps within a process, or it can branch across processes. For example, a value chain across processes might embrace the total life cycle of a product or service, including:

- Product design and development
- Product assembly and packaging
- Product distribution and sales
- Product and service management and support
- Product and systems integration

Value chain analysis can also be used as a check on current process validity, to evaluate the extent to which value is created at each step of a process, and it likewise can be used to assess the value-based validity of a new process proposal.

Value chain analysis can evaluate the contribution of all steps within one of the processes, or could evaluate how each process is performed on a total-product scale. Decisions to work in partnership with world-class service organizations or to merely outsource part of the value chain are supported through this analysis process.

Benchmarking analysis. The intention of benchmarking analysis is to improve or redesign a process based on following or understanding the example of an accepted leader in the process. *Benchmarking* involves investigation and selection of best practices from known organizations, and identifies the high-performance or innovative characteristics of selected practices. For example, if a company were to revamp its brand identification and management process, it might attempt to benchmark Procter and Gamble's branding processes, known as a world-class example.

Benchmarking collects extensive information on the process of interest (usually both publicly and through private partnership or consulting) from at least one process leader and sometimes from several leaders. Information on business performance, cycle time, cost management, and customer satisfaction is gathered and evaluated. Analysis of the best practices of leading companies is also a risk-management approach, wherein decisions on process design are held off until benchmarking results can guide the direction of process change.

Benchmarking is also popular as a reengineering technique, although it does not typically lead to radical change in current processes. Since benchmarking evaluates the processes from another organization, the best practices identified can be assumed as integral to that other culture, and are not yet supported in your current processes. In competitive terms, adopting the other organization's practices merely brings your practices up to the point where they were first adopted by the other company. It is difficult to become competitive or world-class by merely integrating the practices of other organizations, since other organizations can be assumed to continually innovate, and are themselves therefore well ahead of the practices benchmarked.

Davenport (1993) identifies two approaches to benchmarking, *quality* and *innovation*. *Quality benchmarking* becomes useful when evaluating the current levels of process performance, and can establish targets and objectives for process redesign based on realistic situations. And, certainly, knowledge of competitors' processes creates new targets for designing processes to surpass a specific known level of quality. *Innovation benchmarking* investigates processes, sometimes across different industries, to discover innovative aspects of processes that might be used to competitive advantage. Sometimes a specific activity used in a process, such as an information system or work distribution, can add value within a very different process, even in a different industry.

Benchmarking itself will not easily be performed within a facilitated workshop, unless you have invited the target organization to your meetings! It is usually conducted through research, personal contacts, and invited visits to target organizations. Team planning for appropriate benchmarking analysis can be an important collaborative group process, and the team should discuss and evaluate findings from benchmarking to extract and trial ideas for adoption in process design.

Process design requirements.   The conclusive step in visualizing creates an initial specification of process design requirements based on the business and problem area analyses conducted through team workshops and offline system analyses. The initial process requirements summarize the team's learning from the process and business analyses, by developing higher-level descriptions of the designed process. The process requirements organize the new functions conceived for the business process as requirements that guide the next phase of work.

Consider how the requirements are to be used in the next step. The usage phase develops various scenarios of possible process designs, and concludes with a prototype and system design approach to satisfy the best scenario. The process requirements developed in this activity must provide a framework for guiding the scenario, for pointing the team in the right direction. A framework of major requirements the team has agreed upon will set the main direction for process design. The requirements framework might be a fairly high-level definition of the key "musts" of the process, and a definition of business value targets and outcomes identified by the team. This framework of "must" requirements is supported by the thinking and analysis diagrams developed in scoping and visualizing.

Process design requirements will include the scoping and context diagrams and current process maps to define the scope and boundaries of the process. The team's thinking and design oriented toward the process redesign is captured in the affinity diagrams, horizontal process maps, workflow diagrams, and other design models. It can also be supported by process analysis models, comparative models describing the current (as-is) process with the redesigned (to-be) process.

Team Design approaches to developing the process design requirements also include nonanalytic (integrating or *synthesis*) methods, as are also used in scoping for exploring the purpose. At this point in the design cycle further depth might not be productive—the team members should reorganize their findings and models from a fresh perspective to ensure that they are meeting the vision and overall direction for the process. A broader view is taken, therefore, and sense is made of the various models already developed. These diagrams and narratives will be used in the following phase of usage, scenario design.

The integrating methods used for defining process requirements can include the following:

- *Brainstorming methods.*   Brainstorming approaches can be used to identify the major requirements from the products of analysis. The facilitator uses a bottom-up approach now to have top-level requirements derived from the more detailed needs described in analysis.

- *Breakthrough Thinking.*   The two approaches that follow the purposes principle used in scoping are (1) solution after next, and (2) the systems principle. These two approaches are effective for visualizing the requirements for a future design that are not constrained by the current process.

- *Dialogue.*   Holding facilitated dialogue can be useful to refresh the team's thinking after a lengthy series of technical analysis and design workshops. Consider using dialogue sessions as needed when the team becomes stuck or loses sight of the larger purpose.

As-is and to-be models.   Requirements for process design are also derived from analytic tools, including the process modeling methods identified in previous sections. A typical methodology for identifying and defining requirements for new processes is by developing detailed models of the current process and comparing these with descriptive models of the planned process. This method is supported by the process mapping tools (is-map and should-map), and it is supported by other modeling methods that should also be available to the team and the facilitator's toolkit.

Process analysis and design is conventionally performed using a methodology that contrasts current processes with new process design ideas. Current processes are defined with an *as-is model,* and the proposed or new design is the *to-be model.* This approach toward process modeling originated in the early 1980s with the IDEF family of analysis methods, and is specifically used in the $IDEF_0$ process modeling method. IDEF stands for *Integrated Computer-Aided*

Manufacturing Definition, and was developed as a rigorous means of structuring manufacturing processes for automation. The $IDEF_0$ method is the initial model in a series of (at one point) 12 fully defined methods, used for defining processes, data, objects, information flow, and various levels of detail for automation purposes.

In actual use, process analysis using $IDEF_0$ is often conducted to model the current process. Process redesign for automation and integration is not always performed by the same team connected with as-is analysis, and is not always done using IDEF, even where it is called for as a standard. $IDEF_0$ leads to well-defined, fine-grained flow diagrams of processes, their decomposed functions, and the inputs, outputs, controls, and mechanisms that drive the process. Process analysts, especially working in teams, find it easy to get caught up in as-is analysis. When taking on large and difficult problems, the tendency exists to overanalyze and identify every potential problem in the process.

Some business process experts who have completed large process definition efforts find extensive as-is modeling counterproductive. As-is definition usually requires more time than the redesign, as details and systems continue to emerge as analysis is pursued. When extensive organizational and administrative processes and systems are in place in a labyrinthine business process, the analyst is tempted to identify and catalog every function, factor, and metric contributing to the problems in the process. Aside from being a tedious auditing task, this approach toward as-is analysis requires an enormous latitude of time to conduct interviews, track down forms, compare procedures, and change models as new information is discovered. So what alternatives do we have with teams conducting as-is process analysis?

First, let's look at areas where as-is current process analysis can be effective. Discussions with business process experts have identified several general principles, as follows:

- Understanding existing business functions and the organizational beliefs and values
- Identifying business rules and the underlying business models behind policy and procedures
- Integrating the perspectives of users and other stakeholders to be impacted by the redesign
- Documenting the effectiveness of current process performance
- Obtaining a performance and procedural baseline from which to compare new process proposals

Problems with as-is analysis. Agreement exists among business process reengineering experts that when too much as-is analysis is conducted (over a long period of time, perhaps, conservatively, more than 15 percent of the total effort time or if an entire project is devoted to it) effective change becomes more difficult. How does as-is analysis become ineffective? How much analysis is too much, and why is it too much? Some analysts and experts agree on the following points:

- As-is analysis leads to becoming an end to itself, and not a means to an end.

- The more time spent on as-is analysis, the more the team begins to feel comfortable with the current process as it is. The underlying rationale of the current process is exposed, and change becomes more difficult.

- The team gets caught up in thinking along analytical lines and does not reach out for design breakthroughs.

- Incremental progress is settled for, and dramatic changes are dismissed as being too risky or radical.

- As-is processes become defined in their ideal state, and actual problems and issues are deemphasized.

As-is models can become rose-colored versions of the current business process unless the analyst or facilitator uses a variety of approaches to angle in on the business problem. Through both interviews and workshops, users and managers connected with the current process will often describe their role in the associated tasks as crucial or, at least, significant. They might have been involved in process improvement over the years, and could feel that a management-led push to reinvent the process *again* is not in their best interests. Team members often have a stake in defending the current process, and facilitators should watch for their sensitivity to this and their defense of status quo. Even when team members appear fully on board with the proposed changes, they will describe the process in ideal terms, or as it will be in the future when the currently unimplemented improvements they are responsible for are in place. And when process automation is being planned, current users or process owners often believe their jobs are on the line and look for ways of maintaining their current practices in the new system. This approach can design in the flaws and inadequacies of the current process, especially if the team does not sufficiently redesign the functions of the process.

For any number of reasons, it may be difficult for some team members to let go of the current business process. Facilitators should realize that time will be needed to allow their attachment to the status quo to phase out. Where the facilitation job is by design fairly neutral, the very act of setting up a team-based analysis of current processes creates a tension between the existing and the proposed. The idea of the workshop itself pits the organizer and facilitator against team members who might have devised the original process and have their work reputation on the line for its effectiveness.

Finally, practitioners have found that when the team thoroughly explores the as-is process, a curious familiarity takes place. As group members continue to pursue as-is analysis, they create a more deeply engrained mental model. However, the mental model tends to be of an idealized version of the process, a process that doesn't really exist, but is assumed to reflect the current situation. After some time is spent on process definition, the as-is model evolves into a natural mental model, and it becomes difficult for people to change from this model.

An example of overdone analysis.   Stories of overdone as-is analysis are common in the consulting community. In working with the Air Force on a new system design for automating document production for requests for proposal (RFPs), I encountered the request to utilize any existing analyses of the RFP or procurement process available. After asking various customer contacts, a captain pointed out an as-is analysis effort with which he was especially puzzled. A half-million-dollar contract for as-is analysis of the procurement process had been completed no more than four months prior to our design work. Being government (public) property, we investigated the documentation, which included two large binders of $IDEF_0$ diagrams and pages of text describing the diagrams. The material was not useful to our effort, in that it was highly abstracted, defining an "ideal" view of the process as generalized across a major Air Force activity. In other words, since different organizations performed the process in different ways, the process analysis was generalized and aggregated into a composite view that did not closely reflect the real work performed. So even as a baseline current process model, it was of little value to our system design.

Discussions with customer representatives revealed that, in fact, the documents had not ever been used by the organization that had contracted the work. Apparently the *functional* organization (procurement professionals) had requested the analysis, but did not specify an analysis methodology. A research organization assisting the procurement functional recommended the use of IDEF to conduct the analysis, since that was considered the standard method. Unfortunately, the pages of detailed $IDEF_0$ diagrams were not readable by the intended users of the information. Too much information was provided, spread across dozens of boxes with flow arrows linked across dozens of pages. In fact, the procurement chief engaged another consultant to convert the top level of information into a standard flowchart so that the information could be used and understood by the functional organization!

More problems emerge from an inadequate analysis of customer requirements than from inadequate process analysis and diagramming. In the Air Force procurement example, the original analysts never bothered to determine how the information was to be used. They did not prepare the information customers for using the IDEF diagrams, and apparently could not easily educate them to use the models effectively. However, given the large contract sum, consultants are tempted to deliver extensive, overly detailed tomes of analysis and diagrams to justify the price tag. A better understanding of the information users' needs might lead to a simpler analysis approach, which, although less lucrative initially, would foster a better long-term relationship by satisfying the customer.

Summary of requirements models.   In conclusion, when cataloging the requirements for the new process design both synthesis (integrational) and analysis work is performed. Requirements can be derived using comparative analysis methods such as process mapping and IDEF models, but these approaches can be analysis-intensive, and should be adopted with caution. Especially if the facilitator has not worked with the techniques previously, the team should consider using the minimum analysis that effectively documents the requirements.

Process requirements can require several models to cover the dimensions of a complex business process. Functional, business, activity, economic, and system dimensions all contribute to the complexity of defining the business needs and business value for a new process. Maintain a clear target of the team's goals—continually ask, "What are we doing this for?" Remember, the end product, the new process, is the result of many well-formed ideas and decisions, and clear communication is more critical than elegant analyses in reaching the target. Each phase in the format contributes to the target goal—evaluate your planned outputs from this phase and consider what's required to feed into the next phase of process operation. A shared view of requirements is important to develop effective process scenarios in this phase, but having detailed requirements going into this phase can defeat the purpose of scenario design.

Team Design allows facilitators to tailor the facilitated workshop or design process that best fits your system's and organization's context. Remember that not every analysis and design activity described in any of the formats and their phases will be performed. Some methods will be more useful in your environment than others, and some experimentation will always be necessary when adopting new methods. Consider using a cost-benefit approach to the methods described in the book. An analysis-intensive method such as IDEF is not always more costly if, in fact, your team already knows and uses IDEF tools. But if your team has not used these methods previously, the less technically involving approaches will prove more productive and satisfying for all involved.

Usage: Process scenarios

The usage phase of analysis completes the analysis and leads into process design by constructing process models and models of usage. These models of usage are based on developing scenarios that describe views of the future application of the process from the users' and managers' perspectives. *Scenarios* are concrete descriptions of the process in action, sequential stories of usage that enable the design team members to envision their emerging design in its context of use. They also describe operational characteristics of the process that can be used in the next phase, packaging the design.

When redesigning large-scale business processes or user work practices, the scenario approach provides a mechanism for all team members—technical, management, and designers—to discuss the process on equal terms. Scenarios envision how the process will be performed in its revised context, and how users will interact with systems and other actors in the process. As described by Carroll (1995) they are "couched in the lingua franca of end-user action and experience, and therefore it can be a meeting ground for communication and collaboration between developers and users." Imagination and application are more important than systems or data in this approach, allowing the process to be developed from a business perspective *using* technology, not being *determined* by it. Process scenarios can be developed using several approaches. The established approach of scenario analysis is recommended for business process design. This approach provides a business context approach to developing scenarios, based on creating business value. Among other methods, process mapping and other process modeling tools can be used to document the team's results and selected candidate scenario, as outlined in Table 7.4.

Other variations of scenario development are discussed in Chap. 8 as requirements methods. Future workshops and the ideal system are described in its usage phase as envisioning processes that support a user-oriented process design, bringing together the users', designers', and systems' perspectives in designing new work processes.

Usage starts with the analysis products and requirements from

TABLE 7.4   Business Process Design: Usage Phase

Usage: Process scenarios	Methods	Inputs and Outputs
Developing process scenarios	Scenario analysis Scenario design methods Process mapping	In: Initial requirements, process models Out: Process scenarios
Selecting scenarios	Scenario design methods Process mapping	In: Process scenarios Out: Detailed scenario
Documenting scenario design	Scenario design methods Storyboarding Process mapping	In: Detailed scenario Out: Process candidates, scenario process design, process requirements

visualizing, and uses these ideas and shared understanding to build scenarios of the process. Alternative scenarios are defined and discussed, and a best scenario is derived from the scenarios analyses. This selected scenario becomes the best-fit description of the process design, and is used to develop process candidates for consideration for process design in the packaging phase.

Developing process scenarios.   Process scenarios are developed to establish a shared view of the evolving process from the perspective of the business and its goals, products, and existing processes. The initial process requirements and process models are used to start building the scenarios, as materials from which to construct a detailed "story" of the new process.

Scenario analysis is the recommended method for business process design, and it is generally also useful for other formats, such as application design, planning, and decision making. Scenario analysis is well suited for use in facilitated workshops, integrating the knowledge and experience of the multiple disciplines required in any thorough business analysis. Scenarios can be documented as narrative descriptions, and many frequent users of scenario methods adapt templates for identifying the necessary pieces of information and story components for effective scenarios. The completed scenario package might also include process maps, workflow diagrams, system matrix diagrams, or pictorial diagrams keyed to the narrative process descriptions.

Scenario analysis.   Scenario analysis is often used in strategic planning as a method for identifying risks, market opportunities, and potential implementation problems in business proposals. As the name suggests, scenarios are generated and analyzed for their potential impacts by a team. When investing in major process redesign or reengineering, scenario analysis provides considerable value to the decision makers regarding the direction and effectiveness of process design proposals.

As described by the Wharton School's Eric Clemons (1995), scenario analysis offers its adopters a view into their own futures, in the following ways:

- It acknowledges uncertainty and focuses on the key sources of uncertainty.

- It develops a "range of possible future scenarios for exploration, acknowledging that not all are equally likely, and that the future may indeed have aspects from more than one scenario."

- It develops strategies and "future indicators of which strategies may become most critical."

- It acknowledges that discontinuities may be generated from adopting the scenario as a future model, in which metrics, sales figures, and current customers cease to matter. "Rapid and widespread adoption of fax equipment did not just alter Federal Express's plans for Zap Mail, it caused its cancellation."

Scenario analysis can be used in a workshop setting, as it supports group dialogue and discovery. Scenarios for process change are developed and discussed in the team setting, and are compared against key goals and priorities. Competing scenarios are compared, and the possible impacts of each process design are evaluated. Operational and environmental uncertainties are highlighted and elicited with the team. Each scenario in turn is explored, with the team identifying advantages and problems, responses and investments, systems and resources for each one.

If the exploration of each basic scenario has narrowed down the field, the remaining scenarios are examined by simulation. Team members test out the scenarios as a group, encouraging *what-ifs* and relationships to other strategies. As scenarios are fleshed out and understood through the workshop, the relative uncertainties of each approach are defined, and the payoffs of each are estimated. Scenarios are compared, but the goal is not to select the best one and dismiss the others. Uncertainties about the future environment and key vulnerabilities to change are defined through scenario analysis. Contingency planning and strategic planning can follow to address risks and opportunities surfaced through the analysis. Much can be learned from each scenario, and a revised strategy may evolve to incorporate elements of several processes.

Scenario analysis for business process design follows a general team process, the steps of which depend on the complexity of the business process. It is a complete set of activities, that within the following steps defines a method for developing and selecting scenarios and then generating alternatives. The steps in this method conform to the three activities in usage, and can be used without further analysis in some process designs.

Scenario analysis method

1. Identify the business process and its subprocesses for scenario analysis. User-intensive system functions are best, since user interface and process issues are among the most difficult areas in most requirements models. Areas such as customer support, user intervention of any process, or functions involving more than one user group or interface to the system are good candidates.

2. Note the candidates on a chart with the team, and discuss the priorities and business value of each one. Sometimes the priority is driven by design complexity, other times by schedule or customer interest. Select one or two topics to begin creating scenarios.

3. Identify the key conditions for the scenario. What are the business goals, user tasks, user preferences, and organizational conditions around the topic area? Brainstorm each topic, noting responses on whiteboards or charts until a single sheet of conditions are listed (about 10 to 15) for each topic. Select a single topic to begin working the exercise with the team.

4. Use a diagramming method with which the team is familiar or you are comfortable. Process mapping or task sequential diagrams are excellent for scenario definition, depending on the level of detail necessary for the solution. Identify the method you suggest for use, and lead the team in defining the starting point for the scenario.

5. One or several large whiteboards or multiple sheets of chart paper will be required to draw out the scenario model with the team. Work quickly to generate several alternative versions of a process, rather than just a single "best" model on which everyone can agree. If necessary, build a separate scenario for each point of view in the team. Once they are drawn out, discussion and analysis will modify and select the best approach.

6. Discuss the pros and cons of each alternative with the team. Don't overanalyze, just walk through and evaluate each alternative to foster understanding of the objectives and advantages or disadvantages of each alternative scenario. Usually one alternative makes the sense, if the business goals and conditions are defined up front.

If more than one scenario solution appeals, a subteam can break out to investigate technical options further, allowing the selection of a best alternative in the near future.

7. Select the best-fit alternative scenario and add other details as necessary to build a more complete picture of events and conditions satisfied by the process. Develop a summary diagram, and have team members draft readable models for use by the team.

Although the steps in scenario analysis might seem abbreviated, they are provided as representative steps. Scenario design methods are not step-by-step exercises. A general sequence of activities is used for scenario development, but each group and each process design will require local variations that cannot be anticipated by the methodology. Other methods and further details are also provided in Chap. 8, and original sources referenced in the bibliography will prove useful for the practitioner new to scenario design methods.

In scenario analysis, both inventive and analytical team members are necessary and valued. The inventive, creative work is required in generating the model scenario's alternatives and presenting them to the team. The analytical process is required in walking through and evaluating the scenarios to determine how well they fulfill the business goals and conditions specified.

Process design scenarios.   You know you've turned the corner from analysis to design when the team begins exploring scenarios for the new process design, as the process is to-be. This activity can occur spontaneously as the team carefully considers the possible impacts of proposed redesign changes. When evaluating the alternatives for process change, an immediate reaction from current process users and stakeholders is often "What is the impact on our jobs and the business?" As an organizer or facilitator, this natural and expected response can be used to generate creative approaches to redesign.

The first activity in usage discusses scenario analysis for eliciting and analyzing scenarios, based on the method used in strategic and organizational planning. The basic process requires inventing scenarios and evaluating and discussing their impacts. Process design scenarios are similar in function, although applied at a finer level of detail. Where business planning considers more strategic activities (where to invest, buy-or-build, long-term goal setting) process design scenarios consider alternatives and their future implications for a single business process only.

The following general types of methods are involved in building process design scenarios, in a representative sequence of use:

1. Brainstorming and idea generation

2. Visualizing, future projection, and generating alternatives

3. Envisioning work and organizational life in the near future

4. Creating stories, possible scenes and other initial scenarios

5. Selecting a set of process scenarios

6. Tinkering with, exploring, and evaluating scenarios

7. Identifying one or two scenarios, and building details

8. Designing systems, jobs, tasks, and contingencies for scenarios

The usage format shows several identified inputs feeding into the phase to support scenario building. The context and physical models are useful tools for focusing the team's attention on basic aspects of the design problem, and they provide a basis for agreement that moves the design forward. Affinity diagrams show the various factors and influences on the current process, using visual cues in the diagram. The relationship map and is-map provide useful tools for understanding and evaluation, and lead into diagramming the *should* process, itself a visual process scenario. Task flow or sequential models describe any necessary tasks to be redesigned. All of these or any might be key to your team's definition of the business process, providing the base from which to create.

Process and system design requirements.   Requirements for the process and its systems will determine much of the direction of the design scenarios. Requirements describe the business needs from the customer's viewpoint, including must-have capabilities, performance criteria, and completion time. Requirements are based on a vision for the business tempered by budgets and timeframes. The tabulated system or business requirements provide both the design-to capabilities and the constraints for the process.

If the requirements have progressed through agreement and approval, and are baselined, design scenarios might be rather constricted without much room for modification. However, this is atypical for process work. Usually, the requirements at this stage allow the design team some freedom to generate various proposals based on requirements for the business and compatible system technologies. Either way, requirements are a necessary place from which to start with process scenarios.

Requirements for our example might become fairly detailed as the team continues to explore the problem. Looking at a simple example, let's assume a business process problem for the Popular PC Company requiring a redesigned process for communicating and updating product information to their sales and distribution channels, as well as to end customers. The current process uses a central configuration database at the production center to track the various PC configurations as available, but this information is distributed manually to sales staff and distribution channels, such as stores and catalogs. Some examples of business process requirements and criteria based on the example might be among the following:

- Reduce time for information availability by more than 50 percent.
- Provide a means of capturing PC configurations at a single point and reusing the data throughout the process.
- Reduce incorrect PC configurations released to the field by more than 50 percent.
- Provide immediate availability of product data to customers.

The requirements associated with the process then guide the direction of technical solutions and design ideas. Although numerous creative solutions should be encouraged, during scenario selection the requirements and criteria help determine the best scenarios and ideas to adopt for process design.

Models of understanding. By this time, your team has developed several models for understanding the business process as-is. A set of scope and structural models (context, physical, and affinity) and process maps (relationship map and is-map) serve as some of the process models available. These might be refined, printed, and distributed or posted to the wall, but should be discussed and understood by the team when moving into process design.

The next task requires drawing on the understanding developed by this point. Engage the team in a dialogue, using several applicable questions to stimulate the conversation into a group dialogue. In advance of scenario development, you want the team to be thinking outside of the familiar, in new territory, exploring possible paths. Games and exercises, diversions (such as moving the team off site), and group activities (such as physical events outdoors) help to bridge from the last stage to the new.

Upon starting into scenario building, leverage the models of understanding. Probe the team to question and challenge their beliefs about the current process and its models. Point to the most current and well-defined model and ask the team questions such as the following:

- Where will the process break? What's the weakest point of the process?
- Are all the organizations impacted by the process shown? Who have we left out?

- Who are *all* the users? Who are all the customers?

- Can the process handle new or unexpected customer contacts?

- Are all the information systems used in the process identified? Which systems are the most unreliable, or contribute to problems or user errors?

- What ad hoc tasks, user software packages, or process work-arounds are not shown? What else is missing from the model that we can use in redesign?

Following the Business Process Design format, a number of team documents will be available. Current process information includes context and physical process models, a relationship map (similar to the preceding example diagram), and process maps (is-map). Process redesign information might include the should-map, other to-be process diagrams and associated narrative, and lists of requirements.

Creating new process ideas.   Questioning the current models opens up the team's thinking about possible better process options and opportunities. New process ideas are best generated in a team setting, using brainstorming and the synergy of different contributors. Start off the ideation with one of the brainstorming methods described in Chap. 5, or with visualizing exercises that draw out ideas in a meaningful sequence of related concepts. Two other scenario design approaches are presented briefly as useful variations for design teams to consider using.

The future workshop.   The *future workshop* approach has been described by facilitation and design researchers in recent years (Madsen and Kensing 1991). Future workshops are a goal-directed combination of brainstorming and visualizing exercises used within a participatory design orientation. The future workshop is an explicit scenario generating technique, used to create visions of future conditions that test the new process being designed. A future workshop is run by experienced facilitators that ensure involvement of all participants in developing scenarios. Mixing management and technical workers is not recommended with this approach, due to the need to critique existing processes.

The facilitator introduces three phases of activities for the workshop—critique, fantasy, and implementation. The critique phase is used as a means of describing problems and concerns in current work processes. The fantasy phase facilitates the team's creation of visions and scenarios for a better design in the future. Implementation requires the team to narrow down workable strategies for coordinating resources and solving the problems. Future workshops require an investment of workshop planning and commitment to achieve effective results. It is a complete team process in and of itself, and is described here as an alternative for the facilitator or organizer to consider its use with creative and committed design teams.

Ideal system exercise. An effective tool for automation-oriented processes is the *ideal system* exercise, a visualizing approach that engages the imagination and requirements with systems thinking. This method is described in more thorough detail in the Requirements Definition format, but is also useful at this point in scenario development. The essential idea revolves around having users or stakeholders envision the ideal system that would automate all their requirements and improve their jobs in the way they desire. Participants have free reign to describe how the process is fulfilled in every way by this new system. Have the team break out into small groups for each group to explore a different chunk of a large scope scenario. Or, each group could handle their own start-to-finish approach to generate a complete sequence of ideas.

The ideal system exercise is a much simpler technique that can be used within a single workshop as a simple approach for less-complex business processes. If your team has previously used the ideal system technique, or has made progress using it, consider continuing to explore the implications and consequences of this approach.

Selecting scenarios. Selecting scenarios is an integrated part of the process design scenario method. As pointed out in the scenario analysis description, selection of appropriate scenarios follows directly after initial scenario building. Using the narratives developed in scenario analysis, the team identifies one or several scenarios to be the primary representation of the process. The selected scenarios become the models used for prototyping, evaluation, and reality testing for the system or product.

Scenarios can be broad-ranging, and can easily represent activities affecting more than one business process. Several scenarios might also combine to represent a more encompassing business process. Business processes as well as scenarios cut across organizational and system boundaries, and multiple processes will often show up in a single scenario. These interactions are worth documenting, as they point out the realistic overlaps that occur when any process is actually deployed.

Process mapping can be used to document the scenario selection, and the facilitator and recorder might work together to maintain a process-map view of the selected scenario as it is further defined. Using multiple boards or easels, the key two or three scenarios can be mapped out to represent their process flow and differences at a glance. As the team works through the various functions and pros and cons of each scenario, lists or matrix tables can be drawn to score the attributes of the scenarios. A final composite scenario map can be prepared as the output of this activity.

At some point, within a day's workshop, or longer if complex or multiple scenarios are explored, the team will have developed rough cuts of one or several process design models from the scenario exercises. If a single process scenario has been developed, then selection is no problem. However, the inherent value of scenarios is to position various alternative models against requirements, performance criteria, and possible future conditions. If the team settles on just one scenario for process modeling, it might withstand scrutiny by the design team, but it will not be tested against alternative approaches that could lead to a better overall design.

After an initial draft or rough cut model of the scenario has been established, find a break point in the proceedings and have the team reflect on its design.

- Walk through the scenario for the process design with the team. Review the model in its interim state and have the designers describe it to the overall team.

- Ask questions about the process as designed: What *should* the process or system do? What other systems does this design impact?

Documenting scenario design.   Scenarios can be documented throughout the design process. Several approaches can be used to define and document the process scenarios, including process mapping, narratives with diagrams, and storyboarding.

When documenting the team's results of process design, assess the needs of the document customers and other users of the design. If you're making recommendations to an executive committee or continuing with a process reengineering effort, process mapping and organizational diagrams might be especially useful. If a systems solution is contemplated for the process, deeper description of the system requirements for the process might be necessary. If a system requirements document is developed separately, your delivered model might be a process map, not necessarily a specification.

Scenario narratives supported by diagrams are useful for system and process design, and are readable by a wider range of potential design customers. Narratives can follow a template designed for capturing the elements of the process scenario, providing an outline of the process with supporting narrative description. Process diagrams created during the workshops are integrated within the document to support defining the process design. The process mapping approach can be used throughout the scenario analysis and design process.

Process mapping leads to a readable specification of process flow, roles, and interactions. It can be used with the narrative description, or narrative can be used to support the process maps. Scenario analysis and design are not standardized methods. No "best method" can be recommended for scenario design—much of the practice is tailored for the organization and development situations using the methods.

Storyboarding can also be used, as a creative self-documenting approach. Storyboarding can start using an analytical, procedural approach or it can proceed more informally. A storyboard might be developed for each major scenario or proposal, or scenarios can be loosely storyboarded, discussed, and documented following the full storyboard method. Storyboarding creates a highly readable map of the new process, which can be documented by a recorder during the storyboarding exercise or following the workshop. Storyboarding requires team and facilitator discipline, but is powerful and productive if the team is comfortable with the process. Storyboards help the abstract designed process come to life for participants and readers, creating a visual and narrative story of the process and system. Teams already familiar with storyboarding (described in Chap. 5) might prefer it as a method for visualizing the representations of the new process or system.

Most of the analysis and design techniques described in this chapter can serve as documentation as easily as work products. For your team's formal documentation deliverables, not every diagram will be necessary or communicative. Evaluate the extent of information that best tells the story and communicates the direction and decisions of the project. A process design documentation package for management and organizational readers might not describe every diagram in detail, and should be heavy on graphical process maps and light on narrative. Assemble a package for technical readers that includes most of the diagrams and details, possibly with appendixes including raw data and transcripts to show the decision process.

Team Process Design

Process *design* is, in the (literally) final analysis, what this format is about. Although in practice it is not always clear when analysis ends and design begins, this section on process design highlights the distinction. Since most of the methods and tools described for analysis are also used in design, the distinction becomes less clear in actual use. A rule of thumb for design might offer that design begins when the team is spending more time *creating solutions* than in understanding the current process or determining problems in the process.

A review of process design approaches suggests that the design methods are not as methodical as the analysis methods. A creative leap of faith is undertaken when the gap between analysis and design is crossed. This is well known in software, but in business process design it is less understood. Of the process design methodologies in current use, most rely strongly on the analytical model development for the formation of new process designs. Many also presuppose the implementation of systems or software solutions as part of the process design itself.

The different Team Design contexts also account for differences in process design approach. The business context requires a solid business strategy and value foundation as the basis for new process design, and does not necessarily require a system solution. In practice, a system implementation is usually investigated as a business process solution. The systems context requires more of a strategic application of technology to solve process problems. It presupposes a systems solution due to the focus of it being a system-oriented application of Team Design. The user context typically utilizes systems solutions as its key to process design, since it is largely focused on improving user (worker or operator) work processes. Finally, the product context does not often use the process analysis and design model. A business process approach might be required if a customer's business process changed and required a breakthrough design from your team.

What are the successful and proven methodologies used in business process design? From both reviews of the forward-thinking business literature and the applications of practitioners in large organizations, several approaches emerge to the fore:

- Process redesign (Hammer reengineering approach)
- Process innovation (Davenport reengineering)
- Process mapping (Rummler-Brache)
- IDEF methods (U.S. Air Force, Knowledge Systems Corp.)

The purpose of this book is to provide the practitioner with the tools to conduct creative, innovative breakthrough team workshops and design. Rather than elaborate deeply on these approaches, the essential tools and structures from them will be integrated into a common framework that applies to each approach to some degree. References point to the applicable sources, and the practitioner is encouraged to investigate the original sources for further value if a cited tool is found to be especially useful.

Packaging: Process design

Business processes become automated and redefined as business information *systems*. Systems become the means of enabling a business process from their initial moment of use until the process or system is changed. Process and system design often become intertwined and functionally blended to the point where the process cannot be described independently from the system. Processes become integrated in part or as a whole within growing, evolving corporate information systems. Especially to the users of the system, the system *is* the business process.

Essentially, what starts the packaging phase are process design requirements—and requirements for the process redesign are the system requirements, to a large extent. These are defined in business terms through scenario design methods. The process design must also account for applicable systems and technology. The structure of the packaging phase is shown in Table 7.5.

As discussed previously, requirements describe the business needs from the customer's viewpoint, including must-have capabilities, performance criteria, and completion time. Requirements are based on a vision for the business tempered by budgets and timeframes. The tabulated system or business requirements provide both the design-to capabilities and the constraints for the process.

The candidate business process design, process requirements, and

TABLE 7.5 Business Process Design: Packaging Phase

Packaging: Process design	Methods	Inputs and Outputs
Charting the new process	Process mapping Simple prototyping	In: Process candidates, scenario process design, process requirements Out: Primary process model, simple prototype
Demonstrating the process	Process mapping Interactive prototyping	In: Primary process model, simple prototype Out: Process design proposal
Designing the process	Interactive prototyping Process definition Workflow modeling	In: Process design proposal Out: Process requirements and design, system or process prototype
Validating: Process evaluation		
Process prototype evaluation	Interactive prototyping Process evaluation planning Prototype evaluation	In: System or process prototype, defined process Out: Evaluated process prototype, evaluation plan

initial process design are developed and available to this phase. Charting the new process involves prototyping and process modeling to construct a prototype of the process as a system.

Demonstrating the process makes the prototype a shared and visible product, and the prototype becomes extended and demonstrates the characteristics of its planned role as an information system. The prototype can be maintained as part of a proposal package, allowing for further negotiation and modification through discussions with other stakeholders. Or, depending on the business environment, the workshop's prototype product might be the final outcome.

Designing the process completes the packaging phase, with the team splitting into its roles and constructing the products of process design. Process requirements are reviewed and baselined. The prototype is updated to include the current requirements model, the latest decisions and modifications. A design package is prepared as a high-level specification defining the process to be implemented. The design package might include the scenario design and its narrative and diagrams, descriptive process models, and workflow models of the revised work processes.

The validating phase is included with packaging, as the final task of evaluating the process design. Planning for process evaluation considers the requirements for system development, limited deployment, user and system testing, and installation. The prototype is placed into environments where it can be tested by independent users, or evaluators who represent the users. Feedback is gathered on the prototype user interface and its business process as viewed by the users. If user representation has been involved in the team all along, as is recommended, this testing might be welcome validation. If users have not been involved with the Team Design process, be prepared for revising the prototype or the process. Teams cannot afford to learn at the conclusion of design that the new process will induce new kinds of errors or has serious acceptance difficulties. User representation throughout Team Design is vital to ensure effective user-oriented design and acceptance.

Charting the new process. Charting the new process starts the packaging phase by developing models of the process as envisioned through scenario workshops. The scenario process design is evaluated and a rough prototype is drafted as an initial system design. Process and system requirements are provided with the scenario process, and these are reflected in the prototype model. Process maps and models are updated or created to specify the input/output relationships and data managed in the process.

Two major design approaches are used in this phase:

- Drafting a paper prototype or storyboard of screens and user interactions
- Developing process models to construct a systems view of the process

The process models used for charting the new process include those described throughout the process design format. They are brought forward in this stage as guides for the process design and for constructing prototypes. The simplest process models are often the most effective, since they will be readily understood by other stakeholders and allow a wider range of contribution. These models include the following:

- Physical process model
- Process information flow
- Process redesign diagrams (should-map)
- Scenario storyboards

Any of these diagramming methods communicates a story to a diversity of readers, and each type offers a different view of the same process. For the next activity, simple prototyping, the two most useful diagrams might be the process information flow and the scenario storyboards or other scenario diagrams. These diagrams show the users' view of the process, which can be translated to attributes of the user interface. The physical model is too system oriented and the process maps are too abstract to offer effective user interface design concepts.

Simple prototyping.   A simple, noninteractive prototype is used to describe the process and to communicate the design to the team. There are reasons not to move quickly into developing interactive prototypes of the process. A simple paper mock-up or pictorial storyboard of user interaction is useful at this stage, since it allows the team to continue working at the process design level without committing to a particular system model. It enables your customers and sponsors to interact and comment on the process without getting caught up in details over how the system functions and the user interface appears.

The simple prototype of the process serves two purposes of communication within and outside the design team:

- The users and process experts communicate to the team what they require of the process design in a tangible form.
- The design team communicates to users and experts about their understanding of the process and its requirements.

As indicated, a paper prototype is a model of the process, represented by screens and user transactions mocked up in pictorial or storyboard form. It can be initially drawn on the whiteboard or easel sheets, then refined and transferred to good freehand drawings or PC-based drawings of possible views of the system. The simplicity and plain representation of this model allows the design team to work with it directly on the board, so it is not perceived as being owned by IS staff or designers. Users and process domain experts will be more comfortable as codesigners of the prototype while it is maintained as a pictorial version. Also, building the prototype with the team as a cooperative process serves to build a shared vision of the emerging system, gaining buy-in and requiring less modification once it is actually built as a software model.

This simple prototype model will be used as the basis for the interactive user interface prototype in the next stage of work. At this point, however, the simple prototype typically works best as a tool for use in the workshop.

Demonstrating the process.   At some point between *charting* and *demonstrating* the process, the team will review and refine the prototype and process models within the team and with sponsors, customers, managers, and others. The simple prototype is used as a communication tool, and is revised as needed during this review and discussion period. This is done to intentionally keep some flux in the design, before agreements have been reached on numerous details and emerging requirements. This allows the design team to maintain progress while any other organizations, having now learned enough about the process effort to contribute to it, offer their requirements or suggestions. Depending on your development model, these evolutionary changes might be incorporated, negotiated, or kept out of scope. But the packaging phase for process design will support this continuous interaction with other organizations as required.

At some point your team must prove its ideas will work, and demonstrate the process to other stakeholders. Since new requirements are not being invited, an interactive prototype developed as a software program becomes a key part of the demonstration process. A process definition, or package of the team's current design products, is prepared and distributed to reviewers. The team will want to reach fast closure on approvals and feedback, so good project management skills are put into play to defend the design and maintain the schedule.

The output of this activity is considered to be the process design proposal, which is actually the process design package. In practice, the process design can be treated as an investment and decision-making proposal by management review committees. However, since the design is nearly complete by this point, some teams might skip the proposal option altogether and start preparing the process design package.

Interactive prototyping. Simple prototyping uses paper mock-ups of screens to gain broader participation in the system design; interactive prototyping uses software tools to build more realistic (and interactive) prototypes. In business process design, this activity becomes considerably broader than prototyping for requirements or application design. In this format we maintain the focus on business process, and systems are not specified until the business process is planned. By proposing the more conceptual views of simple and interactive prototypes, the system design proposal does not overshadow the process design plan. Interactive prototypes can be built during the workshop as a team activity or constructed offline by a designer and critiqued as a team. Make sure the prototype designer has tools available for rapid construction and linking of screen layouts, and has sufficient training to quickly mock up concepts using the tools as they are described by participants on the board. Visual programming tools, CASE tools, or development environments can support rapid design in the workshop given sufficient expertise with the tool. This process is supported when the designer has libraries or examples from which to draw to minimize the in-workshop time of prototype development. The same tools might also be used offline by a designer to construct a *baseline* interactive prototype with the purpose of discussing and modifying it during workshop sessions. The baseline prototype should be initially built using the simple prototype mock-ups as guides for user interaction and screen layout.

Visual programming tools offer rapidly built environments and allow design of realistic controls and data displays. Realistic interface elements are not important, and can even distract the group from the intent of the prototype; more critical is the ability to configure realistic data entries. Participants often argue about screen look and feel, but consensus can be achieved by mocking up accurate data relationships.

Building at least some of the prototype in a design workshop delivers advantages to the design, such as the following:

- Cooperative design involvement leads to better ideas and team agreement.
- The team understands the issues as they emerge, reducing review and explanation.
- The prototype is built with group feedback provided in real time, avoiding the delay of reviews and integrating comments later.

- When the workshop is completed, the prototype is nearly done and can be demonstrated soon afterwards.

The converse process involves developing the prototype offline, and reviewing it during the workshop. This also offers some advantages:

- The team can work in parallel on different issues, allowing the prototype development to be done offline by a designer while working through issues that don't require the designer's participation.

- If the team is already comfortable with the mock-ups, a designer can construct a draft interactive prototype that maintains the intent of the prototype drawings.

- The team can avoid the long design discussions that will arise during any type of codesign process using software prototypes.

- Workshop time is not spent on prototype design issues that might have already reached agreement.

These two modes of developing the interactive prototype represent two quite different scenarios of work. Consider these issues when planning the agenda identifying team members. A more technical team might appreciate the cooperative design aspects of working together on the software prototype model. A more business-oriented team might not understand or care about the interface design issues that consume much of the prototyping process, so the offline development would be more suitable.

Designing the process. This activity, like many others in any design process, is not a discrete step. It is a culmination of the team's ongoing activity of design and process modeling, which must at some point be completed. Depending on the amount of detail and system definition required, completing the design package can be a matter of integrating the documentation or of completing extensive process definition. The final deliverable is highly dependent on the needs of its users, and a blanket statement cannot be made regarding appropriate depth of process definition.

If further detailed definition is required of the process design, it will probably be pursued in this activity, based on models that have specified the process structures and functions to this point. Detailed design definition can use the process design proposal, and all associated models, prototypes, and scenarios developed. Two approaches to further definition are identified:

- Process definition performed in further depth, by adding and defining functions in the evolving design documentation

- Workflow modeling, defining the work practices associated with the new or redesigned business process

Criteria for acceptance and quality of the deliverable package should be negotiated and understood from the very start of the Team Design workshops. Your organization and internal requirements will set the scope and constraints for the package, which should be tightly defined as part of the design *project*. The final design package can include several sets of documents for different readers and users, and at the minimum will contain the following:

- Executive summary and overview
- Business process requirements
- Business process design model

Optional components of the package or attachments to the deliverables might include the following:

- Implementation project proposal
- Process or system prototype
- Documented scenarios
- Detailed process design document

Process definition.   Process definition involves building a case for the new process design based on business and functional effectiveness. The new process must meet the business goals while providing major advantages over the current process, or the investment will not be considered worthwhile. A process definition based on process maps or other comparative analysis methods will clearly show the planned changes. The methods for process definition include the same as in *charting the new process*. For this purpose, they might be simplified for a different readership, integrated together to show a more complete view, or just revised based on decisions or feedback.

More complex business processes will require more time for process definition, depending on details required or the level or understanding required by sponsors or internal customers before delivering a final design. Throughout the design process, a vast amount of effort in analysis and design might potentially be performed outside of workshops. For example, highly complex and mission-critical processes and systems, such as are found in health care, military, transportation, and similar domains, have highly developed networks of processes that evolved over many years. These complex logistics processes require in-depth process analysis and extensive process and system design, most of which will not be conducted in workshops. Although the same process definition methods can be used in analysis and design of these mission-oriented domains, they require extensive documentation and an extended analysis period.

For the majority of business processes, a process definition will integrate and present the models, design diagrams, and scenarios into a readable document to accompany the prototype. This definition document can be prepared as the final process design deliverable.

Workflow modeling. Workflow design is a more detailed process definition method, applicable to design of complex tasks and work processes that integrate automation and supervision. *Workflow* can be considered to include several analyzable components: flow of work as directed, flow of information, flow of materials, and the task flow, all of which are modeled using diagrammatic techniques. Workflow modeling is supported by the different design-oriented CASE tools available, all of which use proprietary diagramming methods that are not well known or already used by most analysts.

The premise of most workflow design is that work processes in routinized, data-driven activities can be deconstructed and redesigned as more efficient processes. Workflow design seems to be in favor in processes where a large number of users are involved, with the promise of increasing productivity and reducing costs by using a more efficient processing scheme. Some of the assumptions behind workflow modeling support this scientific management viewpoint, and most of the workflow tools support a limited number of flow constructs and controls, which tend to limit the possibilities in process redesign.

Peter Denning and Pamela Dargan are two proponents of a different workflow design approach, having developed an approach they call *action-centered design*. Based on Winograd and Flores' (1986) concepts of system *transparency*, action-centered design supports system and business process design from evaluating the actions through which people actually work. Action-centered design addresses the activities of thinking, speaking, using tools, adopting standard practices, and evaluates the errors (or *breakdowns*) incurred in the process. A significantly different approach to design than any traditional methods, action-centered design has influenced much of the current thinking in workflow systems.

An action-centered approach to business process mapping is discussed by Denning and Dargan (1994), in which they offer an interpretation of workflow based on patterns of communication and repetitive actions. *Speech acts,* language behaviors expressed as commitments through speaking, are considered key to the performance of a cycle of work. In principle, workflow occurs when a person makes a request for action and another agrees to fulfill the request. This simple cycle of conversation is modeled as a transaction, and this and other transactions are joined to construct the workflow design.

These performative speech acts are the basis of all business processes, and they become embedded (and therefore invisible) in business practices after countless repetitions of the request-fulfillment cycle. When analyzing workflow patterns in this way, the rationale and essential purposes of work transactions are clarified. Steps in a workflow process are maintained when they contribute to the purpose of the *conversation* of work, and they can be dropped when the steps are unneeded. A physical task analysis cannot elicit the purpose and transactional structure of workflow as does this method.

Business process mapping of workflow patterns supports the design of systems to coordinate workflow in the business. Winograd, in discussing Denning and Dargan's approach, describes three domains of process engineering applicable to workflow design:

- *Material processes* are those in which raw materials and physical items are moved and manipulated through manufacturing into predefined output products. Material processes are the foundation of steel production, automobile manufacturing, and machining processes.

- *Information processes* are those for which data and information components are entered, managed, and manipulated as part of required business. Information processes are the foundation of handling forms, data entry, customer information requests, and hundreds of repetitive operations involving the movement and management of data.

- *Business processes* coordinate actions that support the management of the larger enterprise, the business itself. From the business process level, most of the material and information processes can be seen as supporting higher-level business processes. A telephone order placed to a catalog sales outfit requires a customer request for an item, an order form, the promise for delivery of the item, instructions, or payment. All these items are separate information processes, but in total they combine to form a single transaction or business process at the workflow level.

Workflow design provides a methodology for the further detailed definition of business processes. Structured, repetitive processes require a design method that captures both sequential and concurrent activities among roles in the process. Effective redesign of workflow should also consider enabling exceptions and individual decision making into the workflow, so as not to expressly routinize every step of a process.

Workflow modeling describes the transfer of information and work products, and can specify the process value flow using time or value metrics as required. The diagramming methods for workflow design are unique and available only with the workflow design tools, so diagram examples are not provided here. Although no standard diagram or representation has emerged yet for this type of description, other commonly used methods (operational sequence diagrams, process mapping, and flowcharts) have been used to diagram workflow designs. If the use of a workflow method is appropriate for your team, consider evaluating the workflow design tools and selecting one that meets the specific needs of your organization's processes. Evaluate the tools closely to ensure that the criteria, assumptions, and values of your organization's processes are supported by the workflow modeling representation.

Validating: Process evaluation.   In the three design formats, *validating* recognizes the need to evaluate the design, as the final phase in the design cycle. Evaluation of the design assumes the ability to establish a baseline in a current process, to set target evaluation criteria, and to measure variables in the new design. However, a business process cannot easily be evaluated in its operation, let alone in a workshop setting, due to the inability to isolate variables for measurement. So how do we validate a process design in practice?

Although the activity description for validating might seem limiting due to its few activities, it is intended to offer a structure for planning, not a methodology for testing and evaluation. Any process design comes from a unique and situated context of systems, organizations, policies, goals, and established processes. Evaluation of any new design must assume that some variables in that context are more important than others, and those more important ones will be evaluated as target criteria. Broadly, one can state that this phase offers a method for evaluation planning, so that an organization has an approach to use in selecting criteria and measuring results emerging from implementation of a process design.

Design validation in the workshop should focus on the evaluation *process:* planning for evaluation and offering valid test methods, criteria, and measures to be used in actual evaluation. Validation of the actual process design can be planned as an activity to be performed after the implementation, to measure the results of the actual process. Brainstorm the evaluation criteria most applicable to the process, and organize an evaluation matrix that allows scoring of process variables against the criteria. The team is in the best position to recommend evaluation approaches; propose an evaluation method that covers the significant business goals as well as the human and system variables.

Process prototype evaluation.   Prototype evaluation can be planned within the workshop and performed within the design cycle. The facilitator can guide the team in evaluating the system or process prototype using a script or scenario to walk through all the critical functions and to review the flow and data of the process design. Comments, issues, and scores can be gathered from the group, and priorities set to address any changes necessary before rolling out the prototype or presenting the proposal package.

To evaluate the process, establish a process testbed, using an advanced version of the prototype or using a test version of the system. Evaluate the process with real users using the test system for a significant period of time, at least a month, to work out the process, system, and user interface bugs. This test period also helps make sure that people are satisfied with the new approach. Positive word of mouth evaluation provides the best encouragement for reluctant users with a new system or business process. Use the evaluation period to build up some goodwill as well as good results.

Chapter

8

Capturing and Defining Requirements

Requirements analysis and definition are such fundamental processes that they become invisible to many practitioners. When an activity becomes institutionalized through many years of performance, it becomes part of the routine, and is not refreshed through periodic examination. Managing the requirements process is a critical activity for system projects, and is a natural process for analysis and design workshops. This chapter covers the requirements definition format and encompasses the entire requirements process, also known as *requirements engineering*. Requirements engineering is closely allied with business process design, since systems are designed to fulfill business needs and work requirements. In this regard, requirements and business process efforts might be conducted concurrently. Fred Brooks (1995), in his treatment of software development and its management, *The Mythical Man-Month,* declares the importance of sound requirements practice:

> The hardest single part of building a software system is deciding precisely what to build. No other part of the conceptual work is so difficult as establishing the detailed technical requirements, including all the interfaces to people, to machines, and to other software systems. No other part of the work so cripples the resulting system if done wrong. No other part is more difficult to rectify later (p. 199).

Requirements engineering is covered by numerous treatments in the business, computer science, management science, and human factors disciplines. A basic model of the requirements process that spans the different views includes the following stages:

- *Requirements gathering.* The initial identification of applicable stakeholders and users and the acquisition of requirements in raw data form.

- *Requirements identification.* The first step in identifying valid requirements, the first iteration of a requirements document and assignment of initial priorities.

- *Requirements analysis.* Investigating the details of identified requirements, enumerating and decomposing requirements statements into discrete elements.

- *Requirements definition.* Specifying requirements in a complete and precise form, enabling their use for system and process design.

- *Requirements management.* The process of establishing requirements baselines from which all changes to requirements are controlled.

Almost any requirements can fit this cycle, using a recognizable series of working steps. In practice, there is rarely much separation between the stages. Although military development processes have typically mandated that contractors follow specific stages for a major project, in commercial systems work the distinctions are typically not followed as clearly. The Team Design cycle used to map design activities to the traditional stages can be used to structure workshops for rapid turnaround projects, providing a single cycle for facilitators and participants to understand and use. This cycle effectively applies in the case of the requirements cycle, as shown in Fig. 8.1:

- *Scoping: Requirements gathering.* Obtaining requirements information from business needs, users and organizations, and planned systems.

- *Visualizing: Requirements identification.* Creating the vision for the system or product from the body of requirements information gathered from the various sources.

- *Usage: Requirements analysis.* Developing models for how requirements will be used and describing the details of identified requirements.

- *Packaging: Requirements definition.* Specifying and prioritizing a set of business, system, or user requirements for the system or product.

A similar design cycle supports the application and process design formats, and many of the same *methods* are transferable among them as well. *Process design* can be conceived as a requirements definition from a business process perspective. In business analysis approaches,

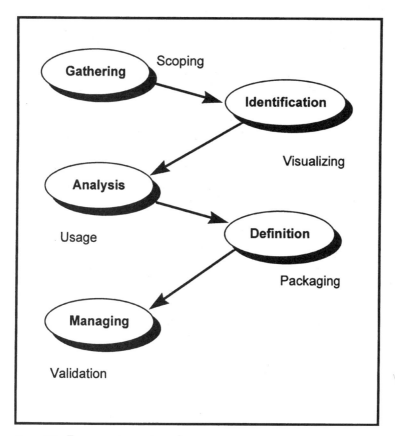

Figure 8.1 Team requirements cycle.

a *process analysis* covers both business processes and requirements definition. An effective requirements package might consist of a process design model and associated system and user requirements. Several diagramming and analysis methods apply equally well to both formats. Note the format description in Table 8.1, where the scoping methods are similar to those in the Business Process Design format. When planning efforts with extensive front-end analysis and design, consider this integrating or *blending* of the formats if the effort will cross over from business processes to system requirements. In workshop planning, extend the visualizing and usage phases to incorporate both business process analysis and user or system requirements. A single package can combine business and system design for a more efficient effort if the extent of design coverage is known in advance.

Typical Problems in Requirements Definition

Chapter 6 describes the Curtis, Krasner, and Iscoe (1988) article wherein large-scale project failures are attributed to problems in requirements management. Specifically, inadequate domain knowledge within the development team and *fluctuating, ill-defined requirements* cause extensive problems in development downstream from the requirements phase. The third problem area identified, communication and coordination breakdown, is addressed by Team Design, but not by most requirements management processes.

In regard to requirements management, Curtis' study resolved that project team domain knowledge is typically insufficient to understand the requirements. Several reasons are given for this insufficiency. One, software developers just don't usually have any background in the business problem domain. Specification mistakes are made without adequate domain knowledge, as a deep understanding is necessary to specify requirements that address the real nature of the work. Some exceptional designers were found who understood both the customers and developers, and who knew the problem domain. However, these designers were not programmers; they were considered interdisciplinary analysts. The exceptional designer was also able to express a *technical vision* to the project team, by articulating a view of working with the system from the user's perspective as well as by identifying details that would escape technical team members who focus only on development.

Requirements drift

Many sources of variation can account for requirements (or scope) drift. As a project progresses, decisions are made that affect specified requirements, and often the implications do not emerge until further into development. This can occur, for example, when a user interface technology is adopted for a project before the implications for its use are fully investigated. As development progresses, standards used for the user interface might force changes to requirements, causing midcourse corrections.

One common problem occurs when customers misunderstand the tradeoffs in the requirements process. They might not appreciate that technical limitations and schedule considerations can scale down requirements in complexity or richness. Also, as the project team and customer representatives haggle over the priorities, tacit agreements are often made that must be clarified in print. Conflicts between development schedules and software features are rampant in negotiating requirements. When decisions are made to drop an advanced feature due to the level of difficulty or inability to meet it within a timeframe, customers might want to fill the void with other features. All these situations require tradeoffs, and without vigilant communication they are not always understood, leading to dissatisfaction following system delivery.

If an internal department is your team's customer (such as product management or marketing), the actual requirements may also differ between it and your buying customers. Development team project managers must be prepared to request validation for questionable requirements, to determine whether the *right product* is being built. Marketing organizations have their own filters on the customer requirements, often due to market or image factors, which might not lead directly to customer satisfaction. Tradeoffs of useful functionality for image-making features must be made with caution.

Requirements can also change between different teams. As a project team splits into subteams responsible for different portions of the system, differing views of the stated requirements emerge. If these differences are not communicated and coordinated at the project manager level, significant drift from the baseline as negotiated may occur. Again, communication among team members is key to managing this process.

Customer learning

Although project managers often believe that the key to successful delivery is gaining agreement quickly on the scope and then holding fast to that agreement, this does not work well in practice. Customers often do not understand the technology they are requesting, and do not know what is possible in the range of solutions. At the requirements stage, they might not understand the implications of making some technology or development decisions. They require a *learning curve,* during which the requirements are initially defined and evolve through iteration between the customers and the development team.

Brooks discusses this problem by pointing out that

> the truth is, the clients do not know what they want. They usually do not know what questions must be answered, and they almost never have thought of the problem in the detail that must be specified....Therefore the most important function that software builders do for their clients is the iterative extraction and refinement of the product requirements. (p. 199).

Curtis' study describes how *new possibilities are revealed to customers* as a result of participating in the requirements process. They learn more about the technology and its limitations, and see how other options become available through choices made during the requirements definition.

This unfolding learning process during requirements applies just as much to the development team. Curtis recommends that requirements not be baselined until the business or problem domain is more fully understood. The team members are not able to freeze a set of requirements or a specification while they continue with a steep learning curve on the problem domain itself. This time for learning and understanding the domain more fully must be justified and fought for—management does not always allow this "luxury," and technical leaders are not accustomed to acknowledging the difficulty of a problem and providing extra time for learning.

Another experience-based recommendation is to build part of the system and learn from it, allowing other requirements to emerge following the initial build. This is a similar process to requirements prototyping, in which a model of the system is built and evaluated during the requirements stage. However, Curtis' team found it useful to actually construct part of the system with known requirements and use the productive development time as a period to identify and define other system requirements. They also recommend developing sufficiently comprehensive early prototypes, to surface requirements problems in the domain early enough in the life cycle to modify requirements and expectations.

Finally, the third major problem in system projects is with communication and coordination breakdowns. As a development team is formed, a layered organization arises with the customer in the center, followed by marketing or product representatives, followed by the development team, followed by management, and by service and others. The more organizations participate, the more remote the communication model. Requirements and technical decisions are made at various levels, but communication among all levels is not typically effective. Requirements and expectations get lost in the web of communications among the numerous subteams. Also, documentation is often relied upon as a means of keeping the players informed, but it can be a weak communicator. Documentation is typically the main source of communication between successive teams (marketing, development, maintenance, and testing). Curtis' study recommends that development teams have people who span organization boundaries. These (usually multidisciplinary) participants are able to create the shared viewpoint *across* organizations, rather than just within a single team.

Curtis points out that an accepted shared representation is required as a point of departure. This is central to the notion of conducting requirements workshops using Team Design or other participatory methods. Participants express that the value of such sessions is that team members share a common viewpoint on the requirements and that everyone speaks the same language regarding the process.

Requirements represent the result of a process, the process of gathering and defining requirements. The approach, skill, and perspective of the gatherer and definer can significantly influence the resulting requirements. Requirements are like any other engineering tradeoff activity where a business process must function as required and some customer or user must be satisfied. The tradeoffs occur during negotiation, which is always present to some degree between the requirements owner (some type of customer) and the solution provider (you).

The Team Design requirements format provides a structure for addressing these known problems in the requirements process. The workshop and team approach allow sufficient face-to-face interaction to enable most teams to create a shared perspective and a venue for agreement and communication.

The Requirements Process

What usually happens in the requirements analysis process? In most companies, it's typically a short period when business analysts or marketing specialists gather up a wish list for a new or enhanced software application. Then, developers look over the list to figure out a best-fit solution to the problems presented. It becomes an exercise of translation with several intermediaries putting their spin on it.

This is a critical area of focus—miscommunication and misinterpretation of requirements is far more costly than any other mistake in the software development process. Requirements analysis and specification is a complex, human-oriented process, and since it happens up front, it affects the direction of every design element and piece of code in a project.

What are the purposes of requirements and how are they used by development organizations? Although many have a single purpose of interest for requirements, many different purposes can be identified:

- To define exactly what functions will be designed and built into a proposed system

- To manage the scope of the project and the system

- To obtain agreement from customers, business representatives, and developers

- To describe the new work processes for users

- As an input document for system and process design

- To define system and business goals and objectives

When discussing the different types of requirements, most methodologies address the requirements in terms of their *function* in the development process or the life cycle. Although this is perfectly valid and expected, it's mainly a distinction of level and not of kind. For example, your product development process might mandate the delivery of *customer* requirements, *product* requirements, and *functional* requirements. Although these might appear to be three different types, in practice they differ more by detail than by content or perspective. The requirements process might yield better requirements, and more quickly, given an understanding of requirements types and of approaches to facilitating the requirements process.

What are the different things we call requirements *in practice?* Some of the distinctions among requirements are described here, all of which might be considered equally valid as requirements documents by the organizations that use them. These are described to provide a sense of the range and scope of requirements models present in different contexts. To some extent, these requirements types can be mapped to organizational contexts, in that each type is oriented more toward one of the four contexts (business, system, user, or product) than the others. However, all or most of the "types" of requirements are often found within a single organization. In large, complex systems projects, all of these requirements types might be present. This also suggests that different functions have different names for the same requirements document. It is not so important to exhaustively define the different types of requirements as it might appear—as a facilitator or project organizer, it's more important to understand the intent and composition of the different types when they are requested as deliverables from a workshop. Although the following nomenclature might not be "standard" and might not even map to your organization's use of the terms, it is intended as a touchstone for thinking about the variations in requirements documents woven throughout business and development teams.

Business or marketing-based requirements. Business and marketing requirements are used as the initial mechanism to define the scope of a product or system. The life cycle of any product starts with an idea that becomes described and approved in these early requirements statements.

Business requirements establish the business needs for the system or product. These requirements provide the goals for a system or product and supply the rationale for development. The term *business requirements* is more typically used in organizations that follow a business context, where an information system is being designed to support an internal operation, such as an accounting system or an operations-oriented system (for example, customer service management). Business requirements are not as much specifications of system functions as they are definitions of business need based on strategy or emerging problems that must be solved. They address the nature of the problem (for example, insufficient customer information at the point of sale), proposals for solving the problem (for example, complete customer database with full transaction histories), and success criteria (for example, must be able to identify customer in database within two seconds of request). Benchmarking criteria may be described, and comparisons made to existing systems performing the functions desired. Business requirements do not typically specify system solutions or define development plans. They can often describe just the very need for a product or system, and therefore lead into the next phase of work.

Customer requirements define a business problem or need from the customer's perspective, and are therefore marketing-based requirements. Typically gathered, evaluated, and defined by marketing analysts or product managers, customer requirements are typically considered statements of the capability desired by a significant number or type of customers. Customer requirements should be market driven, and should not define a system solution. If customer requirements can be defined in more generic or solution-free terms, a design and development team is more free to propose a creative solution to the underlying requirements. Often customers (and users) do not know the capabilities of available technology, and are insufficiently informed to describe their requirements in system-oriented terms. Nor should they be encouraged to do so, since this might significantly limit the effectiveness of development proposals. Customer requirements, from the product organization's point of view, lead right to defining the product requirements.

Product requirements are often market-driven requirements based on customer need and just as often product proposals targeting a perceived opportunity. The term *product requirements* is used within product development organizations to refer to the formal description of the system or product to be built. In different contexts, the product requirements might be the end result of focus groups and product prototyping, or be a proposal dreamed up by a product manager for a new thing the company can sell. Product requirements define a very general specification that can be used by the development team to begin design work. The product requirements should lead the team toward defining a development-based requirements model.

Development-based requirements. Development requirements are created and primarily used by the development team, and provide a great deal more detail for use in design and programming. Although development-based requirements contain much greater detail and analysis than business-based requirements, they must be readable by almost as wide a range of participants. Most JAD processes support the creation of development-based requirements packages, but do not distinguish significantly between the different types.

User requirements is a term that is more often used informally, as a specification of the functions of a system from the user's perspective. User requirements are found more in the business and user contexts, but often find a place in the systems context as well. Very few documents in practice are actually called *user requirements,* although they might be referred to such by the project team. User requirements relate directly to user work processes and specific task needs, and are sometimes developed by a user team or its representatives. Sometimes a section in a functional requirements document will be set aside for specific user requirements.

Functional requirements can be found in all contexts, as this is a common reference to development-based requirements. Functional requirements range in detail depending on the organization and readership. Functional requirements might mean any of the following:

- An analysis of the business requirements with a defined list of functions (basic capabilities) and features (unique abilities) of the system
- A detailed analysis of the entire business process using functional hierarchies and dataflow diagrams to define proposed functionality
- A detailed analysis of business processes plus definitions of software modules addressing system functions, with data definitions as well as dataflow diagrams

Be sure to clarify the level and detail expected in a functional requirements document. This is one of the most common deliverables from a team workshop, and one in which expectations can differ greatly. Identify the ways in which the requirements package will be used after your completion of it—this should clarify the representations and detail necessary for the next phase of work.

System requirements also refer to several different aspects of requirements. At its most general, a system requirements specification (SRS) defines the scope and complete set of functions for a custom system or software effort. The SRS has been used in government projects (MIL-Spec) for two decades, and has a history of standardized usage. That usage might be exemplified by the user or systems contexts, where a custom software product is being developed under contract. The system requirements otherwise define the entire scope of a system, including functions, architecture, related systems and interfaces, and databases. Other more detailed requirements related to the system requirements might be defined as follows:

- *Application requirements.* A specification of requirements for a specific application module as part of an overall system.

- *Software requirements.* A technical specification of requirements for specific software capabilities.

- *Interface requirements.* A specification of requirements that define how software modules will communicate and pass information through developed system interfaces.

- *User interface requirements.* A specification that defines required user interface architecture, user interaction methods, and the initial presentation of screen layouts and look-and-feel design.

Workshops for requirements definition

The team approach to requirements analysis and definition is well established in JAD approaches, and is borrowed from JAD for requirements definition workshop methods. Team Design differs significantly in the following ways:

- The Team Design formats provide a comprehensive set of methods from which to choose, not just a step-by-step or cookbook approach.

- The approach supports both group workshop activities and individual analysis products that support ongoing workshops and team development.

- The workshop formats provide methods for use across four organizational contexts (business, user, systems, and product), addressing a wider band of teams and applications.

- The formats provide agendas and a flexible structure, allowing facilitators to select and integrate their own methods into the structure. Basically, the four general phases of scoping, visualizing, usage, and packaging are structured to generate the necessary deliverables.

Requirements workshops should incorporate the viewpoints and contributions of the various stakeholders throughout a product life cycle. Figure 8.2 shows how different stakeholders are likely to view the requirements throughout the chain of representations. Note that each role in the chain has a different viewpoint of requirements, and represents this viewpoint to the next member of the chain. Feedback is implied by the curved arrows, where confirmation is made or interpretations are checked between the two roles.

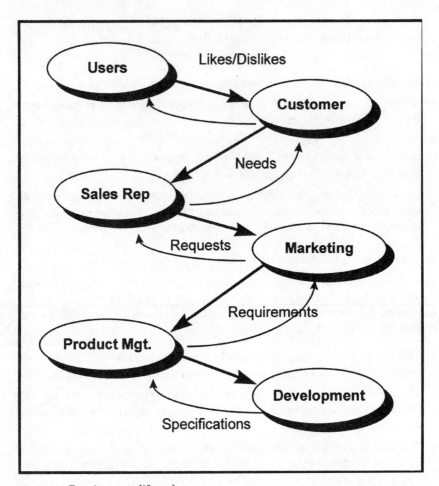

Figure 8.2   Requirements life cycle.

This requirements life cycle adopts a product context view, and it integrates more roles than the other contexts. Starting with users and customers (user and product contexts), a *user* is identified as the person interacting directly with the system, and the *customer* is a buyer, manager, or user representative. In a systems or business context, these two roles might be combined into one.

From the user or customer viewpoint, requirements pinpoint both business needs for their work as well as improvements and fixes necessary to fulfill user acceptance and satisfaction. Following the product context, several other relationships typically unfold. The users or customers express their interests in terms of likes or dislikes and needs for their work. To get their needs into the product, the typical direction is through a sales representative, who has the most frequent contact with the customers. The sales rep communicates customer needs or requests for new features back to the marketing organization. Marketing representatives follow by providing a list of product requirements to product managers, who typically guide the projects for the business. Requirements become specifications as they are provided to developers. In the diagram, each pair of communication links has a feedback channel, expressed by the curved arrows. The feedback channel confirms the communication or requests additional information, and the more active the feedback channel, the greater the ability to acquire useful and appropriate information.

Keep the requirements life cycle in mind when looking through the format and team workshop ideas. Any of the participants along this pipeline of communication would be of value in requirements workshops. All are stakeholders to some extent, and all will have contributions to the product from their own perspectives.

Format: Requirements definition

The phase structure of the Requirements Definition format is shown in Table 8.1.

Analyzing and defining requirements

The practice of requirements analysis is the foundation for developing effective requirements models in a Team Design workshop. Again, this is perhaps the most commonly used and most widely misapplied practice in system development, so providing a basic treatment of requirements concepts should not be considered redundant. Traditional requirements engineering focuses on two primary areas: business needs and functionality. *Business* (and product) *needs* address the necessary changes to the business or opportunity in the marketplace to be fulfilled by the effort. *Functionality,* of course, addresses how these needs are to be met, by specifying the tasks (or functions) that the system must perform.

Requirements activities can be broken out in different ways. A comprehensive example is described, and can be condensed to fit different cases in your practice. This example defines the products as the result of requirements definition activities performed. Recall the Team Design requirements cycle described at the beginning of this chapter. The same activities result in the following outputs:

Scoping: Requirements gathering. *Problem definition* starts the requirements process, and is a business view of the requirements. The problem definition results from the initial gathering and understanding of the user or product requirements.

TABLE 8.1   Requirements Definition Format.

Agenda activities	Methods	Inputs and outputs
	Scoping: Requirements Gathering	
Exploring the purpose	Dialogue, brainstorming methods, Breakthrough Thinking (BT) methods	In: Project goals Out: System purposes
Defining the scope	Scoping diagram, context diagram, process hierarchy	In: Purposes, initial scope Out: Scope definition
User and system goals	Brainstorming methods, BT, affinity diagram	In: Scope definition Out: User and system goals
Understanding the current system and processes	System diagrams, process models, function hierarchy, demonstrations	In: Scope definition Out: Process or system models
Identifying users, objects and relationships	Organization chart, affinity diagram, cause and effect chart	In: Process or system models Out: Process or system models, object and item lists
	Visualizing: Requirements Identification	
Organizational requirements	Brainstorming methods, dialogue	In: Process or system models Out: Organizational requirements
Envisioning task requirements	Task analysis, work descriptions, user process flow	In: Process or system models Out: Initial user requirements
Envisioning system requirements	System matrix, functionality matrix, system process diagrams	In: Process or system models Out: Initial system requirements
	Usage: Requirements Analysis	
Developing user scenarios	Scenario analysis, use cases, ideal system exercise	In: Initial user and system requirements Out: User scenarios
Selecting scenarios	Brainstorming methods, ideal system exercise	In: User scenarios Out: Detailed scenario
Generating system requirements alternatives	Brainstorming methods, system matrix, functionality matrix	In: User scenarios Out: System alternatives
Prototyping user processes	Simple prototyping	In: System alternatives Out: Initial concept prototype

TABLE 8.1   Requirements Definition Format. (*Continued*)

Agenda activities	Methods	Inputs and outputs
Packaging: Requirements Definition		
Defining requirements model	Defining business rules, requirements mapping	In: Concept prototype, requirements models Out: Requirements models
Prototyping requirements	Interactive prototyping	In: Concept prototype Out: Requirements prototype, requirements models
Validating: Requirements Management		
Requirements evaluation	Prototype evaluation, requirements review	In: Requirements prototype Out: Evaluated requirements model

Visualizing: Requirements identification. *Product objectives* are measures of effectiveness, performance, and usage criteria for the system. Product objectives result from the identification of and agreement on priority product requirements.

Usage: Requirements analysis. *Function analysis* is performed to evaluate the problem domain, to provide a clear understanding of all the business or system functions to be accounted for. Function analysis is done to generate better solutions and alternatives, and graphically describes specific requirements.

Packaging: Requirements definition. *Evaluation and synthesis* in the requirements phase is generating alternative solutions and concepts from the function analysis. This activity is characterized by brainstorming ideas, reviewing literature or other products for analogies, and integrating concepts from experts and other sources, and it results in a deeper definition of the requirements model.

Validating: Requirements management. *Specification* defines the baseline description of the system, inclusive of all tasks preceding. The specification must model the system requirements precisely for use by developers and other stakeholders. The specification becomes the baseline for the system or product definition and is managed by change control procedures. *Review* ensures agreement and ownership of the specification as part of the requirements management process.

A requirements specification is used as an agreement between

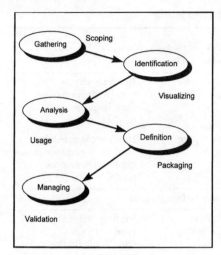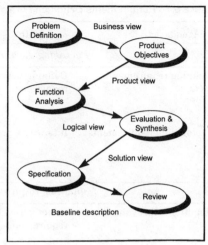

Figure 8.3   Requirements engineering process.

stakeholders in development. It should be treated as a contract of sorts between the owner and the provider. If requirements are not detailed and specified to the extent necessary to ensure adequate understanding, mismatches between customer expectations and the developer's product may result. As Fig. 8.3 shows, a different viewpoint is expressed at each stage in the requirements process. Each stage also represents another interpretation, a transformation of the previous stage's definition, which are points where expectations can differ. Person-to-person communication is required throughout the process to check assumptions and validate the interpretations made from the previous stage. To maintain continuity and communication from stage to stage, analysts develop requirements to meet generally acknowledged quality criteria. Basic quality criteria for requirements include the following:

- *Easily verified.*   Requirements should be verifiable by walkthroughs, tests, or evaluation.

- *Not ambiguous.*   Different readers should have the same understanding of the requirements document.

- *Complete.*   All critical functions must be addressed in the requirements specification.

- *What, not how.*   Requirements state what's needed at a logical level of definition, and do not mandate an implementation or method.

- *Consistent.*   All other known requirements should be referenced and accounted for in the requirements model, and should use the same representations.

- *Appropriate level.* Requirements should be specified at a consistent level for each function described. That is, if appropriate, function 3.0 should be specified to four levels of breakdown if functions 1.0 and 2.0 are so specified.

Addressing the interpretation of requirements. As with business process design, requirements modeling methodological issues arise with regard to the *interpretations* necessary between the stages of development. As the requirements model builds from each phase, a divergent perspective is imposed on the previous model view. There is a necessary political process in this transformation, as the process requires analysts to focus on some functions and to ignore or downplay others. Liam Bannon (1995) logically extends the problem of describing abstracting representations of work processes from the work environment:

> Our critique of modeling argues for the essential limitations of any and every form of representation. In other words, no representation, or set of representations is ever complete. Models are thus seen, in our view, as interpretations, as constructions, which for some purposes, under certain conditions, used by certain people, in certain situations may be found useful, not true or false. Thus, we wished to recast some of the discussion about the uses and limitations of models in the context of "reframing" rather than of simply "describing" or "abstracting from" some external reality (p. 67).

Bannon recommends a participatory design approach for addressing the inherently political issues of interpretation in design practice, understanding that it involves the direct participation of users in the making of representations leading to system design:

> Incorporating the experiences of the workers themselves, or end users, through active participation in the design process...as an antidote to the problems of over-reliance on the normative representations of work that dominate traditional systems development practice (p. 67).

Unfortunately, from the participatory design perspective traditional JAD practice embodies much of what's considered dysfunctional in current development practices. JAD relies heavily on structured analysis methods, and drives toward team consensus instead of educating the development team in the diversity of perspectives. Consensus making always favors project managers and developers, as users are not usually well enough educated in the process and methods to understand the tradeoffs being made, and users tend to go along with the team to support group progress toward agreed goals. Team Design attempts to resolve some of these differences between the two perspectives by proposing the *formats,* with a range of techniques for each activity, allowing for facilitator selection of more participatory or more traditional methods. While this might seem like offering a grab bag of methodological tricks for the practitioner, it can also be seen as a means of culturing the organization through gradual adoption of different techniques, yielding much more diversity in the development perspective than is possible using traditional methods only.

Leading requirements analysis

Team Design workshops are recommended for work across the development life cycle of requirements, including requirements identification, analysis, definition, and review. A different set of team members might be involved in different workshops in a series of sessions, but a core team is typically involved throughout the process. Facilitators should be consistent throughout the workshops, to maintain communication and support a team assimilation and synergy. The facilitator should lead the group sessions, but not be the group leader. The analysis effort itself can be led by a team leader, with shared roles by the facilitator and the project manager.

Chapter 7 discusses some of the capabilities expected of analysts and facilitators leading process design, which can be considered applicable here, it being a similar activity to requirements definition. Requirements processes integrate the ideas, needs, and directives of a diverse and, often, conflicting community of stakeholders. As shown previously, each different role will have a somewhat different outlook on the requirements for the system. Team planning for the requirements phase is crucial to the project. First, make sure enough time is set aside to gather and analyze requirements. If this is a fairly simple enhancement, it may be only three days or a week. If a new concept for a large-scale system is being explored, the requirements phase might involve a month of investigation and analysis, another month of prototyping and review, and another month of refinement and negotiation. Allow time for gathering available appropriate information and documents from users or customers, previous projects, product history, and other sources. Each project has its own ecology of users, customers, managers, and developers, and any product or system has a separate history. In fact, different projects in the same organization will very likely use different requirements analysis approaches. With any approach, a first step requires identifying the customers and end users, and making clear distinctions between them. Requirements must satisfy both groups when software is delivered.

In requirements workshops, representatives from all stakeholder groups can be invited and involved. In the typical development environment, developers don't have the chance to work closely with the customers. The requirements workshop is an opportunity for the developers to work with customers and understand their concerns directly. Therefore, product and customer representatives are necessary team members for the integrated requirements process.

Requirements Analysis Methods

Requirements analysis methods have evolved over time, from the days when MIS analysts interviewed user managers and worked in relative isolation to produce a specification, to today's working environment, where high involvement is expected and many traditional analysis methods are considered overkill and where new technologies require continual revision of approach. In the gap between analyst-driven interviews for mainframe-based information systems and object-oriented reengineering for distributed client-server intranets are many classical methods often overlooked by both traditionalists and newcomers. In my experience, appropriate requirements analysis methods are neglected not due to lack of knowledge so much as they are not *required* by their organizations. People don't do what they aren't asked to do—and the quality of requirements and of resulting design suffers as a result. Team Design is not about doing the least amount of work to design systems—it's about having the best tools available from which to choose for the job at hand.

Consider the methods used in the two major dimensions of requirements definition described previously—business and system requirements. The primary differences are that *business* requirements establish the needs of the business that the system supports and the *system* requirements define the functions of a planned system or product. We look at the representations of requirements in this section, the ways in which human and computer-based activities are described and communicated among the team members and the developers. This establishes the basis for applying the techniques for scoping, visualizing, usage, and packaging described in later sections.

Business and user requirements analysis

In the typical scenario, business requirements are much more informal than system-based requirements. Managers and user representatives are not usually interested in spending the time and effort to perform detailed analyses of usage scenarios; they just want to describe desired functions in their own language and hand it off to be built.

A typical business requirements process might work as follows: Whoever is closest to the customer or user organization identifies some specific needs for a business process or product. This is often a marketing manager (product context) or a user representative (business and user context). They write something up and then "throw it over the wall" to a project manager as their requirements statement. The project manager assembles a team and investigates the problem. They might develop another iteration, reflecting the business needs as a system. This is handed off to developers, who iterate on the specification until they reach agreement. This final version is frozen and the developers build the business system or product from the specification.

A number of interpretations and compromises are made throughout this process, most of which are invisible to the team and its customers. Typically, requirements are accepted in whole when provided by a customer or product manager. If any requirements analysis is done at all, it is done through iteration of the specification until the representative and a developer are satisfied that they can work to that document.

There are many shortcomings to this approach. First, the initial assumptions made by the representative may be biased or filtered through interpretation. People who are close to the customer are often far away from understanding the capabilities of technology. The development request may therefore be undereducated in regard to what's possible.

This first cut of requirements should really be considered a statement of need. When it is handed over to the technical team (or thrown over the wall), it should be considered a starting point. The requirements *analysis* usually starts with this rough material. The analysis process defines the representations that describe the work and define the functions required of the system. These representations, both business- and system-oriented, are the diagrams and definition methods typically associated with technical requirements analysis.

Business process representations. Business process representations of requirements include descriptions, diagrams, and analyses of the business processes automated by the system. Such design artifacts as business process models, process maps, workflow diagrams, and others as described in Chap. 7 provide representations of the business process that reveal requirements. Requirements are often derived directly from these analytical and planning models, since the models define the planned new process from which the business and system requirements are construed. Workshops can build directly on the business process models to generate the system-based requirements that support the newly designed process, and in many workshops this is a transparent flow from process modeling to requirements definition.

Business representations of requirements, to be effective, must be constructed with the involvement and insight of experts in the business area. Otherwise, a cookie-cutter approach to system building will be taken, leading to short-sighted design and insufficient or unneeded functionality. The functional or domain experts should always be involved directly with the team to cut through assumptions and translate the need into detailed requirements statements. Functional experts are analysts or representatives of the product team or user community who fully understand the tasks and procedures of the target work environment and can honestly speak for the users or customers. Their role on the development team is to provide representations of the end users and their tasks, and to describe how information is used in the business.

Functional experts should be incorporated into the team from the very beginning of requirements analysis. They should be available throughout the requirements phase to contribute to the analysis and the specification. They will be the first ones to approve any prototype application or design. They should not necessarily be the project leaders for development, since their expertise is not in the technology domain.

User representations.   User representations of requirements include analyses and descriptions of the planned user community, and include depictions such as user profiles, user analyses, user organizational requirements, and user roles. A solid understanding of users and their tasks is essential to product usability. Development of user representations is critical to system design, especially in user interface design, as the design team must have a model of user needs and behavior from which to determine appropriate usability goals. User representations differ from business and task models in that they enable the requirements necessary to support users in learning the system and using it as a tool with minimal errors and support.

User analysis is necessary in order to better understand the end users and various user types in the community of all customers for your products. Usability and acceptability can never be designed or ensured unless the development team and the product team know the users and their specific work requirements and demands.

Survey questionnaires and interviews are often conducted to gather this information for product development, but with a captured user community, as in large corporations, user information can easily be obtained by working with the intended user organization. Salespeople are likely to work in much different ways than back-office workers, and will have different educations, ages, work styles, and goals than other users. Products, training, and manuals should be designed to fit the intended user group.

User profiles are a common representation of the user for use in requirements models. Profiles of the user include information collected about the intended audience for the product or the end users of the system, including data about their sociopolitical status (demographics) and behaviors and preferences (psychographics).

User profiles therefore establish a picture of the user, defining such characteristics as computer usage, educational background, skills set, specialized training, daily work habits, and other descriptive attributes. User characteristics can be mapped to software usability needs by analyzing the gaps between user background and requirements for understanding the system. Furthermore, user satisfaction criteria can also be extracted for use in requirements planning by identifying the users' effort needed to bridge the gap between their background and productive use of the system. Requirements planning should also account for whether training, tutorials, help systems, and extended learning might be fostered in the requirements to better support user needs.

User representations can be generated within the Team Design workshop when actual users or user managers are involved in the sessions. Human factors analyses of the user population and specific user groups often suffices for development teams when a publicly available product is being designed. However, even human factors engineers are limited by the availability of users and user representatives when describing user characteristics and usability goals.

Task representations. Task representations extend from understanding the user—the user of a system or product has an implied purpose, which is embodied in the various tasks performed in day-to-day work. Task representations are developed to provide clear direction to system designers of the tasks the system must support. Systematic examination of work tasks is conducted to ensure appropriate design for both manual and currently automated tasks. Task representations include task analysis descriptions and diagrams, workflow models, user information flow models, and similar artifacts from which task-based requirements are derived. Chapter 7 describes the use of task sequential models, allowing for both in-depth and informal task analysis.

Task analysis is often overlooked during the requirements phase, typically because development teams have little experience in this area. Essentially, task analysis is a detailed definition of work processes, based on systematic observation and description of tasks. Software designed to rework business or task processes improves user productivity by considering all the manual and automated task functions in their work. Task analysis is *logically* independent of automation. It can be used by itself to improve work efficiencies or to reorganize workers' tasks. It is also the ground-level work for any business process reengineering activity, as it has a direct impact on individual worker productivity.

As with requirements collection, several techniques are used in task analysis, and, often, more than one technique is used in analysis. Several methods commonly used include the following:

- *Content analysis.*   Evaluation of the technical content of documents and manuals.

- *Interviews.*   Structured interviews with key workers involved with the task studied.

- *Questionnaires.*   Designed for use when a larger population of workers is studied.

- *Task observation.*   Naturalistic field observation of workers while engaged in a task. Can be used in conjunction with periodic interviews, "speaking aloud" analysis, or videotaping.

- *Protocol analysis.*   A structured walkthrough of users' tasks using predefined scenarios, recording task steps or activities.

- *Job diary.*   Detailed notes kept by workers during typical job performance. This technique might be more appropriate for workers in environments where output is not measured on a time-per-unit or high-pressure basis.

- *Mechanized measurement.*   Automated recording processes built into machinery or computers to record specific task steps, times, errors, or additional steps. This might be more appropriate for time-intensive industry, where interference with workers would not be tolerable.

Human factors and industrial engineers are trained in task analysis methods, and should be involved on the team and in workshops when called for. Task analysis is useful for most large-scale applications automating business processes, and for any development that seeks to radically change a work process. But it can be a time-consuming and therefore expensive process. Task analysis is usually a fieldwork activity, and not facilitated by team workshops. Field-based task analyses can be supported by the team by developing and planning the approach for task analysis, and by evaluating and discussing the results in a review session.

System requirements analysis

The purpose of system requirements analysis is to develop technical specifications for the product or system. The system requirements specification (or functional specification) is basically a detailed definition of the system, organized in a readable breakdown of functions and topics. Although the specification is itself not typically developed in the workshop session, the system requirements planning and many of the component model types can be developed within the Team Design context.

A functional requirements specification defines the requirements for software development. Functions are defined and are often supported by function hierarchy charts and dataflow diagrams detailing the information flow of data among functions. Within each function, procedures are written to define its logic. These are traditionally defined according to input-process-output definitions. Definitions are written in structured English (terse logical statements that read like a programming language) or brief prose descriptions. Functional specifications also define all the global system requirements, such as for application security or data conversion. Performance requirements are also defined within the functional requirements specification, including the following:

- Data volume and transaction rates
- Frequency and availability
- Planned growth
- Data retention
- Performance objectives
- Hardware constraints
- Communication performance

Systems analysis is conducted both within and outside the workshops, and involves a series of processes (such as Team Design, JAD, and analysis studies) and methods resulting in requirements documentation. System requirements component documents often include CASE diagrams and object or data dictionaries, usually supporting functional process models and logical data models.

The primary models in systems analysis are shown in Fig. 8.4, as they are typically positioned in the development life cycle. The user interface design is conducted as a parallel design activity in conjunc-

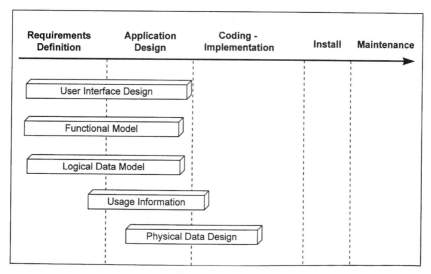

Figure 8.4 Systems analysis in the life cycle.

tion with systems analysis. The functional and data models comprise the traditional systems models generated from systems analysis over the life cycle. All these representations of requirements become integrated into the requirements models at an appropriate level of detail. Systems analysis continues further in supporting design and development beyond requirements analysis and into the application design cycle.

Functional representations.   Functional representations of requirements describe business processes in detail, using function hierarchies or dataflow diagrams to define component functions. Both are traditional structured analysis diagrams that support requirements models, and have been in use much longer than other de facto standard analytic tools. Many organizations maintain these diagramming methods as standard representations for process and functional analysis, and they continue to enjoy a widely shared use and understanding.

Functional hierarchies represent the scope of an entire business process and identify the fundamental needs as abstract functions that can be referred to throughout the design process. Functional hierarchies are produced by *function decomposition,* or breaking down the functions within a given process. Decomposition allows the team to consider and evaluate alternative functions and solutions, with the analysis goal of supporting numerous possible solutions. This is performed to understand all the specific activities that comprise a process that may be suitable for automation or might require a manual or alternative solution.

Functional hierarchies instantiate a basic framework which becomes used in function analysis in building dataflow diagrams, the most widely used functional representation. Dataflow diagrams show the relationships of functions to each other, and their use of data among the functions. Input and output flows of data among functions are described, and the events and data usage are mapped to defined functions. This structured analysis method provides a useful mapping of system and task procedures for system developers, making it a valuable part of the specification.

Functional models are criticized by recent methodologies, especially in object-oriented modeling and process flow modeling. Functional models do not support an object view of the system, yet they can be used as a complementary view to an object model. A true object-oriented system, however, is not designed or built using structures compatible with functional models, so they are not used for object-oriented systems. Some process flow models capture end-to-end processing and sequential temporal information, providing a view of business processes not supported by functional models. Function analysis diagrams do not show precedence or *process* flow, but data flow, so again the models might be seen as complementary, and not as exclusive.

Data representations. Data representations are among the most critical components of any requirements definition. Data requirements include *conceptual data models* (depictions of high-level data required by the system), *logical data models* (such as entity-relationship diagrams), and *data definitions*. Data requirements can often be substantially described and defined in the workshop, and evaluations and refinements of data models are often conducted within a facilitated design session.

The primary goal of data analysis is typically to identify all the components of data, entities and attributes, that are required for the success of the system as a whole. Again, a successful data analysis depends largely on relationships developed within the larger team of domain experts. They provide access to broad-based and detailed information about data used in work processes, and about the normal and anomalous uses of data.

Data analysis requires investigation of numerous sources outside of the workshop, but most of which can be represented by appropriate team members. Figure 8.5 shows some of the sources used in defining data representations for a logical data model. Evaluation of business forms, current data usage, and business regulations provides some of

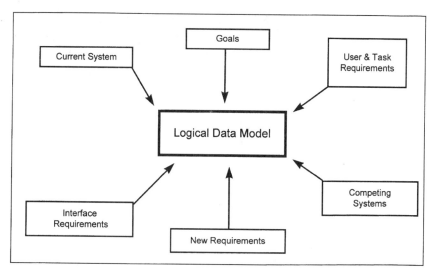

Figure 8.5   Sources for data analysis.

the sources for analysis of data sources, which are described in data dictionaries and logical data models.

Entity-relationship diagrams (ERDs) remain the most common data representation in use across nearly all types of database design. Although several versions and notations of ERDs are supported by available CASE tools, all ERDs follow similar logical rules. Therefore, once people learn to read one version, any flavor of entity diagramming can be understood. ERDs are a stable representation, useful throughout the system life cycle, and are used as the guiding representation for team discussion and design for system data.

User interface representations.   User interface (UI) representations are defined using a functional prototype or a user interface specification. Interactive prototypes are acceptable among development groups as a visual specification for use by developers in programming the user interface. As graphical interface prototyping tools have gained acceptance, the interactive prototype has become the best mechanism for UI specification. In shops where the paper specification is also required by development (at least for sign-off, if not for coding) a document with prototype screens captured and annotated is often used.

Throughout the life cycle, different prototypes will be designed to represent the views required at strategic points in development. The same UI prototypes serve to represent the various views during the design process. During the phases of design and development, the following views or representations of the user interface can be produced:

- *Project planning.* An early concept prototype is developed to represent product requirements.
- *Requirements definition.* The concept prototype is developed continuously through the phase as a requirements model showing emerging requirements and a preliminary design.
- *Design.* An application prototype is developed as a visual specification of the user interface.
- *Development.* A functional prototype is developed for usability testing of the system.

The prototypes and the user interface specification (if prepared) must provide a model of user interaction and describe the software requirements for the user interface. Some of the following descriptions are used in user interface representations:

- *User interaction model and process flow.* Based on a task or scenario description, a diagram and narrative describing the user's interaction points and navigation through the system.
- *Screen display formats.* Based on the prototype or screen documents, the format design specifies the physical layout of all representative screen types designed for the system, and defines all menus, fields, controls, buttons, labels, terms, field names, positioning, and colors.
- *Report formats.* Report formats are typically specified as layout requirements and data requirements, and can be included as part of a specification.
- *System and error messages.* Messages are part of the user interface, and are defined as part of the specification or prototype.
- *Help documentation.* Although Help can be written by documentation writers, the design of the Help interface and the requirements for type and level of Help are part of the user interface representation.

Requirements analysis products

The products of requirements analysis generate several documents, some informal and some considered to be deliverables. Informal requirements analysis products include interim working documents circulated within the team and parts of specifications that are generated when gathering and analyzing requirements. Summaries of interviews and JAD sessions, long lists of issues and potential requirements, and numerous diagrams are often attached to these partial documents. Workshop documentation such as design mock-ups, lists of data elements, forms and screen design concepts, data-flow diagrams, and process flowcharts are summarized and transformed into formal products.

Formal products include any documents considered to be deliverables, as well as plans and reports. Formal requirements documents endorsed by different organizations go by several titles, including the following:

- *Business requirements.*   A statement of business need (not a specification), representing the goals of the business.

- *Product requirements.*   A statement of product definition (also not a specification), representing the strategy of the product positioning.

- *System requirements specification.*   A higher-level definition of system requirements often used as a directive for the technical specification, representing the system to be built to satisfy the goals and strategy.

- *Functional requirements specification.*   A detailed specification that defines the functions of a large system, including data, process flow, or interfaces.

- *Software requirements specification.*   A specification that with related technical specifications (interface, hardware, and embedded systems) defines other detailed technical specifications for software design.

Requirements definition is primarily an exercise in communication. Documentation can be a precise means of communication, but the most effective means of communicating exactly *what* and *how* is a visual representation using a prototype. An application prototype delivered as part of the specification package serves to demonstrate the intentions of requirements and design. Since it shows the product concepts, initial user interface, client-requested functions, data display, and potential output functions to be developed, the prototype is a powerful tool for communicating requirements and building consensus within the team. A type of prototype can be identified with each of the preceding requirements documents as follows:

- *Business requirements.*   Slide show, or paper prototype for presentation purposes.

- *Product requirements.   Product concept prototype,* showing the look and feel and demonstrating possible design ideas.

- *System requirements specification (SRS).   User interface prototype,* defining interface standards or guidelines for the product and representing known requirements.

- *Functional requirements specification.* *Functional prototype,* demonstrating the proposed design of significant system functions and proposing design models.
- *Software requirements specification.* *Design prototype,* a working model of the system as it might be designed, with realistic data and final-form user interface.

In each case, notice how the prototype not only embodies the requirements at the same level documented, but pushes one step further into the process than the requirements. The prototype leads the design by testing out ideas in advance of their definition, while at the same time it *baselines* the previous system definition document. So, the functional prototype baselines (or signs off on) the functions defined in the specification, but it also leads further into software design than the specification.

Finally, as an organizer or facilitator, you must identify your customers for requirements deliverables and prepare packages accordingly to satisfy their particular needs for use. Your customers and their usage needs might include the following:

- *Product managers.* As team members, they should be involved with the design process. As customers, they will require each specification package (but not all associated detail) and will access the prototypes to demonstrate to *their* customers.
- *Executives.* Also your customers, executives will typically require only formal deliverables, and usually without appendix materials. However, they might also expect frequent informal updates about workshop progress and the design process, to gain a level of comfort throughout the process.
- *Marketing representatives.* If marketing plans are integrated with the product development (for example, product context), marketing staff might require access to the latest prototype, or at least demonstrations as needed. The only specifications they might use would be the product requirements, possibly the SRS.
- *Business analysts.* Will typically develop the SRS and functional requirements, and will be customers of the business and product requirements.
- *User representatives.* Will be customers of the specifications they review, typically the SRS and functional requirements. They will also be heavily involved in prototype design and demonstration (for example, user context).

- *Developers.* Customers and users of the SRS and functional requirements; drafters of the software requirements specification. They are also primary customers of the prototypes, since what is prototyped is similar to the expected product.

- *Interface designers.* Customers of the product and system requirements; developers of the prototypes. They will typically be involved throughout the phases requiring prototyping.

- *Documentation writers.* Customers of the prototypes; will also require use of the functional requirements.

- *Test teams.* Customers and users of the functional requirements and software requirements. The test team might also heavily use the prototypes as references.

Team Requirements Cycle

The Team Design requirements cycle is based on the four-phase design process described in Chap. 6. Starting with *scoping,* a design team can select requirements activities associated with the four phases as necessary to produce the appropriate models for the scale and approach of their effort. *Visualizing* uses creative methods for identifying requirements and mapping out process models. The *usage* phase pushes these models into frameworks of use, testing out the unfolding design using scenarios and analysis. *Packaging* formalizes the models after requirements and design decisions have been made, and creates prototypes of the new design.

When the Team Design *workshop* approach is used, two more phases are added. *Initiating* is added to support team building and the kickoff of team activities. *Validating* is an optional phase used with the team as a means to test the requirements using process and system prototypes.

The four phases defined in the cycle describe applicable techniques for requirements definition exercises. Many of these will be familiar from the general workshop methods described in Chap. 5 (scoping, brainstorming, and diagramming) or from the Chap. 7 format for business process design (context and affinity diagrams, process mapping, and scenario analysis).

A method detailed in this chapter, Breakthrough Thinking (Nadler and Hibino 1994) is a complete process for creative collaborative thinking designed to lead to radical effective breakthroughs in process and product. It is a solution-oriented methodology, and not a problem-solving approach as traditionally understood. Several Breakthrough Thinking techniques are highly effective in the Requirements Definition format, and are specified in their appropriate phases in the cycle.

Breakthrough Thinking, however, is not designed to be broken up into component methods, and it would be unfair to the design and the intention of its creators to represent it in this way. It is a problem-solving and creative thinking approach that uses a series of principles for individuals and teams to engage in their own processes. Because of its designed-in flexibility, Breakthrough Thinking is an excellent approach for requirements definition and application design and the Team Design formats that support these processes.

Breakthrough Thinking defines seven principles of creative problem solving, each with its own techniques in Nadler and Hibino's treatment:

1. *Uniqueness.* The uniqueness principle recognizes that each problem encountered is different from others. Regardless of apparent similarities, problems and designs arise from a situated context that differs from that of even highly similar problems. Robust solutions are not copied and applied from other situations. Available solutions should only be considered if the purposes and future needs are also appropriate.

2. *Purposes.* The purposes principle elicits concepts of purpose for the effort, and creates a hierarchy from those purposes. The list is expanded, and the meaning of purpose is explored. Consensus is reached about the level of purpose to pursue, and the uniqueness of the problem emerges within the purpose.

3. *Solution-after-next.* The approach to design and problem solving is based on finding solutions in line with the purpose that satisfy the needs for the future. While meeting the requirements of the present problem, the solutions for the future, or solutions-after-next, are created to meet the projected needs following the immediate solution. The team creates better solutions and is given direction by working backward from an ideal target proposal.

4. *Systems.* The systems principle recognizes that all the necessary elements and relationships must be defined to understand the system in which they interact. The solution's system is contained within a greater system, and problems stemming from one system are related to other systems. The systems principle provides a framework for managing the complexity of difficult and complicated systems, and enables understanding of the relationships among the dimensions of the problem.

5. *Limited information collection.* This principle recommends evaluating the need for collecting and analyzing data before expending this effort on a fruitless pursuit. What are the purposes achieved by gathering and analyzing extensive data? The focus again should

be on the solution, and only as much information as required to support the solution should be collected. Too much knowledge about the *problem* can actually prevent finding innovative and creative solutions, as the team becomes overwhelmed by data and versions of the problem.

6. *People design.*   The people design principle recommends the cooperative involvement of the people affected by your solution in the design and development process. The people who will implement or use the solution in their work should become involved in its development on a meaningful and continuous basis. To better allow interaction with the solution proposals, only critical details should be presented, allowing some design freedom for the people expected to apply the solution.

7. *Betterment timeline.*   The betterment timeline principle indicates that planning for a sustainable future is necessary for long-term and continuing success. A program of continual change must be planned, with scheduled revision throughout the life cycle of the system or solution.

Breakthrough Thinking is a recommended approach for the first two design phases in the cycle, *scoping* and *visualizing.* It is unique among requirements definition approaches, in its clean-sheet creative approach to design. As described by Alan Scharf (1996), a practitioner and consultant, "the most amazing aspect of Breakthrough Thinking is that it gets superior results without collecting, charting, documenting, and analyzing what now exists. The time saved is employed in enhanced creativity and teamwork for unique and surprisingly cost-effective results."

Several other analysis and design methods have been described fully in preceding chapters, and will only be touched upon here as a reminder to the reader of their effectiveness in requirements definition.

Scoping: Requirements gathering

The *scoping* phase of the requirements cycle gathers information for requirements, and uses different analysis methods to fully investigate and understand the background and goals of the process or product. Scoping the requirements is a linchpin activity—it builds the platform of assumptions and priorities upon which the system is conceived. Table 8.2 specifies tools for scoping requirements as a team, supporting group processes in generating purposes and goals for the system and its users.

Team processes used in scoping include many techniques described in the Business Process Design format in Chap. 7. Details on these

TABLE 8.2   Requirements Definition: Scoping Phase

Scoping: Requirements gathering	Methods	Inputs and Outputs
Exploring the Purpose	Dialogue Brainstorming methods Breakthrough Thinking (BT)	In: Project goals Out: System Purposes
Defining the scope	Scoping diagram Context diagram Process hierarchy	In: Purposes, initial scope Out: Scope definition
User and system goals	Brainstorming methods Breakthrough Thinking Affinity diagram	In: Scope definition Out: User and system goals
Current system and processes	System diagrams Physical process model Process mapping	In: Scope definition Out: Process or system diagrams
Identifying users, objects and relationships	Organization chart Affinity diagram Relationship map	In: Process or system diagrams Out: Process relationships, object and item lists

techniques are referenced back to that chapter to reduce some of the inherent redundancy across the different formats.

Capturing and defining requirements are among the most frequent applications for JAD and facilitated group processes. In most situations, a clear need is found for representation across multiple user and operational organizations, and agreement among cross-functional stakeholders is critical. Facilitators will find that most of the techniques in this format support extensive group interaction in requirements definition. Especially in scoping, a high degree of interaction and involvement among team members is necessary to gain early agreement and to cover as many perspectives and inputs as practical until the field of options narrows in subsequent phases.

Exploring the purpose.   Exploring the purposes for requirements definition starts with the scope and considers the overall purposes before breaking it down into function and task models. The team identifies the goals, assumptions, and business needs for the system using methods that surface problems, constraints, and guiding policies very early into analysis.

Having a defined purpose statement anchors and guides the team throughout scoping and visualizing. Team agreement on purpose helps maintain the scope and guides the team's direction and vision for the system. The facilitator can use the same methods to explore purposes as are described in business process design. The methods and their context for use are similar to requirements definition, and the need is the same for establishing team work style and relationships.

The inputs available to the requirements definition team at this point are typically high-level business or user needs, and project goals that might not be well defined as of yet. These inputs become the framework for creative team exercises for meaningful direction and system purposes. Purposes bring together the team's thinking, enabling a complete shared understanding of the goals and purposes of the system.

As described in Chap. 7, several methods can move the team forward in exploring purposes. *Dialogue* is a fundamental process that every facilitator can use to establish a forum for sharing and listening to ideas in the team. Facilitated *brainstorming* methods can be used in conjunction with dialogue, as an exercise to elicit brief statements of purpose and other ideas. And the purposes hierarchy of *Breakthrough Thinking* provides a complete process for working through purposes in a solution-focused approach. Any or all of these methods can be used in requirements definition.

Defining the scope. Scoping the project and system or product can be accomplished using any of several techniques described in Chaps. 5 and 7, especially the scoping diagram or context model. These diagramming methods are useful during the beginning stages of work when the team is building a shared understanding of the domain.

Some will find it more useful to start with the purposes hierarchy exercise and develop the scope and context diagrams from the resulting purposes and objectives. The purposes hierarchy leads to rethinking the scope from multiple perspectives before the scope is finally locked in. It also defines numerous criteria and objectives useful for allocating resources and determining priorities.

Depending on the system analysis methodology your team is using, other approaches might be used to move into the next phase of work. If using structured analysis and design methods, develop a process hierarchy diagram to initially define the basic processes supported by the system, and then break down processes into a hierarchy of related functions. The process or function decomposition represents the scope in more detail once the component functions can be determined, and provides a structure for analysts and developers to refer to requirements by function identifiers (name and number from function charts).

User and system goals. Defining user and system goals is a useful way to construct the high-level framework for requirements definition. Articulating and understanding the goals of users supports the team in making functionality decisions and in making informed tradeoffs among the requirements. Some requirements are more important than others—defining the goals of the *users* based on their work and the goals of the *system* (strategic or organizational goals, actually) assigns value to functions and allows the team to clarify directions and decisions.

Using the Breakthrough Thinking approach, the purposes hierarchy generates a set of goals from the stakeholders' purpose perspective. By working one level deeper with the team, goals can be constructed down to the objectives or milestones defined to reach the goal target states. The focus purpose guides and clarifies the goals, allowing for specific actions to be planned to reach the goals. Using the purposes hierarchy through to its conclusions results in defining most of the process and system goals, plus criteria and measures for accomplishment.

Understanding the current system. Requirements analysis in the scoping phase allows the team to create a shared understanding of the current system. This necessary step also does not demand extensive analysis of *current* processes and systems, a similar approach to that taken with process design approaches in Chap. 7.

If your team has followed business process analysis and design into the requirements phase, you invariably have conducted some measure of current system analysis already. In the form of a process map (as-is diagram), function charts, or dataflow diagrams, some analysis will be available and will save steps in requirements definition.

The *as-is* process modeling approach is a common method used in understanding the current system functions. As described in Chap. 7, as-is process models are a sequenced mapping of the current business process. This model is compared to the *to-be* process design models later in analysis. A process map or other diagram method can be used to document the as-is model. However, these maps can be very abstract, and do not capture the user's viewpoint of the work practice. If as-is process maps are used, only a limited analysis of *current* processes should be conducted for most systems efforts.

The analysis tools recommended for building the understanding of current systems and processes include those used in business process design, as well as those more commonly used with information systems. The following methods can be used effectively in understanding the current system:

- *System diagrams.* Variations of current process models, such as context and scoping diagrams and physical process diagrams, as used in all design scoping.

- *Process models.* Process maps and other as-is models of the business process, as used in business process design.

- *Function analysis.* Analysis of process structure, used to establish scope and functional organization for systems analysis. Function hierarchies are constructed and decomposed functions are identified, and analysis continues into developing dataflow diagrams.

- *Ethnographic methods.* Participant observation, documenting system usage and processes by interacting directly with the users. Ethnographic methods are useful for systems with extensive interaction by teams of users, where systems are just one tool used in complex work practices.

- *Demonstrations.* The simplest approach is also quite effective. The team arranges to review demonstrations of current systems and to observe people working in the processes considered in the scope of analysis. All affected systems or systems to be redesigned or replaced should be demonstrated and discussed by system users or experts.

System diagrams and process models have been discussed to some extent in the previous chapter, in their application to process design. Requirements definition uses a different approach for the same methods.

Process modeling. Process modeling was previously covered as a method for developing analyses of current processes and comparing them with new design models. Within this general yet well-accepted methodology for analysis and design, the primary techniques remain function analysis (dataflow diagramming) and process analysis methods (such as $IDEF_0$).

Process modeling refers to the analysis and modeling of processes in a business enterprise, and usually begins with the highest level of abstraction for an entire business area. For example, the customer billing process or order fulfillment process are large processes with, perhaps, dozens of constituent functions. Process analysis identifies the most basic needs in a business area, and supports discussion of alternatives well in advance of solution definition. In this methodological approach, an analysis of the current business process is performed first, followed by a redesign of processes to focus on a preferred process approach or business solution. In Chap. 7, "As-is and To-be Models" in the "Visualizing: Business Vision" section describes the method and offers recommendations for its use.

Function analysis. Functional decomposition is a fundamental systems analysis concept with near-universal applicability in structured business and system problems. Primarily useful in process design as

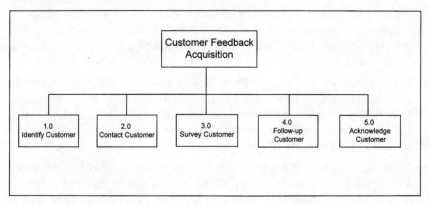

Figure 8.6   Function hierarchy.

a documentation and verification tool, a functional model can be developed by the team to facilitate requirements specification and system design. The method is easily taught to the design team, and it readily communicates required process changes to management or process owners.

Function analysis charts a hierarchical diagram of all defined functions flowing down from a process, each function being subdivided to the appropriate level. Functional decomposition starts with this function hierarchy, as described in Chap. 7 and shown in Fig. 8.6. A top-level function hierarchy is derived from a diagram of business processes that organize a top-level process into significant categories of functions. In the diagram shown, the top-level process is *customer feedback acquisition,* which is composed of five constituent functions.

Functional decomposition typically starts from a single defined process (a high-level business process, such as product development or customer service) which is broken down into its component functions, which are all the activities comprising that process. The same technique is used at different levels of description, depending on the starting viewpoint and the level of detail required to communicate the design. For example, process decomposition remains at a higher level of business process, decomposing a major process or an enterprise into its component processes. The functional level is closer to the definition of systems, and it is this level that supports the requirements analysis.

Although this model does not provide the process *flow* information that is so useful in the process mapping models, it does allow the team to define a more formal process description for system design. The process maps do not define process or system functions in a precise and inclusive way. Different activities that might belong to the

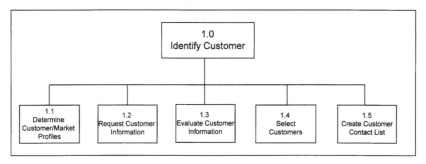

Figure 8.7 Functional decomposition model.

same function are modeled somewhat sequentially, based on the chain of events describing the process flow. In the customer feedback example, several functions might be included in any one of the process steps. *Survey customer* is shown as a single box on the flow model in Fig. 8.6, but might break down into six to eight functions when designed as a system approach, as shown for the *identify customer* step in Fig. 8.7. Language used in functional definition is often different than in a process map, leading to a more system-oriented model.

A function is a separate discrete activity, with a beginning and an end. Functions are named as active tasks, with a verb-noun format, specifying an active task. The minimal action required of a function is to take an input and produce an output. Functions are defined in the hierarchy diagram and are used in dataflow diagrams, mapped one-to-one by name and number. Dataflow diagrams can be considered part of requirements analysis, but are not necessary in *understanding the current process,* the specific activity under discussion. This is due to the basic recommendation to invest the effort of preparing dataflow diagrams in defining the new system, not in analyzing the current system.

Analysis products of the function analysis include basic components of a requirements specification. The team can pursue function analysis in workshops to the point of defining functions and agreeing on their definitions. The specification will require offline work that establishes further details, such as the following:

- *Process.* The process name and definition is documented to support the diagram.

- *Intermediate function.* These include all the levels of functions from the first level to the bottom. The function name, number, and narrative is associated with each function on the diagram.

- *Elementary function.* Elementary functions are the lowest-level functions, and are defined further by specification languages. The function name, number, and narrative is associated with each function on the diagram.

Function names are a focused description of the activity or system behavior defined. Their precise definition is important, as they will define a view of requirements that will be used throughout analysis and design. Functions can further be identified as *automated* or as *human* functions, which are manual tasks.

If a function remains as a manual task, a process map representation is probably sufficient definition for the task. If a process does not require a change of systems, communications technologies, or infrastructure, a functional model to define the system is probably overkill. When an information technology approach is being considered or is required, the functional decomposition communicates the process design at a level of detail consistent with the system design. It becomes the model for system requirements, and can save the system design or development team time and prevent the miscommunication of design requirements.

Ethnographic methods.   Ethnographic methods have been discussed previously as a social research method employed in situations where complex systems and team interactions are involved. *Ethnography* is a technique of observing and studying work practices as they occur in their natural environment of work through actual participation in the work. It has been used for the purpose of deeply understanding the nature of current work practices, by investing the time to learn about them and experience the work from the perspective of the user.

Proponents of ethnography claim that most work practices are situated within the unique context of an organization, with its history, goals, and social order. Basically, system design is work design; therefore, a thorough understanding of the social nature of the work practice is called for to inform system design.

Randall and Rouncefield (1996) describe ways of bringing ethnographic methods into use with system requirements and design. Having studied air traffic controllers, they consider the impacts of system design on complex multiuser systems. Their claims for ethnography can be summarized as follows:

- Systems are by their design an intervention within organizations, and have an impact on the social aspects of work. The actual work practices performed by users have social implications and assumptions that can limit system effectiveness when not understood.

- Ethnographic studies can educate analysts and designers in understanding the real-world context of work, causing them to reevaluate the way work is designed.

- Ethnography informs analysis and design of complex systems to enable the appropriate separation of work into automated and skilled components. Ethnography can provide information to enhance the work of users with systems.

- Finally, ethnography can create possibilities in design that are not available through other means. By designing systems within the context of the work practices, a different set of possible solutions emerges that can result in systems that offer much more value to the users than merely streamlining processes in the name of efficiency.

Randall and Rouncefield discuss the possible use of a design-oriented approach to ethnography they call "Quick and Dirty Ethnography." Essentially an iterative cycle of ethnographic study, their approach allows designers to use a familiar process similar to that used in other areas of requirements definition. Before starting the ethnography, designers familiarize themselves with process models or initial specifications in the target process. They then conduct a short ethnography with the user group of interest for an appropriate period of time—generally more than two days, but perhaps less than a week. During and following a series of ethnographic observation sessions, the designers debrief with the team to discuss what they are finding and to gain feedback on the value and direction of information required for design. This iterative cycle results in revised design and process models.

Identifying users, objects, and relationships.   The eventual results of requirements engineering include documents, designs, and output products that meet the expectations of the stakeholders for the next development activity. Obviously, identifying users and their attributes becomes a critical task for guiding the requirements effort. A thorough understanding of the users, their organization, their work processes and individual tasks serves as the foundation for product and system requirements. User profiles and demographic descriptions help to produce this necessary understanding, but nothing replaces having users available to the project team and involved in concept and prototype evaluation.

Models of system objects, their definitions, and their relationships are also constructed for technical guidance of the team. System data and objects cataloged and defined might include any of the following:

- *Data.*   Entities, attributes, and relationships.
- *Functions.*   Functional models and data flow.
- *Object models.*   Object-oriented models and class-object hierarchies.

- *Architectural models.* Network models, infrastructure models, and database interfaces.

In requirements analysis, these data and object information sources are identified and pulled together for analysis and reuse. In some efforts, existing data definitions and functional models might be organized at this stage and evaluated for reuse. For analyses that concentrate more on *user* requirements, only the identification of system data and objects will be pursued, and further definition will be conducted during the packaging phase.

The depth to which analysis continues for system objects relates to the organizational context. A business or user context might concentrate more on processes and analyze data and objects later, in the Application Design format. Prototypes are used in these contexts, and data must be identified for use in the prototypes, but not necessarily defined in detail. A systems context might focus more on data needs earlier in this format. These methods are more fully detailed in Application Design, where data analysis is performed in support of designing the system.

Several methods are useful for identification of users and user-level objects and relationships for use at the appropriate level for requirements modeling. For Team Design workshops, these methods include the following:

- *Organization charts.* Find existing organization charts to better understand the work environment and reporting constraints of the user community. These are also valuable for identifying key allies in the user groups to obtain technical advice and domain expertise during requirements definition. Also, appropriate use of organization charts might be useful in constructing new proposed views of the organization as conceived following automation or full system implementation.

- *Affinity diagrams.* Recall the affinity diagram described in Chap. 7. This technique affords a rapid approach to organizing concepts, building a shared model of the design, and identifying priority requirements. Affinity diagrams allow the team to structure the ideas, concepts, and issues collected from interviews or brainstorming. They are useful in the front-end analysis of information gathered from customers and users, and provide a method for the team to contribute to the requirements model.

- *Cause-and-effect diagram.* The Ishikawa fishbone diagram (Chap. 7) is also useful in this context, for uncovering elements related to problems or processes in the user environment that might be addressed by the system. Two of the branches of the typical fishbone chart are *people* and *environment,* which can lead to identifying critical components of the requirements model.

Visualizing: Requirements identification

Visualizing generates ideas and constructs a representation of requirements shared by the team as a whole. The *visualizing* phase of requirements definition moves the team into specifying details of user tasks and system needs to support the goals and processes identified in the prior phase. The methods described in Table 8.3 are tools that define requirements by describing the business and work processes supported.

As a team, we want to identify the requirements for conducting certain types of work, especially where new processes are established. Choices are made in the selection of requirements based on satisfying these business processes. When defining requirements for products, market and strategic requirements based on internal business factors are often weighed against customer or user-based requirements. Without a structure in place to assess the effectiveness of requirements, decisions can be made to emphasize requirements that do not add value to the product. Techniques such as the Breakthrough Thinking system matrix provide a means to evaluate the relative value and contribution of requirements against the product concept.

The output of this phase is the initial system requirements package. This document describes the requirements defined and includes the diagrams and models selected by the team to be used to represent the requirements and system design.

Organizational requirements. Organizational requirements are described during requirements definition as a means of understanding what the business and the owner organization are expecting to gain from the effort. These are not always part of the formal requirements

TABLE 8.3   Requirements Definition: Visualizing Phase

Visualizing: Requirements identification	Methods	Inputs and Outputs
Organizational requirements	Brainstorming methods Dialogue	In: Process/system models Out: Organization requirements
Envisioning task requirements	Task analysis Work descriptions User process flow	In: Process or system models Out: Initial user requirements
Envisioning system requirements	System matrix Functionality matrix System process diagrams	In: Process or system models Out: Initial system requirements

definition, but they should be surfaced within the team so they become part of the tacit understanding of *why* the system or product is being built. Organizational requirements can be derived from all of the business functions represented in a project, and for a major internal information system they should be actively solicited by the project team from the management of all organizations impacted by the system.

Organizational requirements might be reflected in the purposes and objectives defined during scoping, in goals such as "need to cut process costs by 20 percent" or "need to have a presence on the World Wide Web." These requirements might never be traced to the design as system and user requirements are, but they have an influence nonetheless and deserve recognition. Perhaps even more important, if left undefined their influence can turn negative, as they become unspoken assumptions that affect the direction of the project and can diminish project leadership.

Dialogue and brainstorming are recommended as methods for surfacing and identifying organizational requirements within the Team Design process. *Dialogue,* described in Chap. 5 as "facilitated storytelling," is a valuable tool for understanding the background and values among business needs and organizational relationships. It is often treated as a two-way conversation between the teller and the group, and becomes an ongoing communications process within the team. Recall that dialogue requires the team members to withhold their assumptions, to not engage from their normal positions. The facilitator maintains the flow of the dialogue, if necessary, and encourages participants to create the proper attitude in speaking and listening.

Envisioning task requirements.   By envisioning task requirements, a team generates concepts, models, and descriptions of the user's work processes and specific tasks supported by the system or product. If a business process analysis or design has been performed, the results of that work and its requirements feed directly into the task level. When reaching this stage of the requirements definition, it's useful to assess whether business process analysis should be pursued, to redefine the work processes from a businesswide perspective. This stage is probably the last chance in the life cycle to cost-effectively make any significant redesign of business processes, as much of the effort can be worked in parallel with requirements definition.

In practice and in concept, progress ensues from defining task requirements first and then following with system requirements. Systems are designed to support tasks, and even if a specific system architecture is planned for the new process or is imposed on the organization, tasks should be analyzed and redefined without relying on special artifacts of technology. Two benefits arise from this process: (1) the task itself benefits, since the team can discover opportunities for design based on true requirements without the constraints imposed by technology-driven solutions, and (2) a better system process is usually created, in that the users are more likely to be satisfied with the result.

Many work processes and user tasks already involve some degree of automation, which also tends to impose or reinforce a certain technological approach. The current technology will often drive much of the thinking about the task, making it difficult for users or analysts to separate the task from the tools.

Start by evaluating the process or system flow diagrams generated in the scoping phase or by prior process analysis work. Determine what level of definition detail is required to move forward most effectively. If a system process being defined is currently a manual or knowledge-intensive task (such as document editing, health care, or financial planning), some work process and task analysis will be necessary to capture the methods, knowledge, and lessons learned from years of task performance. If the process is more data-intensive (such as budgeting, or loan processing), analysis of the use of data might be a more productive use of analysis resources.

The basic output of this activity is initial *user* requirements, based on user work processes and task descriptions. These initial user requirements are instrumental in developing scenarios and use cases in the usage phase.

Task analysis models. A *task flow model* or *sequence analysis model* describes a task or set of tasks across the dimension of time. It is a simplified version of task analysis, and can be used in more situations than the traditional task analysis approach. Task flow and sequence analysis approaches are called for when time-related objectives are important in the new process or automation design. If the process has high-priority objectives for improving response time or saving time overall, or has time dependencies imposed by upstream or downstream processes, a sequential task diagram should be developed.

Task analysis provides a fine-grained model for user task description. Task analysis can be performed for significant software applications in a new domain, although a much less involved analysis can typically be done for existing automated systems where the work processes are already guided by a computer-based task. Task analysis is applied in improving workflow efficiency or in improving the users' effectiveness by redesigning applications. Although some task modeling can be performed in workshop sessions, it is more likely to be limited to higher-level work process modeling and flow diagramming. For many applications, this level of task analysis and redesign might be sufficient. The team's domain experts, again, are the most qualified members to advise the team as to the level of task analysis necessary to generate models for requirements and design.

As with any analytic technique, the more details the method requires, the more challenging it is to engage a workshop team in the exercise. Not every team member has the patience or background to appreciate the work required to conduct sequential task analysis. As with the process information flow diagram, if fine-grained detail is required for effective design, much of the analysis can be performed outside the workshop, and shared and discussed with the team during a review session. The results of detailed analysis can also be presented and used during the design stage of the process design activity.

Task flow model. Task flow modeling is performed to understand the possibilities for redesign of time-dependent tasks. Several task analysis diagramming methods are adaptable for the specific needs of the design effort. Variations of flowcharting are commonly used, with a timeline positioned along the top or bottom of the diagram to indicate time increments as the task's steps are followed from left to right. The operational sequence diagram (OSD) is unparalleled for detailed analysis, where fine-grained increments of task and time must be modeled (Kurke 1961). For most business purposes, that level of detail will never be necessary.

Task analysis is typically utilized when the process design requires a detailed breakdown of the steps and dependencies of a single task from start to end. Although this level of detail is required for user interface design, the method is also useful (with somewhat less detail) for evaluating the impact of the process redesign. The basic method for sequential task analysis is to start with the context diagram or a similar model already developed that shows the broader process and the tasks it includes. Select the task that requires this focus of analysis based on the team's criteria or identified need.

Task flow diagrams are also useful for defining system tasks for prototyping further into the requirements process. Some task flow analysis is necessary for effective user interface design, and it also serves to test the scenarios designed for the larger process. Developing task flow diagrams *within* a Team Design workshop is not the most efficient exercise, but it is still very effective, because it helps everyone in the workshop get on the same page with regard to the task definition. Consider having an analyst develop the diagrams outside of the sessions, and present them to the group in advance of user interface prototyping. Conduct the task flow analysis roughly following these steps:

1. Identify roles and roughly describe the users in those roles. Define any attributes of the users that are relevant to the task design. Useful attributes might include statements such as "task-oriented," "too busy to read manuals," or "measured on timeliness."

2. Identify and define the organization of work in the task area. What are the priority goals of the work process? What is the management structure and reporting responsibility for the task? How is work processed—continuously; in bursts of work; or as parts, forms, or other inputs are handed off to the users?

3. Identify a typical scenario for the task, a story that fits the experience of a user performing that task. Walk through the scenario with the team or a small group of users. Start with the first input or trigger event to the task, and follow the scenario through to the conclusion of the task.

4. Break the task down as far as necessary into discrete actions and the objects used to satisfy those actions. Decompose the task only to the highest level of detail necessary for redesign information (for an office process, this would be at the *form* level, for example, not at the level of data on the form). Identify how work products are completed and handed off to the next role in the chain of tasks.

5. At each point in the decomposed task, identify the *expected* time and typical *actual* time required to perform the action. Identify any exceptions to the action. Review the chain of actions and add the expected times and the typical actual times as two separate sums.

   Compare these sums against known times for full task completion (or heuristic rule-of-thumb time estimates). If there's a large difference, assess whether it is due to the additive task times or the overall time estimate.

6. Summarize the analysis in a task sequence diagram and a short descriptive document, if necessary. Make sure the diagram is easily readable by managers and stakeholders who may not have been involved in the analysis.

When task flow has been completed sufficiently, evaluate the task breakdown for potential areas to change with the new process. Use a diagram of the proposed new process or system and begin to compare the new and the current. Look at the differences in use of information and elimination of task steps in the current way of doing things. Ask the workshop team to contribute answers and brainstorm the following types of questions:

- What is the most basic change to the task? What will go away with the new system?
- What will end users be doing in the new process?
- What current jobs will this change? What others will *that* change impact?
- What new tasks are added? Are there any not yet identified?
- How does the proposed system or process streamline the current process?
- What are the savings or benefits created by the new system or process?

Document the results of task flow analysis in the requirements document. For practitioners new to this technique, use familiar diagram types; adapt a flowcharting technique with which the team is already familiar. Figure 8.8 shows a very simple model that can be used to communicate task flow.

When the task flow diagrams are completed, present them to the workshop team via projection onto an overhead screen. Facilitate discussion about the task flows, and be prepared to modify the diagrams on the fly during the session. Ask the team to describe how certain tasks will be represented by the user interface, and to contribute design ideas by drawing interface concepts on the easels or whiteboard. The results of this process should lead into system requirements or user interface prototyping.

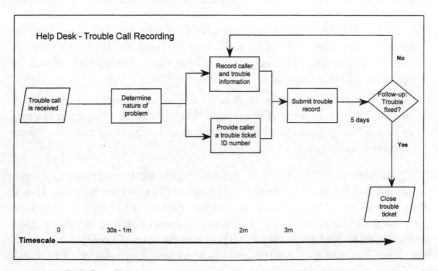

Figure 8.8 Task flow diagram.

Work descriptions. Work descriptions are task models as seen from one level higher—from the process viewpoint. Where *tasks* are the specific sequences of steps taken by a system user in performing a job, *work descriptions* entail groups of tasks oriented toward performance of a larger, more complete function. Where task models are diagrammed using *low-level* flowcharts, work descriptions use *process-oriented* diagrams that might show tasks and roles, relative task completion times and dependencies among tasks, and relationships among inputs and outputs to the work process.

User process flow. Defining a user process flow creates a pictorial view of processes from the user's perspective. Chapter 7 shows examples of the process mapping approaches to process flow, and variations of these diagrams can be produced that focus on the user requirements in the process.

Instead of describing business functions, the user process flow describes activities from the user's workflow. Any user process can be described by a flow diagram, including any set of activities performed by specific individual users fulfilling a job role, or by user or organizational groups performing a complex task or work process.

Several critical elements of a user process flow should be modeled, regardless of the flow diagram method:

1. *Defined roles.* Any specific job roles should be identified and shown on the diagram.

2. *Inputs to process.* Show all necessary inputs—data, forms, orders, paperwork, and customers that initiate a task sequence.

3. *Task sequence.* Show the chain of events triggered by inputs or required of the user.

4. *Process outputs.* Show any physical, electronic, or other defined outputs of the task sequence.

5. *Timing and dependencies.* Specify part-task times, task completion times, scheduling delays, and dependencies among tasks in the flow diagram.

6. *Tools and techniques (optional).* Show any computer-based or physical tools, programs, and defined techniques used to complete each segment of the process.

7. *Information sources (optional).* Show any databases, data sources, or other information required for task completion during normal execution of the process.

From the different models of user work practice, including process models, ethnography, task models, or any combination of these, the initial user requirements and work process requirements are derived. The user requirements model is maintained as part of the requirements definition, and is used again in the usage phase, for scenario design.

Envisioning system requirements. System requirements modeling follows definition of *user* requirements, to drive technology needs from the discovered needs of users. However, some activities can and should be performed in parallel with the user-centered requirements study. These techniques can all be conducted within the Team Design workshop, by bringing together appropriate systems professionals and guiding the group processes to develop these models.

System requirements differ from user requirements in their focus on system solutions to previously identified user needs. System requirements necessitate a technical approach, requiring the involvement of system professionals to portray the possible range of directions to the team. However, at this point in requirements definition the system requirements should not be so restrictive as to constrain effective alternative solutions. Process diagrams from business or systems analysis provide the primary input to system requirements, along with initial user requirements that will have been largely specified by this point. This activity also closes the visualizing phase by generating the *initial system requirements,* a skeleton model of proposed system solutions and constraints.

Three methods are described for team development of system requirements. The *system matrix method* from Breakthrough Thinking ties together system and user requirements across several dimensions, revealing new relationships and system solutions. The *functionality matrix* is similar in its two-dimensional tabular format, but lays out system functions and maps system design options to the functions. Finally, *system process flow diagrams* map out system processing and transactions from the system architecture.

System matrix. The system matrix technique provides a format for teams or individual analysts to creatively generate ideas and options for system design. As with other Breakthrough Thinking techniques, it is part of an ongoing process of team inquiry and creation. The system matrix arises from the systems principle, which holds that all problems and designs exist as parts of multidimensional systems, in which only parts of their structure are ever accessible. No problem or solution ever exists in isolation. The systems principle requires the analysis of interactions and relationships among numerous elements of the design problem, arriving at a total picture through exploration and definition of its manifold components. The systems principle provides an approach for creating solutions, specifying detailed structures to support the solution, and operational requirements for the solution. It also supports team projection of the solution into planning for future use, using scenarios and the *solution-after-next* principle, which looks for the solution envisioned that follows the current design solution.

Figure 8.9 shows an empty matrix similar to Nadler and Hibino's (1994) example in *Breakthrough Thinking*. The use of the system matrix is essentially to support team thinking about problems or design in multiple dimensions, leading to a thorough system-oriented view of the design. Leading this process in workshop practice is an effective approach to generating structured information leading to tremendous insights as well as detailed requirements definitions. Note how the matrix is divided into eight elements (rows) and six dimensions (columns), allowing high-resolution analysis of requirements within a *solution space*. Each cell of the system matrix can also be viewed in terms of its elements and dimensions, inviting thought processes that incorporate the big picture as well as extreme detail, and in the same diagrammatic method. It is not recommended that a single-sheet diagram be used to show the entire problem matrix—the diagram itself can be used as an index to an appropriate body of design information generated from it.

Nadler and Hibino provide guidelines for using the systems principle, based on using the matrix:

1. Start with an empty matrix. Make the assumption that no elements or requirements have been defined yet, and use the clean-sheet approach with the team to generate a mind-set of uniqueness.

2. Don't attempt to fill in every cell. A requirement or relationship will not be necessary for every cell in the matrix. As a facilitator, move the team through the process of defining requirements thoughtfully but quickly. Limit the amount of brainstorming or discussion for the exercise, and don't worry about filling it in.

3. Start by working through the elements (rows), and expand the elements as required by using dimensions that apply to the solution. If you are documenting or diagramming the results, separate sheets should be drawn for each element, and these will map to the system requirements.

4. Manage the complexity of the system matrix—move details from the matrix to separate diagrams or minimatrixes that focus in on a particular area of interest.

5. Use the system matrix as a communication tool within the workshop team and among your internal customers and stakeholders.

Dimensions

Environment	Fundamental:	Values:	Measures:	Control:	Interface:	Future:
Purpose: mission, aim, need, focus, primary concern						
Inputs: people, things, information, triggers						
Outputs: desired to achieve purpose, also unexpected or undesired						
Sequence: process steps, handling inputs, process flow, operations						
Environment: physical and organizational, political, setting, etc.						
Human agents: skills, personnel, roles, responsibilities						
Physical catalysts: equipment, facilities, enablers						
Information aids: manuals, books, instructions, documents						

Figure 8.9 System matrix. (Adapted from Nadler and Hibino, 1994.)

6. Use the system matrix as part of the deliverable—incorporate it into the requirements or other documents as a formal means of defining the system solution.

7. Use the matrix to explore problem causes and relationships among events and functions. The system matrix was invented by an Air Force intelligence officer looking for relationships in difficult problems. It is a successful tool for exposing hidden information, especially in relationships between functions that are not otherwise accessible.

8. No one tool is the best or the only tool to use. Having a large toolkit from which to draw the appropriate tool for the job is the most successful approach. Nadler and Hibino recommend "an integrating and coordinating framework to handle the many available techniques, tools, and analysis models." An integrating framework (such as Team Design formats) can provide an effective means for coordinating the use of the different tools.

9. Encourage the team to adopt quality and productivity *values* while working from a *total system* approach.

Using the system matrix in a workshop moves the team from general to specific, from diagrams and high-level objectives to fairly substantial detail. The matrix approach provides a way to gather information about all the important dimensions of a design, organized in a single format. Once a design problem is laid out in this way, patterns and opportunities emerge that were not visible before. The whole system is visible, not just disconnected parts.

Functionality matrix. The functionality matrix is another type of tabular matrix format useful in defining and managing requirements. Whereas the system matrix is used more for collecting, organizing, and relating requirements within a matrix format, the functionality matrix provides a schema for assessing completeness and fit of requirements. As shown in Fig. 8.10, this matrix type lists specified functions down the leftmost column and common attributes across the top row. *Attributes* consist of design characteristics or product considerations that are mapped to the list of functional requirements. The method is used for checking the coverage and completeness of requirements, for matching requirements against a proposed technical design, and for managing defined requirements. It can easily be used for other purposes by teams and analysts, due to its general applicability.

The functionality matrix shows the extent to which user and system requirements are rated as sufficiently met or not met by the proposed design. It should be used to demonstrate the sufficiency of

Attributes

Functions	Architecture:	Data:	User Interface:	Communications:	Other ...
1. Provide group calendar of events					
2. Integrate with current email system					
3. Notify user of current To-Do items					
4. Generate list of available reports					
5. Provide access to external data sources					
6. Show current account status					
7. Support user-defined object lists					
8. Provide seamless Internet access					

Figure 8.10   Functionality matrix.

requirements for the specific user and task characteristics within the defined user groups. The matrix catalogs the requirements, but does not provide a mechanism for design—scenarios and prototyping are used to move the requirements documented in the matrix into design models.

System process flow diagrams.   By this point, process flow diagrams will be a familiar tool. The system process flow provides a pictorial view of system requirements, interactions, and processes from a system architect's perspective. Chapter 7 describes two approaches easily adapted for system process flow: physical process models and information flow models.

A *physical process model* (see Fig. 7.3) shows how physical system processes interact (computer hardware, software, and networking). The flow of process events can be modeled by showing specific inputs, events, and outputs. *Process information flow diagrams* (see Fig. 7.7) show more flow details, from the perspective of communication and the transmission of information through a system or an organization. Instead of describing business functions, the user process flow describes activities from the user's workflow. Any user process can be described by a flow diagram, including any set of activities performed by specific individual users fulfilling a job role, or by user or organizational groups performing a complex task or work process.

The system process flow models similar elements to the user process flow, but typically excluding the user:

1. *Inputs to process.*   Show all necessary inputs—data, forms, systems, orders, paperwork, decisions, or events that initiate a *system* sequence.

2. *System sequence.*   Show the chain of system events required triggered by the inputs or required of the user (user interface only).

3. *Process outputs.*   Show any data and electronic or other defined outputs of the system sequence.

4. *Timing and dependencies.*   Specify performance criteria, program or response times, delays, and dependencies among system events in the flow diagram.

5. *Other systems or interfaces.*   Show any other systems or interfaces required to support the defined flow or to complete the process.

6. *Data sources.*   Show databases, data sources, or other information required for the process.

As in any Team Design format, not all the modeling methods described need to be used. The goal should be the team's deliverable requirements and the models required to support an effective design. The conclusion of this phase provides initial user requirements and initial system requirements to the team. These models guide scenario design and prototyping in the next phase.

Usage: Requirements analysis

Usage methods in the Requirements Definition format involve the team in analyzing the newly visualized processes by creating scenarios and definitions of system use. The goal of this phase of work is to transform the wish list of visualized requirements, the initial requirements statement, into descriptions of designed usage. By collaborating on scenarios or other depictions of expected system events, a realistic picture of the system is created that projects the requirements onto models of the user environments and tests the assumptions of the designers. While scenarios generate user-centered process descriptions, system design alternatives are envisioned to support the

TABLE 8.4   Requirements Definition: Usage Phase

Usage: Requirements analysis	Methods	Inputs and outputs
Developing user scenarios	Scenario analysis Use cases Ideal system exercise	In: Initial user and system requirements Out: User scenarios
Selecting scenarios	Brainstorming methods Ideal system exercise	In: User scenarios Out: Detailed process scenario
Generating system requirements alternatives	Brainstorming methods System and functionality matrixes	In: User scenarios Out: System alternatives
Prototyping user processes	Simple prototyping	In: System alternatives Out: Initial concept prototype

scenarios. This phase also introduces *requirements prototyping* of the scenarios and user tasks as a means of filling out the design. Table 8.4 shows the usage phase's activities and methods, again with several methods adopted from Chap. 7 and earlier phases in Requirements Definition.

Developing user scenarios.   User scenarios create a team understanding of the ways a system will be used in the real world of the users, through building models of their actions and consequences. User scenarios are essentially projections of the new tasks into the user environment, which will have been defined in the visualizing phase. Initial user and system requirements are available to the team from which to construct the scenarios; user tasks and possible system solutions, new procedures, tools, and data sources are now defined from which to build somewhat detailed scenarios.

Three approaches to scenario building are portrayed. *Scenario analysis* is the most generic of the techniques, and is an approach that can be employed in other situations such as design and decision making. Scenario analysis applies across all organizational contexts, but is also fairly analytical and is best in business and user contexts. The *use case* is a type of scenario analysis method brought into use through Jacobson's (1995) object-oriented analysis methodologies and the emergence of business rules analysis. Use cases typically involve detailed analysis, and are well suited for business and systems contexts. The *ideal system* is a JAD exercise useful for energizing all types of groups to generate concepts of product or system use from the user's viewpoint. The ideal system is best applied in the user and product contexts.

The key function of scenarios is to begin defining requirements in realistic terms, to uncover new solutions, needs, and issues affecting your design. If scenarios are not constructed by the team in the workshop environment, they will eventually be needed to add meat to the bones of preliminary requirements models. Scenarios are more powerful when devised by a workshop or team than by individual analysts, as other experiences and points of view are integrated into the model. Scenarios can readily be built as part of the Team Design workshop agenda, as another group activity following initial requirements definition. They might also be drafted in skeletal form by a lead analyst and user representative, and presented to the team as straw models to be redefined and elaborated. When completed, scenarios often include flow diagrams, matrix diagrams, or pictorials accompanied by descriptions of user activities.

Scenario analysis. Scenario analysis brings the value of visioning, planning, and task sequence analysis together into a powerful team method for working with requirements models. Whereas most requirements analysis approaches in system development use traditional specifications, studies investigating the typical specification approaches have found them inadequate to capture the complexity and issues inherent in designing systems and redesigning work processes. Scenarios describe processes from a depth borne of experience in the business. Scenario analysis essentially creates possible stories of system usage, with the system users as protagonists. The scenario resembles a playwright's script more than a technical specification, in that it communicates the dramatics of system potential, user behavior, consequences of errors, and implications for the future.

Scenario analysis begins by posing thought-provoking questions about the system, positioned in the future. By analyzing the scenarios, opportunities for system or product requirements and design become tangible. By walking through alternative scenario stories, difficulties in one path become clear; competitive value in another emerges. Scenario analysis requires significant time and intellectual commitment; team members bring to the scenario sessions their knowledge and experience, invention and description, and analysis and critique. The payoff for the effort is in clarifying requirements and testing out their implications well in advance of prototyping and user evaluations. These descriptive scenarios of use are refined through feedback from business experts and users, as they challenge assumptions and add the details that result in realistic portrayals. The scenarios are used later in the process to guide prototyping of the user interface.

Scenario analysis is described in the Business Process Design format as a workshop technique supporting group dialogue and discovery of ideas. That is a more business-oriented scenario analysis approach, which compares competing business scenarios and looks at the impacts of process designs. The requirements modeling approach to scenario analysis builds scenarios of user and system behavior, and leads to models that show the necessity of certain business solutions. Like the business process scenario, it is *solution-driven*. Unlike that model, this approach necessarily envisions a system solution.

Scenario analysis for user and system requirements involves several general steps, which are easily modified depending on the complexity of the business process or envisioned system:

1. Identify several candidate topics for scenario building and analysis. User-intensive system functions are best, since user interface and process issues are among the most difficult areas in most requirements models. Areas such as customer support, user intervention in any process, or functions involving more than one user group or interface to the system are good candidates.

2. Note the candidates on a chart with the team, and discuss the priorities and business value of each one. Sometimes the priority is driven by design complexity, other times by schedule or customer interest. Select one or two topics to begin creating scenarios.

3. Identify the key conditions for the scenario. What are the business goals, user tasks, user preferences, and organizational conditions around the topic area? Brainstorm each topic, noting responses on whiteboards or charts until enough conditions for a single sheet (about 10 to 15) are listed for each topic. Select a single topic to begin working the exercise with the team.

4. Use a diagramming method that is familiar to the team or with which you are comfortable. Process mapping or sequential task diagrams are excellent for scenario definition, depending on the level of detail necessary for the solution. Identify the method you suggest for use, and lead the team in defining the starting point for the scenario.

5. One or several large whiteboards or multiple sheets of chart paper will be required to draw out the scenario model with the team. Work quickly to generate several alternative versions of a process, rather than just a single "best" model on which everyone can agree. If necessary, build a separate scenario for each point of view on the team. Once the alternatives are drawn out, discussion and analysis will modify and select the best approach.

6. Discuss the pros and cons of each alternative with the team. Don't overanalyze, just walk through and evaluate each alternative to foster understanding of the objectives and the advantages and dis-

advantages of each alternative scenario. Usually one alternative makes the most sense, if the business goals and conditions are defined up front. If more than one scenario solution appeals, a sub-team can break out to investigate technical options further, allowing the selection of a best alternative in the near future.

7. Select the best-fit alternative scenario and add other details as necessary to build a more complete picture of the events and conditions satisfied by the process. Develop a summary diagram, and have team members draft readable models for use by the team.

In scenario analysis, both inventive and analytical team members are necessary and valued. Inventive, creative work is required in generating the model scenario alternatives and presenting them to the team. The analytical process is required in walking through and evaluating the scenarios to determine how well they fulfill the business goals and conditions specified.

Use cases. Use cases are a class of requirements analysis and design methods based on generalized scenarios of user interaction. Use cases are derived from the object-oriented modeling methodology of Jacobson (1995), who defines them as "a complete course of events in the system, as seen from a user's perspective." Although use cases have been allied with object-oriented design, the object model is not necessary for using this technique. Use cases are an especially effective type of scenario model for unraveling complex systems or when pursuing the technical requirements for a system solution. Use cases should be used as an effective alternative to scenario analysis when pursuing detailed analysis with a more technical workshop group. Because it requires a fairly rigorous process, it should be employed with smaller teams (no more than six participants) to better maintain group focus on scenario definition. It is also a useful approach for technical teams (as in the systems context), where the user's perspective is often overlooked.

Use cases express system requirements through analysis of the user's interaction with the system functions from an external perspective. System functions are treated as "black boxes"—the inputs and outputs are defined but not the inner workings of the function. Each use case represents one complete transaction, a single case of use, which identifies all the interactions and events a user might observe when the case is implemented. Use cases have enough detail to identify all the necessary interfaces, data, and interactions needed to support a function. A simple example might be taken from a typical software interaction, such as creating and sending electronic mail:

1. Launch mail package by selecting icon.

2. If the user name is given, type in a password. Otherwise, enter a user name and password.

3. Select the *Compose New Mail* option.

4. In the body of the mail window, type in the text of the message.

5. Select the addressees to which to send the message. If they do not all exist in a list, enter the new names and e-mail addresses to add to the list.

6. Select any addressees to add as "courtesy copy" (CC or BCC).

7. Compose a theme for the note and type it into the *Subject* field.

8. Specify any additional options, such as *Priority* or *Return Receipt to Sender.*

9. Select the *Send* button.

From the simple example, a model of interaction is revealed whereby physical, concrete interactions are described. Each action assumes a physical software interface (buttons and icons), certain objects (fields and lists), and actors (user and addressees). Use cases can be seen as another type of scenario or task flow model, and have been adapted for use within object-oriented modeling, lending the technique current value in many organizations.

Jacobson advocates use cases as an effectively comprehensible method, understood by all the participants involved in a system project. As an object-oriented design methodologist, Jacobson assents that object models are too complex to use with a mixed audience across a development team. He advises use cases as the alternative, satisfying both technical and usage objectives. Use cases describe the task sequences for each class of user. Object models describe the objects with which they interact. Since a complete collection of use cases defines all the functionality of a system, they can be used to define the functional specification. In a workshop process, use cases are the preferred modeling approach to integrate an object model with the workflow as defined by users.

Use cases fulfill the needs of external design by providing a specification language usable by all members of the design team. The specification of functions is expressed by natural English descriptions of usage actions, supported by simple diagrams to communicate the scenarios with more immediacy. For each use case, Jacobson recommends that a simple object diagram be drawn indicating the objects used by the case and the relationships among objects.

Although use cases are developed at a finer degree of granularity than scenarios, they are especially effective for capturing functional requirements and supporting an object view of the system. By organizing the use cases around the requirements model and object models, complete coverage of requirements and the use of objects is supported.

Ideal system exercise. The *ideal system* exercise is a more informal group technique for creating scenarios of use. In the ideal system, team members, particularly user stakeholders, invent pictures of system use based on an envisioned ideal system that exceeds all possible requirements. While this method does not result in refined analytical models, it is more of a participatory design approach that highly involves users and product customers. Participants create pictures of processes, rough diagrams with people and computer screens, user interfaces showing data displays, and other artifacts based on the facilitator's guidance or suggestions.

The ideal system technique was used for joint application design sessions at TASC for several different types of customer groups, as it was a useful way to enter directly into discussions of system possibilities. One of the tensions apparent with stakeholders in design workshops is the unspoken question of "When do we get to say what we want the system to do?" The ideal system can be used fairly early in workshops (first day's afternoon, for example) to involve participants and bring their ideas and assumptions to the surface. If presented so that users do not feel as though the ideal system results represent the requirements, this exercise relieves the frustration of many who wish to move quickly and don't understand the development process or have the patience to work through more analytical approaches.

The following steps illustrate how the exercise has been successfully used. With 10 or more participants, split the group up into teams of 4 or 5. Randomly assign members so that a mix of backgrounds and viewpoints are available in each group—homogeneous expert groups work well when defining detailed requirements, but are a hindrance in inventive exercises. Part of the reason for using imagery-oriented team exercises is to generate understanding of issues and priorities among different stakeholders, a group dynamics process that becomes immediate when mixing members in working groups.

Assign each group one or more major system functions or business process areas to define in the exercise. Each group will require some guidance for the exercises. If cofacilitators are used, provide a facilitator with easel pad and markers for each group. Use analysts, recorders, and other workshop assistants otherwise.

1. The lead facilitator describes the process for the whole team once subgroups have been assigned. Set a time limit of one-half hour or one hour, and monitor the time. Explain that the purpose is to create useful ideas from their "perfect" system images that will lead the team into better design models of the actual system.

2. Start the process by asking the teams: "Visualize the ideal system for your function. Pretend the whole system does everything you need to make this happen. Imagine how this system will work, how it will look."

3. Lead the teams to think about how the system impacts their work processes and job. "Imagine your job five years from now, in the best of all possible worlds. What does your work look like? Where are you located? What do you do all day? What do you do and what does the computer do for you?" Have each subgroup brainstorm these ideas and list their thoughts and assumptions on the easel pads. Give the group 10 minutes or so and go to the next step.

4. Ask the groups: "Imagine this perfect solution we're building has been delivered and you're seeing it now for the first time. What's the first thing you do when you turn it on? What kinds of data, communications, critical information does it display? What does it let you do? What does it do for you?" Ask other imagery questions as necessary to start the groups thinking about the ideal system for their business functions.

5. Within each group, facilitate the process of drawing process flow diagrams, screen display concepts, and reports or displays that represent their ideal solution. Once a concept is drawn out, extrapolate from that and draw out the next screen or process that must happen. Draw out all participants to contribute to the design, either by going round-robin with different functions around the group, or by working on one function at a time and having each member contribute an idea to the perfect solution.

6. When the time limit has been reached, each subgroup might describe its processes and design to the whole group. Have the group appoint a spokesperson to stand up and show the group's design model to the whole group. Have them entertain feedback and new ideas for their process from the whole workshop group, using a separate sheet to capture the ideas contributed.

7. An advanced approach may also be used, where the lead facilitator then works with the whole team to organize all the functions into a more integrated whole system. This exercise brings the workshop participants back into the whole group identity again, and allows all members to visualize the emerging design ideas and the implications of the solution.

Selecting scenarios. Selecting scenarios is a straightforward activity that follows directly from scenario building. Using the scenarios created in the previous discussion, the team identifies one or several scenarios to be the primary representation of the process. The selected scenarios become the models used for prototyping, evaluation, and reality testing of the system or product.

Sometimes multiple user and system requirements can all be represented by a single scenario. Other processes might require five or six scenarios split across the functions to describe the requirements. The complexity and organization of the system will usually lead to a well-defined set of scenarios.

Each subgroup that developed scenarios describes its pictures in turn. The facilitator can have the subgroup choose a team spokesperson, who walks through the scenario for the whole team. The subgroup should describe its approach, assumptions made, liberties taken, and any recommendations. The facilitator can probe with questions or describe relationships between scenarios that might not have been mentioned. Group discussion follows after all scenarios have been presented.

The team typically selects scenarios by consensus. Perhaps no single scenario captures all the requirements, such as in scenarios that were intentionally separated by function. Several scenarios might be combined to form a larger cross-functional scenario. If the scenarios overlap, they might be combined at interface points and described together.

Another approach uses team brainstorming to generate a detailed process scenario from a single scenario that was not fully defined to begin with. For a software product or system not divided into compartmentalized functions, this gives the whole team a chance to envision the process and contribute to its scenario of use.

Reserve plenty of time to conduct scenario building. Generation and selection of scenarios can easily take a day, and up to three days or so for more complex exercises. Remember that they are used as communications tools for defining requirements, and the more detail envisioned in the scenarios, the deeper the refinement of requirements the team will discover. At this stage, you want to surface issues and potential disconnects in the system solution. The more problems that can be surfaced within the scenario exercises, the better the design team can plan and design solutions to address a more complete set of requirements.

Generating system requirements alternatives. At this point in the process, technical team members might already have mentally designed the "perfect" system solution addressing 90 percent of the requirements. It is typical of scenario exercises to lead into technical solutions, since generating scenarios forces the team to drive out ambiguity to some extent. And developers and systems analysts live to create new ideas, so they can be counted on to offer multiple propositions.

In fact, for this activity facilitation of system solution alternatives is appropriate. With user and task scenarios created, and at least one fairly detailed scenario describing system usage, alternative requirements are brought forward within the team process. The desired output of this activity is a set of system alternatives representing system requirements.

Techniques for creating requirements alternatives include brainstorming, the system matrix, and the functionality matrix. Two of the same techniques described (or used) previously in envisioning system requirements are used to define alternatives. Following the initial use of the matrix approach to specify initial system requirements, the team need only revisit the system matrix and identify those components that changed with the scenarios.

Prototyping user processes.   Prototyping user processes follows as a requirements definition activity. *Prototyping* is defined in the most broad sense for this activity—it refers to any representation of the designed process in a way that explicitly shows a visible model of the user's behavior with the system. It can lead directly from scenario building, so that the scenarios become scripts used to build prototypes. Therefore, the prototyping methods in this stage are early design models based on simple user interface prototyping. Task flow diagrams or other user process diagrams also support prototyping with explicit task information.

In the *business* and *user* contexts, prototyping might involve a strong user process component. In the *system, user,* and *product* contexts, a definite emphasis on the user interface is important. With scenarios defining the user process and requirements addressing both technical and user needs, the workshop team can be broken out into subgroups to design prototypes of tasks and systems for complex processes. For less-complex systems, and many software products intended for a general consumer market, user interface prototyping might be done by user interface designers or analysts and discussed with the workshop group as a participatory process.

Simple prototyping.   Prototyping during requirements definition should be kept fairly simple, since system solution ideas and design concepts are still in the early stages of formation. In many cases, a paper prototype or a preliminary software model (a "slide show" prototype) is sufficient to communicate the user interface ideas to support defined interaction requirements. The goal of this prototype is to reflect the team's grasp of the problem, not to communicate a finished design.

Erickson (1995) describes the use of rough prototypes to facilitate envisioning the design, and portrays their value in creating ambiguity and enhancing design discussion. A working prototype with ambiguous definition of the user interface allows designers to contribute to resolving the ambiguity with innovative or, at least, competing ideas. Initial ambiguity in the design is deliberate, to support a more effective interface design as the model evolves. Prototype roughness also allows different team members to discuss the use of different features. Where an interaction might otherwise have been considered a foregone conclusion, leaving the dialogs, buttons, and wording intentionally unfinished leads to more discussion about the feature than if it were rendered complete. This approach is especially useful when designers or users are uncertain about the best design approach, and new ideas are favored. According to Erickson, roughness also decreases "the level of commitment to the design," giving designers more flexibility:

> With a rough working prototype designers are less likely to feel like they have invested in the prototype, and more open to considering changes. If someone criticizes an idea, it's easy for the designer to discount its seriousness. Users, too, are likely to give feedback more readily because they're criticizing something that is obviously rough. A rough prototype has built-in deniability.

Prototyping methods are highly effective within Team Design workshops to demonstrate to the team and to stakeholders (especially management) how the system or product might appear to users. However, if a realistic prototype is developed that resembles a complete product, unreasonable user expectations can result. At this point in the process, don't worry about user interface realism. For requirements definition, produce a prototype showing how requirements are envisioned in the user interface without nailing down the design details. Design details will emerge through feedback and review, through iterations of the prototype. Build a flexible prototype, and be prepared to change it often. Once the technical considerations of the design are integrated, and the data model and functional details are further defined, the user interface prototype will change drastically.

During requirements definition, two types of prototypes are useful: a *concept model* and a *requirements prototype*. During this early stage, simple interface prototyping is used to demonstrate *concept feasibility*. It is a simulation of the application, a throw-away prototype used to show ideas and surface usability problems. A concept prototype does not actually capture the requirements yet, since requirements are still being defined. It is used to capture the team's ideas along the way, and to demonstrate the feasibility of user interface and interaction concepts. This level of prototype can be built in the workshop, especially with the support of an experienced user interface designer using a portable computer attached to an overhead display.

The concept prototype proves to *customers* that you understand the business need and have progress toward solutions for their specific goals for the system. It involves users by integrating their feedback based on their need for an effective system that improves the work process. The key to serving both needs in the concept prototype is by focusing on highest priority or highest benefit elements of the system. Represent the most critical 20 percent of requirements for (roughly speaking) 80 percent of the benefit. The rule of thumb in interactive conceptual prototyping is to start simple and continue working with users to iterate as many times as necessary to arrive at a satisfactory initial model.

Simple prototyping can be used in a team process known as *codevelopment* or cooperative prototyping, in which designers invite users to try out different interface concepts and test methods of interaction. With codevelopment practices, user engagement in the design process is considered more useful than technical sophistication or the "perfect solution." Mock-ups, drawings, and simple props are used more frequently than computer-generated screens. Storyboarding (discussed in Chap. 5 as a general workshop technique) is another useful process and interface prototyping method. Madsen and Aiken (1993) discuss cooperative prototyping from the perspective of participatory design, using storyboard prototyping instead of computer-based models. Their less-technical approach reduces the intimidation effect on non-computer professionals (such as consumers, in a product context). Madsen and Aiken describe the effectiveness of what they call *cooperative interactive storyboard prototyping* and relate it to other design practices:

> As in film production, the use of storyboards in the development of computer systems is a way to "sketch out" the future system early in the development process. In an effort to verify the requirements, the developer uses nonfunctional mock-ups, a technology dating at least to the 1930s, to illustrate a task-driven view of the proposed system for the user. The concept of iteration as a discovery process is the key to prototyping: each successive iteration brings the prototype one step closer to correctly representing the user needs (p. 57).

Although some storyboard prototyping processes actually start and finish with a paper prototype drawn out on cards or easel pads, Madsen and Aiken move into using a simple graphical prototyper program. Prototyping software and visual programming support concept prototyping for many applications, since it is easy for designers to make rapid changes and simple for most users to work directly with the screen representations. The tool also provides a way for the designers to reuse graphical storyboard components, a time-saving plus over a typical period of extensive design iteration.

The concept prototype can start as simply as drawings, and can end as an interactive user interface in a simple tool that the users can work with directly. However, don't expect this initial concept prototype to do everything the users want to see demonstrated. A deliberately less polished (low-fidelity) prototype will encourage user feedback and new ideas, since it will not appear finished, thus affording the contribution of users' ideas. This level of prototype can also be used to test the product concepts with focus groups and potential users. By keeping the prototype flexible and portable, it can be modified to reflect different users' input as necessary.

A software product prototype should be designed in the same development environment as the product, so that interface ideas are achievable and constrained somewhat by the planned environment. However, remember that this is a *simulation* prototype only, and should not necessarily be managed as a beginning prototype or even as a deliverable. You don't want this level prototype to evolve into a formal prototype, even if it is a simple Web (HTML) prototype for an Internet-based system. It is a tool for demonstration, and must be capable of rapid development and change.

Packaging: Requirements definition

Packaging activities include four classes of methods with five new techniques introduced. As in other phases, not every activity and method is used during workshops or analysis, but one or two methods might be especially useful or necessary. The phase is outlined in Table 8.5.

Packaging the requirements definition involves finalizing the model of system and user requirements to be established as the basis for development. If at least one method from each activity was used in prior sessions, packaging will be a straightforward documentation of requirements models. The level of detail necessary is now the guiding factor; this can depend on the project type (contracted, fixed-price, internal, or research and development), and development life cycle (waterfall, incremental, iterative, or rapid). Rapid, internal projects will not require nor endure the detailed definition needed by a contracted project with several increments defined in advance. Therefore, not every requirements effort *should* be supported by detailed definition.

In the packaging phase, the decision to pursue further analytic

TABLE 8.5   Requirements Definition: Packaging Phase

Packaging: Requirements definition	Methods	Inputs and Outputs
Defining requirements models	Defining business rules Requirements mapping	In: Concept prototype, Requirements models Out: Requirements models
Prototyping requirements	Interactive prototyping	In: Concept prototype Out: Requirements prototype, requirements models
Validating: Requirements evaluation		
Requirements evaluation	Prototype usability evaluation Requirements review	In: Requirements prototype Out: Evaluated requirements model

detail can add significantly to both team and individual schedules. The first activity, formalizing the requirements model, might entail extensive requirements documentation or just a basic mapping of requirements to objectives. The team and your organization must decide what's appropriate for the project and for the receiving *customer* at the conclusion of the phase. To a large extent, the needs of the next phase determine the current phase efforts. If the customer for requirements definition is a development project team that has been involved with the workshops, very little detailed definition might be done. Much of the necessary detail (data and architecture definition, for example) can be done as part of the software design process instead of during requirements. Other project scenarios require a different approach. If the customer for the definition is an outsourced contracting group or, as in many government projects, a management team that must approve detailed requirements before progressing to the next level of funding, a formal definition document will usually be necessary. In any case, some requirements document will typically be delivered in packaging, but the type and depth of the documentation is highly dependent on the business and project needs.

From the organizational perspective, organizational contexts also play a role in the decision to detail. In the business and user contexts, a detailed specification supports larger-scale efforts where funding issues are at stake and larger development teams expect a certain confidence in the defined requirements. In the systems context, a requirements-level prototype with a requirements mapping document might support purchase decisions and implementation planning for a major software package. The product context is variable, but a requirements prototype can typically suffice, supported by documentation prepared from preceding work in the other phases.

Group facilitation issues also play into the packaging phase. Detailed requirements packaging documentation is typically done offline by individual analysts, and not within the team workshop. Packaging activities can be performed individually or in the team, but are usually developed offline and presented and reviewed in meetings. Much of packaging involves generating approved deliverables that meet the team's criteria and satisfy a given organizational customer. These deliverables are planned and reviewed in the workshop, but are all often *developed* individually. Therefore, the packaging phase requires less involvement from the workshop team than the other three major phases.

Defining requirements models. Defining and documenting the requirements is the primary focus of packaging, whether for final use, distribution, or as deliverables. In this phase, the requirements definition becomes defined and usable by others to continue development. The inputs to this activity are the requirements prototype and the requirements model, which might be at any level of detail depending on the team's direction. Regardless of the methods selected, the basic products of this activity are a requirements document and a product prototype. Two activities are presented that teams can use to define requirements in significant detail, *business rules definition* and *requirements mapping.*

Defining business rules. *Business rules* are facts and definitions of a business process, and are considered to be detailed requirements definitions. Practitioners have developed numerous approaches to defining business rules, from extensions of data modeling to scenario-based business rule modeling. Business rules have gained favor as an advanced requirements modeling method, primarily because they allow more precise definition of data and processes. They define the actions and events supported and disallowed in the business; they define the rules for business operation, the use and meaning of data, and the definitive source of terms and facts. They specify requirements to the level where data and process analysis can use the rules and relate them to database and system design.

Barbara von Halle (1995), a proponent of the use of business rules in system and database design, describes a four-part schema for defining business rules, based on their *intent* or desired impact on business behavior:

- Definition of business concepts

- Relation of business concepts to one another (facts)
- Enabling or prohibiting new facts (data or knowledge constraints)
- Enabling or prohibiting actions or behavior (action constraints)

Business concept definition and relationships are already covered well by entity-relationship modeling and its definitions (although data analysis starts during requirements definition, it is discussed in the Application Design format, where it is used more). The definition of constraints is considered fairly new in business modeling; although techniques for knowledge acquisition abound in artificial intelligence disciplines, they have not been applied in business rule definition to a great extent.

David Wright (1996) discusses the application of business rules in requirements definition, explaining that a business rule embodies a business *truth*. Once a truth is established, it can be used in all cases in business systems:

> Because a business truth is basically a statement that can be said to be true all of the time or conditionally, it should also follow that a business rule is a self-imposed constraint.
>
> In short, a "high-quality" business rule can be defined as being atomic, expressed in business terms as opposed to database terms, is not redundant with other business rules, is expressed in precise and unambiguous language, represents the full intent of business users' meaning, is declarative inasmuch as not implying unnecessary sequencing, and is consistent with other business rules.

Wright describes how business rules are different among various practitioners, which can lead to difficulties when defining business rules across disciplines on the same team:

> DBA's may define business rules as the attribute definitions, constraints, cardinality, and verb phrases attached to relationships in database diagrams. To software developers business rules may embody various levels of pseudocode, such as inference rules written in IF...THEN...ELSE format. Business users themselves may define business rules as business policies, business goals, calculations, or step-by-step instructions.

Getting good definitions of business rules in a workshop setting can be a daunting task. What conditions should be defined as rules? What rules are important enough to warrant the work to define them? How precisely should they be defined? Whenever formal definitions are pursued within a group, achieving agreement can be difficult, since participants view the rules from the perspective of their own functions. General business rules are defined from an enterprise viewpoint, so that they can cover all the cases of use in the business.

Specific business rules are defined to cover the conditions for scenarios, and are directly associated with specific use cases. Have the team reach agreement about the goals and uses of business rules from the outset of the activity. Facilitate the process by holding the group members to their goals and definitions. Use a system model such as a function hierarchy and entity model as a structure to support eliciting and defining useful rules.

Requirements mapping. Requirements mapping relates the list of defined requirements to other aspects of the emerging design, such as a business process design or application functions. Generally, mapping of requirements is done to enable tracking of requirements against the design as the system is built. Mapping is a method with numerous approaches, however, depending on the team's intention and use. Some mapping can be conducted as a team exercise, but this would usually be limited by detail and time. The recommended approach for teams is to map requirements offline, and to review results within the team context. Reviews are necessary to point out any missing, inconsistent, or mismapped requirements.

Requirements mapping approaches include the following:

- *Requirements traceability.* Traceability is supported when all functions in a design document can be traced back to their requirements. During requirements definition, however, the need is to define requirements explicitly and precisely so they can be mapped and traced later.

- *Mapping requirements to design.* During preliminary design and prototyping, requirements are associated with design elements that emerge as part of the system solution.

- *Mapping product requirements to user or business requirements.* Different levels or types of requirements documents can be mapped or compared to determine coverage of treatment. This allows the team to see how well they are meeting the business need or customer expectations.

Often, mapping is done to associate requirements with development schedules and increments, as a project management tool. Here, mapping is done to milestones and development goals, instead of to actual defined functions.

Instead of traditional facilitation, requirements mapping review can be conducted by technical peers, since less controversy or new ground is likely to emerge. A lead analyst might typically walk through the requirements mapping, noting changes and clarification, and leading discussion around any concerns that might arise.

Prototyping requirements. The requirements prototype demonstrates the baseline user and system requirements, many of which were obtained by iterative evaluation of the concept prototype. This is also called the *product* prototype, since it is used to show the design of the emerging product by reflecting requirements and design decisions. Whereas the concept prototype is used more to obtain feedback and direction on an iterative basis, the requirements prototype is used to demonstrate the requirements in software to reflect the product baseline. Whereas the concept prototype is often a throw-away design tool, the requirements prototype can be used to demonstrate and refine the requirements model; in a RAD process, the requirements prototype evolves into a final product.

An interactive prototyping process develops a working model of the application as a visual specification, which can be treated as a deliverable. As with the concept prototype, user interaction is invited to help define application behavior. User evaluations are somewhat more controlled, in that blue sky idea generation at this point will only expand the product scope and lengthen the product cycle. A requirements prototype should confirm the previous work on the design, and embody the requirements very closely. A walkthrough of the requirements prototype should proceed like a requirements review—each requirement from the document can be checked off on the prototype, and vice-versa. The requirements prototype developed in this process is normally developed outside of the workshop, and thus development is not as interactive with the team as in developing the concept prototype. However, the prototype will frequently be used for demonstration, review, and critique in workshops, so it should be portable and easy to access for impromptu demonstrations. To support these reviews, the prototype should demonstrate a user scenario that covers all of the requirements and follows a scripted path of screens, data entries, and product functions.

One of the first considerations is whether to adhere to defined user interface standards or to use a custom approach. User interface standards might be internally defined by the organization, and a style guide would typically be available for designing to the standard. Otherwise, industry "standards" established by the dominant user interface platforms can be designed to by using published standards and guidelines. If truly interested in adhering to standards, use the published reference—do not attempt to generalize from individual software packages that are assumed as standards. Even the dominant software companies break their own standards in some products, and there are major differences between packaged software and custom systems. There are also differences between packaged productivity tools (such as word processing and spreadsheets) and tools that support a specific task (such as reference managers, electronic libraries and graphical design tools). These differences must be understood and decisions made whether to follow the standard or to use a different approach.

The interactive prototyping process described in Chap. 7 can be used to build and manage the requirements prototype. Visual programming tools in the appropriate development platforms are used to construct an interactive model of the system as conceived from scenarios and requirements models. The requirements prototype is designed using the concept prototype as a visual guide, and design proceeds by building a prototype that demonstrates the design of user interaction and screen layouts.

Validating: Requirements evaluation. Validating completes the cycle, providing an approach for the team to evaluate the requirements model. Requirements evaluation is the single activity in validation, and offers two evaluation procedures. Validating the requirements model can include evaluation planning or requirements prototype evaluation. Requirements review is typically performed as a team approach to evaluating and signing-off on the requirements model. In a Team Design workshop, requirements evaluation continues logically from the requirements prototype. Evaluation can consist of one or several test and evaluation activities planned with user and development team members. Planning might take into account the following evaluation methods:

- *Requirements review walkthroughs.* Facilitated review sessions for the team to go through the requirements document one point at a time and to evaluate the clarity, accuracy, and specificity of each requirement as written. Similar in intent and structure to a code or document walkthrough.

- *Interdisciplinary prototype evaluations.* Review of the prototype by an interdisciplinary team specifically assembled to evaluate the prototype from an expert opinion perspective. This subteam might include the project manager, requirements analyst, database designer, user interface designer, and other developers. Disciplines not included in the requirements workshops should be included in the prototype evaluation sessions, to ensure that the prototype does not introduce problems in technical areas unknown to other team members.

- *Requirements prototype usability evaluations.* Internal usability evaluation of the prototype conducted by the human factors or usability analyst to validate and acquire feedback on the user interface design. Testing is typically conducted with internal subjects (customer service staffers or secretaries) who have had no prior experience with the product. Other user issues, such as installation or integration with workflow, can be tested through this process.

Prototype usability evaluation.   Evaluation of the requirements prototype provides necessary feedback to revise the user interface in line with *usability* data, and to perform a final check on meeting requirements. Without conducting an evaluation at this point, a prototype might meet all the product requirements but fail usability testing. Numerous factors must be considered in the evaluation, and feedback should be gathered on as many aspects as possible. There will never be a less-expensive opportunity to fix usability design problems.

In most product prototypes, the evaluation emphasis is on testing the product features and functions. However, in usability evaluation the use of features and functions is tested, by evaluating at least the following areas of user interface design:

- Screen layout, length and alignment of fields, and use of appropriate controls (selections, buttons, checkboxes, and others)
- Navigation among windows, flow of defined tasks, the number and levels of depth of dialog boxes, and integration of options on screens
- Presentation of data, field labels and other wording, and menu options
- Use of input devices, mouse buttons, function keys, and standard inputs
- Graphical design, use of color, and design of icons

Early usability feedback on the prototype is essential to supporting the design effort that follows requirements definition. Feedback, even from internal users, provides useful direction for the design, requiring many slight modifications to the interface and retesting with other users. Iterative informal evaluation of the user interface design should be performed until only minor changes are required, or perhaps until users are split in their opinions over minor design features.

The product requirements prototype often becomes the vehicle communicating the requirements, and the design, to developers. Reading requirements documents leaves a lot of room open for interpretation—the product prototype reveals how the requirements might be met in the design, at the user interface level. It is much easier for most design teams to point to screens in the prototype and discuss how things should be changed, rather than to argue the fine points as written in the requirements documents or described in diagrams. The prototype can be used by the project manager to manage the scope, by using it as the definition of the baseline. Therefore, evaluation of the prototype becomes a critical point in the movement from requirements to product design.

Requirements review. Requirements reviews are a traditional and effective method for evaluating requirements, and are especially useful for reaching team agreement for sign-off on the requirements package. Team workshops for requirements reviews have been recommended and described (Freedman and Weinberg 1982), and the use of facilitated process is well accepted. Review processes are often termed *walkthroughs, inspections,* or *reviews,* depending on the type of review and the deliverables. Facilitation is especially useful with product requirements and design walkthroughs, as the session leader is then unbiased and can maintain some distance in the evaluation of the product.

Formal and informal technical review processes can be used with requirements packages. Informal requirements reviews are held with the direct team at any time, and do not require extensive preparation. Informal reviews can be used throughout the packaging and validating phases to evaluate the technical requirements package, to gather issues and areas that require further attention. Informal reviews can be held on sections of documents, diagram packages, the requirements prototype, and other components. Formal technical reviews, such as walkthroughs, have a specific meeting and agenda for evaluating the requirements within a given period of time. Walkthroughs typically involve a larger number of participants (10 or more), and they are more formal due to their larger group size and the need to use a formal procedure to move through the documents. Using a facilitator or presenter, participants do not have to prepare in advance, as many reviewers will be invited and not regular team members.

One review method based on a round-robin procedure requires responsible analysts or experts to each discuss their particular functions and descriptions during the review. The facilitator then guides the discussion, manages the group memory of issues, and keeps the dialogue moving so that the team doesn't spend too much time in details. As explanation or definition is required, the expert or analyst handles the discussion. The facilitator is always available to move the conversation back on track.

Requirements verification can be performed through a small group audit or with a larger team walkthrough. This process is used to verify, trace, and account for requirements. It can be done informally, with the team, or formally, with customers or other stakeholders. Verification sessions should not be allowed to grow too large—fewer than 10 people is typically appropriate.

9

Designing Applications and Software Products

In the software industry, many of us have stories about our dream projects where all aspects of design and development flowed productively along, bringing into being an innovative and high-quality product and resulting in team euphoria. More frequently, we have stories about projects from hell where nothing worked as planned, a lack of leadership prevailed, and a distant customer changed their minds daily. Although we'd like to maximize the former and minimize the latter, in a true team situation we have more ability to bring the former into reality. A team model allows various members to function in leadership roles throughout the project, and can evolve into an environment of openness and productive cooperation.

In a design team, the elements of success consist of clarifying the roles played by team members. Communication and coordination, according to studies and to experience, are the cornerstones. Without coordination, the best group members will fail to work as a team and the project will suffer. With coordination, even a workaday group of designers and developers can parcel out necessary tasks and produce something special.

Although all the methods described in Team Design contribute to a system's design, in this chapter we focus on *software* design. All applications are software, with the primary distinction being that software can be any program run on any computer system, whereas an *application* is typically a set of related programs within a single user interface that automates some business process. In the Application Design (AD) format, most applications and software systems with a user interface are supported. Application Design activities cover the range of practices and methods spanning from requirements definition to implementation of the product.

As the formats move closer toward actual *development,* we might question Team Design's applicability. What is really involved in laying out a system design? When the team's workshop is completed, what remains for the developers? Can a complete design model be constructed by team design work, or is a significant amount of individual work required? Can design work even be done effectively by a team— "design by committee," as some might claim? If so, which parts are best done in the workshop, and which are specifically individual?

Team Design takes the view that in a mixed attendance workshop, primarily the *external,* or visible, components of the design will be productively defined. A detailed *comprehensive* design, such as is required by extensive documentation, will be a difficult and time-consuming process in most workshops. It will also require extensive education of customer or user participants, necessitating an undue time commitment to start working productively as a detailed design team. In addition, major components (system architecture, networking, hardware device integration, and operating systems) that are incomprehensible to almost all except system and software engineers pervade almost any complex system. The workshop practices therefore focus more on *functional* design, by orienting the team toward specifying product functionality. In this view, functional design describes the user interface, input and output transactions (displays, reports, and prints), initial database design, and top-level system architecture. This external design is often documented in a functional specification, used as the application or product description by developers in constructing the software.

So, distinctions are made between design and development, between functional and detailed design, and between individual and team design activities. These distinctions establish guidelines for organizers and project managers to make decisions for project planning and team development. These decisions become important in coordinating involvement to ensure that team members can contribute effectively.

Mitchell Kapor, in *Bringing Design to Software* (Winograd 1996), offers a view of the need for changing the way software is designed:

> The lack of usability of software and the poor design of programs are the secret shame of the industry. Given a choice, no one would want it to be this way. What is to be done? Computing professionals themselves should take responsibility for creating a positive user experience. Perhaps the most important conceptual move to be taken is to recognize the critical role of design, as a counterpart to programming, in the creation of computer artifacts. And the most important social evolution within the computing professions would be to create a role for the software designer as a champion of the user experience (p. 3).

Although Kapor puts the responsibility for the user's positive experience on the software designer, in any large software effort a number of participants play important roles.

Contemporary system development supports many design approaches. Large enterprises such as AT&T and insurance companies develop applications to manage their operations on a continual basis, replacing legacy systems when they become outmoded. These applications are typically developed by large teams (50 to 100 + members) with people from several functional organizations participating. Groundbreaking new software products are created by groups at Microsoft, IBM, Lotus, and other development companies using highly intensive team-oriented processes. In many businesses, management information systems (MISs) are developed by small teams using database management system tools and development templates. In almost no scenario today are major applications designed by one individual and developed by another, the exceptions being primarily research systems or advanced prototypes.

The team application design cycle outlines a workshop approach to conducting application design activities. As with the other formats, workshops create advantages and disadvantages. The disadvantages are generally that most work in the workshop itself proceeds at the pace of the entire team, and tasks are often performed in sequence rather than in parallel. The other primary disadvantage for AD is that detail is forgone during the pursuit of breadth and consensus on design concepts. The advantages are powerful, however, and can be seen as outweighing the downside. First, communication and coordination gained in the workshop typically persist throughout the development lifespan. Design concepts and artifacts are developed by a consensus process, and the team becomes educated in meaningful technologies and distinctions through this process. Parallel design work can be accomplished by small groups or individuals throughout a series of workshops, and the team is available for review and discussion at scheduled points. Finally, in workshops the team benefits from the synergy of the members and their availability for contributing to design and decision making.

In the Application Design format, the workshop can incorporate both requirements and design, or primarily design activities, depending on the project phase or the team's needs. Figure 9.1 shows the system design cycle of activities for this format's workshops:

- *Scoping: System analysis.* System analysis defines the scope of the application, including analysis of functions, data, and objects. It builds on the requirements definition, and in a combined

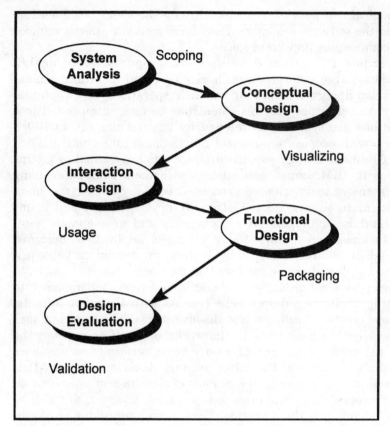

Figure 9.1 Team system design cycle.

requirements and design workshop, this phase represents a rapid
requirements process.

- *Visualizing: Conceptual design.*   Conceptual design represents the
  bridging of analysis to design, and begins to define *how* the system
  will work. Design of user processes and tasks, transactions and
  data, and architecture emerge from this phase.

- *Usage: Interaction design.*   Almost concurrent with conceptual
  design in this format, interaction design starts the design of the
  user interface and user interaction based on usage scenarios soon
  after defining the system structure.

- *Packaging: Functional design.*   Functional design defines the necessary components of the system in sufficient detail for developers
  to construct software. The packaging of the design results in a
  specification or set of diagrams and descriptions that accompany
  the design or product prototype.

- *Validating: Application design evaluation.* Validating, if done as a workshop, involves planning test activities and interpreting the results of development. This phase validates the design but, of course, requires working software for actual testing.

To support this integrating of design needs and project activities, the Team Design formats are designed to be used separately or within a single integrated cycle. As described in Chap. 6, projects can hold workshops for the different formats sequentially or cumulatively, where each workshop phase uses only a single format. Two or more formats can also support a project that requires both types of analysis; for example, requirements and business process design or requirements and AD. Integrating two or more formats into one project streamlines the overall process by reusing techniques across formats where applicable. Formats can also build one on the other cumulatively, which is necessary when a project is conducted across several stages requiring approvals, or if outsourcing or other distribution of project work is envisioned. This *stacking* of formats allows a separation of deliverables into those supporting process analysis, system requirements, and application design. Figure 9.2 shows how the formats can be integrated or stacked.

In the AD format, stacking the Requirements Definition format and the design work that follows produces a sequential schedule of activities. This approach serves incremental and traditional development life cycles effectively, whereas a more integrated approach bringing together two or more formats supports a rapid or evolutionary life

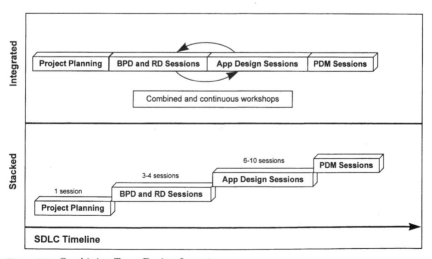

Figure 9.2 Combining Team Design formats.

cycle. Figure 9.2 shows the relationships among formats for both of these approaches.

Application Design Processes

Consider the spectrum of application design. An incredibly wide array of processes are used across companies and organizations to build interactive systems and applications for their designated users. How will we know which design processes work well in our corporate and development environments, and which lead to difficulty?

For the purposes of Team Design, application design processes of interest include methodologies used by individuals and groups to produce design artifacts (prototypes and logical models) and specifications (documented design models, diagrams, and spec packages). The design practices can be compared by constructing two dimensions, *group involvement* and *design practice,* as shown in Fig. 9.3.

Group involvement describes the extent to which the method is *typically* performed in a group, and ranges from individual to the cross-functional team. Individual work includes developing analysis models or programs using single-user applications or methods that require a single thread of work at one time. Small groups include groups of

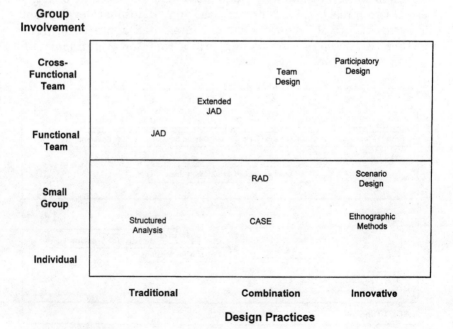

Figure 9.3   Team organization and design practices.

analysts, designers, and developers, mixed or not, but they are considered to be working not as teams but as workgroups. The middle line in the figure distinguishes *teams* from the small group. The functional group is a larger group that includes only participants from related functions; for example, developers but not users. Cross-functional teams are those with a full representation of disciplines, and their team methods are those in which the mix of participants makes a difference in the results of the method.

Traditional team software development starts with functional teams, where analysts and developers are pulled from their distinct organizations and are organized into subteams. The cross-functional team approach is recommended for Team Design, where all representatives of different functions are required to work together for the project, and are accountable to the project, not to their functional organization as such. For example, analysts and customers or users might be brought together with designers and project managers in the early stages of the team. As developers are required a little further down the schedule, development leads are integrated into the intact team, maintaining its tightly cross-functional organization.

Design practice methodologies include the traditional and the innovative, with the distinctively *combined* in the middle. The dimension of methodology implies a range from traditional to innovative, but these practices do not necessarily adapt to a scaled dimension. Many methodologies are available to development teams, and it is a judgment to place any of them in the traditional or innovative category.

Developers and analysts already use a wide range of methodologies, and are not reluctant to change methods if a new one proves effective. A review of how best-in-class CASE tools are used shows not only that methods in both categories are supported by most of the tools, but that users report using a mix of methodologies even on the same project (Vessey, Jarvenpaa, and Tractinsky 1992). These methodologies could be considered design practices to be selected for use by the analyst or team when appropriate.

The diagram shows a number of well-regarded design and development methods as fairly low in team involvement (below the middle line). *Structured analysis and design* can be regarded as low for team use and as traditional. *CASE* is also usually a single analyst's tool, and only rare CASE tools support team integration (which is not the same as multiuser access). CASE provides a combination of methods, both traditional and innovative. *Rapid application development* (RAD) methodologies involve more of a small group orientation, and use a combination of design practices. Two innovative methods, *scenario design* and *ethnographic methods,* to show just two, are still basically small group or individual practices.

Team design methods are those in which the team is really necessary to produce results. *JAD* uses traditional methods, and extended
JAD (various JAD consultants) uses a wider range of methods, but
they are team practices. *Participatory design* is highly cross-functional, and highly innovative, but has not gained wide acceptance—perhaps due to these very factors! And *Team Design* combines traditional
and innovative practices within a cross-functional team orientation.

This dimension of design *practice* is more challenging for many
organizations. With any new practice, it's straightforward for individual analysts to test the new method's utility for a project. However,
adoption of *team* methods into design and development practice
involves different project risks and management considerations.
People who have worked only as individuals are not always readily
comfortable on design teams. Working more closely with users, or
even analysts, requires a different, more communicative style of
working. Team processes might require training for specific members
or for the entire team, incurring necessary delays. Team building
might also be required to ensure that members can work together
effectively. The benefits of adopting new practices are continually balanced against the costs of integrating them into the project and the
organization.

Workshops for application design

Joint application design methods used over the last 15 years have
established the "traditional" group design workshop, leading to a
well-accepted and common practice. As in Requirements Definition,
the Application Design format adapts some of its structure from JAD.
Chapter 2 discusses how participatory design methods have gained
acceptance in more recent years, and constitute the other major force
in user-oriented development practices. Team Design integrates
methods from these practices in the Application Design format by fit-
ting methods to a context, then applying appropriate design tools.

In most contexts, application design workshops must satisfy at
least two groups: (1) application customers, including internal or commercial users and managers, and (2) software application developers.
The first group, the application customers, will have already had the
opportunity to participate in and approve the results of requirements
definition. Developers will not always have the chance to participate
in the requirements process, and then, typically, only the lead developers participate. For many developers, the application design workshop will be the first point of interface with designers and users, perhaps even with the project team.

Unlike the other formats, application design workshops will involve different team members at various points. Typically, a series of workshops will be planned, with early sessions heavily involving users and customers with the core team, and later sessions involving systems analysts and developers. Workshop sessions can be adapted using the AD format as a starting agenda and plan. Initiating phase workshops might require a day or less, depending on the level of team integration needed. Scoping workshops might require two or three days; less if a simpler application is planned. Visualizing workshops could require five days or more if working with one team; up to two weeks if a complex application with multiple organizational functions is involved. Usage workshops, using prototyping and scenarios, are more intermittent, with a series of perhaps three workshops of one or two days each, with individual design work continuing between sessions. Finally, the packaging phase workshop might require up to eight or more workshops of one or two days each to accomplish the final design. Packaging is highly variable, depending on the extent of depth and level of detail required for final deliverables. These workshops might be extended over a period of months in some cases; for example, if incremental design work is performed for a set of applications.

Application design differs significantly from the other formats. It is less conceptual or creative, and more of a hands-on workshop, with the concrete goal of completing a useful and usable system design. It does not lean toward any one primary organizational context; it applies to all four equally. It also involves fewer *roles* than the other contexts, since development does not require as many participating voices in the process.

The description of the AD format that follows shows the Team Design cycle with traditional and innovative design methods for each phase. As with the other formats, evaluate the outputs your team will require as deliverables, and consider other output products that might further team goals for quality or communication. Work your way back from the deliverables to determine the steps and methods needed to accomplish these.

With the AD format in particular, be sure to consider methods from the other formats that might be integrated into your design approach. Use the methodology as a set of flexible tools to lead to better design.

Format: Application design

The phase structure of the Application Design format is shown in Table 9.1.

TABLE 9.1   Application Design Format

Agenda Activities	Methods	Inputs and outputs
Scoping: System analysis		
Defining application scope	Scoping diagram, context model, process hierarchy	In: Requirements model (RD) Out: Application scope, revised requirements
Understanding the current system	System diagrams, demonstrations, function hierarchy, process map or other as-is model	In: Requirements model (RD), application scope Out: Process/system diagrams
Identifying objects, data and relationships	Function hierarchy, affinity diagram, data identification, object identification	In: Process/system diagrams, requirements prototype (RD) Out: Function model, object model, data descriptions
Visualizing: Conceptual design		
Planning system architecture	System diagrams, pictorial diagrams	In: Requirements model (RD), object and data descriptions, function model Out: Initial architecture model
Envisioning process and task design	Task scenarios and use cases, workflow analysis, interactive prototyping	In: Requirements prototype (RD), user or process scenarios Out: Process models, concept prototype
Envisioning system design	Data flow diagrams, system and transaction diagrams, entity-relationship modeling	In: Initial architecture model, process models, concept prototype Out: Initial system design
Usage: Interaction design		
Creating system scenarios	Scenario design methods, use cases, ideal system exercise	In: Requirements model (RD), user scenarios (RD) Out: Detailed system scenarios
Prototyping system scenarios	Process diagrams, interactive prototyping	In: Detailed system scenarios, requirements prototype Out: Initial design prototype
Integrating design models	Interactive prototyping, System and dataflow diagrams, data and object modeling	In: Initial system design, design prototype Out: System design models, design prototype

Software, system, and product design

With a format titled *Application Design,* a reader's expectation might be for it to cover design practices for information systems, such as traditional software engineering and structured methods. Software engineering methods are integrated into the format, but are not the

TABLE 9.1   Application Design Format (*Continued*)

Agenda Activities	Methods	Inputs and outputs
Packaging: Functional design		
Architecture design	System process diagrams, initial build cycle, design evaluation	In: Initial architecture model, design prototype Out: Architecture design model
Database design	Database design mapping, initial build cycle, design evaluation	In: Data models, system design models, design prototype Out: Database design
Object design	Use case mapping, initial build cycle, design evaluation	In: System design models, use cases, object models, design prototype Out: Object design model
Function or transaction design	Transaction mapping, initial build cycle, design evaluation	In: System design models, design prototype Out: Functional design model
Validating: Application design evaluation		
Evaluation planning	Test scenario definition, test and evaluation planning Group planning sessions	In: Detailed system scenario, requirements model (RD) Out: Application evaluation plan
Application or product design evaluation	Design review, prototype usability evaluation	In: Design prototype, prototype evaluation plan Out: Evaluated design model

strength of this approach. Team Design emphasizes emerging software design approaches derived from the human-computer interaction discipline. Given that perspectives from both software *engineering* and software *design* are supported by the format, a reader might find well-known methods mixed with the unfamiliar.

Application design involves planning and specification for the development of *interactive* computer software systems. Embedded software and programs with no user interface are not included in this definition, and are also not typically built by cross-functional teams in a workshop approach. Group design practices are often used in application development, such as in management information systems, custom database or software tools, and commercial software packages. The quality of user interaction with the application is a key criteria for the success of these applications. Many of the newer design practices, from software design or usability engineering (and not software engineering) stress this view of software quality. We start by identifying quality as a function of *the customer's acceptance* and not of software coding elegance. Then, our methods to achieve this type of quality must be selected to fulfill this perspective.

Integrating best practices from the different software design disciplines results in better products over the long run. Learning achieved through studying numerous software projects has led to recommendations to *use what works*. Bill Curtis (Curtis, Krasner, and Iscoe 1988; Walz, Elam, and Curtis 1993; Curtis and Hefley 1994) has recommended integrated organizational methods in research spanning most of a decade. Keil and Carmel (1995) recently studied the use of different methods in custom and packaged software, and made their own recommendations for expanding the repertoire of methods used in design and development.

No single methodology can fit every project and every environment. Given the rapid pace of computer technology change, the widespread consumer acceptance of the Internet, and the proliferation of creative, highly interactive game products, users are more educated and demanding. Since these new users are tomorrow's customers, development organizations seek to improve their current practices by adopting quality improvement and standard development methodologies, and by following the latest software engineering directions. Following these traditional paths of advice is probably insufficient, based on the reports of successful product developers. Software design that results in user satisfaction is not development-centered but user-centered. The best products innovate, but also closely follow the needs and desires of their users, both expressed and *anticipated*. Development team members cannot understand their users by sitting in the lab drawing and coding all day. They must adopt the best-fitting practices from other design orientations that encompass user feedback as an integrated and continuous part of their design process. Examples of these development practices abound in human-computer interaction (HCI) research. Although only a few HCI methods have emerged into general acceptance, such as prototyping and usability evaluation, new practices are adapted from the lessons of research. When looking at the spectrum of software engineering design practices and HCI design practices, many of the innovative design practices emerge from the HCI discipline. When looking at team or workshop-based methods, most of the design tools arise from HCI. While the software engineering disciplines argue over which of the latest object-oriented design methodologies works better for reusable class development, usability engineering practitioners are inventing methods for prototyping and user interaction analysis.

Although the HCI methods are not *standards* in any way, they engage users in the design process, leading to systems and products that users want to use. It is like the difference between construction and architecture. While we need the standards and fail-safe methods of construction (software) engineering, homes and buildings are only interesting and valuable because of the creative (interface) design work of architects. As construction is a coordination of builders, architecture is a collaboration of customers and designers. One of the central disparities in this analogy is that while architecture has evolved over centuries into a practice that integrates creativity with standard procedures, software and user interface design are very new disciplines, with new practices emerging continually.

The key to this comparison is the involvement of designers with users. As described previously in Chap. 3, software development practices differ across various product types. Two of the broadest categories are *custom* software, developed as a unique product to satisfy a specific business need, and *package* software, which is a generic application that is installed and tailored. Designers working on a unique statewide licensing system will use different methods with users than designers implementing an accounting package for use by businesses. Designers building a mapping tool for public use will approach user interaction differently than Microsoft developers making major enhancements to database management software that will be used as a package tool.

When customer-developer *links* were investigated by Keil and Carmel, they found little crossover of techniques from the package and custom development environments. They recommended explicitly that package software developers adopt the most effective practices from the custom software approach, by using facilitated teams and user interface prototyping. Just within these two general practices are hundreds of methods and variations that can be applied in almost any development environment. Team Design enables integration of these user-based practices in your development environment, by selecting and adopting the tools that make sense for the application.

Leading application design

Application design workshops can last for days or weeks; can involve a small group or a roomful of participants; can result in working prototypes or a sheaf of paper specifications. Application design practices are too variable, too customized, to readily characterize in a general way. Also, each team has its favorite existing methods with which designers and developers are comfortable. These methods become part of the unwritten cultural standard and can be difficult to change. Application design methods must be introduced with some caution, especially to developers who might be skeptical as to their value. The

AD and other Team Design formats allow for a minimal usage of methods, allowing incremental introduction of new tools over time.

Application Design workshops are also organized and facilitated differently than in the other formats. Business Process and Requirements Definition formats support front-end analysis workshops, and in these processes an intact workshop team can typically work through most, if not all, the analysis and design methods. Application design rewards invention and experimentation. It supports the design and development of applications and products, and involves a distribution of expertise across the different activities. Involvement of different experts leads to trying new methods they bring from their experience. Mixing content experts, software experts, and user or human factors experts provides a rich source of background and approaches that should be exploited within the team.

However, not every participant will or should contribute to every activity in application design. To make effective use of available time, small groups can break out and work in parallel, coming together as a fully assembled team at least once a week or more often as required. This also allows the team to specialize more, making user and technical experts fully available in the small groups where they can contribute in a more focused process.

The composition of the whole project and the workshop team should be heterogeneous, with participants representing the various development experts and project stakeholders. The whole team breaks down into subteams as required. When deliverables are being prepared, subteams break out to work on the detailed component required. Working procedures for the subteams are different from the whole group. Team Design workshops cannot easily support workshops across the subteams, but what occurs in most groups is that team leaders learn the attitude of facilitation from participating in sessions, and bring this approach to leading their subteam work efforts.

Zahniser's (1993) approach to team coordination from CASELab is described in Chap. 1. He identifies the logical team compositions used in design workshops and associated methods (deliverables) and media with the appropriate size of team. In Application Design, some of the team arrangements shown in Table 9.2 (based on Zahniser) are considered best-suited for certain design activities.

While planning for Application Design, meet with managers, customers, and team members. Planning for AD, as with the Requirements Definition format, includes identifying the workshop goals, deliverables, and dependencies, and determining the schedule for design workshops. Although workshop time is variable, based on the project size and workshop deliverables, the time can be planned by scaling back from the typical nonworkshop design phase. For

TABLE 9.2   Team Arrangements for Design Activities

Team arrangement	Design activities
Solo	Off-line work, such as preparing documents, formalizing diagrams, and refining prototypes
Dyad	Developing detailed models Reviewing and finalizing ER and dataflow diagrams
Small group (subteams)	System architecture design Data analysis and data modeling Function analysis detail Developing detailed scenarios Transaction and database design
Large group (assembled team)	Scoping activities Scenario definition Function analysis Initial design of data model, workflow, and transactions Prototype review and evaluation
Team of teams (distributed development)	Design review Prototype demonstration and evaluation Design planning activities

example, if the external design or prototype for a typical large project requires two months, the duration for using workshops should be about 50 percent of that time, with up to half of that time actually spent in team workshops.

Multiple deliverables are produced in Application Design, and having a wide range of talent on the team will be useful. Workshops using this format might extend for more than three or four times the duration of a requirements workshop, so recruit cofacilitators while planning for the sessions. A variety of technical experts should be available throughout the team in this format, so facilitators are not necessarily required to have expertise in the design methods. Especially if breaking out into parallel subteams, the methods experts can be assigned to the groups as needed. Facilitators will be expected to maintain the pace and flow of the workshop, and to coordinate and track multiple activities following the agenda.

System Design Methods

Team Design focuses on design methods applicable to cross-functional teams. This includes the specific workshop methods discussed throughout the chapters, and also allows for any methods that can be employed with small groups of analysts and developers. The Team

Design cycle allows system designers to expand or contract the processes, facilitation, and workshops as necessary to gain the maximum benefit from working in a project team mode. Not every activity in system design is conducted as a team or subteam; much individual work must be coordinated to fulfill the design needs. These individual design tasks are noted within the process, yet readers should also consider whether their current design activities could be conducted in a team or small group process to benefit from collaboration in design.

The system design approach in this format integrates methods from three disparate forces in software design and development: *structured design, object-oriented design,* and *participatory design* (PD). Although many other categories and subdisciplines could be broken out from them, these three are major current and emerging forces in design for team and workshop-based projects. In some projects only one design orientation might be necessary. In many others, some combination of design approaches will be most effective. A quick investigation of current literature in software engineering, structured methods, or object-oriented design will show how new software design methods are evolving into the methodologies. Structured analysis and CASE proponents explain how they intended to show user and business processes all along, object-oriented methods have pulled in scenarios (use cases) due to the acceptance of Jacobson's approach, and participatory design workshops have incorporated technology-based methods similar to JAD approaches.

All Application Design must start with a requirements definition—it never starts without guidance; it is not a standalone process. Whereas Business Process Design and Requirements Definition can proceed without initial sources, Application Design must start from at least a set of requirements. Where the other formats can also be completed without a following activity, AD must proceed to development to complete its cycle. The requirements analysis approach used in a design effort greatly influences the methods allowed in design. It will be difficult to change the approach midstream—if a structured approach was used in requirements it will be difficult to change in design to a user-oriented collaborative approach based on participatory methods.

There are three approaches the AD format uses to integrate requirements. The first approach stacks AD onto Requirements Definition. Use an RD format workshop initially, performing Requirements Definition as a separate activity, then incorporate the results of RD workshops in Application Design. This has its advantages, such as performing a solid requirements analysis without the impending pressures of moving quickly to development, and using different analysts and, possibly, user representatives in RD and AD.

The next approach is to integrate RD methods into the AD format. This is an effective way to incorporate the requirements activities into a series of workshops using the same team. This approach might be used in smaller projects where general product requirements exist (such as a marketing requirements approach), and more requirements work is required.

Finally, a rapid application development (RAD) process also combines RD and AD. This approach is similar to that preceding, in using a single format for requirements and design. In a true RAD process, requirements activities are pulled into an application design process. Advantages of this approach include continuity, saving time in the development schedule, and being able to rapidly cycle feedback from requirements into design. This approach also allows for iteration within the AD system design cycle, allowing for adjusting the requirements while pursuing aspects of the design itself.

Keep this integration of methods in mind throughout the format. Each design approach has its blind side. Uncertainty is reduced by appropriately using methods from different design approaches, since different views of the emerging system design surface different issues and reveal new opportunities. A prototyping methodology is recommended in all cases as a means of further reducing uncertainty in the design. The RAD approach follows this trend, integrating prototyping, scenario usage models, and a technology-based method (object-oriented or structured design) for specification.

Structured design methods

Structured design methods continue to be the predominant design tools used in most information system development. Even as object-oriented programming has taken hold throughout development shops, requirements and design specifications continue to be represented by structured methods. For better or worse, analysts understand dataflow and hierarchy diagrams, and retraining organizations in object-oriented methods has not yet led to any single generally accepted representation.

In application design, the first significant team activity is *system analysis*. In the context of the Application Design format, structured analysis methods are recommended as a well-known approach for analyzing and documenting the parts of the business being changed. Structured systems analysis continues to be used by many information system development organizations for some of the following basic purposes:

- To define the scope of the system

- To understand and communicate the essential processes of the business
- To evaluate business processes and design improvements
- To provide a baseline model of the business to be used for correct analysis and design

Structured analysis refers to the class of analysis techniques developed in the late 1970s that evolved to become de facto standards for specifying system behavior and data models. These techniques all define system processes and data through graphical diagram specifications, considered far more readable and standardized than text descriptions. The Yourdon-DeMarco methods are considered the basic paradigm for structured analysis, supporting function decomposi-tion, dataflow diagramming, and data analysis. (Yourdon and Constantine 1975; DeMarco 1979) Defined information flow models are typically developed, supported by a data dictionary and processing narrative, documented in specifications.

Although many theorists have abandoned structured analysis in favor of object-oriented or formal methods, structured analysis remains a favored methodology for JAD and group-based design work. Perhaps structured analysis enjoys such a stable continuation of use after two decades because so many analysts have learned and applied these methods and they have now achieved a unique standing among the ever-changing development tools used to build systems. Structured analysis tools are thinking tools, used to map out and communicate solutions to business problems. Other methods have emerged and have found their adopted niches, but the dataflow diagram, function hierarchy, and entity-relationship diagram have grown with the times and have remained effective tools with the advantage of widespread familiarity. Structured analysis tools bring inherent advantages, such as the following:

- Consistent and effective communication among the team members, customers, and organizations involved in development.
- Specifications are readable and usable.
- Techniques have general applicability; once learned, they can be applied to many projects and products.
- Fewer translation errors in design result.
- Better maintainability of the product results from standard analysis and design documentation.
- Techniques differentiate between logical and physical, allowing for separation of concerns among the development staff.

Structured analysis techniques capture the results of analysis at different levels of abstraction, and function as different methods of hierarchical decomposition. For Team Design workshops, diagramming methods are useful as devices to support clear thinking about the problem, and for generating design solutions. They then serve as well-defined structure models for development.

Structured analysis serves the dual purposes of documenting the results of requirements analysis and providing a means of graphical specification of design. Structured analysis includes the following diagramming methods that are useful throughout application design:

- Process analysis

- Function decomposition

- Dataflow diagramming (Gane-Sarson 1979, and Yourdon-DeMarco 1978)

- Control flow diagramming (Page-Jones 1980, and Gane-Sarson 1979)

- Real-time control flow diagramming (Ward-Mellor 1985, Hatley-Pirbhai 1987)

- Logical data modeling (ERD, Chen 1976, Information Engineering, $IDEF_{1x}$)

Any of these methods can be adapted to a workshop environment, if they are known to the team and the technical work warrants their use. In the *systems* organizational context, using structured analysis might not be a problem for any team members, given the stronger focus on technical design. However, in the business and user contexts, only the simpler techniques should even be attempted within a mixed attendance workshop. The recommended methods include process and function hierarchy diagrams, data modeling with simplified entity-relationship diagrams, and simplified dataflow diagramming.

Object-oriented design methods

Object-oriented design methods have received less attention in the JAD world than in the development community, although the object methods have been rapidly adopted by many development organizations. Three factors probably account for their relatively infrequent appearance in JAD development workshops.

First, object-oriented design methods have not yet matured to a state where a recognized standard approach, or even a widely used approach, has taken hold. Therefore, numerous methodologies have proliferated, and analysts and developers often use competing methods or try different tools for different projects to investigate the methods. With this lack of a clearly preferred method, the other methods are often not retained in use long enough to become well integrated into standard development procedures.

Perhaps due to the first factor, business analysts and development managers do not invest time in learning the methodologies, which are therefore not used in cross-functional design sessions. However, other object technologies such as object-oriented programming and reuse libraries become implemented because significant benefits can be achieved without an organizational transition and learning curve.

Finally, where structured analysis and design methods have represented business processes and data for years, object-oriented methods have been developed more recently, and do not offer representations that are well understood by business functions. They are often perceived as highly technical methods that do not communicate with business and user groups, and are not seen as appropriate for cross-functional work.

Perhaps a simple reason why object-oriented design approaches have not worked into JAD and team processes significantly is that object methodologies do not support an accepted conceptual model of end-to-end processing. In cross-functional teams, representations are needed that relate to process views, which are understood by all members of the team. Most object-based methods (Rumbaugh, Booch 1991, and Coad-Yourdon 1991) are highly *data*-oriented, and do not integrate workflow or business process modeling. Jacobson's (1995) use case approach is the closest object modeling method that encompasses usage processes, and even use cases are fairly discrete, and do not support end-to-end business processes.

Some object-oriented processes have been integrated into JAD work using scenario-based methods, which is a similar approach to that taken in Team Design. This approach works with the team to develop scenarios and use cases to reach closure on requirements. Workshop processes support analysis of data and uses of data in the user scenarios, leading to a simple class or object hierarchy as a specification of represented objects. Finally, the user interface is designed from event-driven scenarios based on the use cases. Objects from the simple object model are represented in the user interface, and the design loop is completed.

Participatory design approaches

Participatory design approaches have evolved as useful new practices for involving users and customers in design. Several methodologies have been found useful in North American development environments. These have changed enough from the original European influences to become more acceptable in corporations comfortable with highly structured JAD processes. Some of the methodologies appropriate in the Application Design format are described briefly in the following.

Collaborative design.   Peter Denning and Pamela Dargan championed the idea of *human-centered* design as opposed to *product-centered* design for business process and system design. Similar in intent to the user context described in Chap. 3, human-centered design is based on understanding the social and psychological nature of work as observed, and endorses a design approach to build systems supporting human-centered requirements. Denning and Dargan (1994) list their assumptions, quoted as follows:

1. The result of a good design is a satisfied customer.

2. The process of design is a collaboration between designers and customers. The design evolves and adapts to their changing concerns, and the process produces a specification as an important by-product.

3. The customer is not assumed to be satisfied until he or she declares satisfaction (p. 58).

The customer and designer are in constant communication during the entire design effort, as in a true collaboration. The design team seeks to understand the world of the users as much as possible, and to design products that support their needs as *human* users and customers, not just as performers of tasks. Customer satisfaction is an important by-product of this approach, unlike other design approaches that primarily support technical concerns and do not address the customer perspective as such.

Contextual Design.   Contextual Design is a user-centered prototyping design approach based on Holtzblatt and Beyer's (1993) approach of immersing system designers in the work of the users to better understand the relationship of the system to real work tasks. Contextual Design uses multiple process representations and prototyping for working directly with customers and users in a team environment. This approach is highly proactive in its style, in that analysts and designers work with users in the user environment as much as practical:

> If we wish to codesign with users, we take a previously developed prototype to their workplace. We invite them to work through their immediate work problem using the prototype. Users respond directly to the prototype as if it were real and give much better feedback than would be possible in a meeting room (p. 94).

Contextual Design recommends using a variety of tools to gain information about user work processes. An affinity diagram relating system and process concepts is used in early workshops with the design team, and can be extracted without engaging users directly in the design team. Other work process models are integrated into the approach, such as the context, physical, and flow models. A major strength of the approach is in integrating these models with a team process that works together across the life cycle.

Prototype storyboarding.   Prototype storyboarding (described in Chap. 8) involves developing a fairly rough prototype model of the system and presenting it in a workshop session to generate feedback and ideas. This prototype should show an early representation of user interface, with only a rough idea of the application flow and dialogs, and be presented in a low-tech form. The low-tech prototype approach had been considered valuable by the contextual approach, as it seems to support the participants' comfort level in making changes to the design. In many domains of user work, especially where computers are not yet used, even a simple "slide show" prototype showing screen representations might appear too technical or well planned. Prototype storyboarding advocates a paper or other very simple prototype as an obvious rough cut that can be changed during working sessions.

The paper prototype can be drawn out on newsprint, showing system menu selections and screen concepts. These rough original screens can be elaborated using storyboards, showing a sequence of activities that lead to completion of new tasks in the system. The storyboard approach displays both data entry screens and their sequence in an easily interpreted format, and—most importantly—engages users in workshops they might otherwise fear to attend.

Team System Design Cycle

The Team System Design cycle describes activities applicable across the life cycle of application design and development. As with the other formats, sections are organized into *scoping, visualizing, usage,* and *packaging* phases.

In Application Design more than in the other formats, these phases can be conducted by subteams and worked somewhat in parallel. This type of integration is useful for rapid application development projects as shown in Fig. 9.4. Before scoping is completed, during preparation of system models, visualizing activities such as architecture planning, prototyping, and process design can be started. Separate subteam workshops might be used to work along separate tracks, continuing through the phases at their own pace. In this way, a subteam developing prototypes might use data and process diagrams from an analysis subteam developing system models. A third subteam might

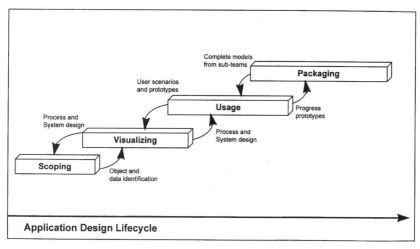

Figure 9.4 Use of the Application Design format for rapid application design.

develop architecture models to be used by the other teams. Regular review and discussion sessions can be facilitated to demonstrate and share models and learning throughout the cycle.

Scoping: System analysis

Scoping activities in Application Design begin with familiar system analysis methods for understanding users, their backgrounds and tasks, and product goals. Application Design scoping establishes the foundation for development—key assumptions are laid out and decisions are made that affect the design for the remaining life cycle. Table 9.3 shows team tools used in scoping the application. As with

TABLE 9.3   Application Design: Scoping Phase

Scoping: System analysis	Methods	Inputs and outputs
Defining application scope	Scoping diagram Context model Process hierarchy	In: Requirements model (RD) Out: Application scope, revised requirements
Understanding the current system	System diagrams Demonstrations Function hierarchy Process map or other as-is model	In: Requirements model (RD), application scope Out: Process or system diagrams
Identifying objects, data and relationships	Function hierarchy Affinity diagram Data identification Object identification	In: Process or system diagrams, prototype (RD) Out: Function model, object model, data descriptions

the preceding formats, team scoping methods also include those described in the format for business process design in Chap. 7.

Scoping starts with defining the scope and requirements for the application. If the Requirements Definition format has been used, the requirements model is pulled in for scoping the application. If the RD format was not used, its methods and approaches can be incorporated into the AD workshops if needed. If a requirements prototype was available, it should be used in the scoping phase.

The overall output of scoping includes a functional model, an object model (if appropriate) and an initial data model, such as data descriptions or an initial entity diagram.

Defining application scope.   As with the other workshop formats defined previously, the first activity the team works through is defining the scope for the effort. In the case of the AD format, the scope of an application involves numerous factors—user environment, functionality, user interface design, installation environment, development cost and customer pricing, increments of delivery, and other elements.

Scope definition uses techniques described in previous sections: scoping diagrams, the context model, and process hierarchies. The main difference between scoping in Application Design and the other formats is that when starting this format, some level of complete requirements definition is assumed. Unless starting Team Design at mid–life cycle with Application Design, a requirements model will usually be available to the team. The primary goal of scoping in AD is understanding the current scope as defined from requirements. In some cases, new information learned since the requirements workshop will lead to some scope redefinition during this phase. Customer feedback, changing market or business conditions, or competitive products might force a rescoping of the requirements model, so at least some form of scoping should be conducted.

At the least, an Application Design workshop should follow the initiating phase by reviewing the agreed scope. The facilitator might lead discussions for reaching group understanding with the new team members who usually join in during this phase. Diagrams and charts used to define the scope of the application might be reproduced and displayed on a board or on easel charts for interactive group scoping.

Understanding the current system.   A team analysis of current systems is necessary for almost any application project. Your team will benefit from having a consistent understanding of any current systems in use as models relevant to the new application. These existing models might include any systems used by the identified user community, any competitive applications available on the market, and any off-the-shelf products that perform similar functions. By reviewing and evaluating these current system models, the team builds a common representation of requirements embodied by the examples. Any ideas that might apply to the new system that can be drawn from other existing products will be useful design material.

The typical inputs to this activity will be the scope diagrams from the previous scoping exercise and the requirements model from the requirements definition. If these are fairly complete, very little new work will be necessary for the team. Review of the requirements model will continue to be useful, especially for new team members. But new analysis might not be performed if it precedes application design.

The extent to which system analysis is performed is highly dependent on the need for a thorough up-front system definition. If the requirements are well defined, an existing system definition might have been conducted and will be available in the requirements model. If existing systems and processes have not yet been defined, consider the depth to which the representation is necessary. You are designing something new, not analyzing something that exists. Use existing models only to the extent that they contribute to the new design, or at least to the team's understanding. In Application Design, breakthrough design ideas are not likely to arise from copying existing models. Existing systems reveal functions and procedures for accomplishing specific tasks, which might be valuable as checks for completeness. Existing systems might also be compared with the new design in terms of usability. However, a thorough current system analysis as discussed in Chap. 7 (as-is process mapping) is not always a good use of the team's time together. Discuss the pros and cons of system analysis approaches with the team before embarking on the journey of understanding. You could end up understanding the current system so well that it will be difficult to design anything dissimilar.

The tools for this activity include system diagrams, demonstrations, function hierarchies, and process maps. These methods are all drawn from the Requirements Definition format. However, the system diagrams and function hierarchy methods might be used to create new diagrams to show a current system's functions from the perspective of the new application design. These system diagrams would represent the main output of this activity from the team.

Identifying objects, data, and relationships. As in the Requirements Definition format, this activity involves discovering and representing the components to be used in the design. During Application Design, however, the team progresses to more concrete examples and develops products that contribute directly to the design. Much of the initial object and data definition can be conducted as an assembled team, so that all participants can contribute their knowledge and a common understanding is achieved. For detailed definition, small groups that include at least one user knowledgeable in the domain and designers or developers might break out from the whole team and work in parallel to continue with the details.

The team can start from process and system diagrams generated through the workshops and the requirements prototype from Requirements Definition (RD). The prototype will especially demonstrate the required functions and will show defined data as used in dialogs and data displays. Primary deliverables or outputs from this activity will include a function model (hierarchy diagram), an initial object model, and data descriptions.

The tools used in this work are the same as in Requirements Definition, but more depth might be pursued with them. For application design (AD), the team seeks not only to identify data and objects, but to validate their use in the application. The tools include the following:

- *Function hierarchy.* Started in RD and developed further in AD for identifying functions and deriving data requirements from the functions.

- *Affinity diagram.* Also available from RD, used to identify new possibilities for usage and to reveal functions and organizations.

- *Data identification.* Started in RD as data identification and continued in AD as the initial data model. Existing systems can support much of the data identification for an initial model.

- *Object identification.* An AD method in which the team identifies classes and objects that might be constructed in an object model.

Only the two methods not covered in previous sections, *data identification* and *object identification*, are described in the following.

Data identification. During the scoping phase, a high-level data analysis is performed within the workshop team to foster a common understanding of the data among all members. While discovering entities, their attributes, and relationships in the data, the team forms a *mental model* of the data. This mental model is useful for all team members, even those not working directly with the data, as it provides a common basis for understanding data needs throughout the application. This initial data model is incrementally built upon throughout the design process, as continued learning and discoveries require changes to the model. In the visualizing phase, a complete entity-relationship diagram is developed as part of the *envisioning system design* activity, and the full process is described in that phase's section. In packaging, a detailed data model is finalized for use in database design and software development.

If leading the workshop process to build an initial data model, it is important to understand the complete methodology of logical data modeling. Although a complete entity-relationship diagram might not be constructed at this stage, the facilitator must understand the eventual use of the model and know practical guidelines for building the diagrams. Otherwise, the team's mental model of the data will be inconsistent, as the initial diagram will not at all reflect the model that evolves through formal data modeling. Basic steps for leading data identification are described as follows:

1. *Entity identification.*   Entities represent physical or conceptual things about which the database will store information. Allow your database experts in the workshop to define the terms if users or other members are unclear; just be sure they translate to the users' level of understanding!

   Many projects will have some basic set of entities from which to start, such as a data listing or diagram from a similar previous project. If this is available, use the materials as a handout to get the group started. Use requirements documents, system diagrams, or prototypes as a means to identify potential entities.

   Start drawing a simple entity-relationship diagram (ERD) on the board to provide a descriptive model for the team. Figure 9.5

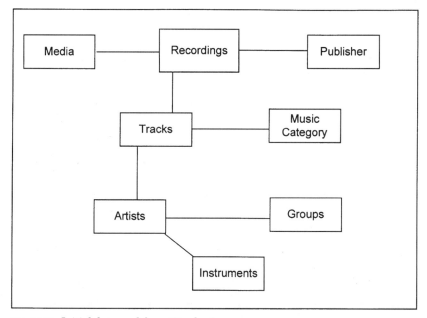

Figure 9.5   Initial data model—entity chart.

shows an example of a simple ERD. This works better than a list of data, since the spatial nature of a diagram enables people to envision links between entities that can be defined as other entities or relationships. Brainstorm with the group to expand the diagram to include as many entities as necessary, based on system requirements and the users' understanding of the work process. Don't worry if the volunteered items are not technically entities—just draw out the items as they are brought out, and keep the team thinking about other possible data items. Items will be resolved into entities or attributes in the next step.

2. *Generating attributes.*   Attributes are data elements, and represent the data fields to be stored in the database and displayed in forms and reports. Once users understand the distinction between *entities* and *attributes,* the design team can brainstorm and identify the first cut of attributes that make up each initially defined entity. Some attributes must be defined for each entity in order to describe it as a valid entity. At least a key identifier must be defined for each entity, with additional attributes that are based on this key.

   This step is called *herding* attributes, since the team surveys the entities and potential attributes and positions groups of attributes into the entity which they fit.

3. *Discovering relationships.*   Relationships are represented by the lines between entities on the diagram, as shown in the simple entity chart in Fig. 9.5. In an entity-relationship diagram, the relationships are specified to represent the business association between the entities. In this analysis of data identification, initial relationships can be shown by a line between entities with a simple name describing the proposed relationship between entities.

The initial data model described by this entity chart establishes a mental view of the data that is shared by all participants. As the design proceeds the more complex ERD models build on this base model, but entity names will typically remain consistent. The importance of this exercise is learning about the use of data, which stays with participants throughout the project. So as the technical design proceeds, the team's understanding of the data is represented by at least this simplified model.

Object identification.   An initial object model is useful if an object-oriented design is adopted for development. Even though this model will be refined and redefined over iterations during detailed design activities, the initial object model should be constructed with the team. The purpose of pursuing this model with the team is the same as with other design models—the system designers benefit from having domain experts available to discuss their ideas and concepts at a very early stage in design. These early conversations establish much of the underlying assumptions that become invisibly adopted throughout design later on. With users and domain experts in the same workshop process, an initial object model can be defined that reflects the nature of the real world of their work.

One of the major assumptions in object modeling is that the system should use objects that correspond closely to the real world in which the work is performed. So a document management system might model the different publications stored in the system (books and journals) and the attributes of each type of document object (articles, paragraphs, and authors) as described in Fig. 9.6. This correspondence with real objects makes it somewhat easier for an interdisciplinary team to discuss and define objects in the model.

Advantages are gained in a design model that incorporates knowledge of the real world in the behavior of the system. Objects are assumed to have identity and have attributes and behaviors associated with their identity, unlike entities (for example) that all behave according to the rules required in the data model. Natural relationships exist among objects that are not supported in conventionally coded representations. Books and articles both are composed of paragraphs and include tables and figures, which can be represented directly in an object model.

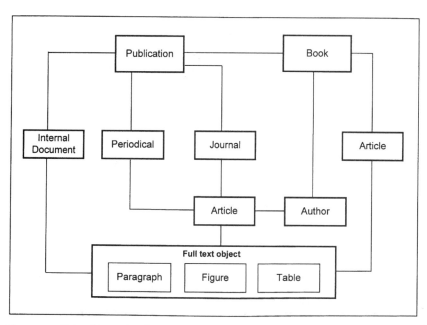

Figure 9.6 Object hierarchy diagram.

Of course, reflecting the *current* state of understanding might not always be the best course of action for a new technology. It is incumbent on the designers to grasp the extent of expected divergence from the current state, and to communicate this effectively to stakeholders. For example, if an object model were defined for an automated publishing process, current users might expect to see the electronic corollaries of typesetting, editing, layout, copy control, and distribution. Many traditional functions might be obviated by the new technology, requiring the system designers to educate the user participants. In Team Design, the new business process would have been designed using a front-end format (BPD or RD), but midstream development efforts will often not have this advantage. A simple object modeling process using a hierarchy diagram can be used in the business, user, or product contexts. Since the inheritance relationships of classes and objects are hierarchical, this well-known modeling method can be used to generate discussion and elicit domain concepts within the workshop itself. Refinements can be made in small groups or by individuals using an object-oriented CASE tool methodology after the rough model is defined far enough to warrant converting it to a more rigorous notation.

Building the initial object model is similar to constructing a data model, since objects represent data and their associated methods (or *allowable functions of objects*). For object-based systems, the object model is the equivalent of the data model; if a relational database is used with the system, an entity-relationship model will also be developed as a complementary view of data managed through the DBMS.

A simple approach to building the object hierarchy chart follows:

1. Identify the purpose and level of description required of the model. Identify the functional requirements model from which to define the object diagrams. System process diagrams, scenarios, process maps, and other representations developed by the team are acceptable.

2. To define the object model, start with the largest, most obvious constructs. These are objects that naturally appear at the top of the hierarchy, or have the largest number of associations. In the example shown, *publications* is the most general object or class, with connections to several other subclasses.

3. List or post candidate objects on the board using a brainstorming or round-robin approach. Objects should have some relationship with the initial objects, but don't judge suggestions as they are given. List the objects and then arrange them in the next step.

4. Arrange objects in categories (like an affinity diagram) and invent new names for groupings if appropriate. Groups of similar objects

might be represented by a class type (such as the *publication* class). Other lower-level objects might be represented as objects that are shared and used by objects of all classes (such as the *full text object*).

5. Remove candidates that are not used or that detract from the categorical organization. Refine the diagram so that any natural hierarchical relationships are made apparent.

The object hierarchy diagram is a simple approach to obtaining team input on meaningful objects that can be used by developers for further analysis and design. Furthermore, it can be redrawn as needed to show the changes to the object model through its evolution during design. Since the team will have been involved with the initial construction of the model, evolutions of the model will be readily understood, and can be used for review and commentary.

Visualizing: Conceptual design

Visualizing is the phase where analysis starts moving into design. Design *concepts* are derived from the previous analysis work and are transformed into design models that define the architecture, business processes, user tasks, and system components. This is a visualizing activity, in that the design becomes created by the group during this stage—it is envisioned through the three team activities using common design methods. Visualizing is not a complicated phase—the whole team can participate in most of the methods.

It is ineffective to make generalizations regarding conceptual design, given the differing needs of development organizations where this activity is concerned. The purpose of visualizing the conceptual design is to construct a meaningful design of system functions with the team, and then to efficiently communicate that design to a development team. In Team Design's organizational contexts, these constructs might include the following:

- *Business context.* In the business context a conceptual design might refer to the overall business system, including the information system, workflow, and business procedures. Technical deliverables such as functional specifications and system diagrams are used to communicate the design to an implementation team.

- *User context.* A user context calls for the definition of a cooperatively defined system that meets the requirements described throughout previous sessions. In this context, a more integrated team will have been involved with the users from the beginning. The conceptual design deliverables from the workshop team might consist of a prototype and user-oriented task scenarios that define the scope of work.

- *Systems context.*   A systems context requires a different set of deliverables than the others. Due to the technical focus of this context, a conceptual design typically consists of system definition documents, system specifications, system diagrams (dataflow and entity-relationship), and perhaps a prototype developed as a testbed application.

- *Product context.*   The product context is variable, depending on product complexity or sophistication and the type of product. This context is treated like the user context, since it is customer-driven. A well-defined functional prototype with system description documents will effectively serve most product context conceptual designs.

Table 9.4 shows the visualization methods for activities associated with conceptual design. Many of these methods are diagrammatic, which is deliberate in this case. Usage activities are reserved for focusing on prototyping and user scenarios. Visualizing is a convenience phase for producing detailed conceptual design models where they are called for, often a strict requirement in corporate information system (IS) organizations. Traditional JAD orientations often plunge into the conceptual design earlier than Team Design might show, but traditional methods do not encourage the cooperation and flexibility of integrating participatory design methods and interactive prototyping that are built into these models.

Planning system architecture.   The goal of planning the system architecture is to define the underlying foundation and shared resources

TABLE 9.4   Application Design: Visualizing Phase

Visualizing: Conceptual design	Methods	Inputs and outputs
Planning system architecture	System diagrams Pictorial diagrams	In: Requirements model (RD), object and data descriptions, function model Out: Initial architecture model
Envisioning process and task design	Task scenarios and use cases Workflow analysis Interactive prototyping	In: Requirements prototype (RD), user or process scenarios Out: Process models, concept prototype
Envisioning system design	Dataflow diagrams System and transaction diagrams Entity-relationship modeling	In: Initial architecture model, process models, concept prototype Out: Initial system design

used for the system as a whole. The initial architecture model becomes a plan for implementing this foundation design. Architecture involves almost anything in the design that affects the system as a whole, and all functions that become dependencies across the design. In a typical large project, architecture definition might include the following analyses:

- Defining geographical and physical constraints for design, especially for distributed business systems

- Defining networking and communications for the system

- Defining program and object libraries for reuse

- Specifying and evaluating integration, system management, and database software

- Analyzing system and data interfaces and data communications with interfaces

- Defining security and access control

- Defining monitoring and system management processes

Architecture *requirements* will have been defined in the requirements model, if available.

Having agreement on requirements and scope will benefit the architecture design by identifying any constraints on the architecture as well as required interfaces, security, and global system factors. Furthermore, the system diagrams, object and data descriptions, and process relationships developed in previous analyses will be necessary for architecture planning, to identify all the areas globally affected by the system architecture.

Outputs of architecture planning are straightforward. Documentation of the architecture can be provided using various system diagrams and pictorial methods. A detailed architecture design is often necessary as a separate deliverable for large applications, especially where the architecture must be defined well in advance of application design. If this is the case, the architecture can be planned and defined incrementally, with completed portions delivered to the team as they become necessary for other design.

Architecture definition is considered a primarily technical undertaking, but it always follows the business and user requirements, and therefore has implications for user-oriented design. When designing the architecture plan in a team workshop, a breakout group or small group of three to six participants will serve better than using the whole team. A facilitated process might still be employed, with a designated cofacilitator working with this breakout team to plan an agenda and organize interactive design sessions. The results of the small group's work can be discussed with the assembled team as tasks are completed.

Envisioning process and task design. In parallel with definition of system architecture, a breakout subteam can pursue process and task design. This is another activity that continues from the Requirements Definition format, where initial task requirements, scenarios, and prototyping will have described many of the planned system tasks. Likewise, the Business Process Design (BPD) format will contribute process models if it was used as a front-end format. Those same techniques are used in this activity if the front-end formats (RD and BPD) were not employed in the development process. Given the availability of these design deliverables, the expected output from this activity (task design model reflecting the users' redesigned tasks) should be readily accomplished.

Envisioning user processes and tasks was addressed by the following methods in the previous formats:

- *Task scenarios and use cases.* From RD; scenarios portray a series of events to complete a task from start to finish.

- *Work descriptions.* From RD; work descriptions detail the whole work process and context in which the task plays a part

- *Process mapping and process flow diagrams.* From BPD; process definitions show the overall business process into which the tasks fit.

In Application Design, two other methods can be used to understand, model, or define the process and user tasks for the system:

- *Workflow analysis.* Used in defining the process design in BPD, workflow analysis describes the actions taken by all participants in a complex set of business transactions that define a work process.

- *User interface prototyping.* Used in RD, prototyping captures the initial vision for how tasks are interpreted in the user interface of the prototype application.

Since prototyping is recommended in both task design and system design, the team should consider conducting these two activities together as an integrated whole. The level to which the other task definitions are investigated depends on how much understanding of the *current* tasks is required to design an effective new process.

Envisioning system design. Envisioning system design is a team activity leading to what's often called *preliminary design*. This work includes the technical design required to build initial system models representing the functions and data of the application. The methods of dataflow analysis, system process diagrams, and user interface prototyping have been mentioned or indicated in other formats, but they are applied more directly in this stage.

The team's current inputs for this activity will include process or system diagrams, the requirements prototype (from RD), as well as the other design products developed through this period. The goal product for this activity is the initial *system* design. In different contexts, the system design achieves a different status.

Regardless of context or approach, the design work in this activity becomes the fulcrum for continuing application development. Development turns on the decisions and definitions made in this activity. Several key methods are used in envisioning system design:

- *Dataflow analysis.* Defining the functions of the system and their relationships.

- *Transaction definition.* Defining the interactive events in the application and the key input and output transactions.

- *Entity-relationship modeling.* Defining a working model of data used by the application.

Since Team Design orients these activities toward team development, complete definitions will not be typically developed during a single workshop. Individual analysts will complete the models offline.

Dataflow analysis. Function analysis and dataflow diagramming have been touched on in previous discussions, but the method has not been recommended in the front-end analysis formats. Although it has been traditionally considered a method with applicability in requirements and business process analysis, Team Design instead emphasizes visual interface prototyping and more pictorial diagrams (process mapping) appropriate for mixed participation teams. Dataflow diagrams (DFDs) are a useful design method for transaction-based systems and management information systems with strong database and user interface components. In the Application Design format, with its focus on functional design, this diagramming method has expressive value not found with other tools. They are not well suited to real-time or object-oriented applications such as process control, simulations, games, or many nondatabase applications.

As a structured analysis tool, DFDs can be used to model any interactive system, and are often used to model existing business systems to provide a baseline model for understanding current operations. In a workshop environment, modeling current systems (as-is modeling) is a considerable loss of potential creativity. In fact, the "father" of structured analysis, Ed Yourdon, has always recommended that

DFDs be used to model the *target* business system, a logical design activity for application definition (Yourdon 1993). Especially within a team workshop, defining the existing business environment can reinforce concepts, business processes, and workflows that are deeply embedded in the old way of doing business. When this path of analysis is pursued, the design might result in no change to business processes or user tasks. It is a common pitfall, and is one reason why DFDs aren't pushed up closer to the front of Team Design formats. By the visualizing phase of Application Design, the new system is halfway designed, and DFDs are unlikely to reflect the current system operations.

Further, although this method is traditionally used in JAD workshops, it should not be considered necessary for all workshop contexts. If your organization currently uses and understands DFDs, chances are they are already integrated into the requirements and design documentation. If they are not used, identify the need for their use and research their value for your environment before bringing the method into the design toolkit.

Dataflow diagramming is an *industry standard* method of modeling the flow of data through a system, and is a fairly abstract representation of a process. It is commonly used to show the logical requirements of system functions, and is not used to show physical design aspects such as modular program construction, function calls, or physical data devices. Dataflow diagrams are built from the functional hierarchies defined in the front-end analysis work.

The hierarchies establish the naming, numeration, and hierarchical relationships of functions. The hierarchical breakdown and the composite functions are preserved in the DFDs, which then extend the model to show relationships of functions to each other, precedence (not control) of functions through the system, and the flow of information between functions.

The data *flow* is shown for functions and interfaces (external entities). Except for the top-level (context) dataflow diagram, all data emerges from or is routed to data *stores*. Data stores show the initial identification of data at a very general level, such as defining storage for *accounts* or *customers*, without breaking these large groups of entities down further. The data stores are evaluated as possible entities in data analysis, but they typically represent a group of entities, or a portion of an entity-relationship diagram.

Dataflow diagramming can be considered to be standardized, since the different methodologies used follow the same analysis and rendering procedures, with primary variations only in notation. The most common methods are Gane-Sarson, Yourdon-DeMarco, Ward-Mellor, and SSADM, all of which are supported by current CASE tools.

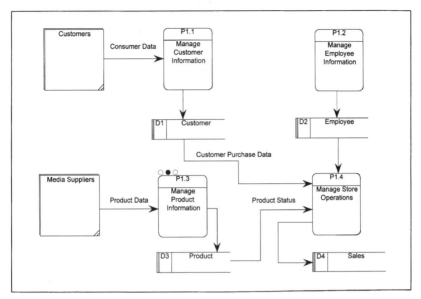

Figure 9.7   Gane-Sarson dataflow diagram.

Figure 9.7 shows the Gane-Sarson method, one of the most widely used DFD notations.

Dataflow analysis shows a flow diagram to model the use of information by functions throughout a defined process. Like function hierarchies, data flows are decomposed into their composite functions. Unlike function analysis, data storage, external processes and interfaces, and data flow are also shown. In fact, this is where data is initially identified in structured analysis, through the high-level data represented in dataflow diagrams. Relationships among functions are modeled with dataflow lines that show inputs from interfaces and data stores, outputs from functions to interfaces, and passing of data among functions through the data stores.

Leading a group through dataflow diagramming requires the facilitator to have a solid understanding of the technique. For effective use of dataflow modeling, some education of the team might be necessary, even if most members have used the method before. Not only will participants forget aspects of the methodology (naming conventions, flow lines, and symbology), but people will forget how to *think* in terms of data flow. Also, the facilitator often must keep the process on track, reminding the team of the purpose of DFDs (to lay out the logical flow of data through the system, not a sequence of steps). Dataflow diagrams are a valuable diagramming method and provide obvious benefits to the organizations invested in their use. User and product context organizations that are not using DFDs should probably consider alternatives to DFDs, except for well-structured applications amenable to the definition of functions in advance of prototyping.

Transaction definition. Transaction definitions for the system design can be based on the dataflow diagrams. In developing the initial DFDs as a team, a catalog of events will be described. System and user input events are identified and incorporated into the dataflow analysis. Many of these events become *transactions,* which define a complete processing of information from input to output or storage.

Transactions can be defined as part of the dataflow diagrams by describing them as each function is defined in the data flow. They can also be defined simply by an interactive team process. Using diagrams from the requirements model (hierarchies, scoping, and affinities), the team can brainstorm together or work in small groups to identify the primary transactions required in the system. Consider the following rapid small group process for transaction definition as a model for a workshop method.

Identify the most effective diagrams in hand that describe the system's requirements and initial design. These might be dataflow diagrams, hierarchy charts, scoping models, process maps, or affinity diagrams. Be sure copies are available for the team to use in transaction definition.

Using a hierarchy chart or function decomposition, identify the top layer of processes from which to define transactions. There should be more than 4 and fewer than 15 in a typical information system. Use a continuation of the hierarchy chart to define transactions, by drawing new boxes from the processes triggering or using the transaction.

Break the team into pairs or other subgroups and have each pair, in order, select a process on which to work. Provide any information as required to support their analysis. Suggest a method for each group to use to identify transactions and define their structure. This should be based on your project's need for this information—in other words, don't set an arbitrary level of detail for the analysis. If the design requires all data to be defined in each transaction, encourage the groups to discover all the data necessary. If information is missing, have them identify what's required to complete the model.

A simple transaction structure might entail the following steps:

1. Identify all events in the process selected. *External events* are actions from outside the scope that require a response from the system. *Internal events* require a response from a function, or provide information to an external entity outside the system. Name events as subject-verb phrases, such as "Loan requested."

2. For each event, define the system transaction that will manage the

information passed into the system. A *transaction* is a complete unit of processing, where all information is collected at once, submitted to a system process, and (usually) stored for later use. Describe the transaction with a verb-object phrase, such as "Record loan information." Describe the external means by which the transaction is used (phone call, forms, fax, or other mechanism) and any current systems used in the process. Describe the transaction as a flow of information from start to finish.

3. Define the data used in the transaction. Describe both minimally required data and optional data collected to complete the transaction. Describe any decisions necessary based on specific data values (e.g., if yearly salary $\leq$ \$20,000, evaluate further for cosigner). These decisions are based on business rules, and, of course, not all decisions or business rules will be definable at this point. The goal is to have the groups identify the conditions to the best of their knowledge during the exercise.

Give the groups a bounded time limit, such as one hour. This might not be enough time to completely define transactions, but it provides a goal toward which to work. At the end of the period, assess progress and have the whole team consider continuing or moving on to the next stage of analysis. Transactions can be refined as analysis continues and data is further defined.

Detailed transaction design should be part of the packaging phase, and can be conducted by experienced systems analysts. The job of the workshop team is to generate the necessary business model for transactions to be used by the analysts. This process saves time downstream in development, since the analysts won't need to conduct interviews and further iterations of definition.

Entity-relationship modeling. Entity-relationship diagrams (ERDs) are widely used for data modeling, and are the accepted standard for describing the conceptual structure for relational databases. Entity-relationship modeling starts with systems analysis, continues as a design activity, and is often done in concert with dataflow diagramming. In typical large development projects, different team members will perform these analysis activities in relative isolation, sharing completed sections of their models as they progress. One of the disadvantages of this traditional process is that coordination among analysts and designers is not consistent, and information shared from each model must be updated and evaluated for impact when received, causing delay in completing the overall analysis.

In a facilitated team process, initial ERD modeling is conducted with a subset of the team to construct an initial data model. During this process, this team builds a shared mental model of the data as well. In team contexts, the mental model is as important as the actual data model, since a common understanding of data used in the system will benefit communications and development productivity throughout the remaining project.

Like dataflow diagrams, ERDs have definite rules and considerations that must be followed for benefit of the technique for development. Even if ERDs are used by system designers, it might not be necessary to use them in a team workshop. If the use of data is extensive, the team should spend time researching the data. If the application design involves extensive use of data, such as hundreds of entities with many relationships, the team will benefit from having some understanding of the structure of the data. After all, every user is likely to be involved on a daily basis with decisions requiring some knowledge of the data. However, if a fairly simple database is envisioned, or one that is transparent to the application or product, then team interaction on ERDs is not necessarily critical.

Developing data models.   Entity-relationship modeling defines entities and their data elements, and shows the relationships among entities. *Entities* are considered to be any "thing" in the business or system that must be known to the system. In a database for a university, entities will consist of the higher-level groups of data such as *student, course,* or *instructor.* Relationships define the way data is used in the business, and are shown as connections between entities showing the relationship with graphical notation. A typical relationship between *instructor* and *course* might show that any given instructor is eligible to instruct one or many courses. The ERD also typically shows the primary identifier (called a *key* when defined for a database), which is used as the identifier for retrieving all attributes of an entity. Figure 9.8 illustrates these simple relationships in an entity-relationship diagram as drawn by a CASE tool.

The entity-relationship diagram is a part of the complete logical data model, which defines the fundamental business information structure. The logical model is a pure data model designed without regard for physical implementation requirements or constraints. In other words, it doesn't show a *database*; it shows the way data is used in the business. The logical data model also includes a data dictionary, with a complete description of entities and attributes defined in the model. The physical data model, on the other hand, is a database representation of the logical data model. It shows the data model following decisions made to optimize structures as tuned for database performance. The physical model is a more technical representation, and is not a typical candidate for team interaction except, perhaps, in a strong systems context workshop.

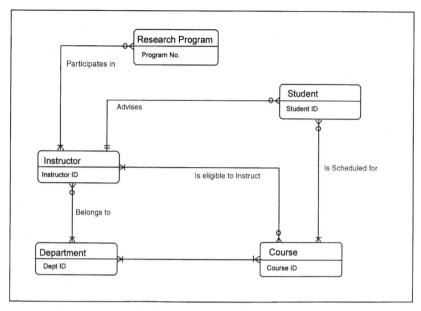

Figure 9.8 Entity-relationship diagram.

Defining a logical data model involves a number of interdependent steps, some of which can be done as a team and others that should be left to individual analysts. A representative small group process for developing the logical data model follows:

1. *Collect information about the data from functional experts.* This information can be collected within a workshop session, if a tightly facilitated process is used to keep discussions on track. A small group is recommended for interviewing or discussions, where the expert's time can be well used by analysts who have some depth of understanding of the data in advance of the process. Some of the questions used to elicit expert information might include the following:

   ■ *User interface.* How does the expert conceive of system use? What users must be satisfied? What Input/Update/Delete privileges are required? What views will each user type require access to? What queries must the user do to be successful?

   ■ *Business process.* What process is used with the forms and reports? What daily, monthly, and annual processes are required by business practices? How would they improve the process? What are the exceptions to the process? How are the exceptions handled?

2. *Identify entities and attributes.*   The first step of the ERD is to define basic entities and to allocate attributes to them. This follows directly from the functional information gathered in the previous step. This step may have been done in scoping, as an earlier session with the workshop team.

3. *Build a data dictionary.*   The data dictionary is an ongoing catalog of data definitions used throughout the project. It is usually documented by an individual analyst, and then used by the team as an evolving, working document.

4. *Build an entity-relationship diagram.*   A preliminary ERD arranges the entities and their business-based relationships visually so designers can begin working with the data conceptually. The preliminary ERD can be developed by a small group in a workshop, and reviewed and revised with other members in subsequent sessions.

5. *Define relationships between entities as one-one, one-many, or many-many.*   The ERD is further defined by establishing relationships showing cardinality, or the relating of an entity to another based on how many instances of one entity are associated with one instance of another entity.

6. *Identify the key identifiers for each entity.*   Candidate unique identifiers are normally assigned in developing the logical model ERD, but they become *keys* during database (physical) definition.

7. *Normalize the entity-relationship model.*   Normalization requires grouping attributes in each entity to eliminate redundancy of data elements across the model. Be sure that every attribute is dependent on a single key in a single entity, and does not appear elsewhere in the diagram. Normalization is an individual task, and is done over revisions of the model.

8. *Validate and refine the model.*   Show the diagram to functional experts, other analysts, and the project team. Conduct a review or walkthrough of the ERD, and refine the model with any required changes.

To effectively use this procedure, a data analyst is involved to guide the team's use of the methodology and to keep the analysis moving toward completion of a workable model. The facilitator must understand the method and be capable of guiding the flow of the work and of managing the group during group data analysis. The facilitator or the analyst might also act as a group recorder for the data model on the board or easel pads.

Usage: Interaction design

As in the other two design formats, usage focuses on developing a use-oriented model of the evolving design and informs the design with real-world scenarios. This interim evaluation of the design model subjects the design to intensive iteration and reconsideration. In usage, the design is pushed beyond just the requirements to determine how well it will satisfy user work practice. Scenario design methods and prototyping are the primary tools in the usage phase, as outlined in Table 9.5.

Why does prototyping fall in the middle of the Application Design format, given that a prototype from the Requirements Definition format might already be available? In fact, prototyping might be carried forward continuously, if your organization uses a development cycle that supports this iterative process. The *usage* phase in Application Design formalizes the prototype further by constructing a prototype model used to communicate the design to developers. We are working from the *concept* prototype, built in visualizing to represent an early model of the information system. The *usage* model can be referred to as the *design* or *product* prototype. Its primary distinction is that of communicating the design to the development team, and acquiring approval from sponsors or customers to move forward with development.

The design prototype is developed through iterations with the team, and may have advanced from a rough requirements model, to a concept prototype, to the more finished design version. Unlike requirements and design documents, prototypes can be iteratively revised without affecting the baseline. Since the prototype visually

TABLE 9.5   Application Design: Usage Phase

Usage: Interaction design	Methods	Inputs and outputs
Creating system scenarios	Scenario design methods Use cases Ideal system exercise	In: Requirements model (RD), user scenarios (RD) Out: Detailed system scenarios
Prototyping system scenarios	Process diagrams Interactive prototyping	In: Detailed system scenarios, requirements prototype Out: Initial design prototype
Integrating design models	Interactive prototyping System and dataflow diagrams Data and object modeling	In: Initial system design, design prototype Out: System design models, design prototype

demonstrates the design approach, the visual representations can be changed without affecting requirements. This allows the team more freedom and creativity in iteration of the design. With documents, it becomes difficult to separate requirements from the design, as they tend to be more tightly coupled in the use of language descriptions.

The design prototype is developed in this phase to show the design decisions, data requirements, and user interaction defined from a more complete analysis. A design prototype is typically developed as a realistic or *high-fidelity* model of the system, and can be used as a visual specification of the user interface. The design prototype serves multiple purposes which the requirements prototype should *not* support:

- A user interface specification for use by developers
- A model for sign-off by customers on the final product design
- A realistic interactive simulation of the product ready for usability testing to acquire user feedback on an early version of the system

Michael Schrage (1996) describes the use of prototyping in different organizational contexts in *Bringing Design to Software*. He describes how smaller, innovative product companies are comfortable using prototypes as the primary means of defining a product instead of an engineering specification. Conversely, the larger corporations supporting large production systems and large installed bases have traditionally used specifications as the driver for development. Schrage further describes the experience of a colleague with prototyping:

> David Kelley argues that organizations intending to be innovative need to move from specification-driven prototypes to prototype-driven specifications. In any event, it is clear that organizations prizing prototypes over specifications have fundamentally different design perceptions and processes.

However, Schrage points out that many organizations have trouble adopting this practice:

> The idea that you can play your way through prototyping to a product is anathema to managers educated to believe that predictability and control are essential in product development (p. 195).

Given more experience with user interface design and evaluation, managers soon discover that the project team has more predictability in product development using a design prototype, since the behavior of the product becomes specified in a way that customers and the entire team can understand. The prototype allows the customers and users to acknowledge their acceptance of the design well in advance of delivery. This demonstration provides far more predictability than hoping a detailed design is acceptable once the code is finished. The only loss of control occurs as prototypes are often iterated well into the development phase, even to the point beyond which additional changes cannot be included in releases. However, from a product design perspective, this allows the team to make a distinction between the release version and functions and design for the *next* version. The evolving design prototype can be baselined into the current version, which can be evaluated. The *solution-after-next* design becomes the model for testing customer interest in a future product release.

Creating system scenarios. Scenarios are described in Chap. 8 as a means of defining complete sequences of business events and user actions for requirements definition. In Chap. 7, they are discussed as tools for designing new business processes. In a twist on the technique, scenarios are used in application design for describing *user* processes that become tangible in design prototypes. In each case, similar workshop exercises can be used to gather ideas through team participation—however, the next step, usage of the scenarios, is different.

Scenarios have received attention from both the research and commercial development worlds in recent years—they have been prescribed as a key representation for joining the user perspective with system development needs. Carroll (1995) describes how scenario-based design is useful in various contexts of design and development:

> Using scenarios in system development helps keep the future use of the envisioned system in view as the system is designed and implemented; it makes use concrete—which makes it easier to discuss use and to design use (p. 4).

Carroll's treatment of scenarios in *Scenario-Based Design* catalogs new design methods arising from the research community. Contributors from schools as divergent as participatory design and object-oriented design have applied scenarios in innovative development projects as a way to understand users' work and to integrate that understanding with the development process. Although the scenario design methods differ in procedure and in representation, some core distinctions apply to all scenario methods:

- The methods can and should be used with teams or small groups to acquire and integrate available understanding of the user tasks.
- The methods require a phase of envisioning possible tasks and work practices, often using new technologies, for future situations and work processes.

- Scenarios (models, scripts, or stories) are constructed to capture a representative sequence of events as described in the envisioning process.
- Scenario models are used to inform design as a model of usage.

Nielsen (1995) studied the use of scenarios in system design and found seven types of scenario tools that emerged from their use across various purposes, media, and situations of use. The following were identified in the conclusion of the study:

- *Diaries.*   Scenarios as observational accounts of work practices used to inform thinking about design.
- *Feature brainstorms.*   Scenarios about features in a usage setting, used to inform thinking about design.
- *Parallel design.*   Scenarios used to communicate the design to stakeholders.
- *Heuristic evaluation.*   Scenarios used to evaluate the evolving design based on expert and designer evaluation.
- *Prototyping technique.*   Scenarios used to design and evaluate the user interface.
- *Structuring user testing.*   Scenarios used specifically to evaluate the user interface.
- *Stereotypes.*   Stereotypical scripts and descriptions used to analyze exploratory data.

In application design, we use four of these types throughout usage and packaging. In the usage phase of the Application Design cycle, scenarios are created to understand and define user interactions, and are then used in prototyping. The design prototype can be developed as a definitive interaction model using team-defined scenarios and use cases as an interaction script. Prototypes are then designed to satisfy all the components described in scenarios, such as classes of users, typical transactions, frequent or important options, possible actions, and user interface characteristics. The design prototype is the natural next step in this scenario process.

If your team has used the Requirements Definition format, a set of initial scenarios should be available for use in continued prototyping. Review the scenario storyboards or diagrams for the business process with the design team, and consider their current validity. Make modifications if required, or scrap outdated scenarios and prepare new ones that show your current thinking.

If using an integrated workshop process, or a RAD approach where requirements and design work are conducted more in parallel, your team will develop their initial scenarios at this point. Refer to the Requirements Definition format in Chap. 8 for workshop guidelines for developing scenarios.

Prototyping system scenarios.   Scenarios alone do not usually represent a sufficient design model to support software development. Although they provide excellent material for understanding user needs for the design, scenarios provide an external view of system function. They have not yet become a part of the typical developer's toolkit as a specification tool. The narrative descriptions or process diagrams from scenario analysis generate an understanding of expected system use, but they do not communicate a design directly to developers. Scenarios as such are also not directly testable by users. Prototypes built from the scenarios are best employed to facilitate both user evaluation and developer specification. A design-level prototype of the user interface and user functions solidifies scenarios into a tangible, interactive software concept.

In the usage phase, interactive prototypes represent the most effective means of communicating a design. Prototypes are easily understood by all team members, especially users and developers. They clearly show the aspects of the design that have been thought through, and leave the rough edges unfinished. They are portable and transportable—a prototype can be taken to meetings and demonstrated, or it can be set up in a user's location where it can be given a hands-on evaluation.

Team Design prototyping methods described previously include simple prototyping methods in Requirements Definition. In this format, one goal was to build a *concept* prototype, showing how the system might meet the requirements during requirements analysis. The other goal was to develop a *requirements* prototype, demonstrating the satisfaction of requirements in a requirements model. In the AD format, the goal of the prototype is to produce and demonstrate a *design* model that satisfies two important objectives:

- It enables interactive design and testing with users and the development team as a participative process.

- It communicates the design details and user interface decisions to developers throughout the design process.

The method for developing the design prototype is *interactive prototyping,* an approach based on user scenarios and rapid iteration of design changes. This prototype is *evolutionary,* in that it continues to evolve through design changes and reflects the latest version of the designers' thinking and the team's decisions.

Evolutionary prototyping can be used to migrate a prototype into the actual software design or to develop the software product from the prototype. An evolutionary process builds across iterations and tests the new functions gradually with users. The *horizontal prototyping* approach is recommended for the evolving design prototype. A horizontal approach builds most or all of the functions for the design, but not all are shown completely. It is a *breadth* design, with maybe only one major function demonstrated in depth. This prototype approach simulates the planned system and surfaces possible problems before implementation of the design.

Developing the design prototype is often approached using the evolutionary approach—building a version, testing it, then revising it again. This process continues horizontally, to cover the breadth of the system design, until a standard interface has been established for navigation and interaction for most of the functions in the system.

Interactive prototyping. Interactive prototyping encompasses numerous techniques for rendering a design prototype. The degree to which the user interface is specified in high-fidelity detail depends on the purpose for the design model. Several purposes typically arise for the design prototype:

- Obtain sign-off on the user interface by product managers and developers.
- Establish an interactive design specification.
- Support sufficient interaction for usability testing.
- Iteratively test user interface ideas with users and developers.

As with several other key processes in Team Design and in software development, much of interactive prototyping is conducted as an individual task. Building the prototyping process into team workshops can be challenging at first, since so much of the product is prepared outside of the team context. The facilitator should view the prototype as a *tool* used interactively in the workshop, and not as a *product* built in the workshop.

The design prototype evolves into a design model used by developers as an interactive specification. The design prototype can grow into the first increment product, depending on the tools used and the type of product being developed. In prototyping, general assertions about development are insufficient. To present examples, if your team is using a database development environment (such as Powerbuilder or Oracle) or an application template (such as with Peoplesoft or SAP), then prototyping is done using the same tools as in development. If the final product will be built in a compiled language (for example, C/C++) then prototypes are probably *throw-aways,* used by developers as specifications but not for code. In Web design, HTML pages can be prototyped and then published live as-is on an Internet server. As indicated, generalization is difficult—new programming languages (for example, IBM's *Visual Age*) and design approaches allow for a high degree of flexibility in prototyping. Many variations exist between these examples, and your team must decide what makes sense for your prototyping approach.

As a cornerstone of the design package, the design prototype is supported by analysis and design models as necessary. This is largely determined by the needs of the project and the standards of the organization, but a design document package typically includes the following:

- System architecture definition
- Narrative description of functional design
- Function analysis and dataflow diagrams
- Logical data model and entity-relationship diagrams
- Initial program module design

The design prototype is held to be a realistic model of the emerging product. It is not usually just an extension to the requirements prototype. The design prototype must communicate all features of the user interface, which can be accomplished through breadth of coverage. Not every possible interaction must be designed, but one of every *type* of interaction should be demonstrated. One of each type of dialog or list might be sufficient; there's probably no need to specify every possible interaction. If the product will use a full-text database, showing one or two sequences of interaction might be sufficient to design the interaction with the database. In other words, the prototyper does not usually create working software to demonstrate a design.

Building the design prototype.   Full attention to detail in the user interface design is essential; the Team Design workshop is not the most appropriate environment for building the design prototype. The design prototype will be built offline and used in the workshops for interactive discussion and feedback. A simple process for constructing the design prototype follows:

1. Establish a working development environment with sufficient computing power and disk space. For building the design prototype, use software tools that have the capability to specify all user interface characteristics expected of the final product.

   It is often best to prototype in the same application language as selected for the product. An exception might be that if software development will be done in C/C++, the design prototype could be created using a compatible application builder or higher-level language that uses identical interface constructs to C/C++.

2. Acquire copies of all current requirements and design documentation. I find it useful to maintain a matrix of baselined requirements with any associated user interface attributes listed next to each requirement. This also enables quick identification of any representation used in the prototype but not yet described in the requirements or shown to the team.

3. Follow a user scenario or set of use cases to build the sequence of interactions. Use scenarios that have been developed in the workshop or that will be used in evaluation. Use cases should show the depth and breadth of the prototype.

4. Model most, if not all, the top layer of interaction with the product. This includes dialogs from every menu option, and all interactions that the casual user is likely to encounter.

5. Create at least one path down to the furthest logical depth. If other paths are similar, develop a realistic model down just one path, and evaluate it before building any further.

6. Provide the scenario as a script for use with the prototype, so that customers, users, and developers are not misled by random interactions not accounted for in the design model.

The most effective uses of prototypes in a Team Design AD workshop are in interactive review and discussion. When the design prototype is available for team review, provide any documents needed to team members in advance of the meeting, along with an agenda. The prototyper can facilitate these sessions, but it is useful to have someone designated as a recorder take notes on comments and discussion during the session. If the prototyper facilitates, consider using the prototyping tool to make rapid changes and try out design ideas as they are presented for discussion.

Use a projection system to display the prototype overhead or on a large screen monitor. Have a whiteboard or easel handy to make drawings or to facilitate design change discussions. Finally, use scenarios as the guides to walk through the prototype and demonstrate the different goals and interactions of typical users.

Another approach to design prototype review is to use the model as a demonstration to customers of how the system will appear when finished. This approach works well during formal design reviews for custom software projects. Use the prototype itself as the design model for discussion. Whenever design documents are provided for customer review, consider simplifying the review by following an agenda based on the prototype. As each area of the prototype is demonstrated and discussed, customers and users can review and sign off on the prototype representation.

Integrating design models. The final activity in the usage phase integrates the design prototype models with the set of related design models. As in integration testing, the purpose of this activity is to make sure all the design products fit together, or at least support one another. Scenarios should explain the processes demonstrated in the design prototype, and user and system models should explain the user interface and system design. The integration of design models involves the following steps:

- Test prototypes (and other design products) to evaluate their effectiveness.

- Assess design products for completeness and quality (check the prototype against requirements to ensure that coverage and functionality are represented).

- Redefine scenario or prototype components to support a complete design model.

Your team will have developed an interactive design prototype, scenarios, and structured analysis and specification products such as dataflow diagrams, entity-relationship diagrams, and object models. A multidimensional view of the design emerges from bringing these components together. During usage, the final goal is to pull together the components and evaluate them to assess the extent of further design required. In a traditional software engineering approach, the specification package would drive the remaining development work. In an integrated system design model, the design prototype is supported by these software specification techniques to describe internal functions, data and objects, and the details of the system design. The user interface design, its behavior, look and feel, and interaction are specified by the design prototype.

Packaging: Functional design

The packaging phase in Functional Design finishes the design work and initiates development. After scenarios and prototyping are completed, and agreement is reached on system design definition, packaging provides a period for designers and developers to evaluate the full design package.

The purpose of packaging is to create and review the set of deliverables provided as the result of team efforts. New analysis and design should not be required—but as design models change, a period is needed to cross-check the impact of design changes from one model against the others. This phase allows for additional design and evaluation cycling should revision be necessary. The other work done in packaging is to develop and test the first functional database tables and software modules. By pushing ahead with some development in this phase, the application design concepts get tested as working software. Following the packaging phase, the development team can fully engage coding, testing, and integration of the application.

Packaging activities are oriented toward development and review. Workshops might be scheduled to support reviews over a period of a week or two to allow for sufficient rework of any functions determined to be misdefined or underscoped. A longer period might be utilized to allow for initial development builds and design reviews covering the builds. The goal for each activity is to provide a final development-ready model of a *design responsibility*. The model for facilitating packaging sessions should be that of a collegial working session, normally facilitated by the technical leader for the design component reviewed.

In the world of development and engineering, as opposed to design, compromises are often and typically made. Developers frequently call for a partial design package to begin working on fundamental system components in advance of a complete design, and each project should determine whether this approach is logical for its system or product. Also, to move a product out the door, a design model is considered to be an *ideal* target and not a fixed entity that must be coded in its every representation. While such in-development modifications are usually discussed with designers, the fact remains that development requires its own creative design, build, and test phases. Designers relinquish substantial control when coding begins in earnest. Involvement of developers throughout the design process, especially in packaging, will lead to a more flexible system design that provides rational alternatives to sometimes idealized design concepts. Sometimes very minor development conditions can require big changes to design decisions during the build process. Packaging allows for sufficient walkthrough to uncover hard points in the design where changes cannot be afforded; it should also shed light on areas where potential difficulties arise, allowing the team to agree on possible alternatives before committing to code.

This format does not specifically show project management decisions affecting development and delivery, such as phased or incremental releases of the design to developers. In larger, complex projects deliverables are often provided to development *as they are completed,* not as an integrated package. This allows development to proceed in fundamental design areas, such as building object classes, libraries, and databases while complex functions or user interface

TABLE 9.6   Application Design: Packaging Phase

Activities	Methods	Inputs and outputs
Packaging: Functional design		
Architecture design	System process diagrams Initial build cycle Design evaluation	In: Initial architecture model design prototype Out: Architecture design model
Database design	Database design mapping Initial build cycle Design evaluation	In: Data models, system design models, design prototype Out: Database design
Object design	Use case mapping Initial build cycle Design evaluation	In: System design models, use cases, object models, design prototype Out: Object design model
Function or trans- action design	Transaction mapping Initial build cycle Design evaluation	In: System design models, design prototype Out: Functional design model
Validating: Application design evaluation		
Evaluation planning	Test scenario definition Test and evaluation planning Group planning sessions	In: Detailed process scenario, requirements model (RD) Out: Application evaluation plan
Application or product design evaluation	Design review Prototype usability evaluation	In: Design prototype, prototype evaluation plan Out: Evaluated design model

models continue in design. Even if this approach is taken, integrating the design package is recommended to understand all impacts among system components, and to detect potential problems as soon as possible. In fact, every design activity in the process can be considered as serving this secondary purpose. Effective and early design serves to specify the *right things to build,* as opposed to just building things right. It also serves to uncover problems in user interaction (user satisfaction) and in software building before the design is committed to extensive development resources and the remaining life cycle.

The packaging phase of Application Design (Table 9.6) contains five basic team workshop activities, not all of which are required for every system or product. Architecture design is considered a fundamental object to which every component must map. Packaging integrates three design components into the development cycle: database design, object design, and transaction design. Evaluation planning is usually conducted throughout the design process starting during development planning, but is formalized during this final step in the design packaging.

Architecture design.   The architecture design model should be packaged and finalized as early as possible, since it contains and constrains the other design components. The architecture design model can provide a separate document or section defining the system structure, communications, system and data interfaces, and relationship of major components. The goal of this activity is to confirm the architecture design, which can be accomplished through design evaluations using documents, process diagrams, and the application design prototype.

Review of the architecture in a workshop setting should be more informative than interactive. At this point, the architecture will usually have been formalized, and in an iterative or RAD project methodology, the architecture might be under development. The purpose of the design evaluation is to cover any remaining issues for the architecture model, and to better understand the implications of architectural decisions in advance of the system mappings and evaluations that will proceed in packaging.

An initial build cycle for architecture might involve a number of modules that are necessary as infrastructure or for other functions to proceed. Local area networking, wide-area communications, and database servers might be established as part of the architecture plan; they can be integrated and tested in this phase. Interfaces with existing business systems or remote servers, file and data sharing, and other interface processes will be defined and tested. Security, system administration, and support systems might be under development during packaging, in order to provide these services to data and transactions when the application functions are developed.

Three system component mappings follow from the architecture, all with essentially equal value. The precedence implied in the format is not a recommended order as in other formats, since evaluation and packaging of the designed components is quite project-specific. The only implication is in evaluating the most fundamental, or far-reaching, components first. These structures will be used to build the system upon, and it will be beneficial to have them finalized and under way as soon as practical. In many systems, especially business and information systems, the database design is necessary as the structure on which transactions will be dependent.

Database design.   Review of the database design can also be performed whenever the deliverables are available; it does not necessarily wait until the phase has officially begun. Packaging and the other phases, remember, are relationships within the design process, and are not stages in project management that require sign-off or review. In most client-server applications, the database design will be the most critical component of the design, in that it must be available for the application functions to use the data. The table structures must be designed and verified and the database must be operational before the other components can be built and validated.

Database design mapping is an evaluation that reviews the data models to consider the impact of any final data model changes and to evaluate whether other design models impact the database. The database design evaluation session can be led by the data analyst, leading a walkthrough of the logical data model, major usage models (such as logical access path diagrams), and database table design. Workshop attendees should include systems analysts, software designers, informed users (especially if they are considered to be data stewards within an organization), and software developers.

Database design mapping checks whether all entities from the entity-relationship diagram conform to and integrate with other system design models. Confirm data access for major transactions using dataflow diagrams or a function-data matrix. If an object model is also used in the overall design, evaluate data access and sharing with specified objects.

The initial build cycle for database table design begins with generating the table structures, primary and foreign keys, and indexes in the database management system (DBMS). The data models and resulting design are essentially coded into the data definition language (DDL) of the DBMS, and the physical tables are evaluated. The DDL can often be entirely generated by using a full-featured CASE tool that supports the creation of entity-relationship diagrams, the data dictionary or encyclopedia, and schema generation. In all cases, these activities are performed offline, and only impacts to other design models are discussed in any continuing workshop sessions.

The database tables are tested by populating with sample data to test the display of data as determined by the table definitions. Test cases based on user scenarios (usage models) are run to determine how record insertions, updates, and deletes are handed. Data integrity rules are evaluated by running the test cases to ensure that records are not duplicated or missing in physical tables or in the user interface display.

These database design activities occurring behind the scenes create the structure for using data in the system, and have major impacts on user interface and system design. Results and critical decisions made by the database designers should be demonstrated to the design team as required to communicate problems or design opportunities for the other development teams.

Object design. The object design also evolves both as a design component and as a development activity. Validating the object design involves the evaluation of object models and their sources. In addition, as developers implement the object design in class libraries for use in a project, testing of the object-based code should include some mapping against the use cases to ensure that the object requirements trace back to the requirements. Finally, design reviews of the object model should be done before development proceeds into building the object libraries.

Object design models consist of a diagrammatic representation of the class or object hierarchy, and typically a narrative description of the objects and their capabilities. A simple object diagram might just be shown as a hierarchy chart, or as a chart of black box objects and their interactions with each other to show object relationships.

A basic mapping test of the object model, derived from Jacobson (1995), entails tracing the objects against the use cases to ensure that all objects meet the requirements for use. A design subteam can evaluate the model by walking through one use case at a time, mapping the objects identified in the use case with objects defined in an object model view. This view shows the objects used just in the single use case. The object view grows as each use case is evaluated for coverage against the object model, while the design reviewers ensure that each object referenced in a use case is defined correctly. Relationships between objects are checked between the use cases, to ensure that an object defined for one use case can support the functionality required of it from another use case. As the mapping continues, a complete object model is derived by superimposing object views from the use cases.

If an object model was already fully defined in advance of the packaging design walkthrough, mapping becomes a validation process. Use cases, object model diagrams, and interaction diagrams are used together in validation mapping. Validation mapping checks the relationships between use case events, the class or object hierarchy, and interaction definitions to ensure that all necessary objects and relationships are defined. An initial build of the object design provides the ability to test some of the operational code against the design. This validates design assumptions and evaluates the emerging object design. Rapid builds allow other development teams (database, transactions, and user interface) to test their physical code modules against developed objects.

A validated object design model is the final deliverable for packaging. As with database design, changes and decisions affecting the object model can have implications for other design teams on the project, and are communicated in project workshop or design meetings.

Function or transaction design. The functional design is produced as a specification and model describing application functions, transactions, or other functional design representations. Only on large-scale development projects will this design effort typically be managed as a separate design effort. With most efforts, functional design is integrated within the database development environment, or is unnecessary due to a true object-oriented implementation. In traditional large-scale business information systems with numerous defined transactions, the functional design model becomes managed as a significant design component that integrates with database and user interface designs.

The functional design model uses system design models and the design prototype from usage as the guiding models for representing the functional design. Transaction diagrams from visualizing are the primary reference for producing a transaction-based functional design. Outputs of the functional design include the transaction process model, defining the coding specifications for transactions, and possibly an initial build of the defined transaction modules.

Methods used in functional design include transaction mapping and functional specification. *Transaction mapping* relates the business transaction definitions to the database design and user interface model. It accounts for input and output data structures for required transactions, and maps user interface events (add, edit, and delete) to transactions. Transaction definition from the functional design work in visualizing provides the input, output, and processing specifications to support transaction mapping.

Functional specification defines the processing that occurs to transform the defined input into output data that satisfies transaction requirements. Functional specifications can be written as structured English for use by developers (traditional large-scale information systems) or defined in the programming language used by the transaction processing architecture (DBMS, compiled code, or development environment).

Initial build cycles can be generated to test the use of data and the integration of transaction design to other developed components. Ongoing builds can be a valuable way to shrink overall development time and to provide the latest working version to other development teams to enable their design testing. Transaction performance and integration evaluations can be conducted on this evolving transaction system as it is built.

Transaction design in packaging is also an offline activity conducted by programmers or analysts that does not allow for workshop involvement. As with the other packaging activities, the results of design and critical decisions affecting other design and development can be discussed at necessary times to inform the design team.

Validating: Application design evaluation.   Validating the application design can incorporate an integration and system test cycle, or can be used instead for team-based test planning and design evaluation. Depending on how team development is used in your organization's life cycles, validating can be used to kick off the development testing phase or might just be used as an independent design evaluation process.

Application design evaluation consists of two approaches that can be used together or separately. *Evaluation planning* is a workshop-based activity that allows the team to determine evaluation processes and criteria for the design and product. This process can include several test and evaluation plans developed with user and development participants. Application or product *design evaluation* performs evaluation on the design package, using either or both design reviews and prototype evaluation. Design evaluation is a critical validating function, but it must be accomplished according to standards adopted by the development organization to ensure rigorous quality control and sign-off. The Team Design process discusses these validating tasks that might be either additional or necessary, depending on the other evaluations performed in your development organization.

Evaluation planning.   Evaluation planning in Application Design brings together test planning and actual evaluation. In the workshop, evaluation and test plans for development are reviewed and finalized. Participants responsible for test planning will have developed plans throughout the phases in Application Design. In this activity, the plans are reviewed and final changes are made before putting them into place. Since the roles of the design team will typically change from design to coordination or evaluation following AD, the evaluation planning step is important for preview of and agreement on the new roles and schedule for completion.

Evaluation planning uses the detailed process scenarios from usage as inputs to test design. The baseline requirements model is also used as a checklist for system and acceptance testing, to ensure that requirements have been met throughout the design. The output of evaluation planning is an application evaluation plan, which might conform to a test planning standard from your organization, or might extend the typical test planning by incorporating scenario-based user evaluations in the application test process.

Evaluation planning can use and plan for the following evaluation methods:

- *Test scenario definition.*   Test scenarios are brainstormed or selected from the set of design scenarios from the usage phase. Test scenarios are specified in as much detail as necessary to test the range of functions of the application.

- *Test and evaluation planning.*   Conventional test and evaluation planning to design appropriate test strategies for the design and the application. Integration and system test design and planning can be conducted by a test subteam and presented and discussed with the whole team.

- *Group planning sessions.* Group planning conducted within the team workshop to schedule and design evaluations to be conducted internally, at user sites, for integration and release testing, and for customer acceptance.

Actual test strategies and testing procedures for the *application* are beyond the scope of this book, as they are numerous and varied, depending on the type of product or application and the development organization approach. In Application Design, we are primarily interested in testing the design package and in guiding and planning the overall testing process.

For evaluating the design, the prototype usability evaluation method is recommended as an approach for gaining early design feedback in advance of final integration and system testing of the product. This strategy allows the development team to uncover any show-stoppers from the customer or user perspective that can work their way into the design model or alpha test versions of complex systems. Major usability findings can be discussed and prioritized for severity and user impact, and critical fixes can be implemented before alpha or user testing.

The output of this activity is the prototype evaluation plan, which describes the plan and procedures for usability evaluation of the design prototype.

Application or product design evaluation. The actual evaluation work performed in Application Design occurs in this final activity in the validating phase. Application or product design evaluation is a team evaluation of the *design,* primarily using two methods: *design review* and *prototype usability evaluation.* Inputs to design evaluation include the design prototype and the prototype evaluation plan. The output is an evaluated design model and prototype.

Design review. Design reviews and design validations can be conducted using facilitated design walkthroughs, using a process such as is described in the Requirements Definition format. Informal or formal walkthroughs are used as a primary means for the team to evaluate design quality as a group process.

Design reviews can be facilitated sessions that require technical leaders to present their parts of the design. Informal design reviews should be attended only by technical contributors, but formal reviews might have managers and customers attend. For contract design reviews, a formal review session must be conducted that allows the customer to understand the design and any implications for fulfilling the contract requirements. Using the requirements specification or a requirements-design matrix as a guide, the application design can be discussed in a structured process that addresses all functions within each system component.

Most design reviews can be conducted within a day's workshop session, although for a complex system design, reviews might require two or more days of walkthrough. To support an effective design review session, some of the following traditional guidelines offered for conducting reviews apply:

- Provide an agenda and readable documentation for following the design review.

- Use a facilitator to maintain the process, pace, and civility.

- Encourage participation—each participant should offer at least one positive and one negative critique.

- Maintain discussion on technical issues only—avoid project management discussions.

- Surface issues and list them—do not attempt to resolve them in the session. Record issues and assign action items.

- Appoint a guardian of standards to critique design and development standards.

Design walkthroughs are a necessary review technique used in most development processes. If using a Team Design workshop approach throughout the development life cycle, a facilitated process will be second nature to the team whenever design reviews are required. Integrating effective facilitated reviews into the team's design cycle will become a regular procedure used in all projects.

Prototype usability evaluation.   Although design reviews are an effective and necessary evaluation process, they are not sufficient. Effective technical designs and requirements can be met, but user acceptance of a product is a primary quality criteria. The design prototype should be evaluated by the team with usability assessments or prototype usability evaluation. This process is discussed in Chap. 8, as it applies to requirements prototypes. For the design prototype, it is more important, since the user interface will (usually) be implemented from this model of the system. Usability evaluation can be conducted using at least three different team processes:

- *Team process.*   Continual team design and interactive prototype review with the project team, making iterative enhancements to the prototype by incorporating the team's latest thinking and design concepts.

- *Focus group.* Moderation of prototype demonstration and discussion with users, customers, and internal stakeholders, representing both *user* and *project* customer and product viewpoints.

- *Usability testing.* Customer-centered design evaluations with end-user representatives using scenario-based scripts to accomplish representative tasks. Following guidance from Chap. 8, usability evaluation procedures can be tailored for the design prototype according to the user needs and project requirements.

For most development teams, the focus group and team process options are the least dependent on specialized expertise within the team, and can be conducted by a larger number of team participants. Interactive demonstration reviews can be facilitated to obtain feedback and responses from the project team or invited participants. A focus group approach uses a neutral or customer location to demonstrate the design prototype, and feedback is acquired through facilitation of questions and probing during the demonstration.

Usability evaluation requires significant planning and preparation, and is typically conducted by a human factors engineer or user interface designer. Well-established usability test processes (Nielsen 1995) can be used or adapted to plan and design effective prototype evaluations. At least three usability evaluation processes are typically used in industry:

- *Field usability tests.* Held at the user's or customer's work location, field usability tests allow the users to maintain their context of work, while evaluating the design at a familiar and comfortable location.

- *Informal usability evaluations.* Held at a neutral location, such as an office or classroom, informal evaluations bring together one or more users to use and evaluate the design prototype. Informal evaluations can use different procedures for testing, ranging from hands-on trials to focus group discussions.

- *Formal usability tests.* Held in a usability laboratory at the product development company, formal tests gather detailed information on usage in a controlled environment. Formal tests are useful for validation of a stable design or in comparing competing designs among a number of participants, where objectivity is critical.

For product designs going into implementation, usability testing is essential. Early feedback on the user interface design prevents problems and issues during development, and is performed at the least expensive point to make needed changes in the development life cycle. Although usability evaluation is conducted as a validating activity, the information gained from the test process should be interpreted by the usability team and discussed immediately. Recommended and accepted changes should then be driven back into the prototype and application design, continuing the iterative design process.

10

Planning and Decision Making

Throughout Team Design our emphasis has been on group design processes that lead to system building, and system design remains a daunting and complex challenge for any organization. In this chapter, we apply the Team Design cycle to planning and decision processes as two separate activity cycles. As in design and development, planning and decision processes require a group consensus, or at least group involvement, and can be significantly enhanced by facilitated workshops. The use of a team process in planning and decision making is effective for the following reasons:

- Major decision making and most planning are already performed by groups—increasingly, by teams involving multiple business functions.

- Team planning processes provide the opportunity for creative thinking from multiple disciplines, leading to plans that take into account a broader view of the business, and perhaps leading to breakthrough strategies.

- Team decision-making processes coordinate knowledge and action from a broader range of individuals, and responsibility for decisions is shared among stakeholders.

Team participation in planning and decision making is in no way a hot new topic. For hundreds of years, indigenous people have conducted tribal councils to plan their future actions for farming, ceremonial, and defense arrangements. Tribal cultures created the processes and rituals of community participation and have long used teams of community leaders for making important decisions affecting the entire community. An article in *Fortune* (Richards 1996) describes the recent acceptance of tribal wisdom in using ancient ceremonial group approaches. Two Native Americans from the Ehama Institute provide their ceremonial approach to planning and decision making to corporate and government organizations. Using a 60-foot circle and fire pit, the pair create an extended working session for participants that approaches planning and problem solving with the wisdom and spirit of the ancient council ceremonial practice.

The effectiveness and experience of the ancestral system cannot just be transplanted into corporate organizations. But such a well-established team process that creates community, educates participants, and preserves and extends a deep value system has significant implications for the learning organization and for organizational thinking. The creative use of team methods can build the groundwork for using team planning and decision making, and can grow into new organizational rituals that educate and express the values held by the group.

Team Planning Processes

Group planning processes of some type are used for significant planning purposes in nearly all organizations, yet many of these processes are informal, without strategy, structure, or definition. It is impossible to evaluate how well the casual planning approach works, since without a defined planning process the plans are only as effective as their results. And although most planning is conducted in group situations, a coordinated *team* approach is not always employed. As we have defined *team,* a team approach to planning establishes a collegial team as a responsible and coordinated group dedicated to the planning effort. A cross-functional planning team should also include such *stakeholders* as the employees and managers affected by the plans, as well as those making the plans.

Planning sessions are frequently managed by executives or managers who use traditional planning processes because they don't have the time to research or experiment with innovative approaches. As with many corporate rituals, the yearly planning cycle or other established planning mechanism becomes the one tool used for planning. Even though business conditions and organizations might radically change, the planning processes comfortably used from year to year are adopted once again, regardless.

Consider the potency and creative possibilities of planning freed from the same old SWOT analysis or bottom-up business planning process. What are the potential advantages of conducting planning sessions with a Team Design process?

Context of team planning

Some of the most common planning situations are the most important. The most critical planning contexts, of course, are those in which the impact of planning affects entire enterprises, business operations, organizations, and large investments. However, a team planning process can be used for any type of planning situation where different stakeholders coordinate goals and ideas for purposes that the group shares. Team planning processes are used in organizations when major changes or new efforts are anticipated, such as when:

- Foreseeable business changes occur due to competitive, regulatory, or other basic pressures.

- Unpredictable business change is evident, due to rapid shifting of essential operating assumptions.

- Changes in organizational culture and direction are required.

- Major new systems or infrastructure are required to maintain the business, or major system redesign at a strategic level is required.

These planning situations are the less-predictable, urgent, action-oriented conditions that emerge in every business throughout its existence. The difference between *urgent* and *visionary* planning situations is often a matter of timing. When an established future planning process is enshrined in the culture, planning for uncertain business conditions creates an environment that is ready for change. When the organization does not plan for changing future conditions, the business becomes caught by circumstances and must deal with change as an emergency.

Some of the basic contexts for team planning are discussed in the following. These range from strategic planning situations to very short-term tactical planning, such as project or development planning. All these planning contexts can benefit from a facilitated or team approach to the planning process.

Strategic business planning. Strategic planning for a business engages a team in determining the best course of action for an enterprise over a long-term period. It is an expensive and often cumbersome process, but is absolutely necessary not only for growth but for survival. There are numerous approaches to strategic planning. Instead of enumerating common techniques, this chapter describes some useful newer approaches that build on the Team Design cycle and methods.

Strategic business planning develops strategies for:

- *Organizational change.* Growth or changing business conditions or management require organizational change planning.

- *Business challenges.* Market, competition, and customer changes force the business to adopt new strategies.

Strategic planning is the best insurance an organization can obtain for future performance. Preparation for an uncertain future is a major force in business planning, but even more powerful is the notion of *creating* the future through effective strategic planning.

Strategic information system planning. Strategic information system planning is a long-term approach that creates a direction for future growth and for disposition of systems used in managing the business. As in strategic business planning, stakeholders are concerned with building future value and maintaining competitiveness as the business moves through phases of growth or technology change. Strategic information system planning is typically led by the information technology organization; however, in many competitive organizations where technology is understood as a competitive driver, information systems strategy is planned by executive committees as critical functions of the business.

Project planning. Effective project planning is essential to effective business plan execution and cost management. Even more so, it is essential to building quality products and delivering them to market in a competitive development cycle. All the assumptions made about strategic business growth or the productivity of new information processes can be scrapped if improper project planning leads to cost and schedule overruns.

Projects begin with the *project plan,* and good project management begins with good planning. The project manager often drives the planning process and can be involved as the leader of project planning workshops. Unlike user participation workshops, project planning does not require neutrality or as much attention to various stakeholder perspectives. The project manager is typically free to conduct the workshops in the most effective way to produce a resulting project plan. A project plan can contain the following:

- Project definition, purpose, or mission statement
- Business objectives
- Strategic and tactical goals
- Description of project scope
- Project schedule and plan for managing schedule
- Project budget and cost management goals
- Management sign-off and milestones

Most of these project plan components are products of a team planning process. The detailed schedule (network or bar chart), budget, and management issues are typically arranged outside of the team planning sessions, but almost every component can be defined in the team sessions.

Development planning.   While often a component of project planning, development planning entails specific process and resource management to ensure effective coordination by development and engineering groups. A tactical planning approach, development planning benefits from the team process by defining the effective use of resources and development approaches as part of the project.

Format: Team Planning

The phase structure of the Team Planning format is shown in Table 10.1.

Leading planning workshops

Team planning sessions vary extensively in scope and participation, and each workshop will be designed to satisfy different goals and success criteria. Facilitation of planning workshops significantly differs from design sessions, although basic facilitation techniques are still used to guide the proceedings. In planning, the facilitator is less likely to be skilled in the domains being planned, whereas in software development, facilitators become knowledgeable guides in software processes. Planning session facilitation is more strictly group-process focused, managing the agenda and providing guidance on group exercises.

Unlike software development, there is no "right way" to run planning sessions. Requirements and software design workshops produce definable outputs to be used by others in development, and quality criteria determine the necessary form and coverage of these products. Planning sessions result in planning documents, which are produced in a specific form only due to preference or tradition. Facilitation of planning workshops allows for creative procedures and products, yet this is infrequent in corporate settings. Interestingly, while corporate leaders might understand that creativity can help in rethinking the dimensions of the business, planning workshops are often treated as "serious" working sessions that deal with solving problems and making decisions, as well as planning the future scope of the business. The problem solving and decision making focus attention on near-term issues, distracting from the purpose of creating a compelling far-sighted planning vision. The quality of long-term planning can suffer

TABLE 10.1   Team Planning Format

Agenda activities	Methods	Inputs and outputs
Scoping: Defining plan scope		
Defining purpose and mission	Situation analysis, mission statement, purposes hierarchy, dialogue, brainstorming	In: Initial goals Out: Purpose, mission statement
Defining scope and objectives	Scoping diagram, system matrix, brainstorming methods	In: Purpose, mission statement Out: Scope and objectives
Visualizing: Shaping scenarios		
Creating scenarios	Visioning exercises, scenario planning	In: Scope and objectives Out: Planning scenarios
Evaluating scenarios	Scenario analysis, quantitative analysis, resource analysis	In: Planning scenarios Out: Strategic options, scenarios
Usage: Defining strategies		
Identifying possible strategies	Breakthrough Thinking, brainstorming methods	In: Strategic options, scenarios Out: Applied strategies, strategic vision
Defining business strategies	Business planning, project planning, SWOT analysis	In: Applied strategies, strategic vision Out: Initial business plan
Packaging: Defining the plan		
Formalizing plan	Plan definition	In: Initial business plan Out: Documented plan
Defining and assigning actions	Action planning, scheduling	In: Documented plan Out: Assigned actions

when its purposes are mixed with those of solving current business problems.

Although most of an organization's planning sessions are for workaday project and development planning, the approach to all planning is influenced by the more aggressive schedule-driven planning necessary for short-term projects. Long-term planning can be more vision-driven, and must also account for uncertainty on the business horizon. These needs point to an opportunity for creative workshops with a more open, reflective, or adventurous approach to facilitation.

To make these determinations for designing the planning workshop, work with the sponsors to understand the background. Who does the planning workshop serve? Who are the stakeholders and the *customers*? Planning usually involves the same group of stakeholders throughout the workshop, and the customers (users of the *plan*) might be senior management, business unit managers, or an entire division or company. Facilitation might be used for one long workshop, or possibly for a series of workshops using defined phases, such as in the planning cycle.

The length of time required for workshops varies considerably. Typically, project planning workshops are concise, but large projects can require up to a week or more. Also, long-term scenario planning should allow for over a week, if necessary; but some sessions could be conducted in a couple of days. Planning for the planning workshop should identify the participants, the planning variables, the cohesiveness and cooperation of the group, and other dimensions in order to judge the workshop period. Planning should also account for gathering all the available information that is required from customers, previous projects, product history, or corporate strategy documents— whatever is required for both the organizers and the participants.

Workshop size can vary remarkably from session to session. Many believe that planning groups should be small, with six to eight participants, to keep the level of commitment high and reduce extraneous issues. Others believe that the widest range possible yields the best results and fosters organizational commitment. Use the best approach for your organization; if just starting with these methods, a smaller workshop will be the most feasible. Once the process is experienced and adopted by the organization, a larger scope of participation might be proposed if a broader representation of perspective is necessary.

The context for team planning will result in using a different spin on planning tools. The contexts described in the design formats have a similar impact on planning. If your organization can be considered a *business* context, scenario planning methods might be the most natural fit for strategic planning. In scenario planning, business process and strategy issues can be evaluated and planned together, making it an especially useful technique for strategic technology planning. The business context should also introduce a strong vision to drive the new process into the organization. Change management and selling the vision are often required with planning in business contexts.

The *systems* context offers opportunities for information systems or infrastructure planning, which *becomes* strategic in most organizations where an information technology (IT) organization supports the business, its products, or its customers. A long-term scenario-driven approach should be used to ensure that the strategy is sound for the future and that uncertainties have been considered. Typically, investment planning is part of the systems context situations, so the selection of alternatives from a small set of equally useful approaches is also a likely planning approach.

The *user* context is oriented more toward organizational development and management planning, where strategic planning from the line user management perspective guides the future work processes and career paths of hundreds of worker stakeholders. Scenario planning is recommended to understand the potential impacts of automation and process change on the users' context of work. Creating strategies is necessary to plan for managing the effects of the scenarios.

The *product* context requires planners to consider product development and distribution in the competitive marketplace, so strategic planning requires significant understanding of the market and customers. Customer and marketing feedback is critical in these sessions, which are also scenario-driven and strategic.

Team Planning Cycle

The team planning cycle is based on the same four-phase cycle as is described in the other formats. *Scoping* initiates the planning process, creating a mission statement (if required) and analyzing the planning horizon. Plan objectives are defined with the scope, as guidance for the planning product. *Visualizing* creates scenarios for the team members to envision the possible forces and opportunities in their future. Visualizing also evaluates scenarios, and selects an appropriate model of the future from which to work. *Usage* identifies and constructs potential strategies to address the conditions of the scenarios. *Packaging* documents the plan for presentation, and creates action plans for the organization to begin working in the necessary direction.

The Team Design *workshop* approach adds the phase of initiating. *Initiating* starts the workshop off by building a cohesive working team, and establishes a positive and creative working environment. Validating is not typically used in planning as it is with the design formats.

Scoping: Defining plan scope

Scoping activities for planning set the bounds for planning, defining a topical framework and direction for the team. In scoping, as outlined in Table 10.2, the team establishes or accepts a mission for planning and defines goals and objectives, criteria for success, and other fundamentals. In defining scope and objectives, familiar design-based methods can be adopted to communicate planning requirements with the team.

Defining purpose and mission.   When starting with a new planning task, some goals are implicit—the plan is to design a path to achieve

TABLE 10.2   Team Planning: Scoping Phase

Scoping: Defining plan scope	Methods	Inputs and outputs
Defining purpose and mission	Situation analysis, mission statement, purposes hierarchy, dialogue, brainstorming	In: Initial goals Out: Purpose, mission statement
Defining scope and objectives	Scoping diagram, system matrix, brainstorming methods	In: Purpose, mission statement Out: Scope and objectives

shared objectives. Going in, we usually have some consensus on general directions; otherwise, we wouldn't have agreed on creating a plan. However, when making the goals and objectives explicit, the plan begins with a commitment to achieve some goals. The achievement is our mission, and this direction toward our mission is the purpose.

For example, if our *mission* is to establish a process allowing all citizens direct input on national issues, our *purpose* might be to fulfill the promise of participative democracy. *Objectives* are specific positions reached that further the mission. *Strategies* are the ways we might meet objectives toward this mission (such as using the Internet to vote or using tax return forms to conduct a referendum on an issue).

Most of us have been involved in planning in our organizational lives at some time, and we often might find it to be laborious, painful, and slow. When planning is driven by the force of personality, by a single decision maker, or simply by uninspiring objectives, the process becomes rhetorical and perfunctory. Group planning processes without a clear mission are hardly worth the group's time. Mere participatory planning results in little more than a well-thought-out plan by an individual, and takes much longer. A more reliable and fulfilling process is called for, a planning model that employs the creativity and energy of the thinkers and doers in the room.

We get what we plan for, and our gains rarely exceed our vision. The very first stages of planning create a shared mental model for the entire planning process, a model that follows through well after the plans are made and are in play.

Creating a mission statement. Creating a mission or purpose statement is a significant activity for any group to undertake, and it should be treated with a sense of privilege and respect. Whether the mission is to be used by your planning team or by an entire organization, specifying the group's mission is an act of bold decision. In effect, you are writing the destiny of the organization. A clear mission invites individual allegiance to the group goals and inspires continuing support and effort toward the common purpose. It is an essential guiding force for a planning group intending to make a real difference.

However, many of us have been in situations where the mission is treated with suspicion, as if the exercise were a politically convenient attempt to shape group thinking. Be certain to clarify expectations and agenda before beginning the process of the mission statement. Your process and mission will fail if the mission is intended to establish interorganizational power. The mission must work for all members of the team, and it must work for the enterprise above all.

Start with the purposes hierarchy as described in Chap. 7. Understanding and agreeing on your general direction, the *purpose,* forges the critical link to the *mission.* When your planning team agrees on the purpose for being, the mission emerges as a logical next step. Many planning groups skip this part—each individual carries a mental model of the purpose, which each believes the others share. Since the existence of this shared model is often not the case, the purposes principle reveals the various degrees of purpose available to the group.

Developing the mission statement often represents a difficult and potentially emotionally involving experience for a group. Facilitation of this process requires practiced sensitivity to the feelings and contributions of all members. Participants are likely to have very strong opinions and attachments; facilitators must work a fine balance between attentive listening and guidance toward the goal.

The purposes array or hierarchy is used as the starting point for the mission statement. The mission statement builds from the purposes, and it differs in that it offers a foundation for the team, project, or organization. The mission states who you are as a team, and defines your commitment to a purpose.

For example, a purpose and its mission statement relationship might appear as follows:

- *Team.* Formed to develop the means to allow voting on national issues using the Internet.

- *Purpose.* To fulfill the promise of participative democracy.

The purpose is simple yet expansive. It provides a direction of intent for the team, along which many paths or missions could fulfill.

- *Mission.* To provide direct democratic participation in issues of national importance for all voters.

The mission defines the role of the team in supporting the purpose, and describes a relationship to its customers (voters). Some mission statements get into details about the type of service or products provided or their unique capabilities or position within the industry or as differentiated in the marketplace. The most potent mission statements are simple expressions of intent that do not bound the enterprise to a particular product or service, but that *provide a sense of significant value and service* for customers, however they are defined. In this way, should the business and its services change dramatically, the mission is not seen as outdated, but as evolved.

Preparing the mission statement. Some organizations prefer to develop the mission statement in a small group and work out most of the issues with the individuals most involved as leaders. Others prefer to work out the mission in a participative process within the workshop itself, thereby gaining complete buy-in and the creative force of the team behind it.

The mission statement should be written down on the board or easel chart in every version as the team iterates on the wording. Read it out loud with every new addition or change to the wording, and let the team think about it after reading it again before continuing discussions. Some teams will want to spend all day writing a mission statement. If you spend your time effectively in the *purposes* exercise, which might take an hour, the mission statement should not take more than another hour or two, depending on the seriousness of commitment or the emotional intensity of the team.

Alternative exercise: The mission mandala. Chapter 5 describes the team mandala as the visual representation of the team's vision. This same exercise might be used to create a visual representation of the mission, as a way of defining the mission in a powerful, nonverbal representation. The mandala can be pulled into the workshop in one of two places, depending on the creative nature of the team. If the team is composed of more visually oriented or creative individuals, have the team create the mandala as a picture of envisioned service *before* defining the written mission statement itself. The mission statement can flow more easily and naturally from this picture. If the team is more action-oriented, the members might be less patient with the imagery exercise and might want to talk things through. Have them create the written statement, then use the mandala exercise as a way to hold the mission in mind as an image of service.

Situation analysis. As with any complex business or organizational endeavor, we define our starting point and fully understand the goals, directions, attitudes, and hardships of our current situation. This is the context from which planning begins. In large organizations, this context is often handed down from executives, who (typically) understand the overall business environment is more acutely, to the operational or business units, which have the ability to act. In smaller or flatter organizations, the context might be generated from within a line group or a team. Although the true team context is usually specific to the team's mission, in some businesses the teams define the organizational future. They are the new context, part of a strategy for growth, change management, or organizational evolution.

Situation analysis identifies the present conditions affecting the enterprise. It need not be extensive, because the focus of strategy is on direction and not on fighting today's problems. But the starting point for direction is localized by the current conditions. Bean (1993) recommends a *valuation* of the business to define the current conditions relevant to strategic decisions. In this approach to situation analysis, four analyses are used to arrive at a complete picture of the enterprise and its state:

- *Valuation of the current conditions.* A strategic enterprise assessment or similar process is used to describe the current situation, health, and direction of the business.

- *Values of the organization and its leaders.* Understanding the values of the organization is essential to planning an appropriate direction, strategy, or mission.

- *Vision for long-term goals.* The vision might emerge from the mission statement, or could grow into a mission. The vision for long-term goals can be a different, more narrowly defined focus than the mission.

- *Understanding the* variables *that impact the business.* Many variables, internal and external, affect the long-term outlook of the business and should be evaluated for their impact on planning.

Valuation of current conditions. Preworkshop interviews and questionnaires are used in this approach to gather detailed input from managers and staff in advance of discussions. Bean suggests an evaluation (using letter grades) of the organization's current status in 16 strategic categories. This process is called the *strategic enterprise assessment* (SEA), and it leads to grading each of the critical areas, then averaging the scores from all inputs for a *grade point average* for each category. Then grades can be averaged across all categories for a total enterprise GPA, which can be tracked over time as a relative indicator of progress in the strategic direction. After engaging the relevant leadership in this sourcing of information, the planning team reviews the inputs and generates a composite view of the current organizational situation.

For some organizations, the interviewing process might be sufficient in itself. Allowing a number of key contributors to provide their thoughts and considerations brings a wealth of deeply held commitments, values, and visions to the process. The interviewing process is not held in a workshop setting, of course, but the workshop-based team might work together on designing the interviews and conduct them in pairs with contributors. Results and follow-up planning will then be discussed in the workshop sessions.

Describing enterprise values. The values of the organization are not abstract statements of what management appreciates about its business and employees. *Values* are the foundation for action and decision making, and drive the choices made in planning and setting direction. Values of an enterprise reflect the values of individuals, but also the inherent value structure in the business based on its history and relationships with customers and the community. Values held by individuals drive individual behavior, and organizational values affect the value making of individuals. Therefore, a constant interplay of values choices plays out in the daily work lives of people in their organizations and teams.

Bean's approach toward values also claims that strategy must "reflect an understanding of the values of organizational members and stakeholders." This he calls the "first axiom of corporate strategy." The second axiom is that "strategy must reflect an understanding of the ethical nature of strategic choice." This simple statement requires the organization to understand the ethical impact of decisions and directions chosen on behalf of the entire organization. Strategic planning must be consistent with the expressed values of the business as a whole.

Long-term vision. The long-term vision can grow directly from the mission statement or from other descriptions of vision. If the strategic plan is to encompass a mission-level operation, then the vision might *be* the mission. However, not all strategic planning grows from the mission; sometimes strategic planning addresses major directions within a business, such as acquisition strategy, or enterprisewide strategic needs, such as information management. A vision for these long-term directions can be quite different from the mission.

However, a strategic planning workshop will typically focus on one type of strategic plan, and that will determine the type of vision or mission developed. Visioning processes and exercises have been discussed previously in Chap. 5, and these techniques also support strategic planning work.

Understanding environmental variables. The last component of situation analysis involves understanding and defining the internal and external variables that affect the business as a whole. *Variables* are any components of the enterprise under the control of planning or that can vary independently. Internal environment factors allow significantly more control than the external variables, which tend to happen *to* the business from the outside.

Internal environmental factors include human resources, products and services, organizational culture, corporate policy, technology, and infrastructure. External variables are those outside of the organization's control, including customers, markets, social movements, government, competition, and the general economy.

Defining scope and objectives.   Scope has been revisited in every format, and should be reviewed as well in your workshops on a continual basis. Since scope is one of the few ways an organizer or project manager (with the team) controls content, scoping is an important means for defining the goals and the limits of the effort. The purpose and mission statement are primary inputs to this exercise—in the workshop, the scoping and objectives can proceed directly following the mission statement.

Defining objectives.   Objectives are target states defined for the mission or the plan itself. Some practitioners think the term *objective* and its partner, *goal,* have been overused and misapplied. After all, every business plan has "goals and objectives." However, the terms have ridden out the course of time, and *participants* understand the need to establish objectives. Regardless of what practitioners might believe, the participants are the benefactors of the process, and are often well served by skilled and insightful use of familiar representations.

An *objective* is considered to be a desired end state achieved by the planned activity, and is a specific, measurable statement of intention. The planning process organizes the efforts of the team toward designing the means to attain each objective. *Goals* are often defined as the milestone points that describe progress toward the objective, and are distinct from objectives in that many goals might be defined to achieve a particular objective. Other practices define these two terms in the reverse—it is worthwhile to distinguish only how they are used in your environment, and how they are understood by your customers. Many workshop practices do not develop tactical goals or objectives in the context of the team workshop—they are saved for small groups or individuals to develop later.

Brainstorming methods can be used to generate the initial material for objectives.

1. Elicit from the group a large list (over 20 items) of potential objectives. If participants wish to redefine an existing candidate state-

ment, write new ones on the board, and don't modify existing items.

2. Review the list when the group has run out of candidates.

3. Draw together related objectives, and review them to determine if the related groupings can be worded into a single objective or a small set of objectives.

4. Refine the list until 8 to 10 clearly framed objectives remain. Then revise each objective to ensure that it meets the well-known criteria associated with the mnemonic *SMART*:

   ■ *Specific.* Be sure each objective fits a specific case. Especially in planning, objectives must not be allowed to drift into generalities that cannot be met.

   ■ *Measurable.* Each item should have some metric associated with it—a count, periodicity, attainable rate, or numeric goal.

   ■ *Attainable.* Objectives should be reachable by the organization (but not easily).

   ■ *Relevant.* Objectives must relate directly to the mission.

   ■ *Time-based.* Each item must have an associated date or time goal.

Objectives can be revised as required throughout the planning session. Often the first set of objectives must be tailored as more information becomes available or as the team makes decisions about strategies.

The system matrix identified in Chap. 8 (Fig. 8.9) is a useful approach for mapping objectives to actions and characteristics required for planning. The system matrix moves the team's thinking from general to specific, from high-level objectives to details directly applicable in planning. Planning elements described by the matrix reveal the whole system, showing new patterns and opportunities, which can lead to breakthroughs in planning.

For a smaller number of objectives, a system matrix can be used for each objective to specify the essential components, resources, conditions, and information for each objective. This process goes far beyond defining the typical SMART attributes of the objectives, and it is useful when a carefully defined set of objectives will advance planning. Determine how mission-critical the objectives and plan are to the organization as a whole. If it is highly critical to future success, the more considerations, issues, and specifics that your team can identify, the better your chance of creating a plan that can be used as a guide into new territory.

TABLE 10.3   Team Planning: Visualizing Phase

Visualizing: Shaping scenarios	Methods	Inputs and outputs
Creating scenarios	Visioning exercises Scenario planning	In: Scope and objectives Out: Planning scenarios
Evaluating scenarios	Scenario analysis Quantitative analysis Resource analysis	In: Planning scenarios Out: Strategic options, scenarios

Visualizing: Shaping scenarios

Visualizing uses scenario planning methods to create the vision and responses of the business in its near future. Scenario planning fulfills the function of visualizing, which is a phase designed to consider the possibilities, both positive and undesirable, that can arise in the organization's environment of products, operations, and competition. By developing plausible scripts of the possible changes, impacts, and growth and of responses by the business, the planning team can evaluate appropriate responses and position the business to face the highest potential opportunities and problem conditions. The visualizing phase is outlined in Table 10.3.

Inputs used from scoping include the plan scope and objectives, as well as any initial *business cases* that might be used in the scenario planning process. Planning scenarios generated by the team will be used to evaluate strategic options and to refine and select the most useful planning scenarios for further definition of business strategy.

Creating scenarios.   Before scenarios were used as a planning method, *contingency analysis* was a primary technique for evaluating uncertainty. When faced with an uncertainty in the organizational future, planners would consider the probable problems that might occur and would propose contingencies for those events. Just in case. A company wouldn't actually plan for a new competitor to reduce its market share by 20 percent, but it would have a contingency plan to mentally and financially prepare for the situation should it arise. A problem with this approach to planning is that it is incomplete, disconnected from the daily concerns of the organization, and is considered to be set aside for emergencies. "What would be the worst case scenario?" is the expression used when evaluating contingencies. However, people do not expect the worst case to ever actually happen, and contingencies are often incomplete in their planning and execution. Finally, contingency planning only analyzes one factor of uncertainty at a time, such as the emergence of the competitor, without considering the joint impact of other factors, such as changes in funding occurring at the same time.

Other strategic planning approaches, such as SWOT analysis, lead to *wish lists* about the future state. SWOT analyzes strengths, weaknesses, opportunities, and threats across the horizon of the business' near term. "What do we see coming down the road at us?" is the mind-set for SWOT analysis. Unlike contingency planning, it addresses multiple factors that could impact the business. However, the typical lack of rigor in SWOT analysis can lead to false impressions of an organization's strength in a rapidly changing market or business climate. SWOT should be used to gather information and attitudes, but as a planning method it can lead to the wish list mind-set, an abstract removal from the potential of major business impacts.

Finally, more quantitative methods, such as sensitivity analysis, bring a rigorous attitude into planning, but often lead to asking the wrong questions. Since only one variable can be adjusted at a time, the interaction of variables is lost. So we make assumptions about what will be the most important issues, and model the impacts of those issues only.

Scenario analysis has emerged as a powerful approach for integrating future visions, contingencies, and objectives within realistic stories of the organization's probable state in the near term. Scenarios are used to envision the state of the business given multiple potential impacts, and the method draws the personal experience and backgrounds of participants into the process. It allows integrating subjective reasoning (values, attitudes, and possibilities) with the basically objective analytic approach.

Scenarios describe potential futures of the organization in useful detail. After evaluating scenarios, the next step is specifying strategies for managing in the new situations brought forth by the scenario.

Scenario planning. Scenario planning has emerged from years of being relatively unknown and little used to becoming an effective first-line strategic planning approach. Scenarios in the planning context are stories of the future, developed by a team charged to investigate the possible futures and to construct effective planning responses to the scenarios.

Two approaches to scenario planning are presented in this discussion, both of which can be adapted for use in most organizations using a team approach. Much of the current thinking in scenario planning stems from the approach developed by Paul Shoemaker (1995). Shoemaker's methodology, designed from work over years of strategic planning, is unique in being firmly rooted in both theory and practice. Honed by his experiences with Royal Dutch/Shell in its long-term strategic planning, Shoemaker presents a methodology useful in major planning efforts as well as in strategic planning far less involved than that of a transnational oil company. A simplified version of Shoemaker's method is discussed initially, as a useful alternative that can be readily adopted for use in the team planning cycle.

Strategic scenario planning. Shoemaker describes the use of scenarios to compensate for two errors commonly incurred in group decision making: underprediction and overprediction of future change. Scenario planning addresses multiple factors that enable thinking between underprediction and overprediction. Scenarios do not address all possible trends and impacts on the plan—they provide a plausible framework from which to evaluate sets of impacts together.

Shoemaker describes the overall purpose of scenario planning as building a "shared framework for strategic thinking that encourages diversity" and broadens the understanding of possible externally driven changes and business opportunities:

> Since scenarios depict possible futures but not specific strategies to deal with them, it makes sense to invite outsiders into the process, such as major customers, key suppliers, regulators, consultants, and academics. Or you can start with trends and scenarios that others have developed. The objective is to see the future broadly in terms of fundamental trends and uncertainties (p. 28).

The complete process for developing scenarios using Shoemaker's approach is described in 10 steps:

1. *Establish the scope.* A planning team can use the scoping processes described throughout Team Design as methods for driving the scenario scope. The important scoping questions include: What is the time frame for scenarios (5 years? 10?) What knowledge will be useful during this period? What sources of uncertainty have given us problems? Where are critical changes likely to emerge from (organizationally, markets, governments, or social trends)? Other scoping questions will arise from the unique requirements of the scenario. Use brainstorming and scoping diagrams to create a visual representation of the scope of the scenario to guide the team's creative process.

2. *Identify key stakeholders.* Describe the most relevant stakeholders for the scenario. Unlike design sessions, where your team can know and include some stakeholders, stakeholders in planning include anybody or any agency that has an interest in the planning issues. This at least involves your customers, users, suppliers, employees, and shareholders. It might also include the government, competitors, and customers and suppliers of competitors. The stakeholders attach names and faces to the stories defining the possible future. Look at the current balance of power, roles, and interests and how they change when tracing the path of your scenarios.

3. *Identify the basic trends.* Basic trends are social, political, and business influences to consider among the forces acting on the future depicted in scenarios. List all the trends and major influences that the team believes will impact the scope of scenarios. Trends are identified from national, social, and community movements, political, regulatory and legal influences, and industry and technology directions. To visualize the effect of each major trend, draw out diagrams for trends showing their current and future influence on the business. Simple line charts can show the expected rate of change as the scenario plays out over the timeframe, allowing the differing trends to be visually compared for interaction with one another.

4. *Identify the major uncertainties.* As part of identifying basic trends, determine the type of events, or specific events that will affect your scenario. Identify the directions in which these events might take the business. What will be the impact of a new Congress; what impacts will occur if interest rates are hiked? Emerging technologies, consumer adoption of an unexpected product or service, or increased oil prices all would be key uncertain events that could interact or directly affect the scenario. Shoemaker recommends identifying relationships among the uncertainties, to point out the more likely combinations and rule out the more implausible. For example, an implausible combination might be the continued growth of Internet services and a flattening of land-based telecommunications services (unless a major event such as cheap cellular transmission emerges as an explanatory function).

5. *Develop initial themes.* How do you start to define your initial scenarios? Where to draw the first line? Using the basic trends and your key uncertainties, prepare combinations of these elements to construct futures that could plausibly occur. Shoemaker suggests that an easy place to start is by collecting all the elements you consider positive and all those negative into two extremes, defining your poles of *best case* and *worst case*. He also cautions that *positive* and *negative* are highly relative to the scenario; events or trends perceived as negative are not necessarily harmful to the scenario, as they might represent opportunities for innovation or for capitalizing on situations. Themes can also be defined by selecting the most important elements, or the most uncertain, and combining them into new themes.

6. *Evaluate scenario consistency and plausibility.* As you review the scenario themes, evaluate them for internal consistency and plausibility. Are the extreme scenarios possible, or even remotely likely? Modify them to correspond more closely with basic trends,

or remove layers of interaction. Look at the underlying trends in the scenarios—are they consistent with the time scale or with the associated uncertainties? Remove trends in the model to improve consistency. Make sure the scenarios have realistic combinations of uncertainties so that the outcomes make sense together. For example, today we know that building nuclear power plants and lowering electricity prices probably do not go together. Finally, look at whether the stakeholders in the scenario have control over situations, or are in positions which they can change. Even if the uncertainties occur, are organizations ready for change, powerful enough to affect the outcomes, or able to adapt?

7. *Construct learning scenarios.* The initial scenarios might be inconsistent or might not apply to the strategic mission. They might be totally unlikely, or have conflicting trends that overlap. The refining of scenario themes into what Shoemaker calls *learning scenarios* represents the step of making scenarios into realistic stories that align closely to the strategic objectives or mission. Identify the scenario themes that are most relevant and adjust the variables, trends, and interactions around these themes.

   Create competing scenarios and give them significant names. These are the stories of the organization's future, and these stories can become the models for strategic thinking for many years. Competing scenarios should be easily identified by their names, such as: *We Buy the Market* (for a proacquisition scenario), *The Market Buys Us* (if we should sell to a larger company, or they want our business as part of theirs), and *We Change Markets* (if our business plan is to adapt to emerging market trends).

   In effect, creating the scenarios and the plans around them is creating the future, or at least the organization's response to the future events. The learning scenarios will be used for research and further investigation, and are not decision models as such.

8. *Specify research needs.* The team is encouraged to research problems in more depth now that actual scenarios have been identified. The learning scenarios become guides to research needs. What might happen in your future with factors your team doesn't currently understand well? Perhaps the introduction of new technologies will change the competitive balance in the industry—these technologies should be researched to understand their potential even if they are never adopted by your organization.

9. *Develop quantitative models.* Depending on the complexity of the scenarios, and what your research uncovers, determine whether quantitative models of business factors are now necessary. Up until this point, the scenarios use *qualitative* data, which many

managers are uncomfortable using for decisions. *Quantitative* models might include economic trend analyses of significant resources, analysis of interaction of key variables in scenarios, or discounted cash-flow models used in operational assumptions. Before this point in scenario planning, quantitative models are less useful due to the lack of context. By this point, their necessity should be clear.

10. *Evolve toward decision scenarios.* Decision scenarios are the ones you select to pursue the evaluation and decision processes further. Your team's process might have constructed five or six scenarios, with research supporting three of these. Select only two or, at most, three to iterate and refine as your *deliverable* scenarios. These scenarios will be used to generate further ideas and business strategy within your organization. Be sure they meet Shoemaker's quality criteria: Are they relevant to the organization and management? Are they internally consistent? Are they archetypal—that is, is each one representative of its own distinct future, not variations on the same scenario.

Simplified scenario planning. Shoemaker's work has been discussed in management publications for several years, and practitioners of scenario planning have recommended refinements to simplify the process. Some observers have suggested that the economic turbulence and shifting of management within organizations in the early 1990s led to a decrease in the use of scenario planning. Probably due to the combination of shorter planning horizons, an ambivalence toward long-term forecasting, and a shortfall of planning skills available, strategic planning has not enjoyed the use it had in the previous decade. Shoemaker's process resulted in considerable success in the Royal Dutch/Shell corporation, where it continues in active use by that world-leading company. But many organizations don't have the expertise or experience in-house to initiate a Shoemaker scenario process from scratch.

Management thinker David Mercer offers a simpler approach, which can be used not only in strategic business and organizational planning, but in any area where futures analysis and forecasting is useful. Simple scenario planning can be used for departmental level strategy, major investments, human resource planning, project portfolio decisions—anywhere in the organization where decisions are affected by future uncertainties.

Mercer's (1995) scenario planning approach presents a streamlined version of the full-scale methodology as described by Shoemaker and used by Royal Dutch/Shell and others. The simplified process begins with an analysis of the environment, recommended as a sophisticated evaluation of current trends and variables in the business. Environmental analysis gathers information from many sources, obtained by all members on the team, and shared and organized through the planning workshop. Typically, team members do extensive reading in the course of their daily practice, and bring together their experience, knowledge, and current research to the planning sessions. Information is gathered, presented, and then analyzed. The analysis is considered to be a learning process, wherein many teams immerse themselves in learning to understand the environment affecting the future as thoroughly as possible.

Streamlined scenario building. The streamlined scenario planning process recommends six steps to prepare scenarios useful for all but the most demanding strategic plans:

1. *Determine the key change factors or drivers.* Brainstorming is recommended as a means of generating a large number of key conditions and drivers for scenario planning. Mercer recommends a simple and highly interactive process where all participants are given sticky notes, write out ideas using large markers, and stick the notes to the wall or whiteboard. Participants are given the supplies, a direction, and a time limit of perhaps 20 minutes. Ideas are created, written on the notes, and randomly placed on the wall. Often, the ideas become less random soon after placement, as participants start to place notes near others that appear to be related.

2. *Organize the key drivers into a meaningful model or framework.* As the sticky notes are all placed, the facilitator can work with the team to organize the ideas into clusters or meaningful groupings. Volunteers can work together to do this for the group, or a model can be constructed as a team. This is a process of discussion and discovery, where patterns are allowed to emerge from the whole. Notes are moved around, ideas are added and clustered, groupings are tried and revised, and titles are added to groups to start defining the forces and influences.

   Mercer recommends taking photographs of the board at various stages to maintain a group memory of this ideation process. The photos will assist the team in rebuilding models (if needed) after they have been totally revised and replaced by new versions of clustered sticky notes.

3. *Develop several scaled-down scenarios (miniscenarios) without elaboration.* The framework of scenario conditions and drivers typically becomes organized into six to nine groupings, which in themselves become the scaled-down scenarios. Each miniscenario represents a set of related drivers from the previous exercise.

4. *Generate two or three scenarios from the larger set.* From the miniscenarios, work with the team to combine and reorganize two or three scenarios with sets of drivers that fit well together. This might involve considerable rethinking of the groups, or copying elements from the groups into all the scenarios if considered significant. Three scenarios have been found by many scenario planners to be the maximum number that teams can effectively work with.

Mercer recommends working with only two scenarios—and making those two complementary to each other. The two scenarios should cover all the key conditions and drivers between them, yet not be polar opposites, which might bias their acceptance. These two scenarios should reflect trends that are equally likely.

5. *Build upon these selected scenarios.* Use a readable format most easily understood by your intended audience. Make sure the narrative tells a story, rather than just recounting the results of the exercise. Scenarios are stories of possibility and the future, and they must be *sold* to others not involved in the process. Add simple trend diagrams and pictures, which always assist in reading and understanding.

6. *Identify the issues that emerge from the process.* Identify the most significant possible outcomes arising from the final scenarios. Determine what issues will have the greatest impact on the business should they occur. Remember, strategic planning isn't just about painting the picture of growth in a rosy economy or a smoothly running organization. It is used to prevent being blindsided by the unexpected or missing major trends that will alter the business.

As with all design processes, scenarios are subject to iteration and refinement. Even the final scenarios will probably be revised through discussions and "what ifs" with other managers. They must also be evaluated for internal consistency, to be sure the story lines hang together, especially after revisions have been made.

Finally, the last activity involves developing strategies to address the conditions and trends foretold by the scenarios. Strategies are developed to address the eventuality of scenarios. Should a pessimistic scenario play out in the events of the real world, the business has a strategy for managing. Strategies are based on the resources that can be made available if required by the scenario. They should be specified within the context of the same planning workshops, so alternative strategies are developed as a group and agreement exists as to their proper usage.

Evaluating scenarios. The final scenarios developed should be highly relevant to current business concerns and have direct meaning for the executive team and others using the scenarios. Each scenario must be internally consistent to have credibility, and each should describe a different story of the possible future. And scenarios should describe conditions that will likely persist over time, and not focus on emergencies or short-term problems.

From the scenario processes we can derive a entire workshop process for facilitated strategic planning. Both the Shoemaker and Mercer approaches map to team planning activities, and are nearly complete cycles in themselves. By mapping these approaches to the team planning cycle, practitioners can adapt group exercises to scenario development, ranging from brainstorming and diagramming to models such as the purpose hierarchy and system matrix (from Breakthrough Thinking). Finally, few (if any) other documented strategic planning techniques support the integration of organizational learning and business planning as does the scenario planning approach.

Usage: Defining strategies

After decision scenarios have been selected and discussed, the usage phase facilitates strategies to manage the scenarios. *Strategies* are mechanisms defined for execution of the plan. A strategy is a broad plan of action, and creates a direction for planners and organizers to follow. Strategies are not actions in and of themselves—they are high-level and large-scale plans that address one or two objectives. Using the scenario planning method, strategies can be generated from the stories of the organizational future.

Inputs to the usage phase, as outlined in Table 10.4, include the results of scenario planning, including scenarios and strategic options from visualizing. At the conclusion of usage, strategies have been defined and an initial business or strategic plan is documented.

TABLE 10.4   Team Planning: Usage Phase

Usage: Defining strategies	Methods	Inputs and outputs
Identifying possible strategies	Breakthrough Thinking Brainstorming methods	In: Strategic options, scenarios Out: Applied strategies, strategic vision
Defining business strategies	Business planning Project planning SWOT analysis	In: Applied strategies, strategic vision Out: Initial business plan

Identifying possible strategies. Strategies are plans in and of themselves to adjust the organization to take advantage of opportunities and to handle potential threats to the business. Possible strategies are generated by brainstorming methods and other techniques for gathering ideas and feedback from the team and sorting it out to make the best choices. Brainstorming and Breakthrough Thinking methods described in previous chapters will serve the facilitator well in leading these sessions.

A strategy might be a plan, a set of coordinated programs, or a framework of actions that accomplish the objectives established in scoping and support key scenarios. Use the scenarios and strategic options discussed during visualizing as the primary materials for working out strategies. Possible strategies are generated by brainstorming, discussion, or dialogue. Have the group list strategies without evaluation until the group feels comfortable with the available candidates. Then discuss each candidate separately, determining whether it is a fit to the scenario and objectives, and whether it is too broad (beyond scope) or too specific (a tactic, perhaps a program or project).

Teams that don't work with strategic planning often might mix the notions of objectives, strategy, and tactics. As a facilitator, don't focus on this distinction too much during the brainstorming or dialogue phase. Instead, allow all ideas to come forth, and use the discussions that follow to narrow down the list. Use the following rules of thumb for identifying appropriate strategies:

- Map every strategy to at least one objective.
- Be sure each strategic objective ends up with a workable strategy.
- Chart the strategies and objectives to show the mapping. Document the chart.
- Narrow the number of strategies to no more than 8 for most organizations, 10 to 12 for large organizations.

When the strategies have been identified (two to four hours total), the typical next step is to define them in sufficient detail to construct the plan.

Defining business strategies. In a typical session the planning group will investigate several or perhaps numerous possible strategies for addressing the scenarios and other business plans. Strategies are basically organized sets of actions directed as a response to foreseeable conditions. They are both plan and prevention, and are not necessarily master plans for business growth or market dominance. As the team develops a set of strategies that applies to the scenarios and plans, these candidate strategies can be selected as the ones to build upon. These strategies must then be defined in enough detail to make decisions about their use.

Defining business strategies might be done within the series of scenario planning workshops. With essentially the same team, brainstorm and construct strategies that best respond to the envisioned futures portrayed in the scenarios. The hard work is in building realistic scenarios—once these are defined, the strategies should almost fall into place. Strategy emerges from corporate culture, company mission, long-term objectives, and human and capital resources. Within a single-day workshop, a management team that understands its mission and resources can define strategies as responses to the two or three scenarios. Have the team brainstorm and develop multiple strategies, leaving out the details until later. Evaluate the possible responses, discuss the details, and then select the approaches that best match the scenario conditions. Brainstorm the details for the strategic approaches selected, and refine these into strategies.

What are the conditions of satisfaction for the strategies? A popular business term for these conditions is *critical success factors*. Either way, they define the necessary milestones for successful implementation of strategies. These are conditions that must be satisfied to enable, realize, or support the strategy.

Using a brainstorming process, the team can spend at least an hour listing and discussing the conditions and assumptions of the business strategies. Allow numerous items to be listed without evaluating the form and type of the contributions. After the team members have listed all their items on the board or easel chart, identify which conditions are critical success factors and which are assumptions or just issues. Assumptions are important to distinguish and should be documented, as are issues, which might be listed on a separate issues area. But the critical success factors are the conditions that must be met in order to possibly develop the strategy into a working plan.

Packaging: Defining the plan

By this point your planning team has created missions, defined objectives, devised scenarios, and developed strategies for meeting the future. Whether for the mission of an entire enterprise or for a large project or program, the process has yielded several key products of planning:

- Consensus on mission, direction, and objectives
- Scenarios describing two or three detailed stories about possible events and impacts, trends, and responses
- Strategies defined to address scenarios and to plan for growth and future uncertainties

TABLE 10.5   Team Planning: Packaging Phase

Packaging: Defining the plan	Methods	Inputs and outputs
Formalizing the plan	Plan definition	In: Initial business plan Out: Documented plan
Defining and assigning actions	Action planning Scheduling	In: Documented plan Out: Assigned actions

At the conclusion of strategic planning, the mission, message, and strategies must be communicated effectively to others in the organization. The planning team is not the business itself, and is responsible to many others in the enterprise for its decisions. Although it is quite effective to share ongoing results with others in management, especially of scenario construction, the results of team planning should be published in a clear, concise package. Packaging pulls together the planning products and constructs a package readable and usable by stakeholders not involved in the planning process. The packaging phase is outlined in Table 10.5.

Formalizing the plan.   Formalizing the plan is a general activity wherein team members build a formal document defining the process, scenarios, and resulting plan for the future conditions. This can be a group-developed document or be composed by one or several individuals using notes and interim planning outputs.

If electronic means of recording have been used throughout the planning process, this step should not require substantial effort. Group conferencing systems used in planning are a useful tool for building objectives, scenarios, and strategies throughout the team planning cycle. Although most of these tools (such as IBM's *TeamFocus,* Ventana's *GroupSystems,* and Enterprise Solution's *MeetingWorks*) are designed as general group conferencing systems, they are excellent systems for generating participation, moderating discussion, and integrating results. With most of these tools the initial documentation can be generated directly into a word-processing format.

Otherwise, a team approach to developing the plan can break out sections of the plan to individuals assigned to prepare and interpret the details of the preceding sessions. Working in parallel, the participants can develop sections and integrate them to create a complete document. The completed plan is read thoroughly in advance of team review. The team review establishes the consensus and sign-off for the plan.

Defining and assigning actions.   Follow-up actions are assigned to participants as a natural conclusion to the planning sessions and to resolve the inevitable question of "What's next?" While maintaining the workshop environment, be sure to facilitate closure and responsible conclusions to the planning process. This might include any follow-up on the review and critique and discussion on the resolution of comments and issues. Discussion might be necessary regarding the reception of the initial plan by management and other stakeholders. Other feedback into the planning process can be resolved during this concluding session.

Provide the opportunity for team members to release expressions of frustration or dissatisfaction, as well as to celebrate the accomplishment. This might be a phase of letting go of withheld communications and straightforward discussion about missed opportunities or disappointments. This allows members to feel closure regarding their participation in the process.

Provide a venue for presentation and discussions with executive and operational management. Before the doors are shut on the planning workshops, set up a meeting to present the final planning results. Typically, some management members will have been intimately involved with the process and will have discussed the results on a regular basis. However, a final discussion session will provide the opportunity to fully engage the management teams in realizing their role in fulfilling the plans.

Hold focus groups with nonmanagement teams and staff throughout the organization to gain valuable feedback and insight regarding the mission, objectives, and plans. Be sure your planning team establishes contact with these individuals early in the planning process and maintains an ongoing dialogue. Contributions from those outside the planning process must be seriously considered, especially if success depends on buy-in from all members of the organization.

Team Decision Making

Although we have primarily dealt with process and system design concerns, the need for decision making arises in almost every facilitated workshop. In other chapters simple group decision methods are discussed, such as consensus, group voting, and nominal group technique. These are specific methods useful for achieving decisions and resolution during design sessions, but are probably too simplified to use when the workshop focus is solely on decision making. The Team Decision Making format provides a framework for agendas and for facilitating workshops designed specifically for decision support.

Dozens of decision-making processes and their variations are available to practitioners, and this chapter does not attempt to present a definitive source of decision-making methods. Instead, as with the other formats, the purpose of Team Design is to provide a framework for practitioners to use their tried-and-true methods within the larger context of a complete design cycle using the workshop setting, as well as to describe emerging methods that others have found useful in the same context. In the Team Decision Making format, the purpose is no different, except the outcome is a much different product than with other Team Design formats. A group decision *process* is similar to that of a design process. The decision becomes a documented deliverable resulting from the team process, as if it were a design document.

If a decision is simple or relatively insignificant to the organization, you probably don't need a team process. Although it might seem obvious, the team process is both effective and time-consuming, and is recommended for decisions where a high degree of importance is understood. Moody (1983) indicates five factors to assess decision importance:

- *Size or length of commitment.*   Major investments have a huge impact on the organization and on the business itself. Significant commitments require a team decision process.

- *Flexibility of plans.*   If the plans can be easily changed as conditions change, an individual can take responsibility and manage the planning and decision process. But if plans must be locked in and become rigidly defined, with associated resources and personnel decisions, the decision becomes important enough to warrant a team approach.

- *Certainty of goals.*   If the goals of the decision are certain, agreement is simple and a team would merely rubber-stamp the decision. However, most decision processes entail some uncertainty. To the extent that uncertainty is present, a team process is necessary to engage a wider variety of experience and perspectives in the judgment.

- *Quantification of variables.*   If variables can be quantified, such as accurate cost estimates, uncertainty is reduced and the decision becomes simplified. In less-definable situations, the quality of decision becomes very important, and a team process reduces the inherent risk.

- *Human impact.*   When a decision affects numerous people or the entire organization, decisions will be significant. In these cases, a larger decision team might be needed to cover the different organizations impacted by the decision.

The typical decision process as described (realizing there is no "typical" decision) involves collecting data until the decision maker is satisfied with the amount and quality of data. A reduction or analysis of the data is performed, and the implications are discussed with others. Often, just single decision makers determine the decision outcome for major and minor decisions for an organization. They consider their experience in the business and their managerial judgment to be all the tools necessary to make effective decisions. Since many managers consider decision making to be part of their job description, they might make decisions individually when they would prefer to use a group process. For traditional managers, concern over sharing the decision process with others can be related to the *job requirement* image of decision making.

For many organizations, moving the decision process to a group venue challenges both management and the team or subordinates involved. Although it is popular for organizations to speak of empowering their teams, in practice the more common approach is to use teams of mixed levels of management, staff, and line workers. Empowerment derives from the ability of all organizational members to freely raise and discuss issues affecting the decision process, whether or not management is involved. In this way all stakeholders have the opportunity to communicate facts and perspectives where they can make the most difference. It is not necessarily being free from management involvement, unless the organization is based on a true autonomous team model—a rarity in North American business. In fact, the team concept as such arises from the sports world, where decisions are usually autocratic and not shared among the players. The concept of full team ownership in decisions has developed more through the needs of business, where much more is at stake than the next play or the game score.

Team decision support processes

The intention of the Team Decision Making format is to support a wide range of possible uses, to expand the approaches used by teams and individual decision makers to make better use of team processes. However, not every type of decision process will fit this model, so it is worth considering the types of decisions best supported by the format. The primary drivers for team decision making include the following:

- Significant decisions affecting product management, product design and development, and the organizations for developing products.

- Significant decisions for establishing, funding, and staffing projects and programs to fulfill products, services, plans, and business needs.

- Major purchases or selections of products, technologies, or tools that support the business, its infrastructure, information management, or product development.

- Decisions affecting organizational structure and process, business (functional) processes, and financial investments affecting multiple organizations.

This chapter provides methods useful in all these areas, but especially for the first three types of decisions, which involve a rational assessment of needs and priorities.

Group decision making has numerous advantages over individual methods, and prevents a number of common decision problems. A team pools together the experience and knowledge of a number of people, bringing more knowledge to the decision than any single individual can. If a team is made responsible for implementing the decision, the members will bring total commitment to the effort, which is certainly not guaranteed in the case of individual decisions. Risk-taking behavior is also moderated in groups, where high-risk behavior is mitigated and risk-averse individuals are encouraged to assume worthy risk. Finally, the collective judgment prevails over individual desires, reducing the effect of hidden or personal agendas.

Individual decision making often results in problems that occur well after the decision, when it is too late to effect a change in direction or resources. These problems can often be avoided by the team decision process. Moody points out some of these problems as follows:

- *Prejudice.* Personal biases affecting individual decision makers are moderated in groups.

- *Showmanship.* Individual decision makers in strong positions are often effective presenters and can argue their case for a strongly held viewpoint. These behaviors are balanced by the group process.

- *Analogy or misdirection.* Some decision makers make decisions and then present their case in terms of analogies or simplistic justifications that would not be allowed to pass within the rigors of a group decision process.

- *Irrelevant information.* When not checked by a group process, individuals can use information that is not directly relevant to support decisions to which they are predisposed.

- *Complete facts.* Individuals do not always have the time and resources to develop the full set of facts necessary to compare several options for a decision.

- *Business familiarity.*   Collective experience and familiarity is brought to bear on the decision when a group process is used, whereas individuals must rely on their personal background only.

Team decision making can be a major change of practice for some organizations. However, for those using Team Design, JAD, or other group participation workshops for development and design, a team decision process is a rational step forward in the same direction. The initial difficulty is initiating the team process. Once established in the organization, the team process becomes appreciated by the organization, and leads to a high degree of involvement. Team involvement will migrate from the development domain to group decisions as a matter of course.

Format: Team Decision Making

The phase structure of the Team Decision-Making format is shown in Table 10.6.

Leading the decision workshop

Decision workshops are a special challenge for facilitators. In design sessions, facilitator expertise in an area can contribute to the product and the process. In decision-making sessions, the facilitator must remain especially neutral to avoid having any undue influence in the outcome of decisions. Decisions often lead to pivotal changes in an organization's direction or objectives. Facilitators find that emotions, concerns, and biases run stronger in decision making than in other types of sessions, since the impact of decisions can dramatically affect the careers and work lives of all involved. Neutrality is a fundamental requirement for decision facilitation.

Decision workshops vary in approach and length to a great extent. Workshops dealing with the selection of software development tools, consulting services, or standard products become fairly rational exercises in establishing criteria and making judgments. When the decision process engages more difficult issues, such as funding business cases or identifying individuals for promotion, objectives can become intertwined with organizational issues and personal goals. The more personal outcomes are at stake, the more sensitive the facilitator must be in leading a fair and neutral session.

Use techniques the team will readily adopt, since a well-understood process will not be seen as being manipulated by any group members. After considering the type of decision to be made by the group members, provide a few optional methods for them to evaluate for use in the decision process. If one approach makes the most sense, offer it to

TABLE 10.6   Team Decision-Making Format.

Agenda activities	Methods	Inputs or outputs
Scoping: Decision scoping		
Determining purpose and goals	Purposes hierarchy, dialogue, brainstorming methods	In: Purpose, initial goals Out: Decision goals
Defining scope and criteria	Scoping, defining criteria	In: Decision goals Out: Decision scope, criteria
Visualizing: Defining alternatives		
Organizing criteria	Prioritizing, grouping and weighting criteria	In: Decision scope and criteria Out: Priorities, criteria weights
Envisioning alternatives	Visioning exercises, system matrix, brainstorming methods	In: Priorities or weights Out: Decision alternatives
Usage: Modeling and selection		
Developing decision scenarios	Scenario analysis	In: Priorities, decision alternatives Out: Scenarios
Evaluating decision models	Ranking, weighted criteria, analytical hierarchy process	In: Scenarios, alternatives Out: Decision models
Making selections	Decision-making methods, voting, rating, points, selection process	In: Decision models Out: Team decision
Packaging: Documenting decisions		
Documenting decision	Decision definition	In: Team decision Out: Documented decision
Assign action plans	Action planning, scheduling	In: Documented decision Out: Assigned actions

the group with adequate description of its applicability to the situation. Allow the team members to own the process, and facilitate their ownership and the decision process.

Managing conflict and agreement

Managing conflict. Conflict should be expected in decision-making settings. People's projects, work, budgets, and personal directions are on the line in any major decision. Although the decision conference might start cordially enough, issues and conflicts will arise as soon as priorities and evaluations are discussed. These are just as much a part of the group process as holding discussions and working through solutions.

Chapter 4, "Facilitating Team Design Workshops," describes facilitation approaches to managing conflict. A facilitator can use one of several approaches to conflict, from confrontation to consensus. First, try to clarify the team's view of the issues at stake. Identify root causes of an issue (or opportunity), and stay away from dealing with symptoms or personalities. Try to understand where the conflict first emerged in the group, and observe its effect on the decision process. Then work with the team toward a mutual solution.

Allow conflict to emerge but don't let it become personal or destructive. Managing conflict typically requires confrontation and, often, intervention. As described in Chap. 4, the facilitator can and must intervene in conflict situations where group integrity is threatened. *Intervention* is confrontation taken to remedy group conflict. The range of intervention behaviors include:

- Nondirective conflict management
- Involving the group members in their conflict
- Confronting the conflict
- Prescribing solutions to the conflict

Conflict often emerges from participants taking a win-lose perspective regarding decision making and decision outcomes. Conflict is natural in this environment, since individuals try to optimize their own outcome at the expense of others. Work from the outset to establish ground rules and an environment that supports win-win decision making. Making the decision process visible to participants is one of the keys to managing conflict. When the agenda, ground rules, and decision-making processes are discussed in the open, the group becomes self-regulating. Facilitation is required to guide the flow and maintain the process, but the usual sources of deep conflict and disagreement are often headed off early in discussions.

In cases where participants come to a decision conference with current and acknowledged conflicts, a different approach might be taken. In these unusual cases, such as in negotiation or bargaining, the initial focus of the meeting is on the scope of the conflict. Even in moderated decision conferences aspects of deep conflict can emerge. Be prepared to use decision-making methods that allow for full and open discussion of all issues and decision factors. Using decision-making exercises, such as scenario building and decision models, gradually reveals the value of all positions evidenced by participants. Closely held viewpoints relax when the personal stakes are removed, and all team members can participate in reaching decisions that support the organization, not just the decision makers.

Managing agreement. One of the major problems with group decision making is in determining when you have true consensus. Consensus can be difficult to assess, particularly in teams with mixed representation. With the typical design or decision team, participants will often be drawn from unrelated organizations and may not have prior relationships. Sometimes this leads to conflict, but usually tends more toward conformance—the new members feel privileged by the invitation and perceive conformity as a way to become part of the team. Also, in mixed teams some members might perceive themselves as having less status than others, leading to artificial conformity. In groups, the pressure to conform may lead to premature consensus.

Facilitators can prevent this situation by creating an atmosphere of openness and free discussion early in the proceedings. The team-building exercises indicated for every workshop format generate an appropriate working environment where participants feel free to express their ideas and concerns.

As with conflict, facilitators also run into trouble with managing agreement. With apparent conflict, individuals at least express their desires and intentions. With apparent *agreement,* the facilitator should cautiously check to ensure that agreement exists, or whether group members are avoiding conflict. When group members fail to test or question the assumptions of their decision processes, a false consensus can arise. A now-classic management fable known as the *Abilene Paradox* (Harvey 1988) points out the fairly common scenario where everybody in the room seems to agree, but each privately disagrees with the decision or direction of the group. This paradox occurs when members believe they understand others' position and go along with the perceived group interest instead of checking to be sure. Without retelling the original story, this situation occurs when all members of a group go along with an idea because they believe the originator of the notion is personally invested in it. The paradox occurs when it is later revealed that no one member of the group actually supported the notion personally, but each felt it was more important to go along with the group. This can happen when a person in authority casually mulls an idea with the group, and then group members acquiesce to what they believe is the individual's highly valued idea. In reality, none of the members—not even the authority figure—actually have an interest in pursuing the idea, but no single member wants to be seen as debunking the idea in favor of another one.

How do we know when consensus actually exists? You can ask, and then ask again in a different way to see if the response is consistent. And check your gut—if the group appears to grudgingly concede to consensus, briefly open up the discussion one more time. Deep issues might still exist that could arise later to interfere with the decision or its implementation. With consensus decision making, the facilitator must often diagnose situations as they arise, since a simple signal will not always be provided. Always check various channels of communication to test for true consensus before moving forward.

Team Decision-Making Cycle

The team decision-making cycle specifies activities and supporting methods for decision making following a common cycle. Outputs *within* the cycle are not typically deliverables as such, as in the other formats. Instead, the objective and output of the cycle is to reach a sound decision as a team, with sound rationale and supportive documentation.

The decision-making cycle uses *scoping* to prepare for the decision, to understand the background, and to identify the goals for the decision. In this phase, the team asks "What is the objective of the decision? What do we want to achieve?" Decision criteria are also defined; criteria lay out the boundaries by screening and evaluating alternatives.

In *visualizing,* two main activities are performed to define alternatives. First, the criteria defined in scoping are organized by grouping or setting priorities. Then, the team defines, elaborates, or brainstorms alternatives from which to select in the decision. If the decision is binary (yes/no), this activity is not significant. Yet if a decision is framed in such a way as to only allow two choices, it is quite possible that expanding the decision space to include other alternatives might lead to better definition and decision approaches.

Usage phases always deal with focusing the process in its domain of actual use. In decision making, various decision models are supported to allow for the different possible types of decisions. For decisions involving significant choices that affect future business, developing scenarios for decision alternatives provides a way to view and predict the potential impacts. Decision scenarios are similar to planning scenarios, but are less time-consuming to build and use. Different quantitative decision models are discussed, as are means of evaluating decision models. Finally, the act of decision, of making selections, completes the usage phase.

As with other cycles, the *packaging* phase is used to document and support the findings and to develop plans of action for moving forward. In decision making, less documentation is developed because the decision itself is typically the deliverable. A support package is prepared to the extent required by the organization and to justify the team's decision.

Scoping: Decision scoping

Scoping the decision refers to establishing the boundaries and assumptions under which the decision will be made. Decision scoping outlines the structure for continuing with the decision process, by constructing goals and rational criteria for the decision. For other workshop formats, the scope is considered to be the definition of the content and the limits for requirements, a design, or a business process. In decision scoping, the team exits when the criteria for the decision are defined. These criteria are initially defined in scoping to serve as guidelines for the decision process. The scoping phase is outlined in Table 10.7.

Determining purpose and goals. Determining the purpose of the decision should be straightforward, but "The Purpose" is a conversation always worth holding with the team. As discussed in prior chapters, purposes are not always simple statements of direction. The purpose is the agreement among all team members as to the best representation of the team's *intention*. The purposes hierarchy approach has been used in the previous formats—it is used to advantage in decision scoping as well.

Once the purpose is clearly understood and documented, the goals of the decision process can be determined. Decision goals are discussed by the team to achieve a basic understanding of the session goals. What, exactly, should the group accomplish to reach the decision? What are the milestones for the decision process itself? Goals establish the method the team agrees to use to pursue the decision—agreement creates a commitment to the results of decision making and prevents second guessing of conclusions.

Let's look at an example. The purpose of the decision might be to identify the top candidate business cases for next-fiscal-year funding.

TABLE 10.7   Team Decision Making: Scoping Phase

Scoping: Decision scoping	Methods	Inputs and outputs
Determining purpose and goals	Purposes hierarchy Dialogue Brainstorming	In: Purpose, initial goals Out: Decision goals
Defining scope and criteria	Scoping Defining criteria	In: Decision goals Out: Decision scope and criteria

In this case, the goals of the decision will be defined as the activities necessary to make the decision:

- *Define the scope and limits of the decision.* Select 20 R&D business cases, rank order them, and allocate money from next year's $10 million R&D budget to each of the projects.

- *Identify criteria for business case assessment.* Specify the most important needs, values, and capabilities for the business for the decision timeframe. Criteria are used for overall assessment and for evaluating each case.

- *Select and prioritize the top 10 to 20 candidate business cases.* Identify the top set of business cases and rank order them in importance, based on the initial criteria.

- *Evaluate the business cases.* Evaluate each of the selected business cases by detailed criteria, and reassign them new priorities if necessary.

- *Allocate funds to the business cases.* Establish a process for allocating funding (full, partial, or percentage) and allocate funding for business case budgets based on priority.

This is a simplified example, but the idea of working through the process from start to finish in the workshop is to build a simple model of the decision goals. What will your team cover in the workshop decision process? What are the activities and decision points planned to reach the desired result? These become your goals, which should be identified with the group, organized into the agenda, and facilitated using the methods best suited to the goals.

Defining scope and criteria. The decision scope is defined by the team's consideration of its purpose, goals, variables, and limitations. It is not defined as directly as in requirements or design, where a constant reminder of scope is sometimes required for guidance and constraint. The scope of the decision emerges through the exercise of defining criteria, and is completed in the next phase, when the decision alternatives are set. At that point the team is constrained by the process put into place, and further scoping is not usually required.

Developing criteria. The team next develops criteria for the decision process. Your team makes its values visible through the decision criteria. For a complex decision, this critical step is approached with some rigor, as the criteria become the keys to selection. For a simpler decision, it is at the very least a thoughtful analysis of the values and needs related to the decision.

As a facilitator, leading groups in defining criteria is an art and an exercise in focused analytical thinking. The decision criteria are the key attribute of the scope—they determine how the alternatives become validated. This approach prevents bias toward particular solutions by deciding in advance what characteristics are important, so that alternatives are fairly evaluated against the values defined in the criteria.

The types of criteria used in assessment are derived from the expertise relevant to the decision, whether from industry standards, the project requirements, or marketing determinations. In making financial decisions, such as funding business cases, the criteria might be largely economic and highly oriented toward strategic business objectives and business requirements. Some criteria derived from this analysis might include the following:

- Business requirements satisfied (type or number)
- Strategic objectives addressed
- Competitive value provided
- Positive customer awareness created
- Return on investment
- Expected market share or gain
- Impact on competitors

Often, the criteria are generated from capabilities or system requirements, such as decisions for the selection of products or tools:

- Capacity
- Flexibility
- Operating costs
- Security
- Usability
- Efficiency
- Maintainability

Many other similar criteria are defined to support technical and functional capabilities: availability, flexibility, integrity, portability, interoperability, reliability, and testability are some of the main criteria used. These attributes can all be defined in operational terms targeted to your business. The team should identify quantifiable values or specifications for each criterion. During the evaluation of alternatives, these values are used as guidelines to distinguish the relative level of satisfaction of each alternative.

When defining criteria, the team becomes objective and considers the entire scope of the evaluation process. The facilitator's job is to move the criteria definition forward and to maintain the flow of discussion. Some of the questions facilitators ask of teams in defining criteria include variations of the following:

- What is to be satisfied by the decision criteria?
- What objectives must be met?
- What are the critical factors?
- Can it be measured?
- What are the conditions of satisfaction?
- What requirements must be met?
- What are the specific and measurable criteria?

Several simple examples of defined criteria follow. Criteria can be operationally defined for rating by the team, or can be defined as "must" criteria used for screening alternatives.

Operational definitions of criteria:

- *Life-cycle cost.* The estimated total cost of purchase, installation, operation, maintenance, and disposal of the system throughout the full period of ownership.
- *Usability.* A characterization of software that is readily learned, that can be used by 90 percent of all users on an intermittent or continual basis with minimal errors, and that has a high reported degree of satisfaction from its long-term users.

"Must" criteria used for screening include the following examples:

- *Timeliness of delivery.* The computer hardware must be delivered to the site, fully installed, and available within two weeks of the signed order.
- *Compatibility.* The development environment must be fully supported in the following platforms (x, y, and z) and must support sharing of files developed in any platform. (In this case, the criteria should read as a specification. Further detail would be associated with "fully supported," the versions of the platforms, and the specific file types developed on those platforms.)

The evaluation method used also drives the formulation of criteria. If a large number of alternatives is considered, use a screening process. A weighted evaluation process might be useful—alternatives are screened out first, and those that remain are rated against scaled criteria. The criteria must be established to both screen out alternatives ("musts") and then to evaluate the remaining candidates. With a

smaller number of more focused alternatives, all mi
"must" screening, so only evaluation criteria are required

Visualizing: Defining alternatives

In visualizing, the goal is to define alternatives from whic
will evaluate and select for the decision. Visualizing bui
from the scope and the criteria, by identifying the most
aspects of the decision to be evaluated. Criteria are organi
or more ways, by ranking, prioritizing, or assigned weighti
to assist in evaluation. The alternatives are next devel
known decision candidates and from creative thinking p
These alternatives become the primary options from which
chooses. The visualizing phase is outlined in Table 10.8.

Organizing criteria. As we continue from scoping, criteria a
nized for use in the decision. The criteria show what t
believes to be important. In this activity, the team arranges t
sion criteria to create a useful model that will sort out the
tives and highlight differences between them. We describe tv
approaches for organizing criteria in the decision cycle.

   Grouping criteria into categories simplifies the decision mod
large number of criteria has been generated. By using sticky no
index cards, the team can rearrange the set of criteria into lo
groupings and then name the groups as new criteria. The deci
process then works through the criteria in each group, one at a tir
The groupings can contain interactions between criteria that mig
be dependent on each other. For example, the criteria in a grou
named user support are all similar, and might vary in the same direc
tion together. If the specific criteria were evaluated separately, undue
influence on the model might result just due to the number of criteria
that relate to that group. By grouping related criteria, these interactions can be minimized, and the decision process might proceed more
rapidly. The steps for this process include the following:

TABLE 10.8   Team Decision Making: Visualizing Phase

Visualizing: Defining alternatives	Methods	Inputs and output
Organizing criteria	Prioritizing Grouping and weighting criteria	In: Decision scope and criteria Out: Priorities, criteria weights
Envisioning alternatives	Visioning exercises System matrix Brainstorming methods	In: Scope, priorities, weights Out: Decision alternatives

ouping assumes that criteria have been written down on cards, cky notes, or some sort of label and are on the board or a table. criteria have been brainstormed on a whiteboard, have a participant write down the items on cards or sticky notes.

Have the team rearrange the defined criteria by moving the criteria labels (on sticky notes or index cards) into logical groups that will reduce the number of criteria or simplify the process.

If items are needed across multiple groups, make new copies of those criteria for the group. Group the items and assign category descriptions as labels for the group.

Another way to organize criteria is to quantify them by assigning them a *rank* (a priority value) or a *weighting factor* for use when rating decision alternatives. Ranking is useful when a rapid or simpler decision model is sufficient. Weighting is recommended when a larger set of criteria (greater than 12) or more sophisticated analysis is required.

If fewer than 10 to 15 criteria exist, *prioritizing* alone might be sufficient to organize the criteria for the decision model. Priorities identify *how important* criteria are relative to one another, and are a simple means of organizing a set of inputs into an immediately useful model for decision making. Merely ranking the criteria as a group exercise facilitates agreement as to priorities, and defines the key variables for the decision. The assigning of priorities to criteria involves judgment and helps define the decision itself.

Weight assignment is done for a more extensive decision model, and is typically used for complex or highly critical decisions. Weights specify a value for each criterion relative to the other criteria. In the decision analysis, participants rate each alternative's criteria, which are factored by the weights for a final weighted score. The weighted ranking process is a straightforward decision analysis that uses both ranking and weighting. The analytical hierarchy process (AHP) or multiattribute utility analysis can be used for complex decision analyses with multiple weighted factors and significant outcomes.

Envisioning alternatives. The first step in envisioning alternatives requires creating an initial set of options from which a decision will be made. Visioning exercises such as those used in requirements definition and design can be used for generating creative alternatives, especially when a wide range of options is necessary for comparison. Brainstorming methods are a simple means of quickly producing numerous alternatives. The system matrix method described in Chap. 8 (Fig. 8.9) can be effectively used to elicit the details necessary to fully define a legitimate alternative. Especially if little information is known or obtainable for the invented alternatives, the system matrix provides a format to fill in sufficient detail for these possible alternatives.

In many cases, your decision options will be preselected due to having only a limited set available, such as with vendor offerings. In selecting tools or technologies, for example, usually only a small set of vendors will have applicable offerings to fit a given need. In this case, the entire range of offerings from vendors might be included as alternatives. In other cases, where commodity items are involved, more extensive research might be required to identify the best cost-benefit options or new options that were not previously considered. The decision scope constrains the alternatives by establishing criteria that sift out many options while leaving those with a reasonable chance of selection.

Once the alternatives are defined, your team must understand them fully. Workshop participants will typically study vendor offerings by obtaining literature and trade information from numerous sources. This information should be validated by real-world experience, such as from observing or using software or systems in operation. In addition, discussing the alternatives with current users of the systems under consideration provides the team with realistic experiential information beyond the vendors' claims. Finally, work with the vendors or consultants by arranging demonstrations or tests of the technologies, or by obtaining research summaries for team discussion.

With more complex decisions, decision alternatives must often be uniquely defined or invented. When selecting among alternative investments or business strategies, for example, the alternatives must be defined clearly enough for all participants to fairly understand each option. When defining the alternatives for complex decisions involving internal business options, require each alternative to list the same set of specifications to support true comparison. Often, ill-defined alternatives are used to fill out the range in decisions, especially where bias exists toward other alternatives. New information comes into play during decision conferences, and even "throwaway" alternatives can emerge as creative solutions when difficult trade-offs are made.

For example, *make-or-buy* decisions are common in development organizations. If such a choice is required for an expensive support system, such as a code reuse repository, management stakeholders might be biased toward a *buy* merely for cost savings. Internal value might be derived from building a custom toolkit that will not easily compare with the vendor tools. Also, vendor information is quickly obtained, and it might take time to elicit complete enough proposals for the internal custom options. To be fair in the comparisons, be sure that the *make* options are defined as well as the vendor options considered. And try to consider the learning and ownership value to the organization in any decision where the choice is to buy or to go custom.

Usage: Modeling and selection

In usage, the decision process continues by developing decision models that enable the team to proceed with making the decision. Two types of models are described that cover the majority of group decision processes—*scenario models* and *quantitative decision models*. Decision scenarios allow evaluation of a decision's future impact. By constructing simple models of the future that describe the resulting implementation, the team can better envision how the decision might affect the business over time. By describing each decision alternative in this way, both short- and long-term benefits and disadvantages can be surfaced and discussed.

Quantitative decision models allow the evaluation of decision models by scoring and comparing models with the criteria established in previous phases. The quantitative approach is more matter-of-fact, and is more typical of business-oriented decision making. Even when using a strong, qualitative decision approach such as scenarios, a simple quantitative analysis should be used as a decision sanity check.

Decision analysts are familiar with other quantitative and qualitative decision modeling methods that are applicable to various problems. Facilitating a group decision process using a multivariable decision model is not recommended for inexperienced analysts or facilitators. Training and practice using the techniques on an individual basis is required before attempting to integrate these methods into decision conferences. Most of the techniques described for Team Design workshops are probably suitable for most facilitators, regardless of background. But complex modeling methods require a significant understanding of the decision method's theory and applicability to the decision problem.

Table 10.9 summarizes some of the most widely used decision-modeling methods, with references and brief notes on their suitable applications.

Finally, a team makes selections after considering all the data, evaluations, scoring, and discussion. The selection itself is a *choice*, and is not necessarily the outcome of running the numbers. Although not always recognized as such, making a selection is independent of the evaluation. It is not a foregone conclusion that the highest score becomes the alternative selected. It might be the safest and most justifiable choice, but it should not necessarily be considered a deter-

TABLE 10.9   Decision Modeling Methods

Decision modeling method	Application	Reference
Weighted criteria	Analyzing and selecting known alternatives	Kepner-Tregoe 1981
Screening matrix	Selection of appropriate alternatives from creative ideas	Higgins 1994*b*
Decision trees	Probability-based decision method for structured decisions	Moody 1983
Force field analysis	Making decisions affecting complex social situations	Lewin 1951
Precedence charts	Structured decision model for simplifying complex variables	Moody 1983
Value-focused thinking	Value-based analysis for organizational decision making	Keeney 1994
Analytical hierarchy process	Strategic decisions Complex decisions with multiple variables	Saaty 1992
Multiattribute utility analysis	Strategic decisions Complex decisions with multiple variables	Edwards and Newman 1982

mined outcome. In making the selection, softer factors can play into the equation, and a decision-making team should pay attention to these factors during the criteria and evaluation process. When group discomfort with a top-scoring alternative shows up, it's time to reassess the criteria or the process. Using a qualitative approach (such as scenarios) in concert with the quantitative usually prevents such reconsideration, but it is always a possibility. The selection of an alternative remains a choice by the team, however, which gives the team its true power in the decision process. Modeling and selection methods are summarized in Table 10.10.

Developing decision scenarios.   Scenarios can be used as tools for analysis and decision support. Developing two or three scenarios for a complex decision can assist the team in understanding the future impacts of the decision. Unlike ranking and weighting, scenarios reveal the possibilities inherent in the decision. Quantitative approaches tend to highlight the decision in terms of value and benefit, but do not portray a holistic view of the situation.

Consider a major personal decision, such as accepting a new job. A

TABLE 10.10   Team Decision Making: Usage Phase

Usage: Modeling and selection	Methods	Inputs and outputs
Developing decision scenarios	Scenario generation and analysis	In: Priorities, decision alternatives Out: Scenarios
Evaluating decision models	Ranking Weighted criteria Analytical hierarchy process	In: Scenarios, alternatives Out: Decision models
Making selections	Decision-making methods Voting, rating, or points Selection process	In: Decision models Out: Team decision

simple decision analysis of the features, benefits, and considerations of each job might provide a view of your valuation of each part of the job, and the new job might score higher just because certain weights or values are rated higher. For a major decision, is this information complete enough? Instead, create two brief scenarios for each job, one a mix of positive trends, the other a mix of more negative trends. Be sure to include descriptions in all domains affecting the decision: quality of work, opportunity, impact of benefits, impact on family, and personal and social issues. Evaluate the scenarios based on your overall values, desires, and directions. The scenarios are also more likely to communicate effectively with others than is a decision analysis spreadsheet. Some decisions are best suited to this approach—other decisions are certainly *supported* by scenarios.

Consider developing scenarios when faced with decisions that have a significant organizational or process impact. If the interactions and possibilities of a decision are complex enough that no one person is likely to anticipate all the potential outcomes, the scenario approach helps to organize the variables into a plausible story. Decision scenarios are used in a similar way as in planning—by developing a narrative story of each possible decision outcome, the team can test the impact of a selection by envisioning its scenarios in use.

Decision scenarios are also developed and analyzed in much the same way as in planning. Teams can use them to better predict the results of selecting a particular decision path. As in planning, scenarios help us understand future trends and the possible impacts and gains to be achieved from adopting a particular decision scenario. They differ in that decision scenarios are less involved than the detailed scenes created for planning, and that typically one per decision alternative is constructed. Two scenarios per alternative can be developed and compared to balance out positive and negative bias, but this should only be done for mission-critical decisions that allow time for extended use of the method. Simple scenario planning, as described in the Team Planning format, can be further streamlined to support team decision making. The following steps can be used in this case:

1. *Determine the key decision factors and* must haves. Use brainstorming to generate key decision factors and *must-have* requirements for decision scenarios. For decision scenarios, you might use the sticky note exercise described previously in scenario planning, or use group brainstorming methods that the team is familiar with. Key decision factors are the main points of the decision, drawn directly from the criteria. The must-have requirements are the conditions every alternative must meet, and these will be described for each scenario.

2. *Develop an initial decision model.* At this point you will have a set of possible alternatives, decision criteria, and background information. Organize the decision factors and must-haves into groups that can be compared with each other in evaluation. Each alternative should include the same groups of criteria and factors drawn from this decision model, so they can be evaluated using the same points of comparison.

3. *Develop a scenario for each decision alternative.* In essence, each alternative is developed as a miniscenario. Each miniscenario describes a set of conditions that might occur, planned or unplanned, if that alternative is selected. A narrative description is detailed that explains the result if that alternative is selected. Questions to ask the team in developing the scenarios include: What benefits or advantages and costs or disadvantages will each option provide? What will emerge in your future situation as a result of the alternative? How will each alternative affect the business, the organization, or the technology platforms? What contingencies are available if the scenario doesn't work?

4. *Identify issues that emerge from the decision scenarios.* Identify the most significant possible outcomes, positive and negative, arising from your scenario narratives. Look for problems and issues that arise from the scenarios that would not be apparent from evaluating only the facts. This is where some of the power of scenarios shows up—real-world issues are identified in its format that are more easily dismissed when looking only at the numbers or at a standard decision analysis. Add these issues to the scenario descriptions used in evaluation.

Essentially, the decision scenarios become decision models in themselves. The predicted results that come forth from the team during this process reveal some interactions with other factors and activities that are difficult to assess when just looking at quantitative models. Of course, not every decision process lends itself to the scenario approach. It can be time-consuming, and not every team will be comfortable with the ranging outside the facts that this process encourages. However, when used as an adjunct to the typical weighted-factor analysis used to score alternatives for a final decision, decision scenarios offer insight and in-depth analysis not found in other methods.

A team might also opt for making the decision based purely on the decision scenarios, in much the same way that scenario planning processes adopt a scenario for use as a core planning model. The last activity in the usage phase allows evaluation of each scenario based on the facts and predictions described in each one. If the team feels that enough information has been described to justify a decision, a group voting process can be used to select the best scenario. A more cautious approach entails developing the weights and scoring each alternative directly against the points defined in each scenario.

Evaluating decision models. Decision models are structures of the decision data organized for ready evaluation using a rating or scoring process. Because the decision-making format describes several methods for decision making that fit into the four-phase cycle, no single method is recommended or defined in entirety. When a quantitative evaluation must be made, decision models are constructed by defining weights or rating scales for the decision variables. Simpler decision models can also be constructed as a set of decision criteria with a clearly defined evaluation path.

Several modeling approaches are described, each with its own level of application to the decision process. These simple methods can be used by themselves or combined as steps in refining a decision model.

Ranking and priority setting. Ranking is one of the simplest approaches to creating a usable decision model. Ranking can also be used anytime a simple list might be evaluated by the team. This is a useful approach in facilitation, where any list of considerations or requirements defined by the group can be ranked to identify the team's values and preferences.

Priority setting is often done using a ranking process, and the processes can be considered equivalent. Whereas *ranking* is the mechanical process of sorting a list in order of preference or importance, priority setting requires more thought about the values important to the team. The word *priority* assumes that some items have significant meaning, while others lower in priority have less value. Assigning priorities when a list is developed encourages more critical thinking about the items, and the priorities provide a record of team values that can be useful further along in the decision or design process.

Simple ranking. Ranking can be used to sort through requirements, design items, and decision points during any of the Team Design processes. Ranking or assigning priorities requires gaining consensus from the team, as it is a rapid approach to defining preferences and should usually be handled by quick consensus. As a facilitator, assess the group's willingness to reach consensus in the area where priorities are needed. If the group reveals points of contention, use a group voting process to vote on priorities. Otherwise, for simple ranked lists, test to see if consensus exists for the top three items. If the top three can be handled easily, the following items follow more readily. A simple approach to ranking follows:

1. Structure the list to be ranked, and discuss the criteria to be used by the team in ranking. Order the list without regard to priority, but assign letters or numbers to the list from top to bottom.

2. Have each participant write down their own rank ordering of the list. For simple scoring, have each participant reverse the numbers of their list beside the ranking. So, from 10 items, write a *10* next to the number one item, *9* next to the number two item, and so forth.

3. For a large list or a large number of people, the participant lists can be given to the facilitator for summarizing. Summarize the numbers by adding the scores (from the reversed rank).

4. Total the scores for each item, and write out the list of items in their ranked order.

Group consensus ranking. The simple ranking process works well when opinions about the items are not consistent across the group. It allows voting to be private, and the ranking cannot then be easily argued. If more consensus appears with the group, use a more discussion-oriented process so the group members can witness the process of their own consensus. A group consensus approach to ranking priorities can be facilitated as follows:

1. Structure a list of all items to be ranked. If more than 12 to 15 items are on the list, reduce the list to concentrate on a smaller number. Items that drop below this number are of lower priority, and can be moved to a list of options to handle in the future.

2. Check whether consensus exists for the top three items or a top priority (also see the *decision selection* methods following). Discuss the top items with the team, and assign ranks according to consensus.

3. If *clear* consensus is not evident, ask the group to use a simple voting process. Vote on the top item, scoring each "number one" item as a single count. The highest count becomes the number one ranking item, and the next three to five items typically will follow. If the following items do not readily emerge due to clustering around the top two or three, have the group vote on the number two and three items. This will usually round out the top half or more of the list.

4. Complete the list through discussion rather than by voting, since the bottom half of the list is less likely to arouse contention and can usually be handled through group consensus.

Weighted criteria. The weighted-criteria method is the traditional decision-analysis approach, considered to be a basic tool of management decision making. This method scores alternatives based on criteria, with weights assigned reflecting their value to the decision. This method is often used in decisions where a rigorous justification is necessary and numerous criteria are evaluated for alternatives. It can be used in conjunction with qualitative methods such as decision scenarios, where it might sort out the variables affecting the decision.

A simplified approach to using the weighted-criteria method is described as follows:

1. Establish the set of evaluation criteria to be used in the evaluation. This will have been accomplished by following the scoping and visualizing phases in the cycle.

2. Break criteria into musts and wants. *Musts* are criteria for the required attributes of every alternative, and are used to screen out options to reduce the selection set. *Wants* are criteria used to evaluate the alternatives that remain.

3. With the team, determine the relative weights to assign to each criterion. Essentially, the criteria will be prioritized, and higher weights will be assigned to the top criteria. A scale of 1 to 10 is typically used, although most criteria worth scoring will rate above 5 in the scale. Don't assign more than 10 percent of the criteria a top weight, to allow the weights to reflect better priorities. Also, criteria with a weight of 10 are very close to musts, and should be minimized.

4. Rate each alternative against the weighted criteria. Use a scale of 1 to 10, being cautious with the assignment of a 10 rating. Work through one alternative at a time instead of each criterion, so that the team can better visualize the characteristics of that alternative.

5. After all alternatives have been rated, multiply the ratings by the weights for scores and total them for each alternative.

6. Typically, teams select the alternative with the highest numerical score. If two alternatives are closely scored (this is for your team to decide), analyze the two items carefully. Assess the ratings for each of the two, and discuss the advantages and disadvantages. If scenarios have been done for the alternatives, choose the alternative with the best strategic value or that satisfies criteria that have gone unrated or unspoken.

At the conclusion of this process you will have a matrix of decision alternatives (in three or four columns) shown with a column of criteria with scores on each row and totals at the bottom. This chart becomes the basic justification for the decision, and can be easily read even by people who are unfamiliar with the weighted-criteria evaluation approach.

Analytical hierarchy process. The analytical hierarchy process (AHP) was developed in the early 1970s by Dr. Thomas L. Saaty of the University of Pittsburgh, and has been widely reprised in recent years through its application in software-based decision-support systems (for example, Expert Choice). Using statistical methods in a readily understandable framework, AHP combines the rigor of statistical decision making and the appeal of well-defined criteria to evaluate alternatives.

AHP helps groups define the types of information required for the decision and sort out irrelevant or unimportant information. Both qualitative and quantitative criteria can be compared using informed judgments to derive weights and priorities. AHP structures the components of a decision into a hierarchical tree structure that makes the branches of the decision visible (see Fig. 10.1). A complex decision can be reduced to a series of pairwise comparisons with rankings. Proponents of AHP claim it is among the most widely used decision-making theories in corporate and government settings.

A detailed discussion of the theory and practice of the analytical hierarchy process is beyond the scope of this book. However, it is an important approach that should be considered when mission-critical decisions or major financial investments are at stake. Decision conferences using AHP generate models for decisions regarding large capital and operating budgets, project portfolios, project selection and funding, workload planning for large scale projects, cost-benefit analyses, source selection, and prioritization of process reengineering and improvement activities.

The basic process for facilitating an AHP-based decision involves the following steps:

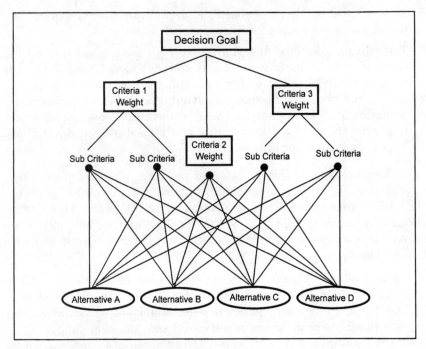

Figure 10.1 Analytical hierarchy process model.

1. Develop the team goal for the decision model (scoping) and document the rationale for the goal.

2. Define the criteria for the AHP decision model, and group the criteria into logical categories (visualizing).

3. Define criteria weightings using pairwise comparisons (usage). Each decision criterion within the model will be compared with other criteria to derive a mathematical weighting for the importance of each criterion in a facilitated team session.

4. Create and assign weights to decision *standards* used for scoring alternatives with respect to each criterion. The standards support choosing the identified standard that best describes how each decision alternative rates. The standards enable the team to look at elements of a problem in isolation with respect to a single criterion.

5. Evaluate and rank the decision alternatives, preferably using computer-based decision analysis to assist in managing the decision model and calculating the scores for each alternative.

6. Select alternatives and document the decision (packaging).

Facilitating an AHP decision process for a complex decision takes anywhere from a day (best case) to a week (not atypical). It requires building a solid model of criteria and standards upon which alternatives will be evaluated, so it must be conducted in several phases. Practitioners and participants in this process generally report high satisfaction with using the process, partially due to its sensitivity to true priorities as defined in the model but also due to its ability to draw participants into thinking completely through all aspects of a major decision process. Like using scenarios, it allows for qualitative judgment, and like the weighted criteria process, it supports using a tightly defined quantitative model. When complete, the result is a well-defined and documented decision model with ranked alternatives that clearly trace their selection back to the priorities and standards defined in advance for the decision.

Making selections.   This final step in usage fulfills the definitive act of deciding. The selection can simply be made from the decision model, or your decision process can be concluded by voting or by some other means of choice. Because the Team Design formats allow the use of multiple methods, not one method followed in isolation, several approaches are described for making selections.

First of all, if the team has decided to utilize a quantitative model such as AHP or weighted criteria, consensus will typically support selecting the highest-scored alternative emerging from the model. Selection in this case will be a simple step of acknowledging the choice, and perhaps reviewing the model to ensure that agreement exists with respect to the process and the outcome. If facilitating the decision process, you might find it useful to remind the team members that even if it appears that the process made the selection, they must acknowledge that this selection was still their choice. In other words, given the evidence of the model, the *team* decided, not the decision model.

Several methods are commonly used in group settings to facilitate choice making. Various types of group voting and consensus processes have been described throughout the book, but in the case of decisions, the following techniques are well received by groups.

Group voting.   *Group voting* refers to any exercise where the team uses a voting procedure to make selections among alternatives. Group voting can be facilitated as a private process (such as *silent voting*) or as a more open discussion. Sometimes the sensitivity of the decision and the subject of the vote drives the need to use a private approach; with other decisions, an open group vote is sufficient.

Silent voting.   *Silent voting* allows team members to maintain anonymity in the actual voting session. Although individual intentions might seem obvious to other team members, the silent process supports an honest selection when a difficult or sensitive decision must be made. This approach is also useful in large or mixed groups, where a vocal process might be cumbersome. Silent voting is facilitated by simply having team members write their votes on slips of paper that are collected and summarized by the facilitator. Anonymity is maintained, and a record is kept of the votes for each alternative.

Voting with points or cash. Assigning points allows team members a certain number of points to allocate among alternatives. For example, each member might be assigned 10 or 100 points for distribution, allowing a range of possible outcomes. This approach does not force ranking, as members can assign equal points to each alternative if so desired. A fun twist to this voting exercise is to actually use money for the voting, either coins or bills. Depending on the group, the use of cash can transform the level of commitment to alternatives—even if using pennies, it causes members to more seriously consider the impact of their choice. Points or cash are summed, and either single or multiple selections can be made.

Dot voting. Dot voting is similar to assigning points except that sticky dots (or other types of stickers or symbols) are given to team members for placement next to the alternatives for which they wish to vote. Alternatives are listed on a whiteboard, or participants can attach sticky notes to a wall. Each member is usually allowed one or three dots, depending on the number of items from which to choose. Some facilitators like to combine dots and points, allowing the use of 10 or more dots to be used visually as points for the voting. Dots are then counted to make a single, multiple, or ranked selection.

Top three. The *top three* approach is used when more than one selection might be made, and team members feel strongly about more than a single alternative each. Each member gets three votes, for first, second, and third place. Points can be assigned to each to allow addition of final scores, or in a small group (less than 15) a show of hands for each option for first, second, and third can quickly resolve the top choices.

Packaging: Documenting decisions

In the Team Decision Making format, *packaging* is primarily a formal conclusion to the decision process. The decision is documented for executive or organizational review, and follow-up actions are assigned to team members as required. The packaging phase is outlined in Table 10.11.

TABLE 10.11   Team Decision Making: Packaging Phase

Packaging: Documenting decisions	Methods	Inputs and outputs
Documenting decision	Decision definition	In: Team decision Out: Documented decision
Assign action plans	Action planning, scheduling	In: Documented decision Out: Assigned actions

Documenting decision. The decision can be supported and justified by several types of documentation. Depending on the recipients of the decision, a formal document can be prepared (for executive committees) or notes from the proceedings of the workshop can be distributed (for internal organizational use). Be sure to address the questions, issues, and concerns of the intended readers. If the readers are executive management, provide only an executive summary document, with full documentation available on request. If the readers are middle management, prepare a full package with summary and details, allowing them to represent the process to other management as needed.

If a software-based decision-support system has been used through the decision workshop, it will typically provide reports of the criteria definitions, weighting and scoring, and final results. Otherwise, the recorder of the workshop can develop a summary of the decision workshop discussing the results, with supporting information drawn from the workshop exercises. If scenarios are used in the decision process, copies of the scenario summaries should be attached for the interest of the readers. Include any other details that might be useful as appendixes to the report or summary.

Assign action plans. The conclusion of the decision workshop should include assignment of the actions required to conduct the next logical activities. These might include preparing the decision documentation, contacting the vendors for selections, or planning for implementation of the decision. Facilitate the action planning, document the actions and dates, and conclude the workshop.

Glossary

activity General term that distinguishes actions taken as part of a business process; in project management, often presented in a work breakdown structure hierarchy as the level between *phase* and *task*. Activities normally have a discernible start and finish that define its bounds.

analytic hierarchy process (AHP) Decision-making process that compares both qualitative and quantitative criteria using informed judgments to derive weights and priorities. AHP structures the components of a decision into a hierarchy, allowing a complex decision to be evaluated by a series of pairwise comparisons.

application template Software that provides a programming environment and program structure for a common business application as a template, enabling application designers to modify only variables and data definitions to produce an operational system.

benchmarking A competitive analysis adopted to improve or redesign a process based on understanding or following the exemplary process of an accepted leader in the industry.

business process A collection of activities performed in coordination to generate value or maintain business operations. A *process* is considered a major activity that is an ongoing cycle, without a specific start or finish (for example, customer service or order management).

business process design Industrial engineering and management discipline of planning and designing business processes, typically to redesign existing processes to maximize value or efficiency.

business requirements A statement of business need (not a specification). These establish the business needs for the system or product. These requirements provide the goals for a system or product and supply the rationale for development.

Capability Maturity Model Five-stage model defined by the Software Engineering Institute (SEI), used in software industry and in government projects to assess the development process capability of an organization.

CASE See *computer-aided systems engineering.*

change management Process of planning for the organizational impacts of major restructuring, policy, system, and personnel changes and managing the implementation of the change program and its emerging issues.

collaboration A purposeful relationship between two or more individuals for working closely in concert to solve problems, create or design artifacts, or produce a deliverable.

computer-aided systems engineering A set of software tools that supports rapid development and organization of software engineering deliverables, including analysis diagrams, design models, code modules, and database schemas.

consensus The state of agreement among all members of a group regarding specific issues, wherein all members either fully agree or assent to support the group's agreed positions. Considered the state where all members can live with a proposal or agreement.

cross-functional team Team organization based on membership from across the multiple business functions that contribute to the overall effort.

customer Any person or organization (internal or external) that functions as the recipient of deliverables produced by the team. The purchaser or user of products or systems.

customer requirements A business problem or need defined from the customer's perspective, a marketing-oriented requirements statement that addresses customer needs.

data definition language (DDL) The computer-based language used by database systems, in which entities and elements are defined and their attributes are specified for use by a database management system.

data model An abstract model of data used in a system, often specified by entity-relationship diagrams and data definitions.

database management system (DBMS) An integrated software system including a database development environment and tools supporting building, hosting, and maintaining databases.

decision support Group processes, methods, and software tools used to facilitate decision making.

deliverables Any written, coded, or constructed product delivered to a customer or recipient.

design (invention) The process of conceiving ideas and the structure for a system or product, establishing a unifying concept, and creating and integrating aesthetic, structural, and process elements.

design (specification) The process of communicating a design in its detailed elements for implementation by engineering or development.

development Typically refers to the process of implementing a product by coding and testing the design specification. Can also refer to the overall process by which software or products are built, from analysis and design through release.

dialogue Process of reflective discussion held with groups to reveal relevant thinking, probe assumptions, and facilitate listening to alternative points of view.

distributed development Development that takes place in multiple locations or involves planned activities directed from a central site and distributed across remote sites.

entity-relationship diagram Diagram of a conceptual data model that represents entities as boxes and shows relationships among entities as lines, using symbology to define meaningful structure of the data.

ethnography A naturalistic technique used in sociology and anthropology adapted for observing and studying work practices as they occur in their given environment.

evolutionary life cycle Also known as the spiral or iterative life cycle, this model supports multiple iterations of design and development. A preliminary design prototype is established and evolved over iterating cycles to add further functions until a desired state of system implementation is achieved.

facilitation Leading group processes as a neutral moderator or guide to assist the group in achieving stated goals.

facilitator Professional group leader who provides independent moderation of processes as required for group design, planning, and decision making.

front-end analysis General term for analyses performed in the early stages of a project or development effort, typically including product definition, conceptual analysis and design, requirements analysis, and competitive studies.

function A system component that performs one cycle of a defined operation, a separate discrete activity with a beginning and an end. They are named as active tasks, with a verb-noun format, specifying an active task. In *function analysis,* a defined activity conducted as part of a business process.

function analysis The methodology and practice of analyzing business functions and describing business and system operations in abstract models used in design and specifications.

functional experts Analysts or representatives of the product team or user community who fully understand the tasks and procedures for the target work environment, and can honestly speak for the user or customer.

functional requirements An analysis of the business requirements with a defined list of functions (basic capabilities) and features (unique abilities) of the system.

functional requirements specification A detailed specification that defines the functions of a large system, including data, process flow, or interfaces.

group support systems (GSS) Group decision support systems, shared whiteboards, and shared document systems, all of which enable team members to work together and see their contributions and responses from others at the same time.

group voting   Any decision-making process in which a group uses a voting mechanism to make selections among alternatives.

hierarchy diagram   A type of diagram that shows items as related in a hierarchical structure, with top-level items established at the top and subordinate items connected by lines below each level.

horizontal process mapping   A diagramming method used to represent business processes, in which activities comprising the process are shown in their sequence of operation from the start to the finish of the process cycle.

HTML   Hypertext markup language, the code translated by Web browsers to display World Wide Web pages across the Internet.

human factors   Discipline that studies characteristics of human beings applicable to the design, evaluation, and operation of systems and devices of all kinds. Human factors is known as *ergonomics* throughout much of the world, and covers a breadth of design applications, ranging from aeronautical controls and automotive systems to software and consumer products.

human-computer interaction (HCI)   Discipline that studies the characteristics and interactions of humans with computer and software systems, applied to the design of useful and usable systems.

implementation   Phase of development in which program modules are coded and tested. Also, any activity where planned actions are executed.

incremental life cycle   Also known as a phased life cycle, the incremental approach uses phases of development to break a very large project into multiple increments of development. Each increment represents a set of functions or additional capability for existing functions.

information systems (IS)   Class of interactive computer-based systems that integrate information received from a set of defined sources, organize the data in formats for use by workers and managers, and provide reports from the data on a regular or as-needed basis.

initiating   Phase in team development in which a group establishes relationships, an initial team identity, and purpose.

life cycle   A representation of an entire product management or development process from a defined start to its completion or retirement, showing major activities and their relationships to one another. Several software life-cycle models are typically identified, including *evolutionary, incremental, rapid application development,* and *traditional* life cycles.

logical model   A set of analytic diagrams and narratives defining the abstract or *logical* processes for system functions, business processes, or data usage. The *what* of the system as defined during analysis, as opposed to the *how* defined during design.

management information systems (MIS)   Information systems designed to support management requirements and processes, by providing interactive access to current business data and reports, and information to support decision making.

mental model   Internalized mental construct of objects, systems, or processes that represents knowledge and understanding of the actual object or system to the individual.

milestone   In project management, a *milestone* represents the accomplishment of a major activity, represented by a critical date in the schedule.

object-oriented design   A software design methodology that views programs as a composition of related objects instead of separate procedures. *Objects* are predefined within a hierarchy of classes and achieve efficiencies by inheriting characteristics from related objects in the hierarchy.

organizational context   The interrelated conditions within an organization that promote distinctive related behaviors, work practices, human relationships, and business approaches.

organizational development   The discipline and process of facilitating organizational effectiveness, including diagnosing organizational problems, identifying organizational improvements, and planning and implementing improvements and interventions.

packaging   Phase of Team Design cycle that completes the design process. In packaging a design model or specification is produced from the analyses, iteration of design, and learning of the prior phases. Packaging produces the deliverables typically used by customers or developers outside of the design team.

participatory design   A discipline of design practice based on complete integrated inclusion of the users or intended work community in the design of their systems and work processes.

problem solving   Practice of identifying and managing problems by some methodology, typically based on problem analysis and resulting in alternative solutions from which a selected solution is implemented.

process   In *function analysis,* the highest level of functional activity performed in a system, typically described as an ongoing series of activities which, as a whole, do not have a designated start or finish (for example, order management or billing). In *facilitation,* process is the distinction of a group's activities as guided by the facilitator, as opposed to *content,* which is handled by participants.

process management   Organizing, controlling, and maintaining business processes using process definitions and life-cycle models for control of product development, engineering, process cycle times, and other process metrics.

product requirements   A statement of product definition (not a specification). Market-driven requirements based on customer need, and used by product development organizations as the system or product description.

project management   Discipline and practice of managing large complex projects, following methods of scheduling, cost management, scope management, and quality control. The Project Management Institute (PMI) recognizes eight disciplines that comprise project management, all of which can be considered applicable methodologies.

prototyping   Developing visual mock-ups of user interfaces (represented by screens and user transactions) for designing and evaluating systems.

rapid application development (RAD) life cycle   Describes a deliberately shortened cycle of development activities designed to quickly implement lower-risk efforts to provide some usable capability with rapid turnaround.

reengineering   The radical redesign of existing large-scale business processes to achieve dramatic improvements in customer service, product delivery, and other fundamental business operations.

requirements analysis   Analysis of requirements information relevant to identified requirements and to specifying attributes of each requirement relevant to the system.

requirements churn   Problem that occurs in managing requirements during analysis and design where requirements remain ill-defined and customer changes force redefinition throughout the cycle, leading to a continual reevaluation and redefinition of requirements.

requirements definition   Process of gathering, identifying, and analyzing requirements, leading to a formal definition of requirements statements.

requirements gathering   Process of collecting requirements from customer, user, and stakeholder representatives, using interviews, surveys, focus groups, and other methods of elicitation.

requirements identification   Identification of requirements from the information gathered, specifically applicable to the domain of analysis.

requirements management   Process of organizing identified requirements, establishing a baseline and tracking their disposition through analysis and development, and handling customer and management inquiries and change requests for the requirements.

scenario analysis   System analysis approach using scenarios or stories of envisioned system use as narrative models to analyze planned system operations, potential fielding and usage issues, and work process situations resulting from the system.

scenario design   System design approach using scenarios to understand the planned system, its users, and work processes as models for use in designing system functions, user interfaces, and operational characteristics.

scenario planning   Strategic planning approach that constructs scenarios of future business, system, or process operations as qualitative models for planning strategies and contingencies, and for use in business decisions.

scoping   Phase of Team Design cycle and analysis method that describes and defines the scope of a project, system, or process. Scoping involves identifying the components and boundaries of the problem or requirements addressed by the design.

Software Engineering Institute (SEI) A federally supported organization located at Carnegie-Mellon University, dedicated to the promotion and education of effective software engineering processes and to establishing quality standards for evaluating software processes.

stakeholders Members of an organization, customers, or users who have a stake in the design and use of a system or process, the implementation of which impacts their job, work practices, or business operations.

storyboarding Design method that plots a system or process design as sequences of activities, drawn visually in a specific storyboard format similar to that used in planning animation and motion picture sequences.

strategic enterprise assessment (SEA) An evaluation of an organization's strategic strength status in 16 categories, using letter grades to construct a grade point average for each category and overall.

strategic plan A plan devised and used by the business to plan for future operations, to identify major opportunities, and to identify and counter possible threats and trends that could affect the business.

SWOT analysis Strategic and tactical planning technique that evaluates the *strengths, weaknesses, opportunities,* and *threats* facing a business or an organization.

system design Planning, analysis, envisionment, and initial construction of software or integrated systems.

system requirements Requirements that define the entire scope of a system, including functions, architecture, related systems and interfaces, and databases.

system requirements specification As used in government applications, a high-level definition of system requirements, often used as a proposal for technical direction for a systems project.

task An activity performed by a system user or worker that is conducted as a complete series of steps, usually performed without interruption from start to finish. In some project planning approaches, the lowest level of effort tracking.

task analysis Detailed definition of work processes, based on systematic observation and description of tasks, represented as diagrams and narrative description.

team A group whose members function as an interdependent collective with common goals and values. Team members work together toward common goals and build upon contributions from all members in pursuit of a collectively held goal.

team building The process of facilitating a group of participants in working together as a cooperative group with commonly held purposes and goals.

Total Quality Management (TQM)   A quality management approach used in many organizations for continual process improvement, focused on improving processes through input from those working with them at the operational level.

traditional life cycle   The traditional software development life-cycle model, commonly called the *waterfall* model, as it is described by a series of stages that occur independently and in sequence, where each stage is completed before passing its output to the next stage.

usability   A quality of systems demonstrated by ease of learning, initial usage, and continued operational use as perceived by the user.

usability testing   An evaluation procedure used to test software for usability by gathering and measuring user responses to sample tasks using prerelease versions of a system.

usage   Phase in Team Design cycle concerned with *applying* the planning and design of systems or processes. Usage addresses the process of designing a system for its context of use within organizations, by users. Usage integrates operational models, scenarios, use cases, and prototypes in order to surface issues, test assumptions, and iterate the design within an identifiable context.

user analysis   Analyses and representations of system users, including profiles of user characteristics, descriptions of user groups, user communities, user organizations, and user roles.

user requirements   An informal specification of system functions from the user's perspective.

validating   Optional phase in Team Design cycle that evaluates the quality and effectiveness of the designed system or process.

value chain analysis   A type of end-to-end process analysis that assesses the business value of components in the *value chain,* a specified series of actions that add value to a product. Value chain analysis is used in cost management or to evaluate the cycle time of business processes.

visualizing   Phase in Team Design cycle that analyzes process representations and envisions the system through designing visual models of the system. Visualizing bridges the design from the analysis of current processes to the new requirements or system or product vision.

work breakdown structure (WBS)   In project management, the WBS is a matrix of project activities associated with project resources or budget categories (from a chart of accounts).

workflow analysis and design   Defining the detailed sequencing of work processes, especially applicable to automation and process supervision. Workflow analysis and design involves several components, including flow of work, flow of information, flow of materials, and task flow.

Bibliography

Articles and Chapters

Anson, R., R. Bostrom, and B. Wynne. 1995. An experiment assessing group support system and facilitator effects on meeting outcomes. *Management Science* 41(2):189–208.

Argyris, Chris. 1994. Good communication that blocks learning. *Harvard Business Review*, July–August.

Bannon, Liam J. 1995. The politics of design: Representing work. *Communications of the ACM* 38(9):66–68.

Basili, V. R., and G. Caldiera. 1995. Improving software quality by reusing knowledge and experience. *Sloan Management Review*, Fall:55–64.

Bennett, John L., and John Karat. 1992. Facilitation as support for partnership in HCI design meetings: A case study example. Research Report, IBM Corporation.

Bjerknes, Gro. 1993. Some PD advice. *Communications of the ACM* 36(4):39.

Brache, A. P., and G. A. Rummler. 1988. The three levels of quality. *Quality Progress,* October.

Brown, John Seely, and Estes Solomon Gray. 1996. The people are the company. *Fast Company,* April–May.

Carmel, E., R. D. Whitaker, and J. F. George. 1993. PD and Joint Application Design: A transatlantic comparison. *Communications of the ACM* 36(4):40–47.

Carroll, John M. 1995. The scenario perspective on system development. In Carroll (ed.), *Scenario-Based Design: Envisioning Work and Technology in System Development.* New York: John Wiley & Sons.

Chen, Peter P. 1976. An entity-relationip model-toward a unified view of data. *ACM Transactions on Databse Systems*, January.

Clark, Herbert H. 1996. Working together apart. Plenary speech, CSCW 96. Boston.

Clemons, Eric K. 1995. Using scenario analysis to manage the strategic risks of reengineering. *Sloan Management Review,* Summer:61–71.

Constantine, Larry L. 1995. Essential modeling: Use cases for user interfaces. *interactions* 11(2):34–46.

Curtis, B., and B. Hefley. 1994. A WIMP no more: The maturing of user interface engineering. *interactions* 1(1):23–34.

Curtis, B., H. Krasner, and N. Iscoe. 1988. A field study of the software design process for large systems. *Communications of the ACM* 31(11):1268–1287.

Davenport, Thomas H. 1996. The fad that forgot people. *Fast Company,* April–May.

Denning, P. J., and P. A. Dargan. 1994. A discipline of software architecture. *interactions* 1(1):55–65.

Driskell, J. E., and Eduardo Salas. 1992. Collective behavior and team performance. *Human Factors* 34(3):27–288.

Drucker, Peter F. 1992. The new society of organizations. *Harvard Business Review,* September–October:95–104.

Erickson, Thomas. 1995. Notes on design practice: Stories and prototypes as catalysts. In John M. Carroll (ed.), *Scenario-Based Design.* New York: John Wiley & Sons.

Erickson, Thomas. 1996. Design as storytelling. *interactions* 3(4):31–35.

Grudin, Jonathan. 1994. Groupware and social dynamics: Eight challenges for developers. *Communications of the ACM* 37(1):93–105.

Holtzblatt, Karen, and Hugh Beyer. 1993. Making customer-centered design work for teams. *Communications of the ACM* 36(10):92–103.

Hughes, J., V. King, T. Rodden, and H. Andersen. 1995. The role of ethnography in interactive systems design. *interactions* 2(11):57–65.

Hutchings, A. F., and S. T. Knox. 1995. Creating products customers demand. *Communications of the ACM* (38)5:72–80.

Jacobson, Ivar. 1995. The use-case construct in object-oriented software engineering. In John M. Carroll (ed.), *Scenario-Based Design*. New York: John Wiley & Sons.

Keeney, Ralph L. 1994. Creativity in decision making with value-focused thinking. *Sloan Management Review*, Summer:33–41.

Keil, Mark, and Erran Carmel. 1995. Customer-developer links in software development. *Communications of the ACM* 38(5):33–44.

Kurke, M. I. 1961. Operational sequence diagrams in systems design. *Human Factors* 1(1):66–73.

Kyng, Morten. 1995. Making representations work. *Communications of the ACM* 38(9):46–55.

Madsen, Kim Halskov, and Finn Kensing. 1991. Generating visions: Future workshops and metaphorical design. In J. Greenbaum and M. Kyng (eds.), *Design at Work: Cooperative Design of Computer Systems*. Hillsdale, N.J.: Lawrence Erlbaum Associates.

Madsen, Kim Halskov, and Peter Aiken. 1993. Experiences using cooperative interactive storyboard prototyping. *Communications of the ACM* 36(4):57–63.

Markus, M. Lynne, and Mark Keil. 1994. If we build it, they will come: Designing information systems that people want to use. *Sloan Management Review*, Summer:11–25.

Matson, Eric. 1996. The seven deadly sins of meetings. *Fast Company* 1(2).

Matthews, Joy. 1995. JAD to the rescue. *Computerworld*, December 4.

Mercer, David. 1995. Simpler scenarios. *Management Decision* 33(4):32–40.

Miller, George A. 1956. The magic number seven, plus or minus two: Some limits on our capacity for processing information. *Psychological Review* 63:81–97.

Miller, Steven E. 1993. From system design to democracy. *Communications of the ACM* 36(4):38.

Muller, M. J., D. M. Wildman, and E. A. White. 1992. Games and other techniques for group design of user interfaces. CHI '92 Tutorial Notes. ACM Conference on Human Factors in Computing Systems. Association for Computing Machinery.

Muller, Michael J. 1991. PICTIVE—An exploration in Participatory Design. CHI '91 Conference Proceedings, ACM Conference on Human Factors in Computing Systems. Association for Computing Machinery.

Muller, Michael J., and Sarah Kuhn. 1993. Response letter to ACM Forum. *Communications of the ACM* 36(10):18.

Nevis, E. C., A. J. DiBella, and J. M. Gould. 1995. Understanding organizations as learning systems. *Sloan Management Review*, Winter:73–85.

Niederman, F., C. M. Beise, and P. M. Beranek. 1996. Issues and concerns about computer-supported meetings: The facilitator's perspective. *MIS Quarterly* 20(1):1–24.

Nielsen, Jakob. 1995. Scenarios in discount usability engineering. In John M. Carroll (ed.), *Scenario-Based Design: Envisioning Work and Technology in System Development*. New York: John Wiley & Sons.

Randall, David, and Mark Rouncefield. 1996. Ethnographic methods in system design. Tutorial notes, CSCW 96. Computer Supported Cooperative Work 1996. Association for Computing Machinery.

Rheinfrank, John, and Shelley Evenson. 1996. Design languages. In Terry Winograd (ed.), *Bringing Design to Software*. New York: ACM Press, Addison-Wesley, pp. 63–80.

Richards, Mark. 1996. Managing, American Indian style. *Fortune*, October 14, p. 130.

Sachs, Patricia. 1995. Transforming work: Collaboration, learning, and design. *Communications of the ACM* 38(9):36–44.

Scharf, Alan. 1996. Purposeful strategies. *The BT Facilitator Newsletter* no. 11, October.

Schrage, Michael. 1996. Cultures of prototyping. In Terry Winograd (ed.), *Bringing Design to Software*. New York: ACM Press, Addison-Wesley, pp. 191–205.

Shoemaker, Paul J. H. 1995. Scenario planning: A tool for strategic thinking. *Sloan Management Review*, Winter:25–40.

Tuckman, B. W. 1965. Development sequence in small groups. *Psychological Bulletin* 63:384–399.

Vance, Rachel. 1996. Characteristics of effective facilitators. Personal communication.

Vessey, I., S. A. Jarvenpaa, and N. Tractinsky. 1992. Evaluation of vendor products: CASE tools as methodology companions. *Communications of the ACM* 35(4):91–102.

von Halle, Barbara. 1995. Life beyond data. *Database Programming and Design,* September: 13–15.

Walz, Diane B., Joyce J. Elam, and Bill Curtis. 1993. Inside a software design team: Knowledge acquisition, sharing, and integration. *Communications of the ACM,* 36(10):63–77.

Wright, David. 1996. Business rules. *Data Management Review* 6(11): 70–72.

Zahniser, Richard A. 1993. Design by walking around. *Communications of the ACM* 36(10):114–123.

Books

Albrecht, K., and S. Albrecht. 1993. *Added Value Negotiating.* Homewood, Ill.: Business One, Irwin.

Arthur, Lowell Jay. 1992. *Rapid Evolutionary Development: Requirements, Prototyping & Software Creation.* New York: John Wiley & Sons.

August, J. H. 1991. *Joint Application Design: The Group Session Approach to System Design.* Englewood Cliffs, N.J.: Yourdon Press.

Barrow, J. 1990. *Process Improvement.* Washington, D.C.: Harbridge House.

Bean, William C. 1993. *Strategic Planning That Makes Things Happen.* Amherst, Mass.: HRD Press.

Boehm, Barry. 1981. *Software Engineering Economics.* Englewood Cliffs, N.J.: Prentice-Hall.

Booch, Grady. 1991. *Object-oriented design with applications.* Redwood City, Cal: Benjamin/Cummings.

Brooks, Frederick P. Jr. 1995. *The Mythical Man-Month: Essays on Software Engineering.* Anniversary edition. New York: Addison-Wesley.

Carroll, John M. 1995. *Scenario-Based Design: Envisioning Work and Technology in System Development.* New York: John Wiley & Sons.

Coad, Peter, and Edward Yourdon. 1991. *Object-Oriented Analysis.* Englewood Cliffs, N.J.: Prentice-Hall.

Crawford, Anthony. 1994. *Advancing Business Concepts in a JAD Workshop Setting.* Englewood Cliffs, N.J.: PTR Prentice-Hall.

Davenport, Thomas H. 1993. *Process Innovation.* Boston: Harvard Business School Press.

DeMarco, Thomas. 1979. *Structured analysis and system specifications.* New York: Prentice-Hall.

Deming, W. Edwards. 1986. *Out of the Crisis.* Cambridge, Mass.: MIT CAES.

Donnellon, Anne. 1996. *Team Talk.* Boston: Harvard Business School Press.

Doyle, M., and D. Straus. 1976. *How to Make Meetings Work.* New York: Jove.

Drexler, A., D. Sibbet, and R. Forrester. 1988. *The Team Performance Model— Blueprints for Productivity and Satisfaction.* Bethel, Maine: National Training Laboratories.

Edwards, W., and J. R. Newman. 1982. *Multiattribute Evaluation.* Beverly Hills, Calif.: Sage.

Erhorn, Craig, and John Stark. 1994. *Competing by Design.* Essex Junction, Vt.: Oliver Wright Publications.

Forbess-Greene, Sue. 1983. *Icebreakers.* San Diego: Pfeiffer and Co.

Freedman, Daniel P., and Gerald M. Weinberg. 1982. *Handbook of Walkthroughs, Inspections, and Technical Reviews.* Boston: Little, Brown and Co.

Gane, Chris, and Sarson, Trish. 1979. *Structured Systems Analysis: Tools and Techniques.* Englewood Cliffs, N.J.: Prentice-Hall.

Gause, Donald G., and Gerald M. Weinberg. 1989. *Exploring Requirements: Quality before Design*. New York: Dorset House.

Halé, Jacques A. G. 1995. *From Concepts to Capabilities*. Chichester, England: John Wiley & Sons.

Hammer, Michael, and James A. Champy. 1993. *Reengineering the Corporation*. New York: HarperCollins.

Hammer, Michael, and S. A. Stanton. 1994. *The Reengineering Revolution: A Handbook*. New York: HarperBusiness.

Harvey, J. B. 1988. *The Abilene Paradox*. Lexington, Mass.: Lexington Books.

Hatley, D. J. and Pirbhai, I. A. 1987. *Strategies for Real-time System Specification*. New York: Dorset House.

Heermann, Barry. 1997. *Building Team Spirit: Activities for Inspiring and Energizing Teams*. New York: McGraw-Hill.

Higgins, James M. 1994a. *The Management Challenge*. New York: Macmillan.

Higgins, James M. 1994b. *101 Creative Problem Solving Techniques*. Winter Park, Fla: New Management Publishing.

Jackson, Michael. 1995. *Software Requirements and Specifications*. New York: ACM Press, Addison-Wesley.

Jacobson, I., M. Christerson, P. Jonsson, and G. Overgaard. 1992. *Object-Oriented Software Engineering: A Use Case Driven Approach*. New York: Addison-Wesley.

Katzenbach, J. R., and D. K. Smith. 1993. *The Wisdom of Teams*. Boston: Harvard Business School Press.

Kepner, Charles, and Benjamin Tregoe. 1981. *The New Rational Manager*. Princeton, N.J.: Princeton Research Press.

Klein, G. A., J. Orasanu, R. Calderwood, and C. E. Zsambok. 1993. *Decision Making in Action: Models and Methods*. Norwood, N.J.: Ablex Publishing.

Land, George, and Beth Jarman. 1992. *Breakpoint and Beyond: Mastering the Future—Today*. New York: HarperBusiness.

Lewin, Kurt. 1951. *Field, Theory, and Social Science: Selected Theoretical Papers*. New York: Harper & Row.

Marshall, Edward M. 1995. *Transforming the Way We Work: The Power of the Collaborative Workplace*. New York: AMACOM, American Management Association.

McCarthy, Jim. 1995. *Dynamics of Software Development*. Redmond, Wash.: Microsoft Press.

Moody, Fred. 1995. *I Sing the Body Electronic*. New York: Penguin Books.

Moody, Paul E. 1983. *Decision Making: Proven Methods for Better Decisions*. New York: McGraw-Hill.

Moore, A. B., and J. A. Feldt. 1993. *Facilitating Community and Decision Making Groups*. Malabar, Fla.: Krieger Publishing.

Nadler, Gerald, and Shozo Hibino. 1994. *Breakthrough Thinking*. Rocklin, Calif.: Prima Publishing.

Nielsen, Jakob. 1993. *Usability Engineering*. Boston: Academic Press.

Opper, Susanna, and Henry Fersko-Weiss. 1992. *Technology for Teams*. New York: Van Nostrand Reinhold.

Page-Jones, Meilir. 1980. The Practical Guide to Structured Systems Design. New York: Yourdon Press.

Peters, Thomas J. 1992. *Liberation Management: Necessary Disorganization for the Nanosecond Nineties*. New York: Alfred A. Knopf.

Peters, Tom. 1987. *Thriving on Chaos*. New York: Alfred A. Knopf.

Porter, Michael E. 1985. *Competitive Advantage: Creating and Sustaining Superior Performance*. New York: The Free Press.

Robey, Daniel. 1986. *Designing Organizations*. Homewood, Ill.: Irwin.

Ross, Ronald G. 1994. *The Business Rule Book: Classifying, Defining, and Modeling Rules*. Boston: Database Research Group.

Rumbauch, J. Blaha, W., Premerlani, W., Eddy, F., and Lorensen, W. 1991. *Object-Oriented Moderling and Design*. Englewood Cliffs, N.J.: Prentice-Hall.

Rummler-Brache Group. 1989. *Process Management Workshop*. Warren, N.J.: The Rummler-Brache Group.

Saaty, Thomas L.. 1992. *Multicriteria Decision Making — The Analytic Hierarchy Process*. Pittsburgh: RWS Publications.

Scholtes, Peter. 1988. *The Team Handbook*. Madison, Wis.: Joiner Associates.

Schrage, Michael. 1995. *No More Teams! Mastering the Dynamics of Creative Collaboration*. New York: Doubleday Currency.

Schuler, Douglas, and Aki Namioka. 1993. *Participatory Design: Principles and Practice*. Hillsdale, N.J.: Lawrence Erlbaum Associates.

Senge, Peter M. 1990. *The Fifth Discipline*. New York: Doubleday Currency.

Senge, Peter M. 1994. *The Fifth Discipline Fieldbook*. New York: Doubleday Currency.

Smith, Preston G., and Donald G. Reinertsen. 1991. *Developing Products in Half the Time*. New York: Van Nostrand Reinhold.

Ulschak, F. L., L. Nathanson, and P. G. Gillian. 1981. *Small Group Problem Solving*. Reading, Mass.: Addison-Wesley.

Ward, P. T., and Mellor, S. J. 1985. *Structured Development for Real-Time Systems*. New York: Yourdon Press.

Winograd, Terry. 1996. *Bringing Design to Software*. New York: ACM Press, Addison-Wesley.

Winograd, Terry, and Fernando Flores. 1986. *Understanding Computers and Cognition*. Norwood, N.J.: Ablex Publishing.

Wood, J., and D. Silver. 1989. *Joint Application Design*. New York: John Wiley & Sons.

Yourdon, Edward. 1993. *Decline and Fall of the American Programmer*. Englewood Cliffs, N.J.: Yourdon Press, PTR Prentice-Hall.

Yourdon, Edward, and Constantine, Larry. 1975. *Structured Design*. New York: Yourdon Press.

Zimmerman, A. L., and C. J. Evans. 1993. *Facilitation: From Discussion to Decision*. East Brunswick, N.J.: Nichols Publishing.

Index

ABOUT THE AUTHOR

Peter H. Jones leads user interface design and user analysis for Reed Elsevier Technology Group, designing new systems for large-scale news, scientific, and legal information services. Mr Jones' work in human factors engineering has spanned over a decade, with research and design in human-computer interaction. His current Ph.D. program in Industrial/Organizational Psychology at the Union Institute focuses on values-based system design.

Previously, Peter Jones was a senior systems consultant at TASC, Inc. until 1966, consulting in project management and development methodologies. His experience in commercial product, large-scale information system, and government developmental projects includes team and design facilitation, systems analysis, software and user interface design, instructional development, and training.

Peter Jones has facilitated and developed tailored methods for user interaction in joint application design (JAD) and participatory design. He developed and instructed complete software engineering and JAD facilitator training curricula, and has published methodologies for development lifecycle management, software project management, and knowledge system development. He holds certification as a Project Management Professional (PMP) from the Project Management Institute.